OXFORD MID-CENTURY STUDIES

The Oxford Mid-Century Studies series publishes monographs in several disciplinary and creative areas in order to create a thick description of culture in the thirty-year period around the Second World War. With a focus on the 1930s through the 1960s, the series concentrates on fiction, poetry, film, photography, theatre, as well as art, architecture, design, and other media. The mid-century is an age of shifting groups and movements, from existentialism through abstract expressionism to confessional, serial, electronic, and pop art styles. The series charts such intellectual movements, even as it aids and abets the very best scholarly thinking about the power of art in a world under new techno-political compulsions, whether nuclear-apocalyptic, Cold War-propagandized, transnational, neo-imperial, super-powered, or postcolonial.

Series editors
Allan Hepburn, McGill University
Adam Piette, University of Sheffield
Lyndsey Stonebridge, University of East Anglia

Red Britain

The Russian Revolution in Mid-Century Culture

MATTHEW TAUNTON

OXFORD
UNIVERSITY PRESS

OXFORD

UNIVERSITY PRESS

Great Clarendon Street, Oxford, OX2 6DP,
United Kingdom

Oxford University Press is a department of the University of Oxford.
It furthers the University's objective of excellence in research, scholarship,
and education by publishing worldwide. Oxford is a registered trade mark of
Oxford University Press in the UK and in certain other countries

First Edition published in 2019

Impression: 1

Published in the United States of America by Oxford University Press
198 Madison Avenue, New York, NY 10016, United States of America

British Library Cataloguing in Publication Data
Data available

Library of Congress Control Number: 2018959055

ISBN 978–0–19–881771–0

Printed and bound in Great Britain by
Clays Ltd, Elcograf S.p.A.

For my parents

Acknowledgements

I am grateful to the Leverhulme Trust for funding the Early Career Fellowship in 2010–13 (award ref ECF/2010/0144) that got this project started, and to the faculty of Arts and Humanities at the University of East Anglia for funding a period of study leave that allowed me to continue work on the book.

Numerous friends and colleagues have helped me at various stages by reading some or all of the book or talking to me about it in seminars, offices, corridors, or pubs. These include among others Rebecca Beasley, Steven Connor, Ben Dawson, Miranda El-Rayess, Tony Gash, Allan Hepburn, Suzanne Hobson, Tommy Karshan, Benjamin Kohlmann, Colin MacCabe, Marina MacKay, Nola Merckel, David Nowell Smith, Rachel Potter, Petra Rau, Stephen Sale, Karen Schaller, Morag Shiach, Lyndsey Stonebridge, Matthew Stratton, Will Viney, and James Wood—I thank them. Thanks also to Paula Clarke Bain, who provided the index.

I am grateful for invitations to discuss this work at research seminars in the English departments of the universities of Durham, Freiburg, and Westminster, and to the organizers of the numerous conferences at which I have presented this work. Certain sections of this book have been published in a different form as 'Cottage Economy or Collective Farm? English Socialism and Agriculture between Merrie England and the Five-Year Plan', *Critical Quarterly*, 53/3 (2011), 1–23; 'Distributism and the City', in Matthew Beaumont and Matthew Ingleby (eds), *G. K. Chesterton, London and Modernity* (London: Bloomsbury, 2013), 203–27; and '2 + 2 = 5: The Politics of Number in Writing about the Soviet Union', *Textual Practice*, 29/5 (2015), 993–1016. I thank the respective publishers for permission to reuse this material with acknowledgement.

Quotations from *The Trial of a Judge* are reproduced with permission of Curtis Brown Group Ltd, London on behalf of the Estate of Stephen Spender Copyright © Stephen Spender, 1938. Extracts from *The Magnetic Mountain* are from *Complete Poems* by C. Day Lewis, published by Sinclair Stevenson, and are reprinted by permission of The Random House Group Limited © 1992. Permission to quote from 'A Plea for Mass Declamation', 'Lenin—1937', *A Short History of Culture*, and *Byzantium into Europe* was granted by David Higham Associates, acting on behalf of the Jack Lindsay estate © Jack Lindsay. I would like to thank the British Library, the Rare Book and Manuscript Library at Columbia

University, the Tamiment Library at New York University, and the Harry Ransom Center at the University of Texas, Austin, for allowing me to make use of materials in their collections.

Thanks to my family Doris Pearce, Albert Taunton, and Oscar Taunton for everything. This book is dedicated to my parents Gloria Martin and Peter Taunton.

Contents

Introduction

The centenary of the Bolshevik Revolution in 2017 raised the question of its long-term legacy for politics and culture, not just in Russia but around the world. This book investigates the resonances of the Russian Revolution in mid-century Britain, showing how literature and culture absorbed, responded to, and reacted against the revolution itself and the subsequent development of the Soviet state. Thinking of Britain in the nineteenth century in relation to political upheavals abroad, E. P. Thompson once memorably remarked that 'the revolution which did *not* happen in England was fully as devastating, and in some features more divisive, than that which did happen in France'.[1] This book aims to stand up a similar claim about twentieth-century British culture in relation to Russia. Britain underwent significant political changes after 1917, but there was no revolution. Thompson's work showed how the absence of a political revolution in the eighteenth century, and the residual trappings of aristocracy and feudalism that this absence left behind, gave English culture its peculiar character. This process continued after 1917 as incremental change in Britain left in place institutional and attitudinal structures which in Russia had been pulled up by the root. But one should add to Thompson's insight that nineteenth-century English culture constantly fed on ideas and attitudes forged in the French Revolution. Shelley's dictum that this revolution was 'the master theme of the epoch in which we live' has become a truism, and 1789 is widely understood as the fundamental precondition for Romantic literature in Britain.[2] It is less common to understand twentieth-century literature and culture as a range of responses to the Russian Revolution, but that is what I propose to do in this book.

---

[1] E. P. Thompson, *The Making of the English Working Class* (New York: Random House, 1963), 197.

[2] Shelley qtd in Simon Bainbridge, 'Politics and Poetry', in Pamela Clemit (ed.), *The Cambridge Companion to British Literature of the French Revolution in the 1790s* (Cambridge: CUP, 2011), 190–205, 204. See also Paul Hamilton, 'Introduction', in Paul Hamilton (ed.), *The Oxford Handbook of European Romanticism* (Oxford: OUP, 2016), 1–12.

The political revolution that did not happen in Britain in 1917 was displaced into the realm of culture. Western Marxism, as it came to terms with the failure of political revolutions in Western Europe, proposed that the cause could best be advanced by a battle for cultural hegemony, and writers and intellectuals across the political spectrum took up arms in that fight. In the resulting politicization of culture, ideas and events in Russia—often explicitly, but perhaps more often implicitly—informed and structured British literary culture at a deep level. In the British mid-century, many areas of cultural and intellectual life became freshly politicized as the reverberations of the Bolshevik Revolution and the subsequent development of the Soviet state were felt beyond the political sphere. To produce a satisfying account of the extent of these reverberations, it is necessary to go beyond the literary text as the primary object of analysis. Rebecca Beasley and Philip Bullock have recently proposed, in an invaluable book, 'shifting attention to the contribution of institutions, disciplines, and groups' in mediating Russian and Soviet culture, that is, shifting attention away from individual authors and texts, and from the model of 'influence'.[3] This book follows their lead by taking in a range of sources that extends well beyond the sphere of literary writers, bringing in works by journalists, travellers, legal theorists, and mathematicians among others. The analysis of literary texts remains an essential part of my method, however, because *Red Britain* is interested in ideas and attitudes and the ways these were transformed, rather than focusing primarily on the institutional mechanisms by which they were transmitted between Britain and Russia. Benefiting from the insights of the archivally driven institutional turn that Beasley and Bullock describe, I aim to leverage this research to produce new readings of literary and cultural texts.

Each of the five chapters of this book focuses on a particular sphere of culture and elucidates the ways in which the Russian Revolution enters that sphere and with what effects. While investigating very particular cultural questions, a diverse range of intellectuals (some of them little-known, many of them not literary writers) have come to the fore, and I put

---

[3] Rebecca Beasley and Philip Ross Bullock, 'Introduction: Against Influence: On Writing about Russian Culture in Britain', in Rebecca Beasley and Philip Ross Bullock (eds), *Russia in Britain, 1880–1940: From Melodrama to Modernism* (Oxford: OUP, 2013), 1–18, 1. Other examples of this institutional turn include Emily Lygo's work on the Society for Cultural Relations Between the Peoples of the British Commonwealth and the USSR (SCR) and Claire Davison's forthcoming work on the BBC's 'Projection of Russia' campaign. See Emily Lygo, 'Promoting Soviet Culture in Britain: The History of the Society for Cultural Relations Between the Peoples of the British Commonwealth and the USSR, 1924–1945', *Modern Language Review*, 108/2 (Apr. 2013), 571–96. Emily Lygo, 'British Cultural Engagement and Exchange with the USSR', *Russian Journal of Communication*, 8/3 (2016), 213–16.

them into conversation with canonical literary texts. Most of the literary texts I examine are by writers who could rightly described as anti-Communists (though in some cases they are ex-Communists too): *Animal Farm, Nineteen Eighty-Four, Pilgrimage, The Trial of a Judge, The Golden Notebook,* and *Darkness at Noon* all receive more sustained attention here than any literary text by a professed Communist. I have taken this course partly because anti-Communist voices have proved so much more influential (for better or for worse) in the British reception of Russian and Soviet politics and ideas. Much excellent work has gone in recent years to excavate a relatively neglected canon of Communist writers, including John Sommerfield, Jack Lindsay, Edward Upward, and Sylvia Townsend Warner.[4] I draw on that work, and Communist writers and intellectuals (as well as various shades of sympathizers and fellow travellers) feature here in important supporting roles. The work of writers such as George Orwell and Arthur Koestler—who came to see the repudiation of Communism as central to their respective intellectual projects, and whose work is particularly important to this book—was fundamentally shaped by their engagements with Communists and Communist ideas. This was not simply a debate between two homogeneous rival camps, but a deeply interconnected and polycentric cultural constellation.

Koestler and Orwell were highly influential on Cold War culture as a whole, and their work was frequently deployed by liberal and conservative cold warriors in defence of the political status quo. My repeated recourse to their work in this book is not intended to amplify a McCarthyist discourse that would treat any and every criticism of capitalism (or some aspect of it) as dangerously subversive, or a stepping stone on the road to the gulag. Instead, I hope to show that Orwell, Koestler, and some of the other anti-Communists and ex-Communists discussed here were more interesting thinkers than this Cold War categorization tends to suggest. Their proximity to Communism meant that they grappled with Marxism and Leninism in ways that mirrored internal debates within the Party (and the wider movement) itself. Indeed, while this is a book that dramatizes intense disagreements, there emerges a surprising degree of

---

[4] See e.g. Andy Croft, *Red Letter Days: British Fiction of the 1930s* (London: Lawrence & Wishart, 1990); Ben Harker, ' "Communism is English": Edgell Rickword, Jack Lindsay and the Cultural Politics of the Popular Front', *Literature and History,* 20/2 (2011), 16–34; Ben Harker, 'Jack Lindsay's Alienation', *History Workshop Journal,* 82/1 (2016), 83–103; Nick Hubble, *The Proletarian Answer to the Modernist Question* (Edinburgh: Edinburgh University Press, 2017); Benjamin Kohlmann (ed.), *Edward Upward and Left-Wing Literary Culture in Britain* (Farnham: Ashgate, 2014); Glyn Salton-Cox, *Queer Communism and the Ministry of Love: Sexual Revolution in British Writing of the 1930s* (Edinbugh: Edinburgh University Press, 2018); Elinor Taylor, *The Popular Front Novel in Britain, 1934–1940* (Leiden: Brill, 2018).

consensus about the terms of cultural debates that involved Communists, anti-Communists, and every intermediate shade of political actor. The rhetoric of Leninism implied a catastrophic break with every feature of bourgeois society—but the way in which Leninist ideas fed into British culture was gradual, giving rise to a range of interconnected, politicized debates that are far from being resolved today. Orwell and Koestler were particularly sensitive to the ways in which Leninist discourse had entered various spheres of cultural life. While the ways they described this were self-consciously partisan and anti-Communist, I have found their work indispensable in helping to show how the Russian Revolution resonated not just with Communist intellectuals, but across a broad section of mid-century British culture.

Each chapter of this book has its own set of questions, and a certain thematic self-containment. Taken together, however, the chapters suggest three overarching arguments, which it will be helpful to set in motion now. First, I argue that the effects of the Russian Revolution in Britain are best understood over a relatively long period. There might be something to be gained by exploring the ways in which the Bolshevik Revolution first impinged on the consciousness of British writers in the months and years immediately after October 1917, but the centre of gravity in this book falls later in the century and it ranges freely over a much longer period. 'Mid-century' is a usefully vague designation and I do not propose to harden its boundaries by suggesting a date range such as '1917–1956'. This would be a long mid-century by most standards, but even so there are good reasons to resist cordoning off the effects of the Russian Revolution in this way. Rather than seeing 1917 as a moment of sudden and fundamental transformation—a 'Leninist event' to use the language of the 'New Communism' touted by Slavoj Žižek and Alain Badiou—this book watches its multifarious cultural effects unfold over a long period.[5] It is written in sympathy with Fernand Braudel's call for a focus on longer term structures in order to move away from what he called an 'événementielle' mode of history—'episodic' in Wallerstein's translation.[6] The chapters to come investigate what Hannah Arendt in *On Revolution* (1963) labelled 'the condensation of happenings into concepts', a process by which the dramatic historical events of a revolution become routinized as part of the general fabric of intellectual and cultural life.[7] I propose an

    [5] Slavoj Žižek, 'Introduction: Between the Two Revolutions', in V. I. Lenin, *Revolution at the Gates: A Selection of Writings from February to October 1917,* ed. Slavoj Žižek (London: Verso, 2002), 1–12, 4.
    [6] Fernand Braudel (tr. Immanuel Wallerstein), 'History and the Social Sciences: The *Longue Durée*', *Review (Fernand Braudel Center),* 32/2 (2009), 171–203, 182.
    [7] Hannah Arednt, *On Revolution* (London: Penguin, 1990), 59.

elastic, long 1917, that reaches back into the political and cultural debates of the nineteenth century, through the Cold War, and into the present. What emerges is a gradual and continuous cultural and intellectual sedimentation, as cultural and political ideas and forms overlay one another and continue to interact. I have found Wai Chi Dimock's notion of 'resonance' useful as a way to think about how the events, texts, and ideas of the Russian Revolution echo through mid-century British culture. Dimock describes the effects of literary texts as 'frequencies received and amplified across time, moving farther and farther from their points of origin, causing unexpected vibrations in unexpected places'.[8] I would only add that, for me, this is not some special quality of literary texts: historical events in the sphere of politics have a similar tendency to resonate, accruing new meanings and interpretations as they travel through time, escaping their containment in the domain of politics.

Second, I seek to explain the processes by which a polarized, binary way of understanding the cultural politics of the period emerged as part of a Cold War mentality, and where appropriate work to resist such a polarized way of understanding the culture. Patrick Wright has posited a 'long Cold War' as a welcome corrective to the pervasive belief that the Cold War began in 1946 with Winston Churchill's 'iron curtain' speech at Fulton, Missouri.[9] John Connor and Michael Denning have suggested in different ways that a 'split in world literature', which saw Moscow emerging as 'the lodestar of a parallel literary universe', opened up in the aftermath of 1917, and not just as a post-1945 phenomenon.[10] This splitting of world culture into two opposing camps is real, and part of the function of this book is to show how such a split developed. However, as Wright suggested, the Cold War needs to be lengthened in *both* directions, if we are to come to terms with the ways that its polarizing mentality continues to structure our habits of thought even after the collapse of the Soviet Union in 1991. Hoping to escape these habits as far as possible, I have tried to resist a tidy-minded division of the writers and intellectuals covered into opposing 'Communist' and 'anti-Communist' camps. As Andy Croft has shown, there was considerable diversity among broadly Communist-sympathizing writers in the 1930s, both politically and in terms of the thematic

---

[8] Wai Chi Dimock, 'A Theory of Resonance', *PMLA* 112/5 (Oct. 1997), 1060–71, 1061.

[9] Patrick Wright, *Iron Curtain: From Stage to Cold War* (Oxford: OUP, 2007), 18.

[10] John Connor, 'Anglo-Soviet Literary Relations in the Long 1930s', in Benjamin Kohlmann and Matthew Taunton (eds), *A History of 1930s British Literature* (Cambridge: CUP, 2019); Michael Denning, 'The Novelists' International', in Franco Moretti (ed.), *The Novel*, i. *History, Geography and Culture* (Princeton: Princeton University Press, 2006), 703–25.

and formal features of their work: it was paranoid to imply, as Orwell influentially did, that Communist-sympathizing writers were 'dancing in unison on the end of strings pulled by the Comintern'.[11] The chapters that follow confirm Croft's insight, but they also bring to light a similar ideological diversity on the anti-Communist side.[12] This book seeks to move beyond the binaristic terms of the Cold War to explore literature's involvements in debates that were profoundly shaped by the Bolshevik Revolution and its aftermath, but nevertheless moved dynamically within and between Communist and capitalist spheres.

Third, I suggest that that British responses to the Bolshevik Revolution should be understood not only as a clash of internationalist or cosmopolitan ideologies, but also as an episode within a longer history of nationally grounded Anglo-Russian cultural and political relations.[13] The idea of Russia loomed large for British intellectuals before 1917, and infatuation with the Soviet Union (as the centre of international Communism) often overlapped with Russophilia, and Russian nationalism. Koestler berated 'Addicts to the Soviet Myth' who had 'a soft spot for Panslavism': these deluded individuals, Koestler mockingly asserted, had come to believe that 'Russian shirts and balalaikas' were 'integral parts of socialism'.[14] Conversely, anti-Communism could become entangled with (or help to foster) slavophobic racism. Despite its professed internationalism, Communism acted as a carrier for Russian national culture and values, becoming the means by which they were transmitted into British culture in newly politicized ways. The way Britain was imagined is also a vital part of this mix, and perhaps above all England. The pastoral and romantic emphases of the 'English socialism' of the nineteenth century—of William Morris and Edward Carpenter—were shaken by the advent of a Bolshevism that was almost antithetical in its utilitarian insistence on rapid industrialization and its critique of 'bourgeois morality'. The story of socialism in Britain after 1917 is fundamentally the story of the tension between these

---

[11] Croft, *Red Letter Days*, 26–7.

[12] The ideological and formal diversity of anti-Communist literature has been explored in Benjamin Kohlmann and Matthew Taunton (eds), *Literatures of Anti-Communism*, special issue, *Literature and History*, 24/5 (Spring 2015).

[13] Recent work that has sought to situate the reception of Bolshevik ideas in the context of the longer history of Anglo-Russian cultural relations includes Beasley and Bullock, *Russia in Britain*; Anthony Cross (ed.), *A People Passing Rude: British Responses to Russian Culture* (Cambridge: Open Book Publishers, 2012); and Olga Soboleva and Angus Wrenn, *From Orientalism to Cultural Capital: The Myth of Russia in British Literature of the 1920s* (Bern: Peter Lang, 2017).

[14] Arthur Koestler, 'Soviet Myth and Reality', in *The Yogi and the Commissar* (New York: Macmillan, 1946).

two models, and the attempts to reconcile them.[15] This tension is not limited to an internecine struggle within the left, moreover: the questions posed by the Bolshevik Revolution—about the politics, the ethics, and the very nature of capitalist modernity—forced a widespread reconceptualization of 'Englishness' in relation to emerging new ideas of Russianness that also resonated in liberal and conservative circles.

These three central arguments are strands that run through the five chapters of this book. Each chapter focuses on one key debate that was energized and given a new political force after coming into contact with Bolshevik ideas. Chapter 1, 'The Radiant Future', addresses the question of the future. The notion that the future would be typologically (and not just incrementally) different from anything experienced in the present, was a crucial component of radical thought before 1917. Indeed Reinhart Koselleck and François Hartog see this attitude to futurity as integral to modernity itself. The term 'socialism' named a state of society that existed nowhere in the world, except as a speculation about the future. After the Bolshevik Revolution, socialists in Britain had to account for the existence of a state that claimed to be implementing socialist ideas. The future was no longer a space of speculation, but became unavoidably entwined with Russia. The effect was all the more dramatic because of so-called Russian backwardness: 1917 provided a destabilizing sense that the future had finally arrived, but in the least likely of places. Exploring works by (among others) H. G. Wells, John Cournos, C. Day Lewis, and Dorothy Richardson, I show how the Russian Revolution entailed—for left-leaning intellectuals—a fundamental shift in the temporality of socialism.

In Chapter 2, the focus is on numbers. The realms of arithmetic, counting, and mathematics might be thought to be highly abstract ones remote from history, and from geographically distant events. Yet as I show here—putting writers such as Koestler, Orwell, and Vladimir Nabokov into dialogue with mathematicians and philosophers—they were politicized in important ways as a result of the Russian Revolution. The Soviet Union presented itself as a planned society in which every aspect of social and economic life could be precisely measured, and tables of statistics abounded in celebration of the successes of the Soviet economy. Against this background, I point to a tradition of romantic anti-Communism that set itself in opposition to all forms of quantitative knowledge and especially their incursion into the political realm. Romantic anti-Communism

---

[15] Attempts to synthesize Soviet-style Communism with Englishness in the Popular Front period have been explored in Ben Harker, '"Communism is English": Edgell Rickword, Jack Lindsay and the Cultural Politics of the Popular Front', *Literature and History*, 20/2 (2011), 16–43.

relied upon an idea of the human (and of literature) as that which is not susceptible to quantification. The chapter's title, 'Two and Two Make Five', is a well-known quotation from Orwell that, I show, has a long heritage both in Russia and in Britain, and reflects a debate about the relationship between radical politics and rationalization. Meanwhile, the institutionalization of dialectical materialism as the official scientific outlook of the Soviet Union raised a vital intellectual question that took on a strong political charge: were seemingly timeless arithmetical or mathematical propositions (such as 'two plus two equals four') part of the ideological superstructure and therefore contingent on their particular historical moment?

Following on from the question of dialectical materialism's attempts to historicize (and potentially to relativize) mathematical statements, Chapter 3, 'Crime and Punishment', pursues this into the realm of justice and law. Legal and ethical norms were subjected to a materialist critique in the nineteenth century by Marx and Engels, who sought to demonstrate that these were a specific product of bourgeois society, dedicated to the defence of capitalist property relations. So what role could there be for legal norms and institutions in a Communist society? The notion of the 'withering away' of the legal apparatus of the state lost traction as the 1930s wore on, and the spectacle of the Moscow trials of 1936-8 offered a fundamental challenge to liberals who sympathized with Communism. They also provided grist to those—like Hannah Arendt—who would theorize a 'totalitarianism' based on a fundamental analogy between Communism and fascism. This chapter sets works by Arthur Koestler and Stephen Spender in context with those including D. N. Pritt, the Duchess of Atholl, Hannah Arendt, and Harold Laski who grappled with Communist law in theory and in practice. Again, the Russian Revolution posed the vital question of whether norms and values are specific to particular cultures, or whether there is an 'Absolute Justice' (as Spender put it) that might be mobilized across national boundaries.

While the first three chapters deal primarily with urban intellectual culture, in Chapters 4 and 5 the Russian countryside and its peasantry come into view—a pervasive obsession for many contemporaries, though comparatively neglected in recent accounts of British attitudes to Communism. Chapter 4, 'Homestead versus Kolchos', is about agriculture, and takes its title from an opposition that obsessed Ezra Pound, between individual peasant smallholdings farmed on a subsistence basis by a free yeoman class, and large-scale, industrial, collectivized agriculture typical of the Soviet Union. Though Pound was an American (and so was the homestead), this opposition is a vital structuring principle in British understandings of the Russian countryside. On the whole, English socialism in the nineteenth century (taking its cue from William Cobbett and William Morris) had been sympathetic to the plight of peasants uprooted by the rise of agricultural capitalism, even idealizing the yeoman as a repository of resistance against capitalist industrialization. This chapter shows that the significant residue of this peasant-oriented socialism had to contend with a new form of socialism with a seemingly antithetical attitude to the land, which celebrated industrialism and made the tractor its symbol. The brutality with which Stalin pursued the collectivization of the countryside added another dimension: anti-Communists such as G. K. Chesterton and Hilaire Belloc were quick to mobilize the peasant smallholder for their cause, and even Orwell suggested that one of Communism's tyrannies was in its attitude to the soil.

The final chapter, 'The Compensations of Illiteracy', combines a consideration of Russian orality and literacy with the question of religion, since these themes were often linked in discussions of the Russian peasantry. The title is drawn from *Undiscovered Russia* (1912) by the Russophile Stephen Graham, who claimed that the illiteracy of the Russian peasantry brought it closer to God. Some intellectuals thought that the Bolshevik Revolution was the force of literate rationality winning a victory over Orthodox mysticism—in a sense, they understood the revolution as a rerun or a continuation of the Protestant Reformation. On the other hand, Communism could often be imagined as a new political religion, capable of providing in a modern, secular form the spiritual sustenance and community that had been the central social function of religion. There was also a strong tradition of understanding the problems of Stalin's Soviet Union as stemming from a residual orality in Russian culture that could partly be attributed to its religious history: the Reformation that did not happen in Russia was every bit as important as the one that did happen in Britain. For some, the absence of a Reformation in Russia left in place a quasi-medieval propensity to idolatry that made possible a cult of personality and leader worship. Moreover, for many writers I consider in this chapter, as for Marshall McLuhan and Walter Ong, modern communications technologies (gramophones, telephones, and typewriters) were powerfully implicated in the shifting relations between speech and writing in modernity, and the socio-political effects with which these were associated. For a writer such as Doris Lessing, the Party was characterized by the routinized habits of thought and conventional speech patterns that were often linked with oral cultures.

Together the chapters in this book demonstrate the manifold influences of the Russian Revolution on our cultural and intellectual life. They describe a constellation rather than an event, as the debates I trace unfold in slow motion across a long period. The questions addressed in each of the chapters came into clear focus in the mid-century, as the 'Red Decade' segued into the early Cold War, but they are still live ones today. Left-wing debates refer back almost inexorably to the role played by the Soviet Union—however bleak the realities of Soviet Communism—in sustaining the idea a future after capitalism, and fundamentally different from it. In Mark Fisher's influential book *Capitalist Realism: Is There No Alternative?* (2009), he argued that 'in the 1980s there were still, in name at least, political alternatives to capitalism'. Following the fall of the Berlin Wall and the collapse of the Soviet system, Fisher argued, that alternative disappeared. 'What we are dealing with now', he lamented, 'is a deeper, far more pervasive, sense of exhaustion, of cultural and political sterility.' Nodding to Žižek and Fredric Jameson, Fisher pointed to a pervasive cultural logic whereby 'it is easier to imagine the end of the world than it is to imagine the end of capitalism'.[16] In some senses Fisher (writing in 2009) captured a quandary the contemporary left still finds itself in, and his project was poised in part to reactivate a culture of speculative utopian thinking that seemed to him to have died with the last embers of the Bolshevik Revolution.

There is much to be gained, I would suggest, by situating the quandary Fisher described in a longer perspective that takes into account the ways Bolshevik and Soviet ideas have been digested and deployed in Britain. As I show in Chapter 1, the Russian Revolution itself—the birth of actually existing socialism rather than its endgame in 1989—could be seen as the moment at which the idea of a socialist future, fundamentally different from the known present, expired. By retrieving older, pre-1917 futures, and showing the Russian Revolution as an embodiment of a still-insurgent and always-contested model of futurity rather than a norm against which our present 'exhaustion' and 'sterility' ought to be measured, this book hopes not simply to historicize mid-century thinking about the future, but to suggest that we still inhabit the discursive universe that was inaugurated by the Russian Revolution. Bolshevism never fully secured the monopoly on the future that Fisher's argument implies, nor did the demise of the Soviet Union wipe it from the face of the earth. Bolshevism proposed revolution as the cataclysmic means by which to effect a break with the capitalist present. But its longer term effect was to force a version of socialism into the present where it became the subject of a debate that was intensely reformist in tone, as writers and intellectuals weighed up competing ways to manage complex modern societies as if they were ordering lunch *à la carte*. In other words, despite its own rhetorical

---

[16] Mark Fisher, *Capitalist Realism: Is There No Alternative?* (Ropley: 0 Books, 2009), 7, 2.

focus on the *means* by which to effect radical political change, the primary cultural effect of the Bolshevik Revolution was to animate a conversation about *ends*. The Leninist idea of a total rupture with bourgeois society was therefore far from being the only legacy of the Russian Revolution for British culture, and to focus on this element ignores questions that were at the heart of the way the revolution was discussed. How ought we to use quantitative data in the management of human affairs? How ought we to agree and enforce legal norms, or can we do without them? How ought we to farm and inhabit the land? How might a literate, secular society replace what is sometimes felt as a lost sense of religious belonging—or escape the feeling that this needs to be replaced? The Russian Revolution ironically helped to generate a sense that the future is contained not in some apocalyptic break with the present, but in the answers to questions like these. The revolution's reconfiguration of the relation between present and future is in a sense a precondition for this set of questions which I pursue in Chapters 2, 3, 4, and 5 respectively, and it is for that reason that I begin in Chapter 1, by turning to the future.

1

The Radiant Future

THE DUTY OF LOOKING FORWARDS

Touring the Future

An advertisement in the *New Statesman and Nation* in 1932 offered its readers the unique experience of travelling to the Soviet Union, a destination that was 'different from the whole rest of the world. Surely', the advertisement continued, 'it is more interesting to see and learn first hand of the dynamic events taking place in the Soviet Union!' Intourist—Russia's state travel agency—offered 'moderately priced tours' lasting fourteen, twenty-one, or twenty-eight days, and many left-leaning British tourists took up these and similar offers.[1] Numbering among these were Kingsley Martin, the editor of the *New Statesman and Nation*, and the political cartoonist David Low, who travelled together under the aegis of Intourist in 1932, with the aim of writing a book. The resulting volume made conventional claims of impartiality, and combined mild, light-hearted criticism of the Communist state with occasionally staggering oversights in terms of reporting the reality of Stalinism. Strolling through the Park of Culture and Rest in Leningrad, Martin and Low were delighted by a vision of peace and prosperity. Their conversation turned on the uncanny feeling that they had arrived in the future. Low asked 'Why is this place so good? It makes me feel positively Bolshevik. It might be the opening scene of one of Wells's Utopias.'[2] The choice of Wells's utopian romances as a lens through which to see the Soviet Union can tell us much about the shifting relationships between literature and politics after 1917. Martin and Low reached for Wells because—as an immensely popular writer of speculative scientific romances—his vision of the future

---

[1] Advertisement: 'U.S.S.R.—The New Travel Land', *The New Statesman and Nation*, 3/60 (16 Apr. 1932), 505. The phenomenon of political tourism to the USSR is discussed at length in Patrick Wright, *Iron Curtain: From Stage to Cold War* (Oxford: OUP, 2009), and Paul Hollander, *Political Pilgrims: Travels of Western Intellectuals to the Soviet Union, China, and Cuba, 1928–1978* (Oxford: OUP, 1981).

[2] Kingsley Martin, *Low's Russian Sketchbook* (London: Gollancz, 1932), 35.

was near at hand. His name, and the fictional genre it evoked, had been synonymous with the future since the late Victorian period. After 1917, in the minds of many writers and intellectuals, the idea of the future became increasingly inseparable from debates about the Soviet Union. Or, to stand this on its head, the future—as a space of possibility, fantasy, and prediction—disappeared, to be replaced by a geographical entity: the Soviet Union. 'I have been to the future and it works', wrote the muck-raking US journalist Lincoln Steffens after he visited Russia in 1919.[3] For Low, entering the Park of Culture and Rest felt just like stepping into one of H. G. Wells's utopian romances. The frontier between present and future—between capitalist reality and utopian dream—had been crossed. This is just one of the ways in which writers imagined the relationship between geography and temporality shifting after 1917.

This chapter documents a number of important sites in British culture at which the idea of the future is transformed by its encounter with Russian socialism. As a result of the Russian Revolution, I argue, the discursive status of the future shifted in ways that shaped debates about political morality, informed a new sense of historicity, and interacted with literary approaches to temporality. Turning to Dorothy Richardson's novel sequence *Pilgrimage* in the final part of the chapter, I show how the ethical and political stakes of her modernist attempt to recapture the sensuous present—with all its implications for literary style and technique—become clearer when seen in the context of a broader debate about the future, and what happened to it after 1917.

In recalling Wells's fiction on their arrival in Soviet Russia, Low and Martin seemed to forget that, in most of the scientific romances, the future is far from the pleasant and carefree park in which they believed them-selves to be strolling. Wells often depicted the future as a dystopian catastrophe. This meant that the parallel between Wells's fiction and revolutionary Russia could also be invoked by those who were more fearful of the Bolsheviks. Responding to Wells's *Russia in the Shadows* (1920)—which recommended that the British Government should recognize and come to terms with the Bolshevik leadership—the émigré Russian writer Dmitrii Merezhkovsky admonished the author in an open letter that suggested a darker parallel between his fiction and the new Russia:

And finally, Mr Wells, let me quote yourself. Do you know what Bolsheviks are? They are neither men nor beasts, not even devils, but your Martians.

---

[3] Lincoln Steffens qtd. in Martin Malia, *Russia under Western Eyes: From the Bronze Horseman to the Lenin Mausoleum* (Cambridge, MA; London: Belknap Press of Harvard University Press, 1999), 340.

This is happening today, and not only in Russia, but throughout the world, this is precisely what you have so brilliantly predicted in *The War of the Worlds*. The Martians descended on Russia openly, but one feels already that they are proliferating everywhere from the inside.[4]

Merezhkovsky subscribed to Martin and Low's sense that the future that had until lately belonged to Wells's fiction now belonged to Bolshevik Russia. But the political meaning for him was reversed: it was the Martian invasion of *The War of the Worlds* (1897), and not the post-scarcity World State of *A Modern Utopia* (1905), that had come into being in Russia in 1917.

Arthur Koestler's understanding of the Russian Revolution was also refracted through Wells's fiction, but his changing attitude to Bolshevism meant that he experienced the political implications of a Wellsian interpretation of the revolution from both sides. A Hungarian-Jewish intellectual, Koestler had been a member of the German Communist Party from 1931 until 1938, when he took British nationality.[5] After leaving the Party, he moved towards a social democracy spiced with the passionate anti-Communism of the repentant convert. Koestler visited the Soviet Union, like Martin and Low, in 1932, at the height of his Communist enthusiasm. Unlike Martin and Low, and most other Western visitors to the USSR—whose visits were carefully stage-managed by Intourist—Koestler visited some obscure corners of the Soviet empire. *Red Days and White Nights*, his account of his travels, extravagantly demonstrated his sympathy with the Communist authorities. Soviet state publishing houses nevertheless refused to publish it, despite having paid Koestler several sizeable advances, labelling the book 'frivolous and light-hearted'.[6] Describing a visit to a new silk factory in Soviet Turkmenistan, Koestler was awed by the women who worked there:

The step across the factory gate takes them in one move from the seventeenth century straight into the twentieth . . . .

Thou and I, we shall die and never learn what news the first spaceship will bring home from another planet. We shall not learn what ideas, machines, and courting habits the citizens of the future will employ. Our curiosity will never be assuaged. But look at these girls. The fetters which had tied them to medieval Islam have suddenly snapped; they rubbed their eyes, sat down in

---

[4] Dmitrii Merezhkovsky qtd. in Olga Soboleva and Angus Wrenn, *From Orientalism to Cultural Capital: The Myth of Russia in British Literature of the 1920s* (Oxford: Peter Lang, 2017), 107.

[5] David Cesarani, *Arthur Koestler: The Homeless Mind* (London: Heinemann, 1998), 325.

[6] Michael Scammell, *Koestler: The Indispensable Intellectual* (London: Faber, 2009), 98.

Wells's time machine, and alighted three centuries later. Their curiosity is satisfied. I envy them.[7]

For Koestler, the voyage from Western Europe to the Soviet Union was a form of time travel. To live and work there was to experience the future first hand. But the young Koestler, still enthused by Communism, did not acknowledge the irony involved in choosing Wells's dystopian fantasy, *The Time Machine* (1895), as an analogue for his experiences in Russia. In Wells's novel, the Time Traveller arrives in the year AD 802,701 to find that the human race has evolved into two distinct species, the Eloi and the Morlocks, descended from the bourgeoisie and the proletariat of Wells's own time. The Eloi are a dim-witted and frivolous species, made soft by millennia of idleness, while the brutish Morlocks live and work underground, and cannibalize the Eloi, their distant cousins. Koestler's version of the story does not explore the parallel. For him, the women of Soviet Turkmenistan have arrived in a future founded on intense industrial efficiency, but one where class divisions have disappeared, in contrast with Wells's tale. These women have arrived in a Golden Age, and Koestler felt himself a privileged guest. The future was no longer a matter for speculation, but a vast country starting at the eastern fringe of Europe and merging obscurely into Asia. The future was now accessible by train.

Koestler continued to write prolifically in the post-war period, now as an anti-Communist. In *Arrow in the Blue* (1952) he retraced the reasoning that led him into Communism: 'the contrast between the downward trend of capitalism and the simultaneous steep rise of planned Soviet economy was so striking and obvious that it led to the equally obvious conclusion: they are the future—we, the past'.[8] The fact that a period of economic expansion in Russia coincided with the worst depression in the history of Western capitalism undoubtedly added to the contrast: capitalism appeared to be burnt out, Soviet Communism was growing stronger. In *The Invisible Writing* (1954), Koestler returned to his memories of the factory in Turkmenistan. He was now 'amazed' by the 'crude naïveté' of his Communist travelogue. For these factory workers, he had come to understand, 'the enforced voyage in the time-machine amounted to their deportation into a disconsolate and incomprehensible world'.[9] Koestler's earlier reference to *The Time Machine* now seemed like an unconscious prophecy of the way he would now—as an anti-Communist—understand

[7] Arthur Koestler, *Red Days and White Nights*, qtd. in Arthur Koestler, *The Invisible Writing: The Second Volume of an Autobiography: 1932–40* (London: Vintage, 2005), 142.
[8] Arthur Koestler, *Arrow in the Blue: The First Volume of an Autobiography: 1905–31* (London: Vintage, 2005), 328.
[9] Koestler, *The Invisible Writing*, 142.

the Russian Revolution. Though it had transmuted from dream to nightmare, Koestler held on to the sense that in the 1930s the Soviet Union had come to be synonymous with the future. In his post-war anti-Communism he was preoccupied with the question of whether it would prove possible to hold off that totalitarian destiny.

In a striking example of the way in which reality can be experienced through the prism of fiction, Russia had become infused with the flavour of a Wells novel. Conversely, the technologized utopias and dystopias that Wells concocted were seen, in hindsight, through the lens of Soviet Russia. Wells's own attitude to the future shifted over the course of his career, with the Russian Revolution an important turning point. His early work was produced in a climate of intense, freewheeling speculation and argument about the possibilities of the future. He acknowledged in his *Experiment in Autobiography*, first published in 1934, that a 'preoccupation with the future' was 'dominant in my conscious life'. In 1902 he gave a lecture to the Royal Institution titled *The Discovery of the Future*, also published as a pamphlet that year. In it he argued that there were two types of mind 'distinguished chiefly by their attitude towards time, and more particularly by the relative... amount of thought they give to the future of things'.[10] Wells called the first type the 'legal mind', which 'seems scarcely to think of the future at all', and can only conceive of it as a 'black non-existence upon which the advancing present will presently write events'.[11] This type of mind, by far the most common, is constrained by the laws and the rules of the present. The second type—the type of Wells's own brain—he called the 'legislative mind', which 'sees the world as one great workshop, and the present [a]s no more than material for the future, for the thing that is destined to be'. Wells believed that the development of scientific thinking—based on the testing of hypotheses and the accurate prediction of experimental outcomes—had reached such a level that humankind's knowledge of its future might begin to outstrip its knowledge of the past. A 'systematic exploration of the future' was now possible, and one could afford to be more confident than ever before in one's predictions, not just in the laboratory but in the realm of politics and society.[12] The future need no longer be a mystery, and the legal mind, with its fixation on inherited rules and existing states of affairs, was becoming anachronistic. 'I believe', he wrote, 'that the deliberate direction of historical study, and of economic and social study towards the future, and... a deliberate and courageous reference to the future in moral and

[10] H. G. Wells, *The Discovery of the Future: A Discourse Delivered to the Royal Institution on January 24, 1902* (London: T. Fisher Unwin, 1902), 7.
[11] Ibid. 8.   [12] Ibid. 52.

religious discussion, would be enormously stimulating and enormously profitable to our intellectual life'.[13]

Regimes of Historicity

Some would argue that Wells's future-orientation was merely a self-conscious and programmatic version of the spirit that had animated the intellectuals of modern Europe in general since the end of the eighteenth century. François Hartog has argued that an orientation towards the future is fundamental to the modern 'regime of historicity', as he calls it.[14] Hartog theorizes three different regimes of historicity in which the past, present, and future (respectively) are foremost on the horizon. Each of these is taken to dominate in a different epoch. In the classical civilizations of ancient Greece and Rome, the present and future were subordinate to the static categories of a mythological past. Hartog's modern regime of historicity—which he claims was dominant from the Enlightenment to the fall of Communism—can be understood in terms of 'the predominance of the category of the future'. In the modern regime of historicity,

> The future is the telos. It is the source of the light illuminating the past. Time is no longer a simple classificatory principle, but rather an agent, the operator of a historical process—the other name, or rather the true name, for progress. This history, which human beings make, is perceived as accelerating. There is thus a belief in history—a belief that is diffuse or reflected, but nonetheless shared.[15]

Hartog's understanding of modernity's temporal regime owes a great deal to Reinhart Koselleck, who described modernity as a dispensation in which a gap opens up between the 'horizon of expectation' and the 'space of experience'. Koselleck argued that

---

[13] Ibid. 70.

[14] Hartog's work has been taken up in Sascha Bru, 'Avant-Garde Nows: Presentist Reconfigurations of Public Time', *Modernist Cultures*, 8/2 (2013), 272–87, Peter Osborne, 'Global Modernity and the Contemporary: Two Categories of the Philosophy of Historical Time', in Chris Lorenz and Berber Bevernage (eds), *Breaking up Time: Negotiating the Borders between Present, Past and Future* (Göttingen: Vandenhoeck & Ruprecht, 2013), and Patrick Wright, 'Preface to the OUP edition', in *On Living in an Old Country: The National Past in Contemporary Britain* (Oxford: OUP, 2009), pp. xviii–xix. Hartog's major work in this area is François Hartog (tr. Saskia Brown), *Regimes of Historicity: Presentism and Experiences of Time* (New York: Columbia University Press, 2015).

[15] François Hartog, tr. Joel Golb, 'The Modern Régime of Historicity in the Face of the Two World Wars', in Berber Bevernage and Chris Lorenz (eds), *Breaking up Time: Negotiating the Borders between Present, Past and Future* (Göttingen: Vandenhoeck & Ruprecht, 2013), 124–33, 124.

during *Neuzeit* [modernity] the difference between experience and expectation has increasingly expanded; more precisely, that *Neuzeit* is first understood as a *neue Zeit* [new time] from the time that expectations have distanced themselves evermore from all previous experience.

Instead of notions of the future being limited by the experiences and categories of the past, in *Neuzeit*, 'expectations that reached out for the future became detached from all that previous experience had to offer'.[16] The modern regime of historicity, then, depends on an assumption that the future will be radically different from the present, and will not operate according to norms, customs, and laws that one might encounter in one's knowledge of the past or experience of the present.

A key intervention of Hartog's theory is his suggestion that, since 1989, we have entered a third regime of historicity, and presentism has taken over from the futurism that was typical of modernity. I argue that, for British intellectuals, the Russian Revolution triggered a widespread and polarized debate that challenged the model of modernity in which 'all the light comes from the future'. Long before 1989—indeed at the beginning of the historical sequence that date is presumed to end—the modern temporal regime was contested by a rival formulation in which the light came from contemporary Russia: geographically distant, yes, but uncontroversially a part of the present. Hartog is happily flexible about his periodizations, and acknowledges that the modern regime of historicity was 'contested' long before its nominal end date in 1989. In any case, he states that 'a regime of historicity has never been a universally applicable metaphysical entity sent from heaven'.[17] Michel Foucault was right to see modernity not as a historical period but as an attitude or an ethos. Foucault argued, moreover, that 'the attitude of modernity, ever since its formation, has found itself struggling with attitudes of "countermodernity."'[18] In British intellectuals' engagements with socialism, 1917 was a key date at which the modern regime of historicity began to be challenged by a presentism based on the idea that socialism had come into being in Russia.

Wells positioned himself as a self-conscious inheritor of an 'attitude of modernity' that traced its heritage to the Enlightenment, and bemoaned the fact that many of his contemporaries were on the side of

---

[16] Reinhardt Koselleck (tr. Keith Tribe), '"Space of Experience" and "Horizon of Expectation": two Historical Categories' in *Futures Past: On the Semantics of Historical Time* (New York: Columbia University Press, 2004), 263, 266–7.

[17] Hartog, *Regimes of Historicity*, 106.

[18] Michel Foucault, 'What is Enlightenment' (tr. Catherine Porter), in Paul Rabinow (ed.), *The Foucault Reader: An Introduction to Foucault's Thought* (London: Penguin, 1991), 39.

countermodernity. He berated these contemporaries in *The Discovery of the Future* because for them, to use Koselleck's terms, the horizon of expectation was fundamentally defined and limited by the space of experience. Modernity was not modern enough for Wells, and so he felt himself a heretic. Nevertheless, Wells did embody for his contemporaries a strong progressive impulse in Edwardian culture. As Beatrice Webb wrote (before the two fell out), 'his work is full of luminous hypotheses and worth careful study by those who are trying to look forward'.[19] A similar phrase was used less sympathetically by Wells's contemporary and interlocutor G. K. Chesterton, who complained of:

> the optimistic official prophecies of the book called, *Looking Backwards* [by Edward Bellamy]; a rather ironical title, seeing that the one thing forbidden to such futurists was Looking Backwards. And the whole philosophy, afterwards sublimated by the genius of Mr. Wells, was the duty of Looking Forwards.[20]

Such debates should be considered as an important feature of the temporal regime into which the Russian Revolution erupted.

Chesterton's own *The Napoleon of Notting Hill* (1904) begins with some 'Introductory Remarks on the Art of Prophecy', which caution about the unreliability of speculations about the future. Chesterton warned against both Wellsian predictions that 'science would take control of the future' and Edward Carpenter's view that 'we should in a very short time return to Nature'.[21] Even so, *The Napoleon of Notting Hill* is itself a work of futurological speculation set in 1984. Chesterton does not turn away from prophecy as such but offers a very different version of the future designed polemically to subvert Wells. Chesterton's protagonist Adam Wayne is surely referring to Wells's *Anticipations* (1901) when he says that 'in the old dreary days, wiseacres used to write books about how trains would get faster, and all the world would be one empire, and tram-cars go to the moon. And even as a child I used to say to myself, "Far more likely that we shall go on the crusades again, or worship the gods of the city." And so it has been.'[22] Rather than the future being driven by constant change, Chesterton sees it as a repetition of a past Golden Age. As such, Chesterton could be thought of as a late representative of a regime of historicity Hartog associates with antiquity, where the past is foremost on

---

[19] Beatrice Webb, qtd. in Samuel Hynes, *The Edwardian Turn of Mind* (London: Pimlico, 1991), 96.

[20] G. K. Chesterton, *Autobiography* (London: Hutchinson, 1969), 25.

[21] G. K. Chesterton, *The Napoleon of Notting Hill* (London: Capuchin Classics, 2008), 16–17.

[22] Chesterton, *Napoleon of Notting Hill*, 180.

the horizon of expectation. But even a future based so determinedly on the past seemed to become swallowed up by an expanding present after 1917. From that date forward, Chesterton's visions of the future were increasingly articulated in opposition to Bolshevism. The idyllic picture of a bucolic lost past was no longer merely an ideal pattern for the future, but a weapon to be deployed against the very present danger of Communism.[23] When Chesterton established his own journal in 1925, he wrote in his inaugural editorial that '[t]his paper exists to demand that we fight Bolshevism with something more than plutocracy'.[24] What that alternative was, I explore in Chapter 4. The point for now is that, as different as their horizons of expectation were before 1917, both Wells and Chesterton were drawn by the Bolshevik Revolution into a polarized debate about socialist Russia in the present.

Wells's work was part of an older debate among socialists about the rights and wrongs of speculation about the future. Writing in the *Communist Manifesto* in 1848, Marx and Engels had lambasted 'utopian socialists' who specialized in 'fantastic pictures of future society' and 'castles in the air', whilst shying away from the class war and from necessary revolutionary confrontations in the present.[25] And in the mid-nineteenth century, English socialists largely followed Marx's lead, dedicating themselves to criticizing capitalism rather than speculating about the socialist utopia of the future. Later in the century, socialists and reformers started to ignore the ban on looking into the future, and produced a series of fictional utopias that combined the features of socialist tract and speculative science fiction. Indeed, as Matthew Beaumont points out, '[i]n the final years of the nineteenth century, hundreds of novels and short stories—each one prophesying a future society from whose imaginary standpoint the present state of affairs seemed manifestly unsatisfactory—were printed in Britain and the United States'.[26] Some of these sold heavily and remain in print today. William Morris's *News from Nowhere* (1890) borrowed a plot device from Rip Van Winkle and saw its narrator falling asleep to wake up over a century later in an ideal future socialist society. For Morris, this involved deindustrialization, with the resettlement of the countryside, a return to handicrafts, and the abolition of money. Morris's utopian romance—clearly shot through with medievalism—was itself a response to Edward Bellamy's bestselling

[23] Chesterton's anti-Communist utopia *Tales of the Long Bow* is explored in Chapter 4.
[24] G. K. Chesterton, 'The First Principle', *G.K.'s Weekly*, 1/1 (21 Mar. 1925), 3.
[25] Karl Marx and Friedrich Engels, *The Communist Manifesto* (Harmondsworth: Penguin Books, 1967), 116–17.
[26] Matthew Beaumont, *Utopia Ltd: Ideologies of Social Dreaming in England, 1870–1900* (Leiden; Boston: Brill, 2005), 1.

Looking Backward: 2000–1887 (1888), a socialist utopia of a very different kind (the same book that Chesterton singled out for criticism). In Bellamy's intensely urban society—set in the year 2000—the machines ruled, and mankind had profited from the increase of industrial efficiency. Similarly, in Wells's novels of the *fin de siècle* and the Edwardian period—the novels that Koestler and Martin allude to in their descriptions of revolutionary Russia—the future's fundamental difference from the present, from 'experience', from 'tradition', was axiomatic. The present was only a stepping stone—all the light came from the future, which could be populated by the dreams and nightmares of the imagination. Wells restlessly explored the different possibilities: the hyper-Fordist urbanism of *When the Sleeper Wakes* (1899), the evolutionary degeneration of *The Time Machine* (1895), the alien invasion of *The War of the Worlds* (1897), the hi-tech commuter society of *Anticipations* (1901), and the benevolent dictatorship of *A Modern Utopia* (1905). As Wells wrote when he was composing *Anticipations*—his first non-fiction book of speculations about the future—he was 'writing the human prospectus'.[27]

Looking back on his pre-war futurology in 1934, Wells acknowledged a significant blind spot: 'I never guessed at the possibility of a modernized planning régime arising in Russia—of all countries . . . . I was quite out about Russia.'[28] And in his less voluminous and largely forgotten futurological work from after 1917, Russia often looms large. In *The Shape of Things to Come* (1929), the new dating system that marks the beginning of the 'Era of the Modern State' takes 1917 as its year zero. Wells can no longer simply turn the brass levers on a time machine and zoom many centuries into the future, as he had done in his early fiction. Instead he debates the rights and wrongs of the Communist regime at some length, before the subsequent history up to 2106, the book's present, can be told, and even then with frequent reference to Soviet Communism.[29]

Wells's increasing preoccupation with Russia led him to visit the country three times, in 1914, 1920, and 1934. This final visit reveals much about the ways in which Wells had changed his orientation to the future. He was still asking the question that had spurred him on as a young man: what would the socialist future look like? But now, instead of writing *A Modern Utopia*, he paid two visits, to the Russia of the Five-Year Plan and to New Deal America, to see where the seeds of the socialist future lay.

---

[27] H. G. Wells, *Experiment in Autobiography: Discoveries and Conclusions of a Very Ordinary Brain (since 1866)*, 2 vols (London: Faber, 1984), 1i. 646.

[28] Wells, *Experiment in Autobiography*, 651.

[29] H. G. Wells, *The Shape of Things to Come: The Ultimate Revolution* (London: Hutchinson & Co., 1933), 27, 30–1.

Wells was anxious to meet both Stalin and Roosevelt 'because I thought that the two of them between them indicated the human future as no other two men could do'.[30] Wells's notion of the writer's role in relation to the socialist future had changed. The world situation—most importantly the rise of the world's first avowedly socialist state—left little room for the free-wheeling fantasies that Wells had produced in his futurological experiments of the pre-war period. Discussing these in his 1933 introduction to an edition of his *Scientific Romances*, Wells admitted a certain exhaustion with the form, arguing that '[t]he world in the presence of cataclysmal realities has no need of fresh cataclysmal fantasies.'[31] He seemed to feel that socialist writers must now engage with world leaders in order to negotiate a position in relation to the existing models, instead of creating 'fantasies'. The legislative mind had no space to work in, and Wells was increasingly and against his instincts forced to think in a merely legal way. His visions of the future were now inexorably bound up with the fate of Russia.

Stalin's Soviet Union would not conform to Wells's vision of the future, and seemed to stand in the way of any further futurological speculations. He was in the awkward situation of knowing everything about what the future ought to be like, but knowing nothing about how to get there. '[U]niversal freedom and abundance dangles within reach of us and is not achieved', he wrote. 'We who are Citizens of the Future wander about this present scene like passengers on a ship overdue, in plain sight of a port which only some disorder in the chart-room prevents us from entering.'[32] The future had materialized, but it was not the future Wells had anticipated. The way to *that* future now appeared to be barred by the intransigence of world rulers, of whom Wells complained: 'I can talk to them and even unsettle them but I cannot compel their brains to see'.[33] Wells's eye for the future had been blinded by a red light emanating from the East.

Socialism, Communism, and the Future

Wells's career in a sense embodies a wider shift I want to describe, whereby the futurist regime of historicity that prevailed among many writers and intellectuals before the Great War gradually foundered in the wake of the Russian Revolution. As Samuel Hynes noted, socialism had 'assumed the progressive role in English political life' during the Edwardian period

[30] Wells, *Experiment in Autobiography*, 804.
[31] H. G. Wells qtd. in Patrick Parrinder, *Science Fiction* (Abingdon; New York: Routledge, 2003), 13.
[32] Wells, *Experiment in Autobiography*, 821.   [33] Ibid. 821.

because, unlike liberalism and conservatism, 'it was not a political party and thus was not bound by either traditions or expedients'.[34] Socialism as a concept was completely unconstrained by Koselleck's space of experience, and existed only as a feature of the horizon of expectation. As an abstract noun describing a particular way of organizing society, 'socialism' can be grouped with 'feudalism', 'absolutism', 'Old Regime', 'liberalism', and 'capitalism'. Yet, as Martin Malia pointed out, unlike all these other examples, 'socialism' was coined almost a century before the attempt was made to bring such a state of society into being. 'Feudalism' and 'capitalism' designated something presumed actually to have existed, so that their meanings could be illustrated with specific historical examples. Before 1917, 'socialism' did not refer to any real society: the word itself was a speculation about an ideal future. To be a socialist, up until 1917, was to believe in the possibility that a state of society never before seen on earth could come into existence. As Malia wrote, '[i]t was only with the Bolshevik October that socialism crossed the threshold from movement to society'.[35] The result was that the word 'socialism' could not be used in the same way after 1917. For one thing, as Raymond Williams noted, '[f]rom that time on, a distinction of socialist from communist, often with supporting distinctions such as *social democrat* or democratic socialist, became widely current'.[36] But on the other hand the Communist parties of the Third International continued to be called, and understood as, socialist. A word whose power derived from its future orientation, its lack of any referent in the present, suddenly obtained an unavoidable referent.

In his book *100 Years of Socialism*, a sweeping history of the Western European left in the twentieth century, Donald Sassoon wrote that

the Russian Revolution provided the Left with a fundamental reference point. Thereafter... every single European socialist group or faction faced the continuous necessity of defining its position not only on the revolution itself, but on each of its subsequent stages. Both revolutionaries and reformists now had a model, positive for the former, negative for the latter.[37]

Or, as Perry Anderson put it in 1980:

the outbreak of the October Revolution transformed the whole landscape of socialist thought. From now on, the construction of a communist society was

---

[34] Hynes, *Edwardian Turn of Mind*, 87.

[35] Martin Malia, *The Soviet Tragedy: A History of Socialism in Russia, 1917–1991* (New York: Free Press, 1994), 34.

[36] Raymond Williams, *Keywords: A Vocabulary of Culture and Society* (London: Fontana, 1983), 289.

[37] Donald Sassoon, *One Hundred Years of Socialism: The West European Left in the Twentieth Century* (London: I. B. Tauris, 2010), 31.

no longer a matter of speculative theory, but of experimental practice....
The deep longing for another human order which had found expression in
the utopias of the nineteenth century had now fastened onto the—often
scarcely less imaginary—society in the USSR.[38]

Before 1917, 'socialism' was nothing anyone had experienced. It embodied the disconnection between the space of experience and the horizon of
expectation that Koselleck argued was definitive of modernity itself. In
1917, when the first avowedly socialist state was created, 'socialism'
became an observable element of the present (albeit a contested one)
for the first time. The horizon of expectation, insofar as it was socialist,
was no longer divorced from the space of experience. The inheritors of
nineteenth-century radical tradition had henceforth to sign up to the
Bolshevik programme, or to use such formulations as 'socialism, but not
that socialism'.

The way in which the Russian Revolution transformed the word
'socialism'—giving a speculation about an ideal future a scrutable reality
in Russia—forms a vital context for debates about language in the Cold
War period. Deconstruction, for example, placed a value on the indeterminate sign precisely because of a desire to keep the future open. '*[I]f there
is* a categorical imperative, it consists in doing everything for the future to
remain open,' wrote Derrida in 'I Have a Taste for the Secret'.[39] When a
term like 'socialism' acquires a discrete referent, its openness to the future
is closed off. Derrida's theory of language thus has a temporal dimension.
A simplistic model of language in which linguistic signs are taken to point
to discrete and final referents—where meaning can be determined and
predicted in advance—is replaced by an open-ended field of *différance*. If
deconstruction has a politics, it is a commitment to this open-endedness,
to what Derrida calls 'the democracy to come':

> What's important in 'democracy to come' is not 'democracy' but 'to come.'
> That is, a thinking of the event, of what comes. It's the space opened in order
> for there to be an event, the to-come, so that the coming be that of the
> other.... 'To come' means 'future,' not the present future, which would be
> present and presentable tomorrow. It means the space opened in order for
> the other and others to come.

Derrida then goes on to suggest that a key characteristic of totalitarian
states is that they close off future possibility:

[38] Perry Anderson, *Arguments within English Marxism* (London: Verso, 1980), 171.
[39] Jacques Derrida and Maurizio Ferraris, *A Taste for the Secret*, tr. Giacomo Donis
(Cambridge: Polity Press, 2001), 82–3, emphasis in original. See also the discussion in
Shane Weller, *Modernism and Nihilism* (Basingstoke: Palgrave Macmillan, 2011), 144.

Non-democratic systems are above all systems that close and close themselves off from this coming of the other. They are systems of homogenization and of integral calculability. In the end and beyond all the classical critique of fascist, Nazi and totalitarian violence in general, one can say that these are systems that close the 'to come' and that close themselves into the presentation of the presentable. What I have said elsewhere about the coming, the event, the 'come here' (viens)—of différance and the deconstruction of presence is where I would begin to try to articulate a thinking of the political.[40]

The formulation 'fascist, Nazi and totalitarian violence in general' hardly gives precedence to 1917 as the moment when the future was closed off: Derrida is referring to mature totalitarian systems, not countries in the throes of revolution. Yet by coining the term 'democracy to come', Derrida attempted to recreate the future orientation that the term 'socialism' held for the Edwardians, even stressing the 'to come' so that nobody can confuse the term 'democracy' with its contemporary instantiations in, say, France or the USA. Deconstruction wants to rescue the indeterminacy of political language—and therefore the future—from the overdetermination of Cold War presentism.

Organizing themselves under the banner of the 'New Communism', Alain Badiou, Slavoj Žižek, and their followers have attempted to salvage some sort of future for the word 'communism'. This term is even more overdetermined than 'socialism', partly because of the operation Williams describes where Western anti-communists were able to defend the (democratic) 'socialism' of the British welfare state (for example) at the expense of the totalitarian collectivism of the 'communist' societies of the Eastern bloc. In *The Communist Hypothesis* (2008, trans. 2010), Badiou berates the French *nouveaux philosophes* (the group of liberal philosophers around Bernard-Henri Lévy who broke with Marxism in the 1970s) for confusing the 'Idea' of communism—and Badiou capitalizes 'Idea' to give it its full Platonic sense—with its various historical instantiations. For Badiou, inverting the procedure described by Williams, 'the communist Idea's only concrete forms' were in fact 'socialisms', whose 'failures' are best understood by analogy with the unsuccessful attempts, over 300 years since it was formulated, to prove Fermat's theorem.[41] Communism is a hypothesis, and 'failure is nothing more than the history of the proof of

[40] Jacques Derrida, 'Politics and Friendship: An Interview with Jacques Derrida', tr. Robert Harvey, in E. Ann Kaplan and Michael Spriker (eds), *The Althusserian Legacy* (London and New York: Verso, 1993), 182–231, 216.

[41] Alain Badiou (tr. David Macey and Steve Corcoran), *The Communist Hypothesis* (London: Verso, 2010), 5–7.

the hypothesis, provided that the hypothesis is not abandoned'.[42] The present—including the experience of socialism's small advances and catastrophic failures as the communist hypothesis is tested—is fundamentally separated from the communist future by 'the event' (akin to Wiles's proof of Fermat's theorem). Badiou's theory of 'the event' can be closely related to Koselleck's description of modernity. Badiou writes that, 'with respect to a situation or a world, an event paves the way for the possibility of what—from the limited perspective of the make-up of this situation or the legality of this world—is strictly impossible'.[43] Badiou advocates an attitude to the future, in other words, according to which the horizon of expectation is not limited by the space of experience, 'this situation or the legality of this world'. As Alan Johnson has argued, all this aims to place the Communist hypothesis 'beyond empirical refutation'.[44] Badiou's attempt to keep the Idea of Communism alive tends towards a future event through which the full Platonic meaning of Communism will be revealed. This is fundamentally different from Derrida's insistence that the future, and the meaning of the 'democracy to come', must always remain open: for Badiou there is a final referent, though it has not yet taken earthly form.

OTHER FUTURES

Science Fiction and Bolshevism

The late-Victorian and Edwardian trend for utopian speculative fiction underwent a rapid demise during the war and failed to revive after it. As Matthew Beaumont shows, utopian fictions continued to be published in vast numbers until 1914 when the trend stopped, 'buried beneath the feet of soldiers fighting trench warfare'.[45] It is hard to overestimate the transformative effects of the Great War, but the Russian Revolution—which after all was itself one of the major results of that war—also played a crucial role in changing the way writers thought about the future, and in holding off any revival of a purely utopian fiction after 1918. The revolution had an analogous effect on so-called 'invasion literature'. This popular genre, which gathered momentum during the late-Victorian romance revival, projected tales of the future that imagined Britain suffering

---

[42] Badiou, *The Communist Hypothesis*, 7.
[43] Badiou, *The Communist Hypothesis*, 243.
[44] Alan Johnson, 'The New Communism: Resurrecting the Utopian Delusion', *World Affairs*, 175/1 (May 2012), 62–70, 66.
[45] Beaumont, *Utopia Ltd.*, 13.

under an occupying foreign force. In the climate of Germanophobia that dominated the Edwardian period, such tales tended to portray Germany as the invading force. Michael Hughes and Harry Wood have shown that 'Red Scare' narratives dramatizing the threat from Bolshevik Russia came to dominate after 1918, occupying the same generic space but locating Russia as the nexus of popular fears and anxieties.[46] They discuss in particular Hugh Addisson's *The Battle for London* (1924), Oliver Baldwin's *Konyetz* (1924) (published under the pseudonym 'Martin Hussingtree', perhaps to conceal that the novel's author was the son of Prime Minister Stanley Baldwin), Horace Bleakley's *Anymoon* (1919), and Charles Ross's *The Fly-By-Nights* (1921). Invasion literature is an intrinsically conservative genre, and by definition only ever imagines the future as the intrusion of one geographically defined part of the present into another, as already-existing empires compete for dominion. Therefore, while I would argue that the fate of invasion literature after 1917 provides an important parallel, the shift that Hughes and Wood describe is a change in the nationality of the projected aggressor, and not the substitution of an abstract and otherworldly notion of a socialist utopian future with Bolshevism.

It would be misleading to imply that Russia maintained a complete hold on literature's capacity to imagine the future. Weird futures unconnected with the debate about Bolshevism continued to be dreamed up by writers, but the work of these genuinely 'legislative minds' tended to be consigned to the genre-ghetto of science fiction, a term coined in 1929 by the pulp publisher Hugo Gernsback and that often had a pejorative connotation.[47] After 1917, those novels about future societies that are classified as literary fiction tended to be deeply engaged with the debate about Soviet Russia (although of course another sub-genre emerged in which Nazi Germany was the target, as in Katharine Burdekin's *Swastika Night* (1937), initially published under the pseudonym 'Murray Constantine'). Where Wellsian futurological fiction thrived, its canonization was linked to its anti-Communism. Let us take the most famous examples, all novels to which I will return later in this book. In Zamyatin's *We* (1924), a novel that profoundly influenced Orwell, the formation of the 'One State' is modelled on the Bolshevik Revolution. Huxley's *Brave New World* (1932) is as much a satire of Fordist capitalism as of Soviet Communism, but as character names such as Polly Trotsky, Lenina

---

[46] Michael Hughes and Harry Wood, 'Crimson Nightmares: Tales of Invasion and Fears of Revolution in Early Twentieth-Century Britain', *Contemporary British History*, 28/3 (2014), 294–317.

[47] Roger Luckhurst, *Science Fiction* (Cambridge: Polity, 2005), 15.

Crowne, and Bernard Marx suggest, his vision of the future is as a nightmare convergence of various tendencies in both monopoly capitalism and Soviet-style communism. In *Nineteen Eighty-Four* (1949), Orwell takes from Soviet Russia (among other things) the Stalinist leader cult, the culture of surveillance, the persecution of a Trotskyite opposition, and many aspects of the operation of the secret police. While Vladimir Nabokov claimed in his introduction to *Bend Sinister* (1947) that it should not be read as an Orwellian allegory of Soviet totalitarianism, the fact that he put verbatim extracts from Lenin's speeches in the mouth of Paduk, his dictator, suggests that Soviet Russia is very much on the horizon. In all of these novels the dystopian futures described are self-consciously aware of their relationship with the Soviet Union. As the battle lines of the cultural Cold War were drawn, instead of asking 'how should the future be?', writers increasingly wanted to know 'whose side are you on?'

There were those who diagnosed and deplored this tendency. Science fiction writers sought to maintain pure visions of the future, attempting to wrest the future free from sectarian debates about the rights and wrongs of Stalinism. Isaac Asimov saw the problem especially clearly, and disliked *Nineteen Eighty-Four* intensely:

> Orwell had no feel for the future, and the displacement of the story is much more geographical than temporal. The London in which the story is placed is not so much moved thirty-five years forward in time, from 1949 to 1984, as it is moved a thousand miles east in space to Moscow.[48]

Orwell 'did not have the science fictional knack of foreseeing a plausible future', Asimov went on, instead 'engaging in a private feud with Stalinism': Orwell's unhealthy obsession with Communism prevented him from seeing the future.[49] The future as conceived in *Nineteen Eighty-Four* was a geographical rather than a temporal entity, and for Asimov this was because Orwell lacked imagination. Orwell might have responded by saying that the eclipse of the future by the shadow of totalitarianism was a part of his subject rather than a defect in his talent. 'If you want a picture of the future,' Orwell's Party man O'Brien says, 'imagine a boot stamping on a human face—forever.'[50]

Asimov's own writing practice showed one way to imagine a future in which Cold War tensions have evaporated. Asimov's story 'Let's Get Together' (1957) imagined that the Cold War would continue for

[48] Isaac Asimov, '1984', in *Asimov on Science Fiction* (Garden City, NY: Doubleday, 1981), 275–89, 279.

[49] Ibid. 289.

[50] George Orwell, *Nineteen Eighty-Four* (London: Secker & Warburg, 1997), 280.

centuries, with a 'We' and 'They' competing for supremacy in the field of robotics, but only behind the scenes of an almost total 'stalemate'.[51] Though in this story Asimov finds in the Cold War a fruitful basis for science fictional extrapolation, elsewhere—in a 1962 essay on Soviet science fiction—he complained that Soviet science fiction tended to fail because it was overdetermined by its Cold War context, which meant that the future had been occluded in favour of a predictable extension of the present.

> The Soviet people are told, and presumably believe, that they are building a new society which is bound, by the sheer attractiveness of its superior workability, to become the dominant society all over the world.... It would amount, then, almost to a lack of patriotism for a Soviet writer to suggest that other societies were possible in the future, or even to look too closely at the present one.[52]

In another essay on the same theme, from later in 1962, Asimov suggested that, for a Soviet writer, a ' "What if—" story might prove embarrassing if it were considered as sign of dissatisfaction with existing institutions'.[53] This time the problem did not derive from the failings of an individual author (Orwell): it was a function of the Communist outlook. For Asimov, a healthy attitude to the future—one that would produce successful science fiction and not just Cold War propaganda—involved asking the question 'what if...?' and then exploring in a rigorous fashion the possible results of a given technological, social, or environmental change. Soviet sci-fi was drastically impaired because the results were always known in advance: the arrival of the 'radiant future' was a scientific certainty.

Asimov's idea of a speculative fiction that achieves its effects by a 'displacement' that is 'much more geographical than temporal' was already evident in early responses to the Bolshevik Revolution. John Cournos's short story *London under the Bolsheviks: A Londoner's Dream on Returning from Petrograd* (1919) appeared as a pamphlet published by the Russian Liberation Committee, an anti-Bolshevik organization. Cournos was born to a Russian-speaking family near Kiev in 1881, and found himself in Petrograd during the October Revolution after Hugh Walpole asked him to join the Anglo-Russian Commission to Petrograd. Cournos was also building a career on the London literary scene, and would later become an

[51] Isaac Asimov, 'Let's Get Together', *Infinity*, 2/1 (Feb. 1957), 64–80.

[52] Isaac Asimov, 'Science Fiction from the Soviet Union', in Isaac Asimov, *Asimov on Science Fiction* (Garden City, NY: Doubleday, 1981), 164–70, 169.

[53] Isaac Asimov, 'More Science Fiction from the Soviet Union', in Asimov, *Asimov on Science Fiction*, 171–7, 174–5.

important contributor to T. S. Eliot's *Criterion*. As David Ayers notes in an invaluable survey of Cournos's career, *London under the Bolsheviks* 'owes a little to Wells'[s] vision of refugees arriving in central London in *The War of the Worlds*'.[54] The story can be read as a strikingly literal foreshadowing of Merezhkovsky's letter to Wells in which he likened the Bolsheviks to Wells's Martians. Cournos's Foreword to the story put it well:

> This is not a fantasy, in spite of the title. It is a true and precise picture of Petrograd during the first few months of the Bolshevist Revolution. The author has placed the scenes in London merely to emphasise the realities of the Bolshevist nightmare, to bring it home to those who do not quite realise the nature of the Russian upheaval. If the result appears fantastic, let the reader beware of blaming it on the imagination of the author. The author would feel flattered, were it not that, unfortunately, he is well aware of what his eyes have seen.[55]

The notion of a 'true and precise picture' of the Bolshevik Revolution being 'placed' in London—and the suggestion that such a geographical displacement in some sense usurps the territory of the 'fantasy' genre—echoes Asimov's later complaint about Orwell: 'The London in which the story is placed is not so much moved thirty-five years forward in time, from 1949 to 1984, as it is moved a thousand miles east in space to Moscow'.[56] Cournos creates British analogues for the key players in the Russian Revolution: Ramsay MacDonald was in charge of a 'well-intentioned but weak' Provisional Government (as Kerensky had been), which was subsequently overthrown by 'MacLenin and Trotsman'.[57] Although this was a game later played by Orwell—Old Major, Napoleon, and Snowball for Marx, Stalin, and Trotsky in *Animal Farm*, and Big Brother and Emmanuel Goldstein for Stalin and Trotsky in *Nineteen Eighty-Four*—Ayers argues that *London under the Bolsheviks* 'should . . . not be mistaken for any kind of lost prototype for [*Nineteen Eighty-Four*]'.[58] However, the symmetry to which I have drawn attention does provide some reason to consider the pamphlet as a predecessor to Orwell's novel, at least in terms of the way it generates a slippage between a science fictional future and a socialist Russia. Both texts use the resources of the

---

[54] David Ayers, 'John Cournos and the Politics of Russian Literature in *The Criterion*', *modernism/modernity*, 18/2 (Apr. 2011), 355–69, 359.

[55] John Cournos, *London under the Bolsheviks: A Londoner's Dream upon Returning from Petrograd* (London: Russian Liberation Committee, 1919), 2.

[56] Isaac Asimov, '1984', in *Asimov on Science Fiction* (Garden City, NY: Doubleday, 1981), 275–89, 279.

[57] Cournos, *London under the Bolsheviks*, 5.   [58] Ayers, 'John Cournos', 359.

Wellsian scientific romance, but they are not products of the 'legislative mind' as Wells defined it in *The Discovery of the Future*, a version of which also seems to be central to Asimov's conception of a properly future-oriented science fictional text. Instead they contend with the threat posed by a political entity that is separated not by time but by space. Potentially, at least, revolutionary Russia falls within Kosseleck's space of experience. As Cournos is keen to assert, the author of his story 'is well aware of what his eyes have seen'. If the reader experiences the story as fantasy, that is not because it radiates from an imaginary future that the reader may not, by definition, visit. It is simply because that reader has not been to Russia to experience it for herself.

Cournos was clearly conscious of Wells as a literary antecedent, to the extent that Wells himself features in the story. As if to underline the notion that Wells's brand of futurological speculation was transformed by the events of 1917, Cournos had his Bolsheviks throw Wells in jail. A cigarette vendor explains to Cournos's narrator that, as one would expect, political figures such as Viscount Grey, Asquith, and Lloyd George have been thrown into the Tower of London:

> And not only they but all the cultured chaps are having a hard time of it. Well, I dare say you've heard of H. G. Wells—to think of a brainy man like that in jail, counter-revolutionary—that's what he is called.[59]

The story dramatizes a rapid change in the meaning of socialism, from a hopeful speculation about the future to the discredited programme of a government that deals in arbitrary violence while it presides over the impoverishment of its citizens. The revolutionary flags that adorn every building have faded from red to a 'dirty black', and the narrator reflects that 'they must have been once as bright as the hopes of the people, and the people's hopes must be by now as faded and tattered as these flags'.[60] Cournos does not stint on the familiar signifiers of dystopian decay, his narrator noting that 'the sidewalk was piled up with discarded tins and all sorts of refuse' and, from the bank of the Thames, observing 'a dead human body floating peacefully along, seawards'.[61] To invert Lincoln Steffens's dictum, Cournos's narrator had been to the future, and it did not work.

The dystopian circumstances that the narrator encounters are not taken as evidence that—for example—the historical circumstances in Britain are not yet ripe for socialism. It is socialism itself that has been blackened, as the dirty flags seem to suggest. Indeed, when he awakes from his

---

[59] Cournos, *London under the Bolsheviks*, 5–6.   [60] Ibid. 7.   [61] Ibid. 7–8.

nightmare, the narrator is glad to see that 'A Union Jack fluttered in the breeze' and remarks: 'It was good to be back in England'—though of course he had never left.[62] This ending seems to point towards a retrenchment in Englishness and the British constitution as the only hope of holding off tyranny: there is precious little hope that an untarnished socialism might be salvaged. In Bolshevik London, what is left of pre-revolutionary English socialism is forced either to throw its weight behind the Bolsheviks (and so lose its distinctive character), or to be classed as hostile. Even socialist newspapers recognizable from before the revolution—the *Daily Herald* and the *Labour Leader*—are now considered 'hopelessly *bourgeois* and "counter-revolutionary"' by the Bolshevik authorities. This causes the left-leaning narrator to reconsider his own position, not because his old views have changed but because they mean something different in the context of a Bolshevik government:

> The things I had learnt in the course of the day depressed me, and, holding what would have been considered in the old days as Liberal, even Radical, opinions, I suddenly realised that I would now be deemed by the new régime to be an excessively dangerous character for holding opinions so palpably Conservative and old-fashioned.[63]

Cournos's narrator thus finds himself in a similar position to many who had identified with radical and socialist traditions in British politics before 1917. Spending only a few hours in Bolshevik London suggests to him that this version of socialism had monopolized the future that his 'Liberal, even Radical' opinions had seemed to make possible. There is no room now for any radicalism that is not Bolshevik, and Cournos's narrator accepts with horror that he will now be perceived as a conservative. And when, at the end of the story, he wakes up relieved to see the Union Jack fluttering in the breeze, the story suggests that this is not simply a question of perception. Embracing this symbol of Empire will be the only defence against Bolshevism: no other future is possible. As the text printed on the back cover of *London under the Bolsheviks* says in large type: 'If you are interested in the overthrow of Bolshevism; if you want to help save civilization from the menace of Anarchy, write to the Literary Secretary, Russian Liberation Committee, 173, Fleet Street, London. E.C.4.'[64] The struggle had become a binary one between civilization and Bolshevism.

Cournos's story underlines the idea that Bolshevism has displaced the utopian futures imagined by English socialism by mirroring—albeit in miniature form—the structure and style of William Morris's classic utopia *News from Nowhere* (1890). After returning from a meeting of the Socialist

---

[62] Ibid. 12.   [63] Ibid. 11.   [64] Ibid., back cover.

League, Morris's narrator, William Guest, falls asleep and dreams a journey through London, transformed according to Morris's socialist ideas. Cournos's narrator, after returning from Petrograd, dreams his own journey through a London that has been transformed according to the purportedly socialist principles of the country from which he has recently returned. In both stories, the narrator perceives social developments that he does not understand, and people he meets along the way explain these in passages of expository dialogue. Cournos even seems to take up particular aspects of Morris's utopia in order to show how they are spoiled in Bolshevik London. One of the most memorable passages of *News from Nowhere* comes when Guest tries to pay a man who ferries him in his boat. The waterman is confused, and then remembers the vague outlines of a money system that no longer exists in this utopian future: 'You think that I have done you a service; so you feel yourself bound to give me something which I am not to give to a neighbour, unless he has done something special for me,' he muses, before dismissing this 'troublesome and roundabout custom'.[65] In *London under the Bolsheviks* the narrator is also astonished to find that his money is not worth anything, but this time because rapid inflation has made it worthless. He is shocked to pay 7/6 for ten cigarettes, and to be told that 'you know what money is—rubbish'.[66] His is given a handful of 'MacDonalds'—notes issued under Ramsay MacDonald's Provisional Government—as change, along with 'sixpenny notes and ... postage stamps, which I noted had no gum on the back but instead an inscription to the effect that they were available as currency in place of the customary copper coins'.[67] Taking his own experience of the collapse of the money system in Russia and translating it into this British context, Cournos also makes it reflect back on the future without money that Morris had imagined. The clear implication of the story is that Morris's version of socialism has been discredited in the process, however distant it may seem from Bolshevism.

The General Strike

Speculative utopian fiction was one field in which ideas of the future were altered by the advent of the Bolshevik Revolution, but there were also more earth-bound examples. As Morag Shiach has argued, for a number of socialist thinkers such as Georges Sorel and Rosa Luxembourg, the transition to a socialist future was bound up with the idea of the general strike.

---

[65] William Morris, *News from Nowhere or an Epoch of Rest, Being Some Chapters from a Utopian Romance* (Oxford: OUP, 2003), 9.
[66] Cournos, *London Under the Bolsheviks*, 4.   [67] Ibid. 5.

Writing in 1908, in *Reflections on Violence,* Sorel argued that 'the general strike has a character of *infinity* because it puts on one side all discussion of definite reforms and confronts men with a catastrophe'.[68] For Sorel, the general strike had an almost mystical ability to disrupt the space-time continuum, opening up new vistas of future possibility. As Shiach writes: 'The general strike . . . has no located place in the unfolding of a continuous historical narrative, but rather breaks down boundaries between past, present and future.'[69] Anindita Banerjee writes that Sorel 'found the European working class stopped in its revolutionary course, artificially frozen by an atomistic conception of change that obscured the essential indivisibility of the present and future': the general strike was to be the way out of this impasse.[70] The millennial potential of the mass strike was also emphasized by Rosa Luxemburg, whose book *The Mass Strike* responded to the first Russian Revolution of 1905.[71]

These radical visions were tested in Britain in the general strike of 1926, and Shiach analyses a number of literary responses to it, showing that it was rarely understood in Sorel's terms as an event that might collapse the boundaries between past, present, and future. Instead, Shiach convincingly argues, 'imaginative representations of the General Strike struggle to constitute the liberating or at least enabling temporality of the future tense', and indeed often tended to display 'a kind of atrophy of utopian thinking'.[72] I would like to add to Shiach's analysis the fact that, when this future disappears, it is often replaced by the spectre of Bolshevism. Let us take one of her examples, *Swan Song* (1928), the sixth instalment in John Galsworthy's Forsyte Saga. During the strike, Soames Forsyte—one of the villains of the saga—arrives in London and goes to his club to eat:

> Opposite the Goya he sat down. No good saying he remembered the Chartist riots of '48, because he had been born in '55; but he knew his uncle Swithin had been a 'special' at the time. This general strike was probably the most serious internal disturbance that had happened since; and, sitting over his soup, he bored further and further into its possibilities. Bolshevism round the corner—that was the trouble! That and the fixed nature of ideas in England. Because a thing like coal had once been profitable, they thought it must always be profitable. Political leaders, Trades Unionists, newspaper chaps—they never looked an inch before their noses!

---

[68] Sorel qtd. in Morag Shiach, *Modernism, Labour, and Selfhood in British Literature and Culture, 1890–1930* (Cambridge: CUP, 2004), 212.
[69] Ibid. 213.
[70] Anindita Banerjee, *We Modern People: Science Fiction and the Making of Russian Modernity* (Middletown, CT: Wesleyan University Press, 2012), 11.
[71] Rosa Luxembourg, *The Mass Strike* (London: Bookmarks, 1986).
[72] Shiach, *Modernism, Labour and Selfhood*, 230.

They'd had since last August to do something about it, and what had they done? Drawn up a report that nobody would look at![73]

The voice of Soames Forstye is that of a conservative member of the commercial bourgeoisie, and his first reaction to the strike is an unpleasant thought about the Bolshevism that is 'round the corner'. The Forsytes, with their many faults, are not called Forsytes for nothing, and it is for a lack of foresight that Soames criticizes the 'Political leaders, Trades Unionists, newspaper chaps', whose inability logically to deduce the consequences of their actions—or their inaction—was part of a fundamental blindness about the future that also prevented them from grasping the inevitable decline of coal. Bolshevism was looming on the horizon: the strike was evidence of that. And Soames had the foresight to see that his kind would not last long in Soviet Britain. In a long excursus on the likely fate of Galsworthy's Forsyte family, George Bernard Shaw opined that

> [t]here is something half tragic, half comic, and wholly pitiable in the spectacle of Soames Forsyte falling into the hands of a communist gamekeeper and being liquidated as vermin; yet such events are inevitable and irremediable under the stern morality of Communism.

Indeed, Russia was to be praised because there, 'forsyte shooting . . . takes the place of pheasant shooting in England except it is always in season'.[74]

The existence of the Soviet Union, and the violence of the Red Terror, enabled conservatives to portray the strike as the gateway to barbarism—not least because men like Shaw were willing to advocate violence in the name of socialism. But it was not only Forsytes who made the connection between the strike and Bolshevik Russia: moderate socialists sought to prove their dedication to parliamentary methods by denouncing Bolshevism, and here, too, the general strike and the Soviet Union were linked. Ramsay MacDonald, Britain's first socialist prime minister, had already been scarred by association with Soviet Communism: the controversy around the hoaxed 'Zinoviev letter', published in the *Daily Mail*, had contributed to the collapse of the first Labour government in 1924. The letter—actually written by a White Russian propagandist—was purportedly addressed to the Communist Party of Great Britain from the head of the Comintern Grigory Zinoviev, and raised the spectre of a Bolshevik-inspired insurrection among the British working class.[75] That year the *Daily Herald*—the Labour paper for which the narrator of *London under*

[73] John Galsworthy, *The Forsyte Saga*, 3 vols (London: Penguin, 2001), II. 582.
[74] George Bernard Shaw, *The Rationalization of Russia* (Westport, CT: Greenwood Press, 1964), 76–7, 82.
[75] Wright, *Iron Curtain*, 223.

the Bolsheviks retains a residual affection—made vigorous efforts to deny the letter's implication that the Soviet Union had effectively infiltrated the socialist movement in Britain. 'Labour is sincerely opposed to the Communist doctrine of "armed insurrection"', claimed the regular column 'From the Worker's Point of View'. MacDonald, meanwhile, was 'vigilant and determined in safeguarding British interests against even the possibility of Communist plots'.[76] Indeed, MacDonald was a committed anti-Bolshevist, yet he was constantly having to reiterate the fact in the face of hysterical accusations in the conservative press. Referring in the House of Commons to the strike of 1926, MacDonald said that, 'with the discussion of general strikes and Bolshevism and all that kind of thing, I have nothing to do at all'.[77] There was a firm connection between the two things in the popular mind. *The Times* reported on 12 June 1926 that Soviet Trade Unionists had donated 3,626,000 roubles or £362,000 to Britain's striking miners.[78] Far from opening up a window to the future, the General Strike of 1926 highlighted the fact that debates about Bolshevism were now implicated in any domestic left-wing agitation. The concept of the General Strike, like the word 'socialism', had lost its potentially useful indeterminacy and its future orientation. Henceforth, it tended to point East to Moscow instead.

THE TEMPORALITY OF COMMUNISM

Birth Pangs

In a variety of contexts, Russia had taken the place of the future in the British imagination. But the realities of Soviet life—which occasionally forced themselves on the consciousness of even the most credulous fellow traveller—presented a problem for the idea of Russia between the wars as a sort of achieved utopia. By most measures, this was a society in crisis. There was widespread poverty amongst a vast, illiterate peasantry. There was a bloody civil war. There were devastating famines in 1921–2 and 1932–4. The fact that trips to the Soviet Union by Koestler, Martin, Low, and the Webbs coincided with one of the worst famines in human

---

[76] Unsigned, 'From the Workers' Point of View: Some People are Never Pleased!', *Daily Herald* (17 Oct. 1924).

[77] Quoted Shiach, *Modernism, Labour, and Selfhood*, 229.

[78] Unsigned, 'British Note to Moscow—Soviet Money for General Strike—a Strong Protest—Communist Plan', *The Times* (12 June 1926). An account of the coercion of Soviet trade unionists by Party officials is in D. R. Trefusis, 'The Stones of Emptiness', TS, Columbia University, 1928.

history, with more than 6 million casualties, did not prevent them from identifying it as the arrival of a utopian future. This seeming conundrum, however, was in fact a vital aspect of the way the Communist regime established its legitimacy, not just in the eyes of Soviet citizens but in those of Western sympathizers. In her book *Everyday Stalinism* (1999), Sheila Fitzpatrick describes three stories that sustained the regime. One of these is the story of the 'The Radiant Future', the name taken from the title of a satirical book by Alexander Zinoviev. This story said that the 'present was the time when the future, socialism, was being built. For the time being, there must be sacrifice and hardship. The rewards would come later.'[79] The idea can be traced back to Lenin's promise, in *The State and Revolution* (1917), that the state would eventually wither away, and that '[o]nly then will a truly complete democracy, democracy without any exceptions whatever, become possible and be realized'.[80] In the meantime, Lenin argued, under the dictatorship of the proletariat, a 'special apparatus, a special machine for suppression, the "state" is *still* necessary, but this is now a transitional state, it is no longer a state in the proper sense'.[81] Famines, repressions, and disasters of every kind were not the result of socialism, this logic suggested: they were versions of what Marx had referred to as the 'birth pangs' of socialism, whose arrival was thereby always deferred.[82] Fitzpatrick's 'Radiant Future' is related to but different from the phenomenon I have been describing, where Russia came to embody the future on earth. On arriving in this newly minted future, it was not uncommon to find it full of people suffering in the name of a future still to come. While of course from 1917 Russia was undergoing a revolution and the word 'socialist' became part of the country's name in that year (it was called the Russian Soviet Federative Socialist Republic from 1917 until 1922, when it joined the other Soviet republics to become the Union of Soviet Socialist Republics), it was not until 1936 that Stalin 'officially declared that Russia had achieved socialism and enshrined this achievement in a new constitution'.[83] Officially in Russia, in the years 1917–36, socialism could be described as a future aspiration or as the prevailing reality, as the context demanded.

---

[79] Sheila Fitzpatrick, *Everyday Stalinism: Ordinary Life in Extraordinary Times: Soviet Russia in the 1930s* (New York; Oxford: OUP, 1999), 8.

[80] Vladimir Ilich Lenin (tr. Robert Service), *The State and Revolution* (London: Penguin, 1992), 80.

[81] Ibid. 81.

[82] Karl Marx (tr. Ben Fowkes), *Capital: A Critique of Political Economy* (Harmondsworth: Penguin Books, 1976), i. 92.

[83] Martin Malia, *Russia under Western Eyes: From the Bronze Horseman to the Lenin Mausoleum* (Cambridge, MA: Harvard University Press, 1999), 306.

The mentality of the radiant future that Fitzpatrick describes can be found in the work of many British writers as they thought about or visited the Soviet Union. George Bernard Shaw, a visitor to Communist Russia in 1931, specialized in this kind of argument. In the preface to his political play *On the Rocks* (1932), Shaw dealt with the various conflicting reports about starvation in Russia in equivocal fashion. On the one hand he sought to deny the famine, commenting that 'I saw no underfed people there; and the children were remarkably plump'. He even claimed to have 'thrown his food reserves out of the window as his train approached the frontier from Poland', in defiance of Western 'propaganda' about starving Soviet villages.[84] On the other hand, he acknowledged that there may have been some 'shortages', which he explained in terms of the radiant future:

> while the grass grows the steed starves and when education means not only schools and teachers, but giant collective farms equipped with the most advanced agricultural machinery, which means also gigantic engineering works for the production of the machinery, you may easily find that you have spent too much on these forms of capitalization and are running short of immediately consumable goods, presenting the spectacle of the nation with the highest level of general culture running short of boots and tightening its belt for lack of sufficient food.[85]

In Shaw's accounts of the Soviet Union, present suffering is invariably explained away in the name of hypothetical future improvements. A certain amount of belt-tightening was inevitable for the sake of what Shaw called the 'sacrifice of the present to the future'.[86] Rather than representing the victory of presentism over the modern regime of historicity, Stalinism was simply, for Shaw, one way of keeping the future—and therefore modernity—alive.

Other writers were more detached and diagnostic in remarking on this phenomenon. As early as 1920 Bertrand Russell, who visited Russia that year, had described the problem:

> [I]n Russia present circumstances tend to obscure the view of the distant future. But the actual situation in Russia can only be understood superficially if we forget the hope which is the motive power of the whole. One might as well describe the Thebaid without mentioning that the hermits expected eternal bliss as the reward for their sacrifices here on earth.

[84] Wright, *Iron Curtain*, 297.
[85] George Bernard Shaw, 'Preface', to *On the Rocks: A Political Comedy* in *Plays Political* (London: Penguin, 1986), 167.
[86] Bernard Shaw, *Plays Political: The Apple Cart, On the Rocks, Geneva* (Harmondsworth: Penguin, 1986), 167–8.

I cannot share the hopes of the Bolsheviks any more than those of the Egyptian anchorites; I regard both as tragic delusions, destined to bring upon the world centuries of darkness and futile violence.[87]

Russell was occasionally criticized for being too indulgent of the Communist government. Certainly he did not advocate that the British Government should pursue an anti-Bolshevik foreign policy. The anarchist Emma Goldman, author of *My Disillusionment in Russia* (1923), wrote to Russell in 1925 complaining of his refusal to condemn the Bolshevik government's habit of imprisoning its enemies without trial, a 'question of life and death to thousands of men and women now languishing in Soviet prisons'.[88] Russell replied that 'I am . . . unwilling to be associated with any movement that might seem to imply that a change of government is desirable in Russia. I think ill of the Bolsheviks in many ways, but quite as ill of their opponents.'[89] There was no more hopeful alternative for Russia: Bolshevism was *destined*—Russell's word—to 'bring upon the world centuries of darkness and futile violence'. The existence of socialism as a viable alternative had been negated by the fact that socialism—however ugly a version—had now been installed in the Soviet Union. Russell had spied in Russia something that was fundamental to the psychology of those who would extend their sympathies to the Soviet government. This allowed residents and visitors alike to put aside the iniquities of 'present circumstances' in favour of a belief in an illusion that had distinctly religious overtones: the 'eternal bliss' that was coming in the 'distant future'. As much as he disbelieved this myth, Russell found little to offer in its place, and seemed content to preach Realpolitik despite his theoretical interest in anarchist and syndicalist models of change.

To-day the Struggle

The callousness of Shaw's later years when it came to Stalin's crimes is legendary. But younger, subtler minds also succumbed to the logic of the radiant future and saw the Soviet Union through this filter. Stephen Spender's book *Forward from Liberalism* (1937), published just before he joined the Communist Party of Great Britain at the suggestion of its

---

[87] Bertrand Russell, *The Practice and Theory of Bolshevism* (Rockville, MD: Arc Manor, 2008), 13.

[88] Emma Goldman to Bertrand Russell, 9 Feb. 1925, in Emma Goldmann Papers, Tamiment Library, New York University, Box 4 Folder 3.

[89] Bertrand Russell to Emma Goldman, 14 Feb. 1925, in Emma Goldmann Papers, Tamiment Library, New York University, Box 4 Folder 3.

general secretary Harry Pollitt, set out an argument that was clearly shaped by this logic. Spender was liberal by temperament and by upbringing, but felt that liberalism could not on its own provide the answers to the political crises of the 1930s. Communism, he thought, had the same goals but was willing to be more ruthless in pursuing them.

> Communist and liberal approach the same freedom from opposite angles. Ultimately they agree in wanting the liberty of the individual, but the communist takes the view that true liberty is unattainable without a socialist revolution to overthrow capitalism; and without setting up a proletarian dictatorship during the transitional period of advance towards the classless society. The liberal refuses to accept the sacrifice of present limited individual liberty for future equality.[90]

Unlike Shaw, Spender did not revel in the violence of the Communist regime: he was understandably squeamish about 'forsyte shooting'. But in *Forward from Liberalism*—to his later regret—he saw the suspension of what Communists called 'bourgeois morality' as a necessary evil, acceptable for a limited period while a dictatorship of the proletariat built socialism. Spender did express some qualms about the Moscow Trials which were then in progress (as I discuss in greater detail in Chapter 3). Still, his wider argument suggested that he was willing to forgo the 'limited individual liberty' of the present, in the name of 'future equality'.

Spender's close friend W. H. Auden flirted somewhat more equivocally with Communism in the late 1930s: he never actually joined the Party. Yet the logic of the radiant future was integral to his brief dalliance. Auden's famous poem 'Spain'—written in a fellow-travelling mood, and later disowned—has a distinctive temporal shape, moving from the repetitious incantation of 'Yesterday', through a bright vision of 'To-morrow' and arriving finally at the moral compromises of 'To-day'.[91] He describes his radiant future:

> To-morrow, perhaps the future. The research on fatigue
> And the movements of packers; the gradual exploring of all the
> Octaves of radiation;
> To-morrow the enlarging of consciousness by diet and breathing.
>
> To-morrow the rediscovery of romantic love,
> the photographing of ravens; all the fun under
> Liberty's masterful shadow;

[90] Stephen Spender, *Forward from Liberalism* (London: Gollancz, 1937), 46.
[91] Auden's later attitude to the poem and his various revisions of it are discussed in Elizabeth Maslen, '"The Menacing Shapes of our Fever": Looking Back at Auden's "Spain"', in Stephen M. Hart (ed.). *¡No Pasarán!: Art, Literature and the Spanish Civil War* (London: Tamesis Books, 1988), 65–82, 66–7.

To-morrow the hour of the pageant-master and the musician,
The beautiful roar of the chorus under the dome;
To-morrow the exchanging of tips on the breeding of terriers,
The eager election of chairmen
By the sudden forest of hands. But to-day the struggle.[92]

This bright vision of a future 'under / Liberty's masterful shadow' is held up as the destination towards which literary efforts must be directed. Auden's vision of the future is manifestly not a description of Soviet Russia as it then was. Indeed, what should perhaps strike us is how far Auden's utopia resembles the bourgeois normality—'the exchanging of tips on the breeding of terriers'—which, the poem argues, had to be suspended in the extraordinary political conditions of the 1930s, when Fascism had to be repelled at all costs. The poem shares a distinctively Communist temporal regime, implying that by looking to the future the darkness of the present can be made meaningful and even morally necessary. Like Shaw, Auden is willing to be frank about the kinds of moral compromises bracketed under his repeated mantra: 'But to-day the struggle':

To-day the deliberate increase in the chances of death,
The conscious acceptance of guilt in the necessary murder;
To-day the expending of powers
On the flat ephemeral pamphlet and the boring meeting.[93]

In this tawdry present, literature is subordinate to the needs of 'the struggle' and murder is 'necessary'. This will be the era not of an autonomous literary art, but of the 'flat ephemeral pamphlet'. The present is a hardship that must be endured, where fundamental ethical compromises must be made. Only 'to-morrow' will there be the freedom to photograph ravens and rediscover romantic love.

In his strange and powerful sequence *The Magnetic Mountain* (1933), which he dedicated to Auden, C. Day Lewis portrayed a world in which the conventional assumptions about the future destination of society had been upended. The titular mountain refers to Magnitogorsk, a mining city in on the edge of the Urals, so called because of its proximity to the Magnitnaya mountain, a freak of geology made almost entirely of exceptionally rich iron ore. Magnitogorsk was a centrepiece of Stalin's industrialization drive, as the city was rapidly transformed into a major centre of steel production during the First Five Year Plan. For Day Lewis, the mountain's

---

[92] W. H. Auden, 'Spain', in *Selected Poems* (London: Faber & Faber, 1979), 51–5.
[93] Ibid.

magnetic quality becomes a metaphor for the drastic reorganization of global time and space:

> Near that miraculous mountain
> Compass and clock must fail,
> For space stands on its head there
> And time chases its tail.[94]

This magnetic force is symbolic of Russia's new role leading the way for workers and intellectuals the world over. This is all the more disorientating—causing the failure of compass and clock—because of Russia's longstanding reputation for historical backwardness, which I explore later in this chapter. Heading out for the Magnetic Mountain in a later poem, the speaker turns back to see 'A world behind us the west is in flames'.[95] The West is now dead and left behind, while the future comes from the East. The final poem in the sequence uses a repeated refrain to suggest the effect of this reorientation on intellectuals like Day Lewis and Auden: 'we turn / Like infants' eyes like sunflowers to the light'.[96] The light of modernity and the future is now coming from the East, and *The Magic Mountain* celebrates this new geotemporal dispensation.

The sequence is divided into four parts. The first part establishes the magnetic mountain as a new gravitational centre, and the speaker sets off on a quest towards Communist Russia, following in the footsteps of his friends W. H. Auden and Rex Warner: 'I'll hit the trail for that promising land; / May catch up with Wystan and Rex my friend'.[97] The second and third parts show the speaker grappling with potential obstacles to his quest, and the poem becomes a dialogue between the speaker and 'Defendants' of the existing order (in part 2) and 'Enemies' of the revolution (in part 3). In part 4, a series of lyric poems attempt to imagine the Communist future. The four 'Defendants' who speak in part 2 of the poem, representing various aspects of British culture—the countryside, education, the Church, and the home respectively—are presented as sirens who might distract Day Lewis from his quest. However 'Those chorus girls are surely past their prime, / Voices grow shrill and paint is wearing thin'. Unlike Odysseus, Day Lewis has 'No need to stop the ears, avert the eyes'.[98] To take 'Second Defendant' as an example, the account

---

[94] C. Day Lewis, *The Magic Mountain*, poem 3, in *Collected Poems 1929–33* (London: The Hogarth Press, 1945), 109.
[95] Ibid., poem 26, p. 142.   [96] Ibid., poem 36, p. 156.
[97] Ibid., poem 4, p. 111.   [98] Ibid., poem 6, p. 109.

of British schooling offered is hardly likely to inspire the idealism of
a young poet:

> Here we inoculate with dead ideas
> Against blood epidemics, against
> The infection of faith and the excess of life.
> Our methods are up to date; we teach
> Through head and not by heart,
> Language with gramophones and sex with charts,
> Prophecy by deduction, prayer by numbers.[99]

The school's primary function, in this account, is the inculcation of
ideology. Pupils do not learn to think for themselves, but are weighed
down with 'dead ideas'. The speaker's lyric in response to this speech is
addressed directly to the 'boys':

> It boils down to this—do you really want to win
> Or prefer the fine gesture of giving in?
> Are you going to keep or to make the rules,
> Die with fighters or be dead with fools?[100]

The question of whether 'to keep or to make the rules' recalls Wells's
distinction between legal and legislative minds. The difference is that for
Wells, it was *before* 1917 that the legislative mind was freer to imagine a
panoply of possible futures: the emergence of actually existing socialism ended
up involving such minds in presentist debates about the rights and wrongs of
Bolshevism. For Day Lewis, by contrast, the magnetic lure of Soviet Russia is
precisely what makes possible a break from the stale institutions and norms of
British society. The emergence of a new magnetic force in Russia highlighted
for Day Lewis the vanity of the hope that educational institutions might
become the instruments of progressive reform, helping to show the way to
freedom and equality in the future. The lure of the magnetic mountain
necessitates a complete break from the institutional forms of British society,
which are associated only with the past and left 'behind us . . . in flames'.

Koestler encountered the problem of the radiant future both as a
Communist and, later, as an anti-Communist. In the ecstatic hyperbole
of *Red Days and White Nights*, he wrote:

Only slowly does the newcomer learn to think in contradictions; to distinguish, underneath a chaotic surface, the shape of things to come; to realise
that in Sovietland the present is a fiction, a quivering membrane stretched
between the past and the future.[101]

---

[99] Ibid., poem 9, p. 118.   [100] Ibid., poem 10, p. 119.
[101] Koestler, *The Invisible Writing*, 66.

Koestler's supreme confidence in predicting the coming of a better future was no doubt derived from what Sheila Fitzpatrick sees as a fundamental aspect of the radiant future story. Believers in this story could be 'confident that there *would* be rewards because of their knowledge of historical laws, derived from Marx'.[102] This bore obvious similarities to Wells's scientific futurology—Koestler even uses Wells's phrase 'the shape of things to come'—but far from freeing us to imagine future possibilities, it laid out a glittering destiny in order to justify the brutal hardships of the present.

Koestler continued to think about the relation between Russia and the future as he left the Party, and as he developed his stridently anti-Communist politics in the post-war period. In the letter he wrote to Kisch, the leader of his party cell, when he had decided to leave the Party, Koestler asked 'What's left?':

> The Soviet Union is left. Not Stalin, but the Soviet Union. It's the only hope offered by this miserable century. It's the foundation of the future. Whoever goes against the Soviet Union goes against the future. But whoever presents it, afflicted as it is by all the flaws of transition and by the adolescent growing pains of Stalinism, as a finished prototype of the future, is offering us a caricature of the future. The Soviet Union is the most precious thing we have at present, but it is no prototype. For its *politics* we must defend the Soviet Union at all costs. But for its *theory*, it is an object of study, and study without criticism is unthinkable.[103]

Later, in the sober and ironic tones of *The Invisible Writing*, Koestler diagnosed the peculiar psychological state that he had entered into. His mind had become a 'sorting machine', he wrote.

> I learnt to classify automatically everything that shocked me as the 'heritage of the past' and everything I liked as the 'seeds of the future'. By setting up this automatic sorting machine in his mind, it was still possible in 1932 for a European to live in Russia and yet remain a Communist.[104]

Koestler attempted to theorize and understand the role that the radiant future played in sustaining Communism, and postulated that the Communist faith required the believer to enter into a very particular psychological state. The 'sorting machine' was, for Koestler, a powerful mechanism that shielded the inner convictions of the Communist sympathizer from the evidence that threatened to destroy them. Such evidence only formed part of a fictional present; the socialist future alone was real.

---

[102] Fitzpatrick, *Everyday Stalinism*, 8.
[103] Arthur Koestler qtd. in Michael Scammell, *Koestler: The Indispensable Intellectual* (London: Faber & Faber, 2009), 163.
[104] Koestler, *The Invisible Writing*, 66.

Like the later Koestler, Orwell took issue with the idea of the radiant future, and the ethical downgrading of the present that it implied. Orwell focused his criticism on Auden's 'Spain' and in particular his phrase 'necessary murder', which seemed to make excuses for extra-judicial killing on the basis of hypothetical future improvements to society. 'Personally I would not speak so lightly of murder', Orwell wrote:

> It so happens that I have seen the bodies of numbers of murdered men— I don't mean killed in battle, I mean murdered. Therefore I have some conception of what murder means—the terror, the hatred, the howling relatives, the post-mortems, the blood, the smells. To me, murder is something to be avoided. So it is to any ordinary person.[105]

Orwell's dismal view of the Auden circle and its flirtations with Communism has popular (and, to an extent, academic) currency, and it even gained support from Auden himself, who repudiated 'Spain' and made, as Frank Kermode notes, 'his own solid contribution to the myth of his own early failure'. Yet Kermode seems right to argue for a more nuanced view, stressing the complexity of the aesthetic and political struggles in which Auden and his circle were engaged.[106] Still, Orwell's insistence on a political morality firmly grounded in first-hand experience, one cognizant of the blood and the smells and the howling relatives of the present, can be seen in this context as a way of warding off the radiant future story that he associated with the Auden gang.

TAKING THE PRESENT

Out of Backwardness

I have been describing two phenomena that coexist in a sort of tension. First, the modern, futurist regime of historicity was contested by the advent of the Russian Revolution, as the future seemed no longer to be an otherworldly space clearly separated from present experience, but to have established itself on Earth, in Russia. Second, in the experience of Stalinism in practice, an exaggerated and accelerated version of that modern regime of historicity took hold. Some left-leaning intellectuals responded to the seeming decline of the future as a space of possibility by signing up to the Soviet myth of the 'radiant future'. If in Britain after 1917 the light seemed to come from Russia, rather than from an

---

[105] Orwell, 'Inside the Whale', 123.
[106] Frank Kermode, *History and Value: The Clarendon Lectures and the Northcliffe Lectures 1987* (Oxford: Clarendon, 1988), 73.

indeterminate 'socialism' that lacked any earthly referent, in Russia the future was almost obsessively invoked as justification for present ills. The third and final phenomenon I want to discuss in this chapter could be seen both as a symptom of the first, and as a reaction against the second. Turning to Dorothy Richardson's *Pilgrimage* (1915–67), I will explore how her modernist prose seeks to grasp the present in order to redeem it from the teleological narrative she associated with Communism.

To do this, I will first need to consider the role that Russian 'backwardness' played in debates about the temporality of the revolution. In 1917 Russia became the future and capitalist Western Europe the past. Yet it is important to note that this was a reversal of the spatio-temporal logic through which European progress had long been understood. As Ezra Pound noted in *The Spirit of Romance* (1910): 'All ages are contemporaneous. It is B.C., let us say, in Morocco. The Middle Ages are in Russia. The future stirs already in the minds of the few.'[107] For Pound notions of history and progress were as much spatial as temporal: one could see the various stages of historical development distributed in different parts of the world more easily than access the past itself. Before 1917, Russia was where the Middle Ages were located, and if you needed to find the future you had to look into the minds of 'the few'—by which we are to understand the modernist intelligentsia. Pound's remark about Russia reflects widely held assumptions about the spatio-temporal relationship between East and West Europe.[108] Marx's philosophy of history sketched out a timeline in which aristocratic feudalism was succeeded by bourgeois capitalism, and the communist revolution was the next stage. According to this logic and to Marx's prediction, the revolution should have happened first in the country with the most 'advanced' capitalist economy—it should have happened, in other words, in Britain. Europe's eastern extremity, a semi-feudal autocracy, and the gateway to the barbarism of Asia, Russia had tended to be associated with backwardness. Imperial Russia was in a sense literally behind the times, employing the Julian calendar which was thirteen days behind the Gregorian calendar used in Western Europe. The Bolshevik government switched to the Gregorian calendar in February 1918 as if to demonstrate its modernity. The knowledge of living in a kind of time lag was built into the Russian language. The Russian term for modernity, *Sovremennost'*, derives from

---

[107] Ezra Pound, *The Spirit of Romance: An Attempt to Define Somewhat the Charm of the Pre-Renaissance Literature of Latin Europe* (London: J. M. Dent, 1910), p. vi.

[108] The idea of 'backwardness' and its relationship with Eastern Europe has been explored in Malia, *The Soviet Tragedy*, 53–9, and, most influentially, in Alexander Gerschenkron, *Economic Backwardness in Historical Perspective: A Book of Essays* (Cambridge, MA: Belknap Press of Harvard University Press, 1962).

the Greco-Latin *synchronos*, and is 'not an absolute term but a relational one', involving the idea of synchronizing with a Western modernity that was implicitly ahead, in the future.[109] The idea that the Soviet drive to industrialization involved catching up with—and perhaps surpassing—Western Europe was widely discussed in Britain. Stephen Graham reported Stalin saying that '[w]e are fifty or a hundred years behind the leading countries of the world' and that '[w]e must cover that distance in ten years... or we shall be swept away.'[110] The specific character of Russian Communism is thus deeply marked by pre-revolutionary Russia's sense of its own backwardness.

Claudia Verhoeven has recently explored Russia's unique temporal landscape:

If modernity is an ethos, and anti-modernity too, then much of imperial Russian history might fairly be framed as a somewhat unfair tug of war between these two attitudes. Tracing this history's trajectory would produce an ellipse, its long sides the empire's frozen political winters, the short turns its vital thaws—the more violent for their very quickness, though at no point quick enough to escape the orbit. The pull of the past is strong in Russia.

This gravity held Russia in its grip until the events of 1917, or the 'event' that was 1917. The year outran the old world with such force that it smashed not only Russia's horizons of expectations, but also—because it produced the world's first socialist revolution in the very last of likely places—all the prognostications of global revolutionary culture.[111]

Verhoeven casts the conflict within Russia between Westernizers and Slavophiles in usefully abstract terms. As she goes on to show, Russian revolutionaries of the nineteenth century developed a capacity for 'wormhole thinking': the belief that supposedly necessary stages of historical progress—most importantly, capitalism—could be skipped, to facilitate an abrupt jump from the feudal past to the socialist future. Lenin undoubtedly drew on this tradition, though to my mind Verhoeven goes too far in asserting that his 'logic kept company with a century of intense intelligentsia efforts—theoretical and practical—to break out of normal time'.[112] The Russian Marxism that emerged in the 1880s distanced itself from the utopian idealism and terrorist tactics of the radicals

---

[109] Banerjee, *We Modern People*, 11.

[110] Stephen Graham, *Stalin: An Impartial Study of the Life and Work of Joseph Stalin* (London: Ernest Benn, 1931), 125.

[111] Claudia Verhoeven, 'Wormholes in Russian History: Events "Outside of Time" (Featuring Malevich, Morozov, and Mayakovsky)', in Berber Bevernage and Chris Lorenz (eds), *Breaking up Time: Negotiating the Borders between Present, Past and Future* (Göttingen: Vandenhoeck & Ruprecht, 2013), 109–23, 109.

[112] Verhoeven, 'Wormholes in Russian History', 111.

Verhoeven discusses, and—as Sheila Fitzpatrick notes—Russian Marxists 'asserted that capitalism constituted the only possible past to socialism'. For Fitzpatrick, Marxism in Russia meant something very different to what it meant in the England of William Morris and Edward Carpenter: 'it was an ideology of modernization as well as an ideology of revolution'.[113] In important senses, the Bolsheviks were Westernizers, and they sought to accelerate the necessary phases on the way to Communism rather than skip one. Nevertheless, the various nineteenth-century arguments for a socialist revolution in a 'backward' country, and then the event itself, had temporal effects in Russia and abroad.

It is not merely that socialist aspirations about a future society fixed onto a geographical entity, then. Russia had been associated with the past and felt itself out of step with European progress. Then, in 1917, it pivoted into the future. 'It was as if', Martin Malia wrote, 'the East-West gradient of European history had been upended'.[114] Compass and clock had failed, as Day Lewis suggested, with the 'magnetic mountain' of Russian industrialization causing a fundamental realignment of space and historical time. Koestler's factory workers, who broke the shackles of 'medieval Islam' and stepped into the bright light of an electrified future, jumped from the Middle Ages to the future without pausing for breath in the present.

The perspectives on modern Russia that emerge in Dorothy Richardson's *Pilgrimage* engage with many of these temporal problems. The sections of the thirteen-volume novel sequence with which I will concern myself are set in 1905–6 and written in the 1920s. In them, Richardson looks back across the frontier of the Bolshevik Revolution, examining Russian socialism at an earlier stage and, through the experiences of her New Woman protagonist Miriam Henderson, putting it into dialogue with other available models in the Edwardian period. Richardson's novel engages with Russia's presumed historical backwardness in two ways. Michael Shatov—Miriam's Russian Jewish lover—acts as both a conduit and a sounding board for Miriam's ideas about Russia. Shatov first discusses Russia with her early in *Deadlock* (1921), and his talk effects an 'irrevocable expansion of her consciousness'.[115] Miriam's thoughts, interspersed with snatches of Shatov's reported speech, take her on a sweeping tour of a Russia imagined very much in the terms of Edwardian Russophilia:

[113] Sheila Fitzpatrick, *The Russian Revolution*, 3rd edn (Oxford: OUP, 2008), 26.
[114] Malia, *Russia under Western Eyes*, 298.
[115] Dorothy M. Richardson, *Pilgrimage 3* (London: Virago, 1979), 45.

she was carried away to villages scattered among great tracts of forest, unimaginable distances of forest, making the vast forests of Germany small and homely . . . each village a brilliant miniature of Russia, in every hut a holy image; brilliant colouring of stained carved wood, each peasant a striking picture, filling the eye in the clear light many 'most dignified'; their garments coloured with natural dyes, 'the most pure plant-stain colours,' deep and intense.[116]

This is Holy Russia, a place of peasant simplicity and religious mysticism—backward, yes, but (for British Russophiles) preserving a form of community which is lost to the advanced industrialized nations. In her mind, Miriam 'turned grievously to the poor cheap tones in all the western shops, clever shining chemical dyes, endless teasing variety, without depth or feeling, cheating the eye of life'.[117] The unflattering comparison with English reality was also a stock feature of pre-war Russophilia. Michael Hughes has described an analogous impulse in the work of British Russophile Stephen Graham, who saw in Old Russia 'a place that could provide a living model for a world that had become too captivated by an overly materialistic conception of progress'.[118] The expansion of Miriam's consciousness that is triggered by her early conversations with Shatov picks up on this familiar Russophile theme, looking into a prelapsarian past that could stand outside history and progress.

However, backwardness also poses a problem for Shatov, a Jewish intellectual from the radical end of the liberal intelligentsia. He wants for Russia the constitutional freedom and democratic institutions that he finds in Britain: 'In matters of justice between man and man *England* has certainly led the civilised world', he says.[119] In one discussion with Miriam, Shatov theorizes that the reason for the strength of 'abstract justice' in Britain is the Protestant Reformation, which he explains as a 'relatively very rapid and unrestricted *secular* development'.[120] On one level, then, Richardson's novel reproduces a familiar picture of Europe before 1914, imagining historical progress distributed on an East–West axis, with Russia lodged in the past and Britain paving the way for the future. For Miriam, Russia poses an urgent question about whether the benefits of historical progress outweigh its costs.

In tension with this familiar picture of Russian backwardness, *Pilgrimage* explores the temporal regime of socialism. Miriam encounters many English socialists and Fabians—or Lycurgians as they are called in the

[116] Ibid. 44.   [117] Ibid.
[118] Michael Hughes, *Beyond Holy Russia: The Life and Times of Stephen Graham* (Cambridge: Open Book Publishers, 2014), 52.
[119] Richardson, *Pilgrimage 3*, 112.   [120] Ibid. 109.

novel—as well as Russian revolutionaries she meets through Shatov. Richardson stages the encounter between English and Russian socialism as an encounter between a plural and dialogic critique, and a unified body of ideology and doctrine. At the beginning of *Revolving Lights* (1923), Miriam attends a lecture about socialism, attended by both Lycurgians and Russian revolutionaries. While for English interlocutors, 'the bare outlines of socialism . . . forced every one to look at the things they had taken for granted in a new light', Miriam thinks that 'to appear before these Russians talking English socialism was to be nothing more than a useful person in a uniform'.[121] Russia's revolutionaries had replaced human sympathy with unfeeling ideology, a coldly utilitarian calculus with which Miriam cannot identify. She goes on:

> Their scornful revolutionary eyes watched her glance amongst her hoard of contradictory ideas. Statements about different ways of looking at things were irrelevancies that perhaps with Russians might be abandoned altogether. . . . Personal life to them was nothing, could be summed up in a few words, the same for everybody. They lived for an idea.[122]

Richardson's novel does not systematically set out the details of the idea for which the Russians lived: she is more interested in attitudes and sensations than ideologies. And perhaps Miriam's specific responses to Russian socialism are less important than the fact that she is an individualist and not a joiner? As Kerstin Fest has argued, Miriam 'is in contact with a number of political groups, yet due to her strong sense of individuality she is unable to join anyone of them wholeheartedly'.[123] Yet it is worth paying some attention to her turn away from socialism—an idea that is bound up with Russia here—because it bears on the questions of temporality and historicity that form the focus of this chapter. By the end of volume 9, *The Trap* (1925), Miriam has turned from socialism to anarchism, explaining to a Lycurgan: 'anarchy and socialism are the same in spirit. Only that socialists think they can define their future and anarchists know they can't.'[124] Miriam turns away from socialism because it appears too confident in defining its future. At the lecture where she meets the Russian revolutionaries, the lecturer expounds on 'the white

---

[121] Ibid. 238.   [122] Ibid. 239.

[123] Kerstin Fest, *And All Women Mere Players? Performance and Identity in Dorothy Richardson, Jean Rhys and Radclyffe Hall* (Vienna: Braumüller, 2008), 49. Richardson's attitudes to Fabianism have been explored in Isobel Maddison, 'Trespassers will be Prosecuted: Dorothy Richardson among the Fabians', *Literature and History*, 19/2 (Autumn 2010), 52–68. Maddison notes that 'she is never wholly seduced by Fabian socialism . . . although Miriam's egalitarian beliefs remain firm, she is unable to relinquish her faith in individuality'.

[124] Richardson, *Pilgrimage*, 495.

radiance of the distant future' and 'the forward march of a unanimous, light-hearted humanity along a pathway of white morning light'. Miriam then reflects on '[t]he land of promise that she would never see; not through being born too soon, but by being incapable of unanimity.' Miriam's resistance to living, like the Russians, 'for an idea' and the turn towards an ever more intense exploration of '[p]ersonal life' is a crucial element of the strand of literary modernism that Richardson belonged to—turning away, in the terms of Virginia Woolf's famous essay, from the Utopia out of the window (or in the future) in order to look more closely at Mrs Brown in the present.[125] Richardson's attempt to preserve the possibility of 'contradictory ideas' and 'different ways of looking at things' in the face of an ideology that purported to explain everything was prefigured by Katherine Mansfield's early stories in the *New Age*, as Lee Garver has shown. Mansfield's heroine rejects the conventional paths of Fabian socialism and suffragism in favour of independence and individualism. Garver shows how this is echoed on the level of style by a rejection of the omniscient narrator and of 'ideational language', in favour of a flowing free indirect discourse that prioritizes the experience of the sensuous present, following the philosophical examples of Nietzsche, Bergson, and Bradley.[126] Richardson's work gives this presentist turn a strong political charge.

Modernism as Presentism

Richardson's resistance to a 'future orientated' notion of historical destiny can be illuminated in terms of Hartog's regimes of historicity. Hartog draws on Lévi-Strauss's widely misunderstood distinction between 'hot' and 'cold' societies. Cold societies, like the tribal cultures of the Amazon Lévi-Strauss visited in his anthropological research, are characterized by 'seeking, by the institutions they give themselves, to annul the possible effects of historical factors on their equilibrium and continuity in a quasi-automatic fashion'. The point is not that primitive, cold societies exist outside of history, but that their shared attitude to temporality is characterized by 'obstinate fidelity to a past conceived as a timeless model', which amounts to 'a consciously or unconsciously adopted attitude' towards historical change. Lévi-Strauss contrasts this with the 'avid need for change characteristic of our own civilization'. The 'hot' societies of Western

---

[125] Virginia Woolf, 'Mr. Bennett and Mrs. Brown', in *Collected Essays*, i (London: Hogarth Press, 1966), 319–37, 327–8.
[126] Lee Garver, 'The Political Katherine Mansfield', *modernism/modernity*, 8/2 (2001), 225–43, 236.

modernity are characterized by 'resolutely internalizing the historical process and making it the moving power of their development'.[127] These different orientations towards history are what Hartog goes on to develop into his notion of regimes of historicity. Where Lévi-Strauss works with a binary opposition between hot and cold, however, Hartog delineates *three* regimes of historicity, which are defined by whether the past, the future, or the present are foremost on the historical horizon, as I have explained. The ancient regime of historicity, where (as Hartog puts it) all the light comes from the past, thus maps onto to Lévi-Strauss's cold societies. The modern, future-orientated regime would be typical of a hot society.

In Lévi-Strauss's terms, the Russia that Miriam contemplated in 1904–5 was cold (even if, internally, as Verhoeven emphasizes, it played host in the nineteenth century to a conflict between cold Slavophiles and hot Westernizers). Russia's coldness, moreover, was one of the things that British Russophiles found to admire in it. For them, Russia—the Russian countryside in particular—was a template for a society that could exist outside of rapid and disorientating historical change. In a utopian moment, Lévi-Strauss looks forward to a time when 'society would be freed from a millennial curse which has compelled it to enslave men in order that there be progress' and 'once more assume this regular and quasi-crystalline structure which the best-preserved of primitive societies teach us is not contrary to humanity'.[128] This anthropological sense that cold societies might have something to teach us is very obvious in the work of Stephen Graham and other Russophiles active in the period Richardson is writing about.

Hartog's introduction of a third regime of historicity into Lévi-Strauss's binary model again draws on Koselleck. Koselleck points out that political discussions until the late eighteenth century were 'bound up in the network of Aristotelian constitutional forms which limited the number of possible variations'. Only in *Neuzeit*, and above all with Kant, did it become possible to think that 'all previous experience might not count against the possible otherness of the future. The future would be different from the past, and better, to boot.'[129] Hartog notes that '[i]n 1975, Koselleck tried to formulate what an "end" or "exit" from modern times might look like'.[130] Hartog proposes that we exited from modernity when the Berlin Wall fell, and now inhabit a new regime of historicity:

[127] Claude Levi-Strauss, *The Savage Mind* (London: Weidenfeld & Nicolson, 1966), 233–5.

[128] Claude Lévi-Strauss (tr. Monique Layton), *Structural Anthropology*, ii (Chicago: University of Chicago Press, 1983), 30.

[129] Koselleck, *Futures Past*, 267.   [130] Hartog, *Regimes of Historicity*, 17.

presentism. The present, and no longer the future, is where all the light comes from, partly due to the collapse of the vision of the future embodied in the Communist International. Hartog describes a contemporary dispensation in which 'the distance between the space of experience and the horizon of expectation has been stretched to its limit, to breaking point'. As a result there prevails a 'sense of a permanent, elusive, and almost immobile present'.[131] While he does cite the demise of the Soviet sphere as the primary reason for the emergence of presentism, these periodizations are not rigid, and Hartog points out that '[t]he twentieth century... combined futurism and presentism'. It 'started out more futurist than presentist and ended up more presentist than futurist'.[132] Richardson's novel is an instance of presentism breaking onto the early twentieth-century scene, precisely through a modernist attempt to resile from the temporal regime of the Russian Revolution.

Richardson's engagement with Russia and its revolution dramatizes the question of conflicting regimes of historicity both thematically and on the level of form. I have already pointed to the way in which Miriam recoils from the Russians who 'lived for an idea', seeking to replace this with a new emphasis on 'personal life'. This was connected with her sense of socialism, and perhaps Russian socialism in particular, as an ideology that sacrificed the present to the future. Her response to this was to assert an ethic and an aesthetic that prioritized the present. Here is Miriam as she leaves the lecture on socialism to walk the evening streets of London.

> The illuminated future faded. The street lights of that coming time might throw their rays more liberally, over more beautiful streets. But something would be lost. In a world consciously arranged for the good of everybody there would be something personal... without foundation... like a non-conformist preacher's smile. The pavements of these streets that had grown of themselves, flooded by the light of lamps rooted like trees in the soil of London, were more surely pavements of gold than those pavements of the future?[133]

Against the future-orientated regime of historicity that she associates with socialists and above all with Russian revolutionaries, Miriam asserts an approach to temporality in which all the light comes from the present. And this has structural and stylistic ramifications. Richardson's paratactic free indirect discourse wants to give us experience in the raw, without seeing it organized through the lens of ideas. It is a manifestation of 'presentism', conceived not as some postmodern, post-historical malaise,

---

[131] Ibid. 17–18.   [132] Ibid. 107.   [133] Richardson, *Pilgrimage 3*, 235–6.

but as a specifically modernist attempt to confront and negate a regime of historicity where the past and present are subordinated to a 'radiant future'.

Richardson's novel-sequence is highly paratactic, both on the level of the individual sentence, where clauses are juxtaposed without subordination and often separated by unconventional uses of punctuation (ellipses in particular), and on the level of the episode and the chapter where—as unsympathetic readers complain—it is one thing after another. The novel resists causal and temporal hypotaxes: we are immersed in a present that includes memory and retrospect but that does not situate these in any perspectival hierarchy.

In this respect Richardson's style should be distinguished from that of her close contemporary Virginia Woolf, with whom she is frequently compared. While Woolf was clearly enthused by *Pilgrimage*, she distanced herself from the novel's intense paratacticity in a review of *The Tunnel* (1919), which can also be read as a manifesto for Woolf's own writing. While conceding that Richardson's book was 'better in its failure than most books in their success', Woolf writes that that 'sensations, impressions, ideas and emotions . . . glance off [Miriam], unrelated and unquestioned, without shedding quite as much light as we had hoped into the hidden depths'. Richardson's refusal to 'relate' and 'question' sensations and impressions, her failure to produce 'depths', is seen as a failure of her prose. Woolf bemoans the lack of a hypotactic sense of 'the conception that shapes and surrounds the whole'.[134] In a work like *To the Lighthouse* (1927) Woolf certainly took inspiration from Richardson's explorations of the shifting surface of consciousness, and like Richardson also attempted tendentiously to subvert the futurist regime of historicity, redirecting readerly attention to the sensuous present and satirizing a tendency to postpone fulfilment to a hypothetical future, in which (in this case) the trip to the lighthouse will take place. Still, *To the Lighthouse* makes a definite effort to impose a hierarchy of significance on the often apparently disconnected consciousnesses of its characters. This is particularly evident in the novel's ending, where there is a sense of completion that is always denied to the reader of *Pilgrimage*. After noting that 'the Lighthouse'—emblematic of a kind of radiant future in the novel—'had become almost invisible', Woolf relays Lily Briscoe's thoughts in the final sentence of the novel: 'Yes, she thought, laying down her brush in extreme fatigue, I have had my vision'.[135] There may be no narrative conclusion (they never reach the lighthouse) but the sense of a completed final perspective in

---

[134] Virginia Woolf, 'The Tunnel', *Times Literary Supplement*, 17 (13 Feb. 1919), 81.
[135] Virginia Woolf, *To The Lighthouse* (London: Penguin, 1964), 236–7.

Lily's painting forms a contrast with the restless and additive mood of *Pilgrimage*. It is also notable that this sentence is itself—like many in Woolf's novel, and unlike most in *Pilgrimage*—hypotactic, with a dependent clause situating the thought within the context of action (the completion of the painting) and mood (fatigue). The possibilities of hypotaxis are elsewhere rather ostentatiously exploited by Woolf when she reports the deaths of important characters (Mrs Ramsay and Andrew Ramsay) in square brackets.[136] The purpose seems to be to invert the normal hierarchy in fiction between a narrative event and the characters' subjective perceptions of it. But it does not abolish hierarchy as such, any more than it abolishes the distinction between a main clause and a subordinate one, which is the tendency in *Pilgrimage*. Richardson's parataxis is therefore not representative of modernism as a whole—it is a specific technology that sets out to resist the radiant future, and with it the attitude to history that is represented by the Russian Revolution.

The argument I am making owes something to Georg Lukács, and in particular his essay 'Narrate or Describe' (1936). Comparing depictions of a day at the races in *Anna Karenina* (1880) and *Nana* (1878), Lukács contrasts the 'narration' he finds in his hero Leo Tolstoy with the mere 'description' practiced by one of his favourite villains, Émile Zola. The great Russian had grasped history as process, and all the events and details presented bear an integral relation to the plot (this is the scene where Karenin and Anna watch from the stands as Vronsky falls from his horse, and Anna's reaction tells her husband about her adulterous infatuation with Vronsky). Sara Nadal-Melsió argues compellingly that Lukács's argument represents an 'implicit reading of Marxism as the discovery of hypotaxis in history, as the reading of the past as a narrative in which all parts are interrelated in unequal ways'.[137] This is narration. By contrast, the horse racing scene in *Nana* is

> a series of static pictures, of still lives connected only through the relations of objects arrayed one beside the other according to their own inner logic, never following one from the other, certainly never one out of the other. The so-called action is only a thread on which the still lives are disposed in a superficial, ineffective fortuitous sequence of isolated, static pictures.[138]

In terms of this distinction, Richardson is interested in description and not narration, and she takes the tendency Lukács notices in Zola to a greater

---

[136] Ibid. 146–7, 152.

[137] Sara Nadal-Melsió, 'Georg Lukács: Magus Realismus?', *Diacritics*, 34/2 (2004), 62–84, 69.

[138] Georg Lukács, 'Narrate or Describe?', in *Writer and Critic and Other Essays* (London: Merlin Press, 1970), 110–48, 144.

extreme. Interestingly, there is a scene in *Deadlock* where Miriam and Shatov read *Anna Karenina* together (in A. C. Townsend's notoriously bad translation).[139] Shatov praises 'a most masterly study of a certain type of woman', but Miriam is drawn to other aspects of the book and resists Shatov's explanation. This sends Miriam into a mental digression about the nature of fictional narrative, where she describes

> reading whole books through and through, and only finding out what they were about by accident, when people happened to talk about them, and even then, reading them again, and finding principally quite other things, which stayed, after one had forgotten what people had explained.[140]

Miriam's reading of Tolstoy is quite different to Lukács's idea of a novel that can grasp historical forces and dramatize them in the experiences of his characters. Instead, her reading is immersive, intuitive, and open-ended: she is drawn to description and not narration. And this method of reading becomes for Richardson a method of writing. Where Lukács would see this as a deficiency in Richardson's prose—raising an objection similar to Woolf's—a grasp of its political context helps us to understand what is at stake.

Richardson's style is a rejection of the futurist regime of historicity that she links with Russian socialism, and the version of Marxism that the revolution promoted. This Marxism embodied a view of historical process, and it was also a way of writing. Like most philosophy, Marxist prose is heavily hypotactic, both on the level of the individual sentence and in terms of the structure of its arguments. But Lukács's version of Marxism is rather puritanical in disparaging parataxis as 'description'. It will help to return to Marx, and I want to focus on this famous passage from *The German Ideology* (1846, publ. 1932):

> For as soon as the distribution of labour comes into being, each man has a particular, exclusive sphere of activity, which is forced upon him and from which he cannot escape. He is a hunter, a fisherman, a herdsman, or a critical critic, and must remain so if he does not want to lose his means of livelihood; while in communist society, where nobody has one exclusive sphere of activity but each can become accomplished in any branch he wishes, society regulates the general production and thus makes it possible for me to do one thing today and another tomorrow, to hunt in the morning, fish in the afternoon, rear cattle in the evening, criticise after dinner, just as I have a mind, without ever becoming hunter, fisherman, herdsman or critic.

---

[139] George H. Thompson, *Notes on Pilgrimage: Dorothy Richardson Annotated* (Greensboro: ELT Press, 1999), 148.

[140] Richardson, *Pilgrimage 3*, 61.

This fixation of social activity, this consolidation of what we ourselves produce into an objective power above us, growing out of our control, thwarting our expectations, bringing to naught our calculations, is one of the chief factors in historical development up till now.[141]

It is no surprise to find a high degree of hypotaxis in Marx's style. Dependent clauses of various kinds explain the logical and temporal connections between the key statements, illustrate causes and effects, and provide context. Historical events, classes, 'progress', are all viewed from the unifying perspective of a materialist dialectic, and thus put into logical and causal relation. The grammar reflects at a fundamental level an outlook that grasps history as a process and as progress towards a future. In Hartog's terms, it is deeply typical of the modern regime of historicity. However, one should also notice that there *is* some parataxis when Marx compiles these lists: 'a hunter, a fisherman, a herdsman, or a cultural critic' and 'to hunt in the morning, fish in the afternoon, rear cattle in the evening, criticise after dinner'. In the latter example, it would not be going too far to say that parataxis appears as Marx's social ideal: one can hunt, fish, rear cattle, and criticise, all in one day and one after the other, without one activity assuming precedence over another, without the need to put all of the activity that falls outside an apparently a priori identity—'cultural critic' or 'fisherman'—into grammatically subordinate parentheses. The undoing of capitalist division of labour entails a decisive shift *away* from a hierarchy of activity, as labour and leisure become interchangeable. Undoubtedly, the instance of parataxis, in a rare discussion of the communist utopia to come, is held in a hypotactic frame. Nevertheless, Marx's movement *towards* parataxis is missing from Lukács's account. Indeed, on this evidence we might go as far as to suggest that hypotaxis is one of the symptomatic contradictions of bourgeois society, in Marx's diagnosis, as much as it marks his approach.

If Marx's method is that of the modern, futurist regime of historicity, the objective of a Marxist politics is to transcend the ordered hierarchies of hypotaxis, and the fixation on a radiant future to come, in order to live in a state of paratactic presentism. One is reminded of Lévi-Strauss's suggestion that a Communist future would resemble a 'cold society', reminiscent of the prehistoric past—that 'quasi-crystalline structure which the best-preserved of primitive societies teach us is not contrary to humanity'.[142] Except that the utopian impulse in Richardson's modernist aesthetic is not

---

[141] Karl Marx and Friedrich Engels (tr. W. Lough), *The German Ideology* (London: Lawrence & Wishart, 1970), 54.

[142] Lévi-Strauss, *Structural Anthropology*, ii. 30.

locked into Lévi-Strauss's structuralist binary. We need a third term: Hartog's presentist regime of historicity.

The tension I have highlighted between hypotaxis as narration and parataxis as description is a version of Michael Levenson's distinction between deep modernism and montage modernism.[143] Richardson's novel is an example of montage modernism, embracing montage as a way of grasping the present while resisting the deep modernism of Marxism, the modern regime of historicity, and the Russian revolutionary sensibility. Unlike Marx's local but utopian use of parataxis, which—as I put it—was held in a hypotactic frame, the presentism of Richardson's novel suggests an achieved utopia: the paratactic, episodic structure of Richardson's novel reflects Marx's ambition 'to hunt in the morning, fish in the afternoon, rear cattle in the evening, criticise after dinner', but this is a feature of the capitalist present, the space of experience, not a part of the horizon of expectation as it remains for Marx. Miriam's thoughts, actions, and memories are held together paratactically, 'objects arrayed one beside the other according to their own inner logic, never following one from the other, certainly never one out of the other', as Lukács wrote of Zola. It seems fitting that Richardson was later drawn to the Soviet filmmakers, including Eisenstein, whose work Levenson makes representative of montage modernism (in contrast to the deep, Bazinian emphasis on depth of field and the long shot). Contrary to the official ideology of the teleological, Stalinist radiant future, Eisenstein and Vertov offered presentist montage, investing the everyday experience of the Soviet scene with intense and immediate significance, tragedy, and joy that was not to be deferred but grasped in the present.

Sascha Bru draws on Hartog's work to explore the temporalities of the Soviet avant-garde. He asks whether both Italian and Russian futurism were futurist, in the sense of Hartog's second regime of historicity. His conclusion reflects what I have argued about Dorothy Richardson and the montage modernism of Eisenstein and Vertov. Bru analyses Tatlin's *Monument to the Third International* (1920) as an example of presentism:

> The upward direction of the spiral in Tatlin's never-realised masterpiece led nowhere; it was diametrically opposed to the teleological sense of time advocated by communist doctrine at the time. Its vortex-like shape led upward, yes, but upward in the present. It did not embody progress, nor did it look back. Or, as Naum Gabo and his brother Antoine Pevsner put it in their 'Realistic manifesto' (1920) that was much debated in the circle

---

[143] Michael H. Levenson, *Modernism* (New Haven, CT; London: Yale University Press, 2011), 143.

around the journal *Lef*: 'The past we are leaving behind as carrion. The future we leave to the fortune tellers. We take the present.'[144]

Bru sees the Soviet avant-garde, in other words, as attempting to enact the paratactic, descriptive, approach to historicity that I have equated with presentism. He concludes—and again this seems to run against Hartog's periodization of his concepts—that 'we can define presentism rather than futurism as the key temporal regime of the avant-gardes'.[145]

Of course, Russia did not have the monopoly on teleological, future-orientated attitudes to history: in a sense, as Hartog argues, these are typical of modernity in general. But at the time when Richardson was writing, for the reasons I have set out, it was Russia that posed this question most insistently, and it is through her engagement with Russia that—like Vertov and Tatlin, Gabo and Pevsner—she determined to 'take the present'.

---

[144] Bru, 'Avant-Garde Nows', 274–6.   [145] Ibid. 277.

2

Two and Two Make Five

THE GREATEST GOOD OF THE GREATEST NUMBER

Quantitative Omniscience

When Western writers thought about Communism, or about the Soviet state, they often also thought about numbers. From simple counting to advanced mathematics, the realm of number and numbers was often disturbed by literary encounters with the Soviet Union, which in turn drew on nineteenth-century Anglo-Russian debates about the politics of number. Winston Smith's final acceptance, under torture, of the proposition that two plus two equals five, is one of the most memorable tropes in Orwell's *Nineteen Eighty-Four*, and it immediately provoked a debate (involving Marxists such as Isaac Deutscher and John Strachey) about the relationship between Soviet Communism and Enlightenment rationality. The example from Orwell is not an isolated one. This chapter explores the range of ways in which mathematics, arithmetic, or questions of number were invoked in analyses and descriptions of the Soviet Union. The level of sophistication at which writers thought about the politics of number varied: some of the writers I discuss in this chapter had knowledge of advanced mathematics, or recent philosophical debates about the foundations of mathematics, and thus their thinking about the political possibilities of numbers was inflected by their engagements with the discipline of mathematics or with the philosophical critique of its presuppositions. Others used arithmetic, or mathematical equations, in a looser way: as a sort of synecdoche for calculative rationality itself. But the uses of numbers I explore are not all categorizable in terms of a static binary relationship between arithmetical rationality and various forms of irrationalism. Numbers themselves, and mathematics too, were often infused with mystical and utopian significance in Russian culture, and this proved to be a resource on which Western writers could draw. This chapter suggests that, when it comes to the debate about the Soviet Union, sophisticated philosophical deployments of mathematics, crude, inexpert thinking about numbers and arithmetic, and mystical beliefs about what mathematics could do, ought to be considered together. The politics of number was, I argue, a key trope that mid-century writers—the mathematically knowledgeable as well as the ignorant—deployed as they reflected on the Russian Revolution and its consequences.

In *The Taming of Chance* (1990), Ian Hacking proposed that, over the course of the nineteenth century, the statistical sciences grew exponentially and came to take a central place in intellectual and political life. Hacking disapproves of this, describing the effect of bureaucracies' increasing 'enthusiasm for numerical data' as an 'avalanche of printed numbers', implying that people in modern societies are effectively buried under a numerical landslide.[1] Behind this argument lies a Foucauldian account of modern 'biopolitics' which—and here Hacking quotes Foucault directly—'gave rise to comprehensive measures, statistical assessments, and interventions aimed at the entire social body or at groups as a whole'.[2] This new numerical way of doing politics seemed to Hacking (as it did to Foucault) to introduce a new and fundamentally modern form of social control, based on 'the notion that one can improve—control—a deviant subpopulation by enumeration and classification'.[3] The modern tendency to measure and enumerate is not limited to the bureaucratic apparatus of the modern state. For Hacking it is a mentality that has become so basic to our habits of thought that we have often failed to notice it:

> The systematic collection of data about people has affected not only the ways in which we conceive of a society, but also the ways in which we describe our neighbour. It has profoundly transformed what we choose to do, who we try to be, and what we think of ourselves.[4]

Hacking's argument is supposed to apply to modern societies as a whole (though at times a distinction between Eastern and Western European understandings of society is important to his argument).[5] For many Western observers after 1917, however, it was Soviet Russia that became most closely identified with government by numbers. Hacking's description

---

[1] Ian Hacking, *The Taming of Chance* (Cambridge: CUP, 1990), 2.
[2] Foucault qtd. in Hacking, *Taming of Chance*, 21.
[3] Hacking, *Taming of Chance*, 3.   [4] Ibid.
[5] E.g. Hacking states that 'Mainline western thought was atomistic, individualistic and liberal. The eastern, in contrast, was holistic, collectivist and conservative.' Ibid. 36. This is seen to have shaped the different ways in which the notion of 'statistical laws' was received in Western Europe (enthusiastically) and in Eastern Europe (with dismissive scepticism) during the 19th century. My argument—among other things—could be taken as an answer to the question of how this East/West contrast (which Hacking admits is a crude one) developed in the 20th century.

of an 'avalanche of printed numbers' is intended as a critique of modern bureaucratic capitalism. However, in the twentieth century, the Soviet Union was frequently understood to be the most archetypal embodiment of this numerical approach to government.

Statistics were everywhere in the Soviet government's self-presentation, and this was reflected in the ways Communism was discussed and promoted in key Popular Front publications in Britain. Victor Gollancz published many reports sympathetic to the Soviet Union, and those in turn often abounded with statistical evidence of the triumphs of the Soviet industrialization drive. *Twelve Studies in Soviet Russia* (1933) was the product of a trip to the Soviet Union organized by the New Fabian Research Bureau, and offered, as Clement Attlee and G. D. H. Cole put it in their introduction, 'a series of independent pictures drawn by experts in different fields of social and kindred studies'.[6] Many of these provided tables of relevant data in an attempt to quantify the success of the Soviet experiment. In the section on 'Power and Industrial Development', for example, written by the Fabian engineer T. G. N. Haldane, we learn that the 'Installed Generator Capacity' grew from 2,900,000 kw. in 1930 to an estimated 5,517,000 kw. in 1932, and a projected 22,500,000 in 1937, among many other quantifiable improvements.[7] Beatrice and Sidney Webb's *Soviet Communism: A New Civilisation?* (1935)—another key Fabian text—contained its own avalanche of numbers, from detailed statistics about the percentage of Shock Brigaders (productive workers temporarily deployed from other industries) in various areas of the economy, to records of the increased total capacity of blast furnaces in the period of the first Five-Year-Plan.[8]

In certain respects, these figures simply played into pre-existing, utilitarian notions of quantifiable efficiency, whose proliferation in the nineteenth century Hacking records. At the more ambitious end, however, writers imagined a fundamentally new mode of statecraft founded on what might be called quantitative omniscience. The Webbs remarked that 'one of the cornerstones of socialist development' was 'an all embracing system of measurement'.[9] Moreover, 'a socialist community must, perforce, have the most scientific system of accounting, and notably one more searching, more candid and more public than that which the capitalist

---

[6] C. R. Attlee and G. D. H. Cole, 'Introduction', in Margaret I. Cole (ed.), *Twelve Studies in Soviet Russia* (London: Victor Gollancz, 1933), 8.

[7] T. G. N. Haldane, 'Power and Industrial Developments', in Margaret I. Cole (ed.), *Twelve Studies in Soviet Russia* (London: Victor Gollancz, 1933), 62.

[8] Sidney and Beatrice Webb, *Soviet Communism: A New Civilization*, 3rd edn, in 1 vol. (London: Longmans, Green & Co., 1944), 608–9, 534.

[9] Ibid. 633.

system contents itself'.[10] For the Webbs, the Soviet habit of quantifying everything made sure that power could be wielded impartially and impersonally. The Revolution was above all a managerial one, and by rigorously applying its ethos of 'measurement and publicity' in every sphere, the Soviet government demanded submission not to the whims of arbitrary authority and capitalist exploitation, but to the entirely neutral realm of numbers. A worker in any sphere may be found lacking, and harshly punished, but such judgements have been delegated to 'statistics impartially arrived at upon objective measurement, presented by trained experts *unconnected with the persons actually wielding power over others*'. The deficient individual may feel 'annoyance' at being so judged, but cannot argue with the objective measurements that precipitated the judgement, and so (the Webbs claimed) can feel 'no resentment' towards the system itself or those charged with running it.[11]

Hewlett Johnson's *The Socialist Sixth of the World* (1939) took a similar view in celebrating the birth of the Supreme Council of Planning Economy, known as Gosplan, in 1917:

> There is centred in a series of buildings in Moscow an organization unsurpassed in the world for the extent and importance of its operations. Its ramifications stretch on and on until they penetrate every corner of a sixth of the world's surface. No factory, no farm, no school, no theatre, no court of law, no hospital, no regiment escapes its scrutiny. By statutory law every public institution in every branch of activity throughout a union which embraces a twelfth of the human race must supply to that central office in Moscow complete data of their present and prospective needs and operations.
>
> The mass of information that pours daily and hourly into those central offices is seized upon, sifted, sorted, and utilized by what is undoubtedly the largest staff of trained statisticians and technical experts in the world, served by thousands of clerks and assistants.[12]

The centralized planning that the Bolsheviks mandated from 1917 onwards, and which what central to the Five-Year-Plans that began in 1928, is seen by Johnson as an unprecedented achievement of modern statecraft. The Soviet Union had shown that there was no sphere of human activity that was beyond quantification. Counting was in a sense the primary function of the omnicompetent state that Johnson imagined. Once established, Gosplan's role was to measure outputs in every sector of society, and then to set targets for increasing them: 'Decisions arrived at in

---

[10] Ibid. 636.   [11] Ibid.
[12] Hewlett Johnson, *The Socialist Sixth of the World* (London: Victor Gollancz, 1939), 114–16.

this way are naturally based upon extremely complicated data and very varying considerations. . . . The ultimate proposals will be the result of a highly complicated balance of forces.' Gosplan promised incremental and quantitative improvements, year on year. Yet, Johnson stressed:

> That office is no dead, cold, scientific, and heartless place of red tape and officialism; it is primarily concerned with the fate of men and women, boys, and girls. Every individual throughout the whole Soviet Union has his or her place among the figures that enter those doors. . . .
> Another set of essential data is the estimation of the needs of all those same multitudes for food, clothing, housing, education, health, or leisure, and of the people as a whole for defence and for capital production in the form of mines, railways, or machines.[13]

Gosplan, for Johnson, existed to serve very human ends. Soviet planning was often seen by British observers as an austere calculus that placed crushing demands in particular on peasant producers who could not or would not meet the quotas the system required of them (as I discuss in Chapter 4). Johnson understands quantitative omniscience from the perspective of the consumer rather than the producer, and thus imagines a state that can quantify not just the demand for grain in a particular region, but every individual's particular requirements for culture and education.

It is relatively difficult to find examples of literary writers who embraced quantitative omniscience as a system of government. This is partly because literature, as I will show, has often been defined partly by its resistance to the realm of number and numbers, providing a warmly qualitative alternative to the number-crunching of Soviet statecraft. George Bernard Shaw was an exception: he seemed to feel entirely at home with Communism's presumed lust for utilitarian calculation. He described Soviet Russia being run in accordance with the 'multiplication table' and celebrated 'the rationalization of Russia'.[14] For Shaw, determining rationally who ought to be exterminated was the key role of the Communist government. Shaw went a lot further than Hewlett Johnson: rather than trying to show how Communist utilitarian calculation was fine-tuned to cater for individual human requirements, Shaw saw Communism as a much needed call to set aside the 'oldfashioned prejudices' of bourgeois humanism so that 'extermination' can 'become a humane science'. 'The notion that a civilized State can be made out of any sort of human material is one of our old Radical delusions',

---

[13] Ibid. 116.
[14] George Bernard Shaw et al., *The Stalin-Wells Talk: The Verbatim Record and a Discussion* (London: New Statesman and Nation, 1934), 41; George Bernard Shaw, *The Rationalization of Russia* (Westport, CT: Greenwood Press, 1977).

he wrote.[15] In *The Rationalization of Russia* Shaw described the need for 'deliberate killing', a 'necessary process politely paraphrased as weeding the garden', and which the Bolsheviks had mastered. This practice he defended as 'utilitarian killing which no sane person dreams of associating with crime and punishment, innocence and guilt, expiation and sacrifice'. It was no surprise, he thought, to find 'the weeds vehemently dissenting'.[16] Shaw embraced Soviet utilitarianism, 'rationalization', and the 'multiplication table' as an alternative to bourgeois humanism. Decisions about who to exterminate were arrived at by a quantitative evaluation of the input and output of each person or social group: 'are you giving more trouble than you are worth?' was the relevant question. '[T]he Cheka had no interest in liquidating anybody who could be made publicly useful.'[17]

Romantic Anti-Communism

For many writers, Communism's apparent reliance on a quantitative utilitarian calculus was deeply offputting. Malcolm Muggeridge had travelled as a sympathetic socialist to the Soviet Union in 1932 and, by his own account, had his eyes opened to the horrors of Communism. He described British friends of the Soviet Union 'repeating, like school children a multiplication table, the bogus statistics and dreary slogans that roll continuously—a dry and melancholy wind—over the emptiness of Soviet Russia'.[18] The image of the 'multiplication table' (echoing Shaw's more appreciative account of the Soviet regime) here becomes symbolic of an arid utilitarianism that has taken over from human morality, at a terrible cost.

Muggeridge's novel *Winter in Moscow* (1934), a savage portrait of the Soviet Union at the time of the terror-famine, is preoccupied with the inhumanity of numbers and the Dictatorship of the Proletariat's attempts to apply arithmetically precise formulae to human society. The novel focuses on a group of foreign journalists, compromised, duped, or bribed by the regime's agents, and contending with censorship. Cooley, one American journalist, protests at being fed statistics:

> 'Tired of figures,' Cooley interrupted. He had often tried to cut a way through the jungle of Soviet statistics, but without success.... 'You can't make a story out of figures...Haven't you heard any gossip?' he asked.

[15] George Bernard Shaw, 'Preface' to *On The Rocks,* in *Plays Political: The Apple Cart, On The Rocks, Geneva* (London: Penguin Books, 1986), 163–5.
[16] Shaw, *The Rationalization of Russia*, 73.   [17] Shaw, 'Preface', 161.
[18] Malcolm Muggeridge, 'To the Friends of the Soviet Union', *English Review*, 58/1 (Jan. 1934), 55.

'Colour stuff for mailed articles. Human interest. Love affairs of the Kremlin. Commissar and Ballerina.'[19]

Cooley's frustration is clearly satirical of the prurience and triviality of the American press: what is needed here is some sordid sex scandal. But there is also a sense that the official Soviet barrage of numbers cannot encapsulate what is really going on in Russia. 'Human interest' is lost in a sea of statistics.

If the novel's weary hacks are simply exhausted with trying to squeeze a story out of a list of numbers, then the true believers who reel off statistics are portrayed as being under the power of a calculative rationality that has completely departed from real human values. Their devotion to the cause is frequently described using mathematical imagery. At a literary party late in the novel, Prince Alexis, an aristocratic Bolshevik sympathizer—'based', as Gerald Stanton Smith writes, 'unmistakably on [D. S.] Mirsky'—is accosted by three young girls: ' "Tell us," the girls chanted together like school children reciting a multiplication table, "how you, a prince, became a Communist." '[20] Their question is itself formulaic and their discourse has become automated, with the multiplication table again being invoked. Muggeridge continues the theme in a set of reflections on Prince Alexis's Communist sympathies:

> The Dictatorship of the Proletariat was, to him, a principle; a law, that he believed in because it was exact. He had come to it at last as some debauchees come at last to join a religious order, or as some scientists or philosophers come at last to absorb themselves in the mathematics of the Old Testament. The more he had come to detest human beings, the more attractive the Dictatorship of the Proletariat had seemed, because it alone opened out the possibility of clearing the world altogether of human beings and leaving only a principle existing.[21]

The combination of mathematical and religious rhetoric is an interesting feature of Muggeridge's novel. The 'mathematics of the Old Testament' (most closely associated with Ivan Panin, a Russian opponent of the Tsardom) points to the frequent intersection of mathematical and religious debates in Russian culture. Communism was often treated as the latest manifestation of the coming together of mathematical reason and esoteric spirituality: Muggeridge's novel depicts a country where rationality itself is

[19] Malcolm Muggeridge, *Winter in Moscow* (London: Eyre & Spottiswoode, 1934), 161–2.
[20] Gerald Stanton Smith, *D. S. Mirsky: A Russian-English Life, 1890–1939* (New York: OUP, 2000), 225; Muggeridge, *Winter in Moscow*, 223.
[21] Muggeridge, *Winter in Moscow*, 223–4.

idolatrously worshipped. Communism for Muggeridge is in the end a cold, inhuman ideology, and its apparent obsession with numbers is an indicator of that inhumanity.

Prince Alexis's arrival at a mathematical certitude about human society recalls a number of other literary depictions of Damascene conversions to Communism. Writing in 1938, describing the events of a decade earlier, a worldly wise Christopher Isherwood ascribed a similar emotion to his friend Edward Upward, who became a Communist. Benjamin Kohlmann has shown how 'Chalmers'—the nickname Isherwood and friends ascribed to Upward—became a key figure for the writers of the 1930s as they debated the dangers that political commitment represented for their art. 'More than any other writer,' Kohlmann writes, ' "Chalmers" was the figure onto whom politicized authors of the 1930s could project their artistic fears about going over to the Communist Party.'[22] Isherwood described Chalmers's search for truth in *Lions and Shadows* (1938):

> He was to spend the next three years in desperate and bitter struggles . . . to find the formula which would transform our private fancies and amusing freaks and bogies into valid symbols of the ills of society and the toils and aspirations of our daily lives. For the formula did, after all, exist. And Chalmers did at last find it, at the end of a long and weary search . . . quite clearly set down, for everybody to read, in the pages of Lenin and of Marx.[23]

Isherwood suggests that for Communists the writings of Marx and Engels were a mathematical formula for the betterment of society. His clear implication is that the very idea of such a formula implies the reduction of all the complexities and nuances of human behaviour to a brutally simple calculus. Such a reduction was inimical to the project of 'literature' as Isherwood and his circle seem to have understood it: part of the agreed narrative around Chalmers's path to commitment (and his discovery of this 'formula') was that it had a mortifying effect on his writing. As John Lehmann put it, the 'imaginative gift in "Chalmers" [was] slowly killed in the Iron Maiden of Marxist dogma'.[24] For both Isherwood and Muggeridge, the attempt to apply Marxism in Russia had confirmed that the aspiration of Condorcet and other Enlightenment figures to apply mathematics to society was intrinsically flawed: literature needed to be rescued from Communism, and also formed part of the alternative to it.

---

[22] Benjamin Kohlmann, *Committed Styles: Modernism, Politics and Left-Wing Literature in the 1930s* (Oxford: OUP, 2014), 161–2.

[23] Christopher Isherwood, *Lions and Shadows: An Education in the Twenties* (London: Hogarth Press, 1938), 274.

[24] Lehmann qtd. in Kohlmann, *Committed Styles*, 162.

These writers participate in a particular version of what Tyrus Miller, in a discussion of E. E. Cummings's *Eimi* (1933), calls 'romantic anti-Communism'. Miller describes Cummings's book as an 'extended romantic protest, in the name of life, individuality and feeling, against the repressive, deadening "unworld" . . . governed by collective thought, industrial technology and repressive statism'.[25] Romantic anti-Communism habitually recoils from the supposed simple certainties of mathematics. The realm that it recoils into is the supposedly complex and uncertain one of literature: the Empsonian province of 'ambiguity' that the multiplication table did not seem to admit. Steven Connor has argued in *Living by Numbers* (2016) that we in the humanities suffer under a 'hysterical institutional allergy to number and all the inhuman, morbid powers it is held to embody'.[26] Literature, as Isherwood and Muggeridge conceive it, is defined by its ability to preserve the humanely qualitative in the face of the inhuman abstractions of quantity. Such an 'allergy to number', Connor argues, remains centrally important to the institutional formation of the humanities today:

> it seems to many, and perhaps especially those who think of themselves as participating in the world of arts, culture, or the humanities, that number has come to be kind of tyrant virus in human affairs, such that the preservation of our humanity, not to mention its earthly vicar, 'the humanities', depends upon our recession from number, and the rescue of what are thought to be qualities from their reduction to mere quantities. . . . [A]n anti-numerical ideology founded on the principle that it should be possible to separate quality from quantity maintains itself with unexampled vigour and self-reproducing virulence.[27]

Connor elsewhere remarks that this allergy to number originates in a 'Romantic protest against the powerful efforts to put social and political reasoning on a firm basis by employing calculative reason, especially in the philosophical form of utilitarianism'.[28] Connor argues for an 'enhanced utilitarianism' that 'recognizes that there is no single unified currency . . . by which pleasures [or pains] can be totted up.'[29] As Connor rightly points out, the suspicion towards number that pervades the humanities disciplines today is generally tied up with a suspicion of a 'capitalism' which is taken to embody 'the reduction of everything in modern life to economics'.[30] Romantic anti-Communism—the elaboration of a refined literary

[25] Tyrus Miller, 'Comrade Kemminkz in Hell: E. E. Cummings's *Eimi* and Anti-Communism', in Benjamin Kohlmann and Matthew Taunton (eds), *Literatures of Anti-Communism* (special issue), *Literature and History*, 24/1 (2015), 16, 14.
[26] Steven Connor, *Living by Numbers: In Defence of Quantity* (London: Reaktion, 2016), 45–6.
[27] Ibid. 7–8.
[28] Steven Connor, 'Blissed Out—on Hedonophobia', <http://stevenconnor.com/blissedout> [accessed: July 2017].
[29] Connor, *Living by Numbers*, 160.		[30] Ibid. 270.

sensibility, descriptive of a humanity that must strive to break free from the tyranny of number—was just as prevalent in mid-century culture. I would suggest that in the twentieth century anti-Communism played a significant part in the development of the humanities disciplines as a locus for the resistance to the application of mathematics to social problems.

So far, the writers I have discussed share a widespread set of beliefs about the relationship between politics, number, and the Russian Revolution. Both sympathizers and critics—from Shaw and the Webbs to Isherwood and Muggeridge—assume either that Marxism is itself mathematical, or that Leninism is a mathematized version of Marxism. The Bolsheviks lent some credence to this idea by deploying mathematical imagery in their own pronouncements, most famously in Lenin's dictum: 'Communism is equal to Soviet power plus the electrification of the entire country'.[31] All these thinkers also rely on a picture of mathematics as an internally consistent, mechanistic science dealing in whole, rational numbers and in equations with predictable, finite outcomes. So when Shaw explains what is wrong with capitalism in *The Rationalization of Russia*, he complains that the experts who are in charge of it constantly contravene the rules of basic arithmetic, and represent a kind of sham rationality: 'The unskilled public are dumb in the presence of experts whom they suppose to be starting from the general premise that two and two make four, though they are really assuming that two minus four makes six.'[32] Shaw and Muggeridge both agree that Communism is the application of a rationalistic arithmetic to society, in contrast to a capitalist West where political and economic decisions are made on arbitrary or qualitative grounds. They only differ over whether it is desirable to manage human affairs according to such an arithmetical mechanism.

EKWILISM

More Equal

Numerical methods can mean different things and be used in different ways. One important use of them is to determine the relative benefit that specific individuals or groups achieve in a given social structure. In these terms, measuring inequalities might be thought of as the first step to

---

[31] Lenin qtd. in Anindita Bannerjee, *We Modern People: Science Fiction and the Making of Russian Modernity* (Middleton, CT: Wesleyan University Press, 2012), 90. Bannerjee argues that 'the seemingly infallible scientific diction of "equal to" and "plus" ... lent the dream of electrification an aura of inevitable prophecy' (p. 91).

[32] Shaw, *The Rationalization of Russia*, 51.

rectifying them. For some, like Hewlett Johnson, the Soviet Union was praiseworthy because it embodied an ideal of equality:

> Complete equality enables citizens, irrespective of their race or nationality, to participate in governing the State according to their ability. Complete equality of sexes, 'equal pay for equal work', is a fundamental law. Equal opportunity for education is provided universally, the school-leaving age is in process of being raised to seventeen, and payment is made to students at universities.[33]

Johnson understood equality as a guiding principle of Soviet society, providing a normative ethical prism through which to view all sorts of different social questions: income, wealth distribution, education, the sexes.

Victor Gollancz had published many books in the 1930s that deployed statistics in defence of the Soviet Union (including Johnson's *The Socialist Sixth of the World*). After the war, having changed his mind about Soviet Communism, he railed against inequality in the USSR in his post-war memoir, *My Dear Timothy* (1952), addressed to his grandson. For the Gollancz of 1952, the precise measurement of social and economic powers retained its importance, but here such measurements are used to condemn the Soviet Union, making manifest the inequalities in Communist society. Gollancz sought to describe 'how corrupt modern socialism is' and pointed out that the 'gap between typical incomes' is 'bigger, it appears, in the Soviet Union even than in America itself'.[34] Perhaps this should not have been news to Gollancz, since statistical presentations of Soviet industrial successes had always tended to highlight relations of inequality: 1934's output exceeded that of 1932; one region, factory, or worker outperformed another in terms of productivity. In particular, the celebration and reward of very productive workers became institutionalized in the Soviet Union as Stakhanovism. As Sheila Fitzpatrick relates, the feats of 'the record-breaking Donbass coal miner, Aleksei Stakhanov' were held up as an ideal for workers to emulate. The institutionalization of Stakhanovism helped to create a social hierarchy based on industrial productivity, such that '[t]he most visible Stakhanovites became members of a new social status group that might be called "ordinary celebrities."'[35] From the perspective of his newfound scepticism about Soviet Communism, Gollancz reflected on the inegalitarian nature of that key element of Soviet industrial psychology.

[33] Johnson, *The Socialist Sixth*, 88.
[34] Gollancz, *My Dear Timothy: An Autobiographical Letter to his Grandson* (London: Victor Gollancz, 1952), 268.
[35] Sheila Fitzpatrick, *Everyday Stalinism: Ordinary Life in Extraordinary Times: Soviet Russia in the 1930s* (New York: OUP, 1999), 74.

Consider, in Russia, Stakhanovism. Somebody produces more than the average: he is rewarded accordingly—with money, not with honour and decorations alone, which would be bad enough: others are encouraged to emulate him: so a few grow as wealthy as film stars, while, down at the other end of the scale, charwomen, let us say, can hardly get enough to keep alive on. The theory is that they are working, the Stakhanovites, for their country, and that being of such value in consolidating socialism they deserve to be conspicuously enriched. Can you imagine a more ludicrous paradox? Or a piece of more distasteful hypocrisy?[36]

In Stakhanovism, feats of productivity were held up as examples for other workers to try to emulate (or used as a stick to beat them with). The system of rewards attached was quite manifestly and deliberately a *cause* of substantial inequality among workers in the Soviet Union.

Koestler—another intellectual whose sympathies with Communism were reversed as the 1930s receded into memory—also castigated Stalin's Russia for failing to live up to standards of equality that seemed important to his version of socialism. He saw this as a narrative of decline from the egalitarianism he attributed to Lenin (who in fact had railed against equality in *The State and Revolution*).[37] Koestler presents data—which must have alarmed egalitarian leftists—to show the extent of income inequality in Stalin's Soviet Union: Stakhanovites 'had separate dining rooms in factories and were paid up to twenty times the average', he noted. Moreover, 'the salaries of directors, chief engineers and administrators in the top stratum are up to 100 times higher than the average wage and up to 300 times higher than the minimum wage'.[38]

Both Gollancz and Koestler condemned the Soviet Union from the perspective of an egalitarian socialism that had considerable emotional appeal for many writers. Orwell was one who took 'equality' to heart. In *Homage to Catalonia* (1938), he described the atmosphere of Republican Spain in these terms:

One had breathed the air of equality. I am well aware that it is the fashion to deny that Socialism has anything to do with equality. In every country in the world a huge tribe of party-hacks and sleek little professors are busy 'proving' that Socialism means nothing more than a planned state-capitalism with the grab-motive left intact. But fortunately there also exists a version of Socialism quite different from this. The thing that attracts ordinary men to Socialism

---

[36] Gollancz, *My Dear Timothy*, 273–4.
[37] V. I. Lenin (tr. Robert Service), *The State and Revolution* (London: Penguin, 1992), 83–5.
[38] Arthur Koestler, 'Soviet Myth and Reality', in *The Yogi and the Commissar* (New York: Macmillan, 1946), 156–7.

and makes them willing to risk their skins for it, the 'mystique' of Socialism, is the idea of equality.[39]

While Orwell laid claim to an instinct for equality and saw socialism as the only means to achieve it, he saw in Communist Russia the betrayal of this principle. This was summed up in another slogan that Orwell projected onto the Soviet Union in *Animal Farm*: 'ALL ANIMALS ARE EQUAL BUT SOME ANIMALS ARE MORE EQUAL THAN OTHERS'.[40] The phrase recalls the 'two and two make five' of *Nineteen Eighty-Four* as it conjures paradoxically with its seemingly simple terms.[41] Orwell's sense of equality is better captured by the qualitative and evanescent feeling that struck him in the streets of Barcelona than by the kind of quantitative totting up that would make equality an easily measurable social virtue. Equality is not, so it appears, a straightforward way of solving social injustice and oppression by recourse to quantitative methods, partly because there exists such a variety of quantifiable social and economic ends, which might be measured in different ways.

Perhaps unsurprisingly, it fell to the Webbs to defend the inequality of the Soviet Union in its own terms. No doubt Orwell was thinking of them when he described a 'tribe of party-hacks and sleek little professors' who dedicated themselves to 'proving' that socialism had nothing to do with equality. A chapter of *Soviet Communism* called 'Not Equality of Wages' set out why wage equality was a thoroughly bad idea and why, therefore, Communists scrupulously avoided it. Riffing on the Marxist slogan 'from each according to his faculties and to each according to his needs', the chapter recruits Marx and Lenin as it rails against an 'abstract equality between man and man'.[42] For the Webbs, Lenin had recognized 'the impulses i[m]planted in the ordinary man ... to better their customary condition of livelihood', and it was Communism's task to ensure that this acquisitive drive was 'directed into channels of public usefulness'.[43] The Webbs hoped, somewhat paradoxically, that 'individual remuneration for services rendered might be sufficiently varied without impairing that general condition of social equality which is fundamental to both socialism and communism'.[44] Inequality of wages was to be used as an instrument to create equality of a more 'general' sort: perhaps the Webbs are not so

---

[39] George Orwell, *Homage to Catalonia* (London: Penguin, 1989), 83–4.

[40] George Orwell, *Animal Farm: A Fairy Story* (London: Secker & Warburg, 1987), 90.

[41] For David Dwan, *Animal Farm* 'raises tough questions about the coherence and viability of equality as a theoretical principle'. Dwan's illuminating article explores the possibilities and the limits of equality throughout Orwell's oeuvre. 'Orwell's Paradox: Equality in *Animal Farm*', *ELH* 79/3 (2012), 655.

[42] Webb and Webb, *Soviet Communism*, 572.   [43] Ibid. 573.   [44] Ibid.

very far from Orwell in feeling that equality was more of a vibe than something one could measure, though they differed over whether it could be found in the Soviet Union.

Against the Average Man

Not everyone felt that equality was an intrinsic good, and some worried that—especially where it was crudely applied—it might have damaging effects. For writers including D. H. Lawrence and Vladimir Nabokov, the problem was that Russia was *too* committed to equality. Lawrence's early infatuation with Russian literature fed into an initial enthusiasm for the Russian Revolution. But, as Olga Soboleva and Angus Wrenn have shown, this enthusiasm waned and then mutated into an outright hostility in the period 1923–6. They argue that Lawrence came to see Bolshevism as a 'dogmatic, mechanical and essentially rationalistic social doctrine, hardly different from that prevailing in the West'.[45] Lawrence's resistance to Bolshevism's 'rationalistic' dimension clearly places him with the Romantic anti-Communists. But where some understood Russia's bureaucratic rationalization as tending to produce and measure inequalities, Lawrence's increasing disaffection with Communism led him to suggest that the brutality of the system stemmed from its failure to understand people as individuals, flattening out important differences so as to understand them as interchangeable units. There was too much equality, not too little.

Lawrence's essay 'Democracy' treats Bolshevism as one symptom of a pervasive modern tendency to seek treat humans as if they were 'automatic units, determined entirely by mechanical law'.[46] 'Let us get over our rage of social activity, public being, universal self-estimation, republicanism, bolshevism, socialism, empire—all these mad manifestations of *En Masse* and One Identity,' Lawrence wrote.[47] Lumping all these disparate movements together in this way might be thought to dilute the specificity of Lawrence's critique of Bolshevism. And it is certainly true that the mentality of '*En Masse*', of equality, and of the 'Average Man' (to whom we will return) was for Lawrence a pervasive feature of modernity itself:

Now we will settle forever the Equality of Man, and the Rights of Man. Society means people living together. People *must* live together. And to live

---

[45] Olga Soboleva and Angus Wrenn, *From Orientalism to Cultural Capital: The Myth of Russia in British Literature of the 1920s* (Bern: Peter Lang, 2017), 223.

[46] D. H. Lawrence, 'Democracy', in Edward D. McDonald (ed.), *Phoenix: The Posthumous Papers of D. H. Lawrence* (Harmondsworth: Penguin, 1978), 717.

[47] Ibid. 709.

together, they must have some Standard, some *Material* Standard. This is where the average comes in. And this is where Socialism and Modern Democracy come in.[48]

Yet elsewhere, Lawrence got more specific about Bolshevism. In his poem 'When Wilt Thou Teach the People' (1929), Lawrence implored a 'God of justice' to 'send no more / Saviours of the people'. Having first disparaged Napoleon and then some unnamed 'later republicans' as false prophets, Lawrence turned on Lenin and reflected directly on the legacy of the Bolshevik Revolution:

> Our Lenin says: You are saved, but you are saved wholesale.
> You are no longer men, that is bourgeois;
> you are items in the soviet state,
> and each will get its ration,
> but it is the soviet state alone which counts
> the items are of small importance,
> The state having saved them all.—[49]

In Lawrence's understanding, Bolshevism converts 'men' into 'items', to be allocated a 'ration'. The punning use of the word 'counts' suggests it is that entity which counts (meaning 'enumerates') that really counts (as in 'matters'). The state itself has become a sort of counting machine.

It is in 'Democracy', however, that Lawrence most clearly articulates his objections to equality, understood as mathematical approach. Lawrence insists that each individual is 'a single, incommutable soul' and that 'there can be no establishing of a mathematical ratio'. Indeed, 'We cannot say that all men are equal. We cannot say A=B. Nor can we say that men are unequal. We may not declare that A=B+C.' In place of comparison, Lawrence invokes a purely qualitative appreciation of human individuality:

> When I stand in the presence of another man, and I am my own pure self, am I aware of the presence of an equal, of an inferior, or of a superior? I am not. When I stand with another man, who is himself, and when I am truly myself, then I am only aware of a presence, and the strange reality of Otherness. There is me, and there is *another being*.[50]

Both egalitarianism and Stakhanovism are culpable here precisely because they rely on a *quantitative* assessment of human capacities and achievements.

---

[48] Ibid. 701.

[49] D. H. Lawrence, 'When Wilt Thou Teach the People', in *The Complete Poems of D. H. Lawrence*, ed. Vivian de Sola Pinto and Warren Roberts, 2 vols (New York: Viking Press, 1971), 442.

[50] Lawrence, 'Democracy', 715.

When Lawrence imagines standing next to 'another being', there is only a qualitative awareness of complete otherness. It is only the 'material-mechanical world' that involves humans in quantification, and that entails a departure from 'integral being'.[51]

For Lawrence, a central problem with the modern discourse of 'equality'—of which Bolshevism was an important proponent—was its fixation on the figure of the Average Man. A scrupulous commitment to the equitable allocation of resources had mushroomed into an all-embracing ethics of sameness based not on any observation of human behaviour, but on abstractions: 'What is the Average?', Lawrence asks:

> As we are well aware, there is no such animal. It is a pure abstraction. It is the reduction of the human being to a mathematical unit. Every human being numbers one, one single unit. That is the grand proposition of the Average.[52]

Lawrence's critique of the 'Average Man' could be illuminated by turning to Ian Hacking's argument about the rise of statistics as a mechanism of social accounting and planning. Hacking points out that the 'average man' was first theorized (as 'l'homme moyen') by Adolphe Quetelet, who mooted the concept in his *Treatise of Man* (1835) and refined it in *Recherches statistiques* (1844). Quetelet transposed the terms of a debate about probability from the exact sciences into 'biological and social phenomena where the mean is not a real quantity at all, or rather: *he transformed the mean into a real quantity*'.[53] This conceptual leap carried with it real political dangers, Hacking implies: 'the average man led to both a new kind of information about populations and a new conception of how to control them'.[54] He also refers to a 'steady chorus' of complaints about the abstraction of the concept—'there isn't really an average man!'—and the 'commonsense reply' of the doctrine's adherents: 'no one says that there is a man who is the average man, divorced 0.17 times and with 2.2 children'.[55] But Hacking is sceptical of this response and his book reacts against the average man both on the technical grounds that no such individual exists and on the ethical grounds that the assumption that one does exist grants the state new and extraordinary powers over its citizenry. Hacking seems entirely in tune with the critique set out in Lawrence's essay. 'An average is not invented to be an archetype', Lawrence wrote. 'What a really comical mistake we have made about him . . . He was never intended to be worshipped.'[56] For Lawrence, Bolshevism had elevated the Average Man, squashing the possibility for complex, artistic individuality in the process.

---

[51] Ibid. 716.   [52] Ibid. 699.   [53] Hacking, *Taming of Chance*, 107.
[54] Ibid. 108.   [55] Ibid. 107.   [56] Lawrence, 'Democracy', 699.

In certain ways it is hard to imagine a writer more different to Lawrence than Vladimir Nabokov. Yet Nabokov followed Lawrence in understanding the Bolshevik party as the party of the Average Man, above all in his dystopian fable *Bend Sinister* (1947). Nabokov, characteristically, took pains to emphasize in the novel's 1963 preface that he had 'never been interested in the literature of social comment' and was 'neither a didacticist nor an allegoriser', insisting that his work should not be compared with Orwell's 'mediocre' satires (although he acknowledged that the novel included 'bits of Lenin's speeches, and a chunk of the Soviet constitution').[57] As Michael Glynn points out, Nabokov was elsewhere 'ready to acknowledge the socio-political import of *Bend Sinister*'. He wrote to Alexander Solzhenitsyn, claiming *Bend Sinister* as a novel that set out 'to mock the philistinism of Sovietized Russia and to thunder against the very kind of vicious cruelty of which you write'.[58] *Bend Sinister* depicts a totalitarian dystopia ruled over by a dictator called Paduk, founder-leader of the party of the Average Man whose tenets are based on the philosophy of Ekwilism. Ekwilism had been developed in the previous generation by a friend of Paduk's father, Fradrik Skotoma. The arguments of Skotoma's 'rambling treatise' are set out in these terms:

> At every given level of world-time there was . . . a certain computable amount of human consciousness distributed throughout the population of the world. This distribution was uneven and herein lay the root of all our woes. Human beings, he said, were so many vessels containing unequal portions of this essentially uniform consciousness. It was, however, quite possible, he maintained, to regulate the capacity of the human vessels. If, for instance, a given amount of water were contained in a given number of heterogeneous bottles—wine bottles, flagons and vials of varying shape and size, and all the crystal and gold scent bottles that were reflected in her mirror, the distribution of the liquid would be uneven and unjust, but could be made even by and just either by grading the contents or by eliminating the fancy vessels and adopting a standard size. He introduced the idea of balance as a basis for universal bliss and a theory called 'Ekwilism'.[59]

This theory proposed to go further than socialism in its total application of the egalitarian principle, on the basis that:

> no levelling of wealth could be successfully accomplished, nor indeed was of any real moment, so long as there existed some individuals with more brains or guts than others; and similarly the priest had failed to perceive the futility

[57] Vladimir Nabokov, 'Introduction', in *Bend Sinister* (London: Penguin, 2010), p. vi.
[58] Nabokov qtd. in Michael Glynn, *Vladimir Nabokov: Bergsonian and Russian Formalist Influences in his Novels* (Basingstoke: Palgrave Macmillan, 2007), 146.
[59] Nabokov, *Bend Sinister*, 55.

of his metaphysical promise in relation to those favoured ones (men of bizarre genius, big game hunters, chess players, prodigiously robust and versatile lovers, the radiant women taking her necklace off after the ball) for whom this world was a paradise in itself and who would always be one point up no matter what happened to everyone in the melting pot of eternity.[60]

Skotoma is in a sense the equivalent of Old Major in *Animal Farm*, a grandee who was 'spared the discomfort of seeing his vague and benevolent Ekwilism transformed (while retaining its name) into a violent and virulent political doctrine'.[61] Readers of *Animal Farm* have often disputed about whether Old Major's social programme was intrinsically doomed to end in tyranny, or whether a benign message was distorted by the megalomania of the novel's own Stalin figure, Napoleon. In *Bend Sinister*, there is little doubt that the theory of Ekwilism itself is fundamentally tyrannical, as the passage quoted makes clear. Ekwilism holds 'that Quality is merely the distribution aspect of Quantity': there is no social or aesthetic good and no human attribute that cannot be assigned a numerical value, and the consequences of that quantification is a moral imperative to redistribute, forcibly if necessary. Paduk promises his subjects 'total joy', to be achieved 'by adjusting ideas and emotions to those of a harmonious majority'. 'Your groping individualities will become interchangeable', he proclaims.[62] Out of a misplaced sense of fairness, Ekwilist politics tasked itself with ensuring that everybody has precisely the same amount of brains and guts.

As flawed as Nabokov makes Ekwilism seem, it is no more than an idle speculation in a little-read pamphlet until it is taken up by a strongly motivated individual. By returning to the dictator's school days, the novel supplies a psychological explanation which accounts for the appeal of Ekwilism to its adherents. Paduk (with his 'pasty face and grey-blue cranium with bumps') was bullied at school, and the chief perpetrator was Krug, the complex chief protagonist of *Bend Sinister*. Krug gave Paduk the nickname 'Toad', and 'used to trip him up and sit upon his face'.[63] The party of the Average Man was founded in the playground, as a group of bullied children gathered around Paduk:

> Every one of his followers had some little defect or 'background of insecurity' as an educationalist after a fruit cocktail might put it: one boy suffered from permanent boils, another was morbidly shy, a third had by accident beheaded his baby sister, a fourth stuttered so badly that you could go out and buy yourself a chocolate bar while he was wrestling with an initial p or a b.[64]

---

[60] Ibid.   [61] Ibid. 56.   [62] Ibid. 72.   [63] Ibid. 49, 37.
[64] Ibid. 54.

Ekwilism is thus painted as a means for the weak to exact revenge on the strong. Communism, for Nabokov, is a kind of macrocosm of the politics of the playground, and the Bolsheviks are self-righteous children, left out of a game, who complain 'it's not *fair*' and lash out against their stronger schoolmates.

The connection that Nabokov draws between egalitarianism and vengeful resentment recalls Nietzsche's condemnations of socialism. ' "If I am a canaille, you ought to be too"—on such logic are revolutions made', he wrote in *Twilight of the Idols* (1889). Ekwilism offers to the bullied children of *Bend Sinister* what Nietzsche called the 'honey of revenge'.[65] For Nietzsche, the desire for equality is one version of a slave morality that has its roots in a feeling of envy and resentment, and is directed by the weak against the strong:

> The doctrine of equality!... But there exists no more poisonous poison: for it *seems* to be preached by justice itself, while it is the *termination* of justice... 'Equality for equals, inequality for unequals'—*that* would be the true voice of justice; and, what follows from it, 'Never make equal what is unequal.'[66]

There seems to me no doubt that Nabokov's rejection of equality—and his implication that the root cause of Soviet tyranny is a rigorous egalitarianism—is heavily influenced by his reading of Nietzsche (as, no doubt, was Lawrence's).[67] Yet if *Bend Sinister* can be read in terms of a Nietzschean critique of egalitarianism, it is less easy to map the genealogical dimension of Nietzsche's critique onto the novel. This would seem to require Krug—the stronger man against whom Paduk takes resentful revenge—to assume the role of 'the magnificent *blond beast* avidly prowling round for spoil and victory', described in the first essay of *On the Genealogy of Morality* (1887).[68] The refinements of modern intellectual culture (Nietzsche argued) were developed as part of a slave revolt against those who were too healthy and happy to bother much with introspection. Krug is no '*blond beast*': he is, as Thomas Karshan puts it, 'blocked in his

---

[65] Friedrich Nietzsche (tr. R. J. Hollingdale), *Twilight of the Idols* and *The Anti-Christ* (London: Penguin, 2003), 98.

[66] Ibid. 113. Ellipses and emphases in original.

[67] Brian Boyd notes that Nietzsche was on Nabokov's reading list in *Vladimir Nabokov: The Russian Years* (Princeton: Princeton University Press, 1990), 76, 150. Michael Rogers has recently made the case that Nabokov's works were profoundly and systematically shaped by an engagement with Nietzsche, in *Nabokov and Nietzsche: Problems and Perspectives* (London: Bloomsbury, 2018).

[68] Friedrich Nietzsche (tr. Carol Deithe), *On the Genealogy of Morality* (Cambridge: CUP, 2006), 23.

writing, ... childishly vain and enmired in memories of the schoolyard'.[69] In these respects, Krug embodies the self-loathing asceticism of the modern intellectual class that Nietzsche also railed against.

Nietzsche's critique of egalitarianism forms an important intellectual substructure for Nabokov's strong commitment to anti-Communism. Recent scholarship has helped to reconstruct a more politically committed Nabokov, contrary to his sense of himself as an apolitical aesthete. Critics have pointed to Nabokov's membership (from 1926) of the secret anti-Bolshevik organization VIR, as well as a series of often unpublished or untranslated writings in which his political identifications seem to be a more of guiding force in his life and work than might have been assumed.[70] Karshan draws attention to a 1927 piece Nabokov wrote for the tenth anniversary of the Russian Revolution, called simply 'Anniversary':

> I hold in contempt the communist faith, as an idea of base equality, as a dull page in the festive history of humanity, its denial of earthly and unearthly beauty, as something foolishly infringing on my free 'I', encouraging ignorance, dullness and complacency.[71]

It is not surprising that these were Nabokov's political views (though the specific characterization of 'base equality' should interest us). But some of the evidence Karshan sets out implies that anti-Communism had a determining influence on Nabokov's craft as a novelist. In a 1925 essay, 'Play', Nabokov related Communism's supposed egalitarianism to an inability to play:

> There is no play without competition ... Which is why the communist system is so absurd, in which everyone is condemned to do the same boring gymnastic exercises as each other, not allowing, that anyone should be better than his neighbour.[72]

Thus, on some level, the aesthetic of play which Karshan identifies as central to Nabokov's work could be described as a reaction against what he saw as Communism's deadening egalitarian unplayfulness. To underline this political commitment is to read Nabokov against the grain: one of

---

[69] Thomas Karshan, *Vladimir Nabokov and the Art of Play* (Oxford: OUP, 2011), 163.

[70] See Karshan, *Vladimir Nabokov*, 79,, and his unpublished paper 'Nabokov and Anti-Communism', delivered at Anti-Communism: Culture, Literature, Propaganda, Institute of English Studies, 28 Aug. 2013, and Brian Boyd, *Vladimir Nabokov: The Russian Years*, 260.

[71] Nabokov, 'Iubilei', first published in *Rul'* ('The Rudder'), 18 Nov. 1927; republished *Sobranie sochinenii russkogo perioda*, 2: 645–7), tr. Karshan, cited in 'Nabokov and Anti-Communism'.

[72] Vladimir Nabokov (tr. Karshan), 'Play', qtd. in Karshan, *Vladimir Nabokov*, 79.

the things that Nabokov most objected to about Communism was its assumption that art must necessarily embody a political position, however concealed. Yet, given this stridently apolitical aesthetic orientation, it is interesting to note how deep Nabokov's anti-Communism runs, and also how rooted it is in Russian debates about the politics of number that run back to the 1860s, to which I now turn.

RATIONALISM AND ARITHMETIC

Twice Two is Four and the Rest's Nonsense

In seeking to counter a deadening Leninist egalitarianism with an aesthetic of playful illogicality, Nabokov drew deeply on the resources of nineteenth-century Russian culture. Nabokov's early work develops a critique of revolutionary nihilism that began in the 1860s with Turgenev and Dostoyevsky, transposing its terms to the Bolshevik Revolution.[73] His last Russian novel, *The Gift* (1937–8), explicitly revisited the debates of the 1860s. The fourth chapter is a biography of Nikolai Chernyshevsky, purportedly written by Fyodor, the protagonist of Nabokov's *Bildungsroman*. Chernyshevsky was the leading figure of the so-called 'men of the 1860s', who were associated with the importation into Russia of the thought of Ludwig Feuerbach, Karl Vogt, Ludwig Büchner, and Jakob Moleschott. These debates were much taxed by the question of the applicability of numerical and mathematical methods to society. For the men of the 1860s—Chernyshevsky foremost among them—the application of strict scientific principles was the key to the solution of social ills. E. H. Carr described Chernyshevsky and his peers as belonging to 'the age of the supreme cult of science'.[74] In *The Gift*, Nabokov's contemptuous portrayal of Chernyshevsky repeatedly emphasizes ways in which he sought to force phenomena into a logical, arithmetical frame: 'he was able to bend the silliest daydream into a logical horseshoe', Fyodor notes, '[h]e distilled his feelings in the alembics of logic'.[75] Fyodor's account—characteristically Romantic in its scepticism towards number—positions

[73] See Thomas Karshan, 'Introduction', in Vladimir Nabokov (tr. Anastasia Tolstoy and Thomas Karshan), *The Tragedy of Mister Morn* (London: Penguin, 2012), pp. viii–ix.

[74] E. H. Carr, 'Introduction', in Nikolay Gavrilovich Chernyshevsky, *What is to be Done? Tales about New People* (London: Virago, 1982), p. xv.

[75] Vladimir Nabokov (tr. Michael Scammell and Dmitri Nabokov in collaboration with Vladimir Nabokov), *The Gift* (London: Penguin, 2001), 202–3., Gabriel Shapiro, 'Setting his Myriad Faces in his Text: Nabokov's Authorial Presence Revisited', in Julian W. Connolly (ed.), *Nabokov and his Fiction: New Perspectives* (Cambridge: CUP, 1999), 19.

'love' as a symbol of unquantifiability. Chernyshevsky is scorned because, in referring to his mother by the plural 'they', he 'attempts to express quality by quantity'. Even in his romantic infatuations, he 'sets his love on a utilitarian foundation'.[76] Translating this drive to rationalization and quantification into a political position, Fyodor points to Chernyshevsky's love of Fourier and his phalanstery: '1,800 souls—and all happy! Music, flags, cakes. The world is run by mathematics and well run at that.'[77] Nabokov also underlined the parallel with Leninism, and Fyodor cites multiple sources to show (uncontroversially) that Lenin owed an immense intellectual debt to Chernyshevsky.[78]

Nabokov's account of Chernyshevsky in *The Gift* owes an obvious political and literary debt to Turgenev and Dostoyevsky, who reacted against Chernyshevsky's ascetic and rationalistic radicalism in the 1860s. The latter found its most memorable satirical embodiment in the figure of the nihilist Evgeny Bazarov in Ivan Turgenev's *Fathers and Sons* (1862). The novel turned around a central contrast between Bazarov and Nikolai Petrovich, the liberal humanist man of the 1840s (Turgenev's own generation). Arkady Nikolaevich, Bazarov's friend and disciple, describes a nihilist as someone who 'approaches everything from a critical point of view...a man who doesn't acknowledge any authorities, who doesn't accept a single principle on faith, no matter how much that principle may be surrounded by respect'.[79] The 'Nihilism' that Chernyshevsky and Bazarov come to stand for, then, is an extreme version of the scientific attitude, applied to social and political problems. Bazarov himself is an amateur scientist as well as a political revolutionary, spending much of his time dissecting frogs or peering down his microscope, and professing himself indifferent or hostile to literature and art, asserting that 'a good chemist's twenty times more useful than a poet'.[80] Bazarov's rationalism means a reduction of all human problems to the mathematical formula which becomes something of a refrain in nineteenth-century responses to Chernyshevsky and the men of the 1860s: 'What's important is that twice two is four and all the rest's nonsense.'[81] Turgenev emphasizes that this involves a fundamental disregard for human feeling and morality. Pressed by the beautiful widow Anna Odintsova (with whom he will fall awkwardly, irrationally in love) on his professed contempt for literature, Bazarov counters her assertion that literature can teach us to understand

---

[76] Nabokov, *The Gift*, 200, 203.   [77] Ibid. 226.
[78] Ibid. 225. Lenin's pamphlet *What is to be Done* (1902) took its title from Chernyshevsky's 1863 novel of that name. Orlando Figes explores Lenin's debt to Chernyshevsky in *A People's Tragedy: The Russian Revolution 1891–1924* (London: Pimlico, 1997), 145–6.
[79] Ivan Turgenev (tr. Richard Freeborn), *Fathers and Sons* (Oxford: OUP, 1999), 23.
[80] Ibid. 26.   [81] Ibid. 44.

people: 'One human example is sufficient to judge all the rest', he asserts.[82] The perfect, mathematical organization of society that Bazarov advocates will render all questions of morality void: 'in a properly organized society it'll be completely irrelevant whether someone is stupid or clever, good or bad'.[83] Turgenev clearly aligned himself with the Romantic reaction against Bazarovian rationalism in his prose poem 'Prayer': 'Whatever man prays for, he prays for a miracle. Every prayer reduces to this: "Great God, grant that twice two be not four."'[84]

This equation and the questions about the social applicability of mathematical reason were taken up again in Dostoyevsky's *Notes from the Underground* (1864), whose narrator spends the first half of the novel berating imagined interlocutors who want to insist that twice two is four, and that society ought to be structured along the rationalistic lines suggested by this equation. Dostoyevsky's narrator—the so-called 'Underground Man'—resists this violently:

> But this twice two's four—it's nevertheless an intolerable thing. Twice two's four, well in my opinion it's a cheek. Twice two's four watches smugly, stands in the middle of your road with his arms akimbo, and spits. I agree that twice two's four is a marvellous thing; but to give everything its due praise, twice two is five can also be a very nice little thing.[85]

Against the tyrannical assertion that twice two is four—and the still more frightening possibility that in some hypothetical, hyper-rational future '[a]ll human action will automatically be computed according to these laws, mathematically, like a table of logarithms'—the underground man asserts that twice two is five, as a way of holding on to his individuality.[86] Who are the novel's imagined interlocutors, insisting on the iron rule of twice two? It would be oversimplistic to limit these to the Russian context—the Chernyshevskyan rationalism that oppresses the underground man is also seen as an imposition from the West.

As should already be clear, nineteenth-century debates about the politics of number profoundly informed the whole range of responses to the Russian Revolution discussed in this chapter. The equation two plus two equals four was frequently used metonymically in English literature as well as Russian literature to stand in for excessive rationalism—yet the political significance of this was entirely different in the two countries.

---

[82] Ibid. 84.   [83] Ibid.

[84] Ivan Turgenev (tr. Constance Garnett), 'Prayer', in *Dream Tales and Prose Poems* (London: Faber & Faber, 2008), 163.

[85] Fyodor Dostoyevsky (tr. Jane Kentish), *Notes from Underground* and *The Gambler* (Oxford: OUP, 2008), 34.

[86] Ibid. 25.

Understanding this difference can help to shed light on the articulation of politics and number in the wake of the 1917 Revolution. In Steven Connor's argument about the humanities' allergy to number, Charles Dickens is made to exemplify the Romantic reaction against utilitarianism.[87] Thomas Gradgrind in *Hard Times* (1854) personifies what Dickens saw as the subjection of the rich complexity of human experience to the unfeeling effect of number. He is described as

> A man of realities. A man of fact and calculations. A man who proceeds upon the principle that two and two are four, and nothing over ... With a rule and a pair of scales, and the multiplication table always in his pocket, sir, ready to weigh and measure any parcel of human nature, and tell you exactly what it comes to. It is a mere question of figures, a case of simple arithmetic.[88]

Reading *Hard Times* in the present context, however, might cause us to question Hacking's argument, because it can easily be shown (as Connor insists) that views like Dickens's were and are at least as widely held as the views he caricatures in Gradgrind. We may be justified in feeling buried not by an 'avalanche of numbers' but by an avalanche of Romantic reactions against them.

The point to underline here is that, in Russian literature (at least, in the enduring works of Turgenev and Dostoyevsky), 'two plus two is four' is a statement aligned with the radical nihilists who wished to tear down the edifice of the Tsarist state and create a completely equal society. In the English tradition of Romantic scepticism, the same statement is associated with the educational, penal, and political institutions of Victorian society, and with the hegemonic values of the capitalist bourgeoisie.

From Arithmetic to Arythmology

Together, both the English and the Russian traditions form the background to Orwell's use of the equation 'two and two makes five' in *Nineteen Eighty-Four*. But before turning to that text, it will be worth our while to dig a little deeper into the Russian side of this question, where the resistance to the idea that 'two plus two is four'—or at least a version of it—progressed beyond the simplistic rejection of number that Connor deplores, and moved into more mathematically sophisticated territory. One of Orwell's key sources for the use of numbers in *Nineteen Eighty-Four* was Yevgeny Zamyatin's fascinating response to the Russian Revolution, *We* (1923). Indeed, in a famous essay of 1954, Isaac

---

[87] Connor, *Living by Numbers*, 137.
[88] Charles Dickens, *Hard Times* (Oxford: OUP, 2003), 10.

Deutscher argued that Orwell's borrowings from Zamyatin were so extensive as to constitute a 'lack of originality', and certainly there are significant aspects of his portrait of a totalitarian society, as well as elements of the plot, which have been taken more or less directly from *We*.[89] Orwell's first written reference to the planning for *Nineteen Eighty-Four* came in a letter to Gleb Struve (an expert in Soviet literature at the School of Slavonic and East European Studies) and he connected it to Struve's account of *We*: 'I am interested in that kind of book, and even keep making notes for one myself that may get written sooner or later.'[90] A few years later, Orwell obtained a copy of the French translation and reviewed it for *Tribune*. He thought that 'Huxley's *Brave New World* must be partly derived from it', since both books 'deal with the rebellion of the primitive human spirit against a rationalised, mechanised, painless world'.[91] Like Shaw and Muggeridge, Zamyatin implied that the revolution works by applying a rigid form of quantitative calculation to social life. But his recoil from rigid utilitarian thinking is supplemented by a use of mathematics more complex than either of those writers. The novel depicts what it refers to as 'the mathematically perfect life of the One State'.[92] The novel's characters (like the pupils at Dickens's M'Choakumchild school in *Hard Times*) have numbers instead of names. While there is no necessary connection between the assignment of an identifying number and either mathematics or the calculative rationality it is often taken to represent, it is clear that for Dickens and for Zamyatin it is freighted with political meaning, signalling the reduction of humanity to interchangeable units. This is a world where 'dreams are a serious psychic disease', because they seem incompatible with an ordered, rational society, and the state declares that 'YOU WILL BE PERFECT, YOU WILL BE MACHINE-EQUAL'.[93] When the rebellion against the One State begins, it is in part a rebellion against numbers. I-330, the rebellious woman with whom D-503 is in love, tells him that 'you are overgrown with numbers, numbers crawl all over you, like lice'.[94]

Zamyatin did not simply equate mathematics with rationalism. In his review of *We*, Orwell was perceptive in noticing that the totalitarian

---

[89] Isaac Deutscher, ' "1984"—The Mysticism of Cruelty', in *Heretics and Renegades and Other Essays* (London: Hamish Hamilton, 1955), 36.

[90] George Orwell to Gleb Struve, 17 Feb. 1944, in *George Orwell, the Complete Works: I Have Tried to Tell the Truth, 1943–44*, ed. Peter Davison (London: Secker & Warburg, 1998), 99.

[91] George Orwell, 'Freedom and Happiness' (*Tribune*, 4 January 1946), in *George Orwell, the Complete Works: Smothered under Journalism, 1946*, ed. Peter Davison (London: Secker & Warburg, 1998), 14.

[92] Yevgeny Zamyatin (tr. Natasha Randall), *We* (London: Vintage, 2007), 4.

[93] Ibid. 30, 158.   [94] Ibid. 144.

society Zamyatin described could be 'mathematically perfect' without being rationalistic. He felt that it was an 'intuitive grasp of the *irrational* side of totalitarianism . . . that makes Zamyatin's book superior to Huxley's'.[95] Orwell's review pointed to a loosening of the association between the idea of rationality and that of mathematics. Indeed, *We* steps outside of the simple arithmetical logic of 'two and two is four' by bringing higher level mathematical concepts such as imaginary numbers into play. An engineer by trade, Zamyatin understood and engaged with mathematics in a profound way that Dickens, for example, was not interested in doing. The novel's central character, D-503, spends much of the novel trying neurotically to fit into the One State's rigid conception of a mathematically ordered polity, and trying to repress the irrational, human sides of his character that don't fit the model. Yet the latter also find expression in mathematical terms. He is haunted by the figure of the square root of minus one ($\sqrt{-1}$); he hates it because it has no real solution.[96] In mathematics, it is a so-called 'imaginary number'. Perhaps, then, the rebellion against the One State is not a rebellion against mathematics and its social applications per se. Gleb Struve responded to Orwell's review by stressing that '[h]is mathematical training is strongly reflected in all his work'.[97] For Zamyatin, there existed the possibility of a more humane mathematics, encompassing phenomena such as imaginary numbers. We are no longer in a simplistic binary situation where inhuman, totalitarian government applies the principles of mathematics rationally, and the Romantic rebellion against it implies the wholesale rejection of reason and mathematics. Instead, there are numbers and mathematical operations on both sides, and these can contain or even inspire a departure from rationality, for good or ill. In Zamyatin's moral universe, a more complex account of the politics of number is achieved by taking the social applications of mathematical thinking beyond the categories of mere arithmetic.

Such a possibility had been suggested by Russian mathematicians who were Zamyatin's contemporaries. Indeed, Zamyatin seems to have been drawing on recent developments in the philosophy of mathematics as it was practised in Russia. Russia had a strong tradition of mathematics dating from the foundation of the St Petersburg Academy of Sciences by Catherine the Great. Some of the most fundamental results of nineteenth-century mathematics were achieved in Russia, notably the development of non-Euclidean geometry by Lobachevsky. At the *fin de siècle*, a number of prominent Russian mathematicians and thinkers were exploring aspects of the discipline that had the potential to test the boundaries of calculative

[95] Orwell, 'Freedom and Happiness', 15, my emphasis. [96] Zamyatin, *We*, 36.
[97] Gleb Struve, qtd. in Orwell, *Smothered under Journalism*, 17.

rationality, or disrupt it entirely. One of the most influential thinkers to develop the philosophical implications of this was Nicolai Vasilievich Bugaev, founder of the Moscow Mathematical-Philosophical Society, who addressed the First International Congress of Mathematics in Zurich in 1897 with a fascinating paper called 'Les mathématiques et la conception du monde au point de vue de la philosophie scientifique'. He argued that the application of mathematics in the physical sciences had hitherto restricted itself predominantly to continuous functions. However,

> Continuity explains only one aspect of the phenomena of the universe. Analytic functions are immediately linked with continuity. These functions can only explain the simplest phenomena of life and of nature. The analytic conception of the world is therefore insufficient. It cannot not extend to all the facts of nature, nor explain all of its phenomena.[98]

But despite its limitations, Bugaev argued that the 'idea of the continuity of natural phenomena has begun to penetrate into biology, psychology and sociology'.[99] It is in the nature of a continuous function—a multiplication table, for example—that its results follow a straight line that is entirely predictable, and Bugaev argued that if social trends and transformations can be expressed as continuous functions, this would give us the ability to know the past and future order of events.[100] Crude attempts to mathematize the human sciences resulted in a rigidly deterministic worldview, then, and Bugaev objected to it on an ethical level because it allowed no space for free will.

The determinism that was inherent in understanding the world in terms of continuous functions is one aspect of what Dostoyevsky's underground man objected to in 'twice two is four': 'science itself will then teach man . . . that . . . he has neither will, nor caprice . . . that whatever he does is not through his own volition, but automatically, following the laws of nature'.[101] And just as Dostoyevsky's underground man sought (in the counterfactual equation 'twice two is five') a mode of resistance against the rigid rationalism and determinism of Chernyshevsky and the men of the 1860s, Bugaev's resistance to the idea of applying continuous functions to social problems was framed as a form of resistance to the deterministic outlook of the Marxism that had taken root among the Russian intelligentsia in the 1890s. However, Bugaev's response was not to seek an escape from the avalanche of numbers by speaking out against

---

[98] Nikolai Bugaev, 'Les mathématiques et la conception du monde au point de vue de la philosophie scientifique', in Ferdinand Rudio (ed.), *Verhandlungen des ersten Internationalen Mathematiker- Kongresses in Zürich Vom 9. Bis 11. August 1897* (Leipzig: B. G. Teubner, 1898), 217. My translation.

[99] Ibid. 213.   [100] Ibid. 214.

[101] Dostoyevsky, *Notes from Underground*, 25.

the application of mathematics to social and cultural questions. Instead he advocated a different approach to numbers. Mathematicians had conventionally thought of continuous functions as beautiful and harmonious, and believed that discontinuous functions were aberrations: the French mathematician Hermite famously called them 'monsters'.[102] Bugaev by contrast emphasized the beauty of discontinuous functions, and their ethical importance. He advocated what he called 'arythmology', the study of discontinuous functions (as opposed to 'analysis', the study of continuous functions), because he saw discontinuity as in some way safeguarding free will: 'Discontinuity appears wherever independent and autonomous individuality manifests itself. Discontinuity also intervenes wherever there arise questions of final causes and in aesthetic and ethical questions.'[103] It seems to me that Bugaev is formulating a mathematical response to the belief, explored by Dostoyevsky, that two plus two is four is a tyrannical statement. If Dostoyevsky's underground man had rejected numbers and arithmetic in the name of spiritual explorations that were fundamentally unquantifiable, Bugaev suggested that mathematics itself—via the exploration of discontinuous functions—might be able to break from the rigid determinism of continuous functions and so open up a space for free will. The discontinuous function could open a space for an ethics that was numerically grounded, but not rigidly bound by the assumptions that continuous functions might foster about the relationship between productivity and human happiness.

Pavel Florensky, Bugaev's student at the Physico-Mathematical Faculty at the University of Moscow, took up these ideas. Florensky made arythmology the centre of a mystical worldview that led him first into the Orthodox priesthood and then into the heresy of Name Worshipping: the belief that repeating the Jesus Prayer—because it involved repeatedly speaking the name of the deity—would bring the devout closer to God (a heresy to which Rasputin would also subscribe). As his biographer explains, for Florensky,

> 'arythmology' did not emancipate the scholar from the 'chain of reasoning' essential to the mathematical process of thought, but it did establish the possibility of breaks in the chain, the legitimacy of the 'arbitrary jump' which left room for intuition as well as speculative calculation.[104]

---

[102] Loren Graham and Jean-Michel Kantor, *Naming Infinity: A True Story of Religious Mysticism and Mathematical Creativity* (Cambridge, MA; London: Belknap Press of Harvard University Press, 2009), 68.
[103] Bugaev 'Les mathématiques et la conception du monde', 217.
[104] Avril Pyman, *Pavel Florensky—A Quiet Genius: The Tragic and Extraordinary Life of Russia's Unknown da Vinci* (New York: Continuum, 2010), 29.

Florensky then went on to study Cantor's set theory and his work on transfinite numbers and 'actual infinity', coming to think that these could only be understood in terms of the 'logic of discontinuity'.[105] As Graham and Kantor have shown, many of Russia's leading mathematicians in this period were, like Florensky, Name Worshippers, and the uptake and development of set theory in Russia was bound up with the belief that naming infinite sets (a central theoretical concern of set theory) was a way of naming God.[106] Florensky 'strongly influenced... the theoretical and philosophical work of many Russian writers at the turn of the last century, including Zamyatin, Bulgakov, and Andrej Bely', and it is thought that he was the model for the Master in Bulgakov's *The Master and Margherita* (publ. 1967).[107] The reciprocal circuits of influence that linked Russian mathematics with Russian literature are clear: the thinking of Florensky and Bugaev both responded to the literary debates of the 1860s, and had a direct influence on Zamyatin's use of mathematics in *We*.

Nabokov's anti-Communism reheated previous critiques of Cherny-shevsky, and also in places drew on mathematical ideas developed by thinkers such as Lobachevsky, Bugaev, and Florensky. In his book *Nikolai Gogol* (1942), Nabokov seems fascinated by an author who—in works such as 'The Nose' (1836) and 'The Overcoat' (1842)—made the fictional text a space in which the expectations of an orderly and rational world could be surprisingly undermined. Nabokov explicitly links Gogol's work to developments in non-Euclidean geometry:

> He may be compared to his contemporary, the mathematician Lobachevsky, who blasted Euclid and discovered a century ago many of the theories which Einstein later developed. If parallel lines do not meet it is not because they cannot, but because they have other things to do. Gogol's art as disclosed in The Overcoat suggests that parallel lines not only may meet, but that they can wriggle and get most extravagantly entangled, just as two pillars reflected in water indulge in the most wobbly contortions if the necessary ripple is there. Gogol's genius is exactly that ripple—two and two make five, if not the square root of five, and it all happens quite naturally in Gogol's world, where neither rational mathematics nor indeed any of our pseudophysical agreements with ourselves can be seriously said to exist.[108]

By aligning Gogol with Lobachevsky and Einstein, Nabokov—like Zamyatin before him—effectively frees the idea of numerical or mathematical knowledge from what he sees as the straightjacket of excessive

---

[105] Ibid. 32.   [106] Graham and Kantor, *Naming Infinity, passim.*

[107] Edna Andrews, *Conversations with Lotman: Cultural Semiotics in Language, Literature, and Cognition* (Toronto: University of Toronto Press, 2003), 84.

[108] Nabokov, *Nikolai Gogol* (New York: New Directions, 1961), 44.

rationalism, associated very closely (in *Bend Sinister* and elsewhere) with Chernyshevsky, Lenin, and the whole ethos of the Russian Revolution.

A similar effect is explored in Nabokov's essay 'The Creative Writer' (1942), which targets a pervasive and limiting notion of 'common sense'. Looking back to the very origin of arithmetic, Nabokov writes:

> Man at a certain stage of his development invented arithmetics for the purely practical purpose of obtaining some kind of human order in a world which he knew to be ruled by gods whom he could not prevent from playing havoc with his sums whenever they felt so inclined. He accepted the inevitable indeterminism which they now and then introduced, called it magic, and calmly proceeded to count the skins he had bartered by chalking bars on the wall of his cave.[109]

Nabokov then sketches a narrative from this prehistoric scene—in which, note, the 'inevitable indeterminism' of certain mathematical or arithmetical operations is simply accepted—to more modern times, when 'mathematics transcended their initial condition and became as it were a natural part of the world', and in fact 'the whole world gradually turned out to be based on numbers'.[110] But Nabokov—perhaps inspired by the non-Euclidean geometry of Lobachevsky—understood the creative process as one in which 'commonsense is ejected together with its calculating machine' and 'numbers cease to trouble the mind'. He continued:

> Two and two no longer make four, because it is no longer necessary for them to make four..., I invite my numbers to an impromptu picnic and then nobody minds whether two and two make five or five minus some quaint fraction.[111]

The tradition of Russian thinking about the politics of number that I have been describing, throws up some interesting possibilities. In breaking the conventional literary association between numbers or mathematics as such and Stalinist technocratic rationalization, it offers a way out of Romantic anti-Communism. When they are not merely dismissed as some restrictive 'multiplication table', counting, measuring, and applying mathematical functions seem to have a more loosely defined, wider range of possible applications. Frequently enough, Nabokov's work does seem to indulge in a Romantic recoil from measurable equality. But it contains, at least in latent form, a suggestion that enumerability might not be the end of the story: that—in the non-Euclidean geometry of Lobachevsky for

---

[109] Vladimir Nabokov, 'The Creative Writer', *NEMLA Bulletin* (Jan. 1942), 23.
[110] Ibid.   [111] Ibid. 23.

example—there might be ways of doing things with numbers that are not simply forms of social control.

If nothing else, the argument I have been making in this chapter demonstrates how ludicrous it is to assume that basing economic and political decisions on numbers is necessarily tyrannical, or at heart a biopolitical mechanism of social control. The Soviet Union was frequently abominated (and less often praised) as a country crawling with numbers, or a 'mathematically perfect society'. Yet it is plain that those who criticize it in those terms fell into (at least) two camps: the ones who thought that counting things encourages competition and exacerbates inequalities (in Stakhanovism), and the ones who feared the crushing force of equality, reducing complex human individuals to interchangeable units and levelling out rich, qualitative variations. Stakhanovism and Ekwilism pull in different directions, and in any case, these by no means exhaust the possible social applications of numbers. As Connor notes, '[t]ranslating things into numbers or giving them number-like qualities and relations, which essentially means dividing wholes up into smaller parts, hugely multiplies the possibilities of what may be done with those wholes'.[112] Bugaev's suggestive arguments did not detail how arythmology or non-Euclidean geometry might help us to understand social phenomena. But he and the Russian tradition that took his lead helpfully underline that numbers are not simply a grid to be imposed on human life with predictably oppressive effects. Counting things is not something we could easily stop doing, but bemoaning its ubiquity—or suggesting that the problem with Stalinism was its propensity to quantify social goods—tends to prevent us from acknowledging that the ways of doing it (deciding what to count and how) are infinite, as are the possibilities of what might then be done with the information.

The Freedom to Say that Two Plus Two Make Four

In *Assignment in Utopia* (1937) the American journalist Eugene Lyons gave an account of his time in the Soviet Union from 1928 to 1934, that included a chapter called 'Two Plus Two Equals Five', describing industrialization during the first Five-Year-Plan. Here, the familiar theme of the Communist obsession with statistics is at issue, but the chapter also suggests ways in which an excessively calculative rationalism might push over into the irrational. Lyons was interested in the celebrations around the completion of the Five-Year-Plan, which gave rise to official slogans

---

[112] Connor, *Living by Numbers*, 33.

such as 'The Five Year Plan in Four Years' and then (on a more surreal note) '2 + 2 = 5'. He wrote:

> The formula 2 + 2 = 5 instantly riveted my attention. It seemed to me at once bold and preposterous—the daring and the paradox and the tragic absurdity of the Soviet scene, its mythical simplicity, its defiance of logic, all reduced to nose-thumbing arithmetic. . . . 2 + 2 = 5: in electric lights on Moscow housefronts, in foot-high letters on billboards, spelled planned error, hyperbole, perverse optimism; something childishly head-strong and stirringly imaginative. . . . 2 + 2 = 5: a slogan born in premature success, tobogganing toward horror and destined to end up, lamely, as 2 + 2 1/4 = 5.[113]

Lyons reproduced the standard complaint that Communism leaned too heavily on quantitative, numerical methods. But he was also captivated by the paradox that the regime could use a slogan that flew in the face of arithmetic. 2 + 2 = 5 represents the victory of the regime's magical power over the dictates of reason and common sense. Lyons's account of the significance of this equation disrupted the classic identification of the Soviet Union with a narrowly rationalistic utilitarianism. Orwell reviewed *Assignment in Utopia* favourably, noting that Lyons 'gives the impression of being more reliable than most' when it came to the USSR.[114] Orwell was certainly aware, when he wrote *Nineteen Eighty-Four*, that '2 + 2 = 5' was a Communist slogan. It has often been assumed that, in that novel, Orwell offered a common-sense anti-Communism in which the stable certainties of simple arithmetic—twice two is four—might hold off the illogical tyranny of a regime that has forgotten how to add. I hope to show, however, that—seeing this slogan through Lyons's account but also in light of the Russian tradition he absorbed via Zamyatin, Dostoyevsky, and others—Orwell produced a more complex version of the relation between Communism and number.

Early in *Nineteen Eighty-Four* Winston Smith writes in his diary a phrase that immediately recalls both Gradgrind and Bazarov, but with a different meaning: 'Freedom is the freedom to say that two plus two make four. If that is granted, all else follows.'[115] Dostoyevsky and Zamyatin had opposed socialist rationalization by invoking equations that defy or twist ordinary logic, just as Bugaev and Florensky had pushed mathematics

[113] Eugene Lyons, *Assignment in Utopia* (London: George G. Harrap & Co., 1938), 240.

[114] George Orwell, 'Review of Assignment in Utopia by Eugene Lyons', in *Orwell, Facing Unpleasant Facts: 1937–1939*, ed. Peter Davison (London: Secker & Warburg, 1998), 159.

[115] George Orwell, *Nineteen Eighty-Four* (London: Secker & Warburg, 1997), 84.

towards the study of discontinuous functions and set theory as a way of
resisting the determinism of the scientific Marxism prevalent in Russia in
the 1890s. Orwell's critique of Bolshevism inverts this procedure: his
defence against Communism was to invoke the most purely rational
equation he could think of.

The agent of the regime who is responsible for interrogating Winston,
O'Brien, has read Winston's diary and picks up the arithmetical theme
during the interrogation. O'Brien attempts to force Winston into believ-
ing that two plus two is five or that he is holding up five fingers when
actually there are only four. O'Brien uses a machine to deliver jolts of pain
measured on a scale of 0–100:

> 'How many fingers am I holding up, Winston?'
>
> 'Four.'
>
> 'And if the party says that it is not four but five—then how many?'
>
> 'Four.'
>
> The word ended in a gasp of pain. The needle of the dial had shot up to
> fifty-five.[116]

The torture is delivered in shocks whose intensity is numbered from
1–100, just at the moment when O'Brien is trying to torture Winston
out of his ability to count. The Romantic critique of utilitarianism had
long insisted that it was impossible to calculate the 'greatest pleasure of
the greatest number' because it was impossible to assign a quantitative
value to either pleasure or pain. Affect—Romantic critics of utilitarianism
insisted—was by definition strictly qualitative. In this case, O'Brien and
his machine seem very capable of adding two and two and getting
four. The progress of the dial towards 100 produces an increasingly
devastating effect on Winston's body and mind. In response to increasingly painful shocks, a broken Winston shouts that there are indeed five
fingers, to which O'Brien replies that 'You are lying. You still think there
are four.'[117] It is not enough, O'Brien says, that Winston should say that
there are five. He must believe it, and, by extension, anything else that the
Party holds to be the case, however contrary to the dictates of reason or
common sense or empirical observation. Orwell's text imagines a regime
that attains a complete mastery of number, but not out of any fidelity to
rationalism. Indeed, as in Eugene Lyons's depiction of the Soviet Union,
Orwell's regime seems to be one in which the rationalistic implementation
of calculative reason has flipped over into its opposite: $2 + 2 = 5$.

---

[116] Ibid. 261–2.   [117] Ibid. 263.

Responses to *Nineteen Eighty-Four* from the left have fixated on the way it deals with the relationship between Communism and rationalism. John Strachey—a leading Communist sympathizer in the inter-war years, and one of the editors of the Left Book club—described the anti-Communism of *Nineteen Eighty-Four* in a fascinating essay called 'The Strangled Cry' (1960). Strachey felt that the mainstream of anti-Communism— including Koestler, Whittacker Chambers, and Boris Pasternak—tended to the view that 'the catastrophe which Communism has suffered proves that reason carried to its logical conclusion leads to horror; that consequently we must retreat from reason into some form of mysticism or supernaturalism'. Orwell's work, by contrast, seemed to imply that Communist doctrine had 'become, precisely, a mysticism, an authoritarian revelation'. Strachey went on:

> For [Orwell], it is not that Communists have discredited reason by pushing it to its logical conclusion. On the contrary, it is that they have betrayed reason by abandoning its living empirical methodology for an unchanging revelation. His whole satire was an exposure of the consequences of pathological unreason.[118]

Strachey blamed Orwell for failing to develop his commonsensical critique of Communism into a political philosophy capable of taking up the mantle of the Enlightenment project—that is, a rejuvenated Marxism. If Orwell had lived, Strachey mused,

> He might have given social empiricism a firmer basis, and at the same time shown us how to do justice to those personal, aesthetic, and religious values about which we can as yet say so little—except that we can all now see that their neglect is fatal.[119]

Strachey's suggestion is that Orwell died too soon to bring the 'social empiricism' that he deployed against a wildly irrational Stalinism back into a meaningful relationship with human 'values'. It is striking that, here and elsewhere, the word 'values' (which would seem at heart a quantitative concept) should be used as a warm and qualitative *contrast* to the cold utilitarianism of quantitative measurement. In short, Strachey saw *Nineteen Eighty-Four* as a departure from the prevailing currents of Romantic anti-Communism.

A key Marxist critic of Orwell in the post-war period—the Trotskyist historian and intellectual Isaac Deutscher—savaged Orwell in an essay called '1984 – The Mysticism of Cruelty' (1955). His argument comes out in a slightly different and equally interesting way as compared with

---

[118] John Strachey, 'The Strangled Cry', *Encounter* (Nov. 1960), 12. [119] Ibid. 13.

Strachey's: he thought that Orwell's problem was that he was not Marxist
enough. Orwell, Deutscher argued, began from a position of rationalism
and recoiled from dialectical materialism because it was 'too abstruse for
him'. Marxism, Deutscher meanwhile maintained, was, whatever the
socialist rationalists might think, 'not at all rationalist in its philosophy'.
Deutscher wrote:

> the authentic Marxist may claim to be mentally better prepared than the
> rationalist is for the manifestations of irrationality in human affairs, even for
> such manifestations as Stalin's Great Purges. He may feel upset or mystified
> by them, but he need not feel shaken in his *Weltanschauung*, while the
> rationalist is lost and helpless when the irrationality of the human existence
> suddenly stares him in the face. If he clings to his rationalism, reality eludes
> him. If he pursues reality and tries to grasp it, he must part with his
> rationalism.[120]

For Deutscher, Orwell had taken the second option: obsessed by the
purges, 'he increasingly viewed reality through the dark glasses of a
quasi-mystical pessimism'. Marxism alone could understand these events
'in their complex historical context'.[121] Orwell held onto the idea that
2 + 2 = 4, but in the face of the massive unreason of the purges, became
increasingly pessimistic about his ability to convince the world of his
gospel of common sense.

Marxist critics like Deutscher and Strachey used Orwell's 'two and
two make five' to think about how the oppositions between rational
calculation and irrational incalculability had become politicized since
the Bolshevik Revolution. A feature of Orwell's text that has been less
frequently commented on is the way in which it raises epistemological
questions about what we can know and how we can know it. During the
interrogation, Winston responds to O'Brien by asking: 'How can I help
seeing what is in front of my eyes? Two and two are four.'[122] Is the
freedom to say that two and two make four different from the freedom to
observe that there are four fingers being held up before one's eyes?[123] For
philosophers from Plato to Descartes, mathematical statements were
viewed as a priori truths, not reliant on experience. The phrase '[f]reedom
is the freedom to say that two plus two make four' seems to adhere to this
view of mathematics, supplementing it with an additional political meaning: the individual's ability to articulate a priori truths, which will be

---

[120] Deutscher, '1984', 45.   [121] Ibid. 46, 49.
[122] Orwell, *Nineteen Eighty-Four*, 263.
[123] One commentator who does touch on this issue in a highly illuminating discussion is
Stephen Ingle, in *The Social and Political Thought of George Orwell: A Reassessment* (London:
Routledge, 2005), esp. ch. 6, 'Two Plus Two Equals Four', pp. 114–39.

universally true in any context and of which mathematical statements are an example, is the test of the extent of freedom available in a given regime. Two things in Orwell's text lead us to question this view of mathematics. First, we are given to understand that, in fact, the Party has the ability to override the individual's ability to know that two plus two makes four. In Oceania, there is no freedom, and that includes the freedom not only to say but to think that two plus two make four—unless the Party wills it. Winston believes that the propositions of arithmetic exist outside the individual mind and any given social formation, but the events of Orwell's novel disprove Winston's notion that clinging to these will in the end do any good in a totalitarian society. O'Brien's contradictory assertion that 'Whatever the party holds to be truth, is truth' in the end holds sway.[124] Winston comes to believe that that two plus two is not necessarily four and to love Big Brother, just as Gradgrind learns that two plus two is not necessarily four and to love his children. Secondly, Winston's question, 'how can I help seeing what is in front of my eyes?', seems to make mathematical statements dependent on empirical observation. Winston's interrogation conflates questions about the reliability of empirical sense data with questions about the accessibility of the unchanging forms of mathematical reality posited by Plato.

Orwell had begun to raise these questions in his journalism before the writing of *Nineteen Eighty-Four*, with frequent references to the question of whether two and two made four or five. In these references, Orwell tends to blur distinctions between mathematical and other forms of knowledge. For example, in his essay 'Looking Back on the Spanish War' (1943), he describes his premonitions about

> a nightmare world in which the Leader, or some ruling clique, controls not only the future but *the past*. If the leader says . . . 'it never happened'—well, it never happened. If he says that two and two are five—well, two and two are five. This prospect frightens me much more than bombs—and after our experiences of the last few years this is not a frivolous statement.[125]

Stalin's attempts to alter the historical record, particularly in relation to events that Orwell saw first-hand in Catalonia, is the spur here for Orwell to invoke the idea that a powerful leader could rewrite not just historical events but also mathematical statements. The parallel between the manipulation of history and of mathematics is implicit in the syntactical

[124] Orwell, *Nineteen Eighty-Four*, 261.
[125] George Orwell, 'Looking Back on the Spanish War', in *The Complete Works of George Orwell*, xiii. *All Propaganda is Lies: 1941–1942*, ed. Peter Davison (London: Secker & Warburg, 1998), 497–511.

mirroring of the two sentences. There is no attempt to distinguish the supposed apriority of the mathematical statement from the empirical grounding of the historical one.

Similar ambiguities are at play in Orwell's review of Bertrand Russell's *Power: A New Social Analysis* (1938), which questioned Russell's naive 'idea that common sense always wins in the end'. Orwell suggests instead that '[i]t is quite possible that we are descending into an age in which two and two will make five when the Leader says so'.[126] Orwell argued here and elsewhere that the persistent rationalism of old Edwardians like Russell and Wells would not allow them to come to an understanding of modern politics and in particular its totalitarian movements. Orwell's engagement with Russell on this point has wider philosophical implications when we consider Russell's important work, earlier in the century, on the foundations of mathematics. In *Principia Mathematica*—a vast, three-volume work co-authored with Alfred North Whitehead and first published in 1910—Russell had attempted to ground mathematics in fundamental logic, attempting to prove, in so many words, that $1 + 1 = 2$ (from which it would follow that $2 + 2 = 4$). 'From this proposition it will follow, when arithmetical addition has been defined, that $1 + 1 = 2$', Russell and Whitehead wrote.[127] There are further epistemological consequences of this for Russell. He wrote in *The Analysis of Matter* (1927), first, that 'clearly we may learn from experience that $2 + 2 = 4$, though we afterwards realize that the experience was not logically indispensable', and then that '[t]he only legitimate attitude about the physical world seems to be one of complete agnosticism as regards all but its mathematical properties'.[128] Like Winston Smith, Russell looks to mathematics as the last refuge of certainty, and in both cases Orwell suggests that even this seemingly secure realm of pure abstract logic stands to be overrun by totalitarian politics.

Russell's arguments responded to a widespread crisis in the foundations of mathematics, as neo-Kantians led by Frege revived a debate about what exactly Kant meant by the category of synthetic a priori knowledge (the category to which he allocated mathematical statements), and whether recent innovations such as Cantor's transfinite numbers could also be contained in this ontological category. The three schools of logicism (Frege, Russell, and Peano), intuitionism (Brouwer and Weyl), and

---

[126] George Orwell, review of Bertrand Russell, *Power: A New Social Analysis*, in *The Complete Works of George Orwell*, xi. *Facing Unpleasant Facts, 1937–1939*, ed. Peter Davison (London: Secker & Warburg, 2000), 311.

[127] Alfred North Whitehead and Bertrand Russell, *Principia Mathematica* (Cambridge: CUP, 1910), 379.

[128] Bertrand Russell, *The Analysis of Matter* (London: George Allen & Unwin, 1954), 174, 270–1.

formalism (Hilbert) all sought to set mathematics on the firm foundations of some stable axioms, a quest that continued until the publication of Kurt Gödel's incompleteness theorems in 1931, which seemed to confirm that the quest to set mathematics on a stable set of foundations would necessarily fail. These attempts to establish the philosophical foundations of mathematics took place against a tide of scepticism within philosophy that argued that mathematical precepts had no objective validity. Edmund Husserl argued in *The Crisis of European Sciences and Transcendental Philosophy* (1936, tr. 1954) that mathematical rationality was a historically specific product of the Renaissance. Galileo, Descartes, Newton, and others were guilty of 'the surreptitious substitution of the mathematically substructured world of idealities for the only real world, the one which is actually given through perception, that is ever experienced and experienceable—our everyday life-world'.[129] Martin Heidegger argued in a similar vein that the mathematical is 'a fundamental trait of modern thought', meaning that our mental habits have become bound up with numbers and calculations to an unprecedented extent, leading us to neglect more qualitative forms of knowledge.[130] Far from having the universal validity of Platonic forms, mathematical and scientific results—Heidegger gave the example of Newton's first law of motion—are to be seen as the historically contingent products of a particular historical moment. The curse of modern humanity is that it can only see the world through the restrictive prism of mathematical reason: phenomenology sought to restore the importance of experiences unmediated by quantitative knowledge.

A different form of scepticism about the possibility of universal mathematical truths was represented in this period by Ludwig Wittgenstein. In *On Certainty* (1969) he suggested that mathematical statements had validity only according to the arbitrary rules of a particular language game. 'Every language-game is based on words "and objects" being recognized again. We learn with the same inexorability that this is a chair as that $2 \times 2 = 4$.'[131] It is true to say that what I am now sitting on is a chair, just as it is true to say that $2 \times 2 = 4$. Nobody would deny that the first proposition is true only given a certain context. According to the culturally specific conventions prevailing in France and among French

[129] Edmund Husserl (tr. David Carr), *The Crisis of European Sciences and Transcendental Phenomenology: An Introduction to Phenomenological Philosophy* (Evanston, IL: Northwestern University Press, 1970), 48–9.
[130] Martin Heidegger (tr. W. B. Barton, Jr, and Vera Deutsch), *What is a Thing?* (Chicago: Henry Regnery Co., 1967), 95.
[131] Ludwig Wittgenstein (tr. Denis Paul and G. E. M. Anscombe), *On Certainty* (Oxford: Basil Blackwell, 1974), 59e.

speakers, this chair would be *cette chaise*; meanwhile, lots of cultures subsisted without chairs and would not recognize it at all. Wittgenstein wants to insist that our intuitive certainty about mathematical propositions is of the same order. Orwell's text seems to play with very similar ideas. When O'Brien holds up the four fingers of his hand, a priori mathematical certainty and empirical certainty are simultaneously thrown into doubt, and are precisely analogous. Certainty, for Orwell (as for Russell), has a positive political value, going against the Romantic belief that it is authoritarian. Nevertheless, for Orwell, certainty cannot be guaranteed. What Russell had failed to grasp, he implied, was that totalitarian government is possible because of its ability to manipulate epistemological *uncertainty*.

For Alain Badiou, whose work has attempted to revive philosophical interest in mathematics as well as politicizing the field, Wittgenstein's thought on this subject is a 'refined form of sophistry' that 'constitutes an affront to the available evidence as well as to the sensibility of every mathematician'.[132] For Badiou, the demotion of mathematics from the ontological ground of philosophy to 'a register of language games, a formal type, or a singular grammar' is a symptom of our 'subjection to Romanticism'.[133] His account of the history of the relationship between philosophy and mathematics runs entirely counter to the accounts set out by Husserl and Heidegger. Rather than positing a shift into an excessively rationalistic, mathematical worldview around the time of Galileo and Descartes, Badiou argues that, from Plato to Kant, mathematics played a fundamental role in philosophical thought. It was only with Hegel and Romanticism, he goes on, that mathematics surrendered the central position it had occupied within philosophy since antiquity. This was an effect of Hegel's 'presupposition . . . of historicism, which is to say, the temporalization of the concept'.[134] Badiou thinks that Heidegger and Husserl are merely symptomatic of a Romantic historicism, then, but he also suggests that certain elements of their critique are valid. In his polemical introduction to *Number and Numbers* (1990, tr. 2008) he bemoans the fact that we live in an 'empire of number' where '[w]hat counts—in the sense of what is valued—is that which is counted'.[135] Badiou picks out the democratic habit of counting votes as particularly pernicious: he prefers revolutions to elections. Utilitarianism, quantitative

[132] Alain Badiou, 'Philosophy and Mathematics: Infinity and the End of Romanticism', in *Theoretical Writings*, ed. and tr. Ray Brassier and Alberto Toscano (London; New York: Continuum, 2004), 24.
[133] Ibid. 23.   [134] Ibid. 25.
[135] Alain Badiou (tr. Robin Mackay), *Number and Numbers* (Cambridge: Polity, 2008), 1–2.

sociology, analytic philosophy, logical positivism, and voting are excessively instrumental deployments of number that can be discounted as mere knee-jerk reactions against Romanticism. They represent mere counting rather than the higher mathematics which Badiou favours. While Connor and Badiou are both in a sense trying to rescue number from Romanticism's rejection of it, their recommendations are radically divergent. Connor explicitly advocates a rapprochement with utilitarianism and a defence of the application of numerical methods (including counting and voting) to social and cultural life. From this perspective, Badiou looks like a part of the (Romantic) problem. Badiou wants, on the other hand, to encourage a philosophical engagement with the concepts of higher mathematics—transfinite numbers, set theory, etc.—which will help in the theorization of a politics that can break away from exactly the utilitarian deployments of number which Connor favours. Both of these positions have their antecedents in the period I am discussing, and both are brought into clearer focus when we turn to the debates surrounding the relationship between dialectical materialism and mathematics.

DIALECTICAL MATERIALISM

Dialectics of Nature

Badiou's argument that it is Hegelian, Romantic *historicism* that displaces mathematics from its rightful place at the heart of philosophy raises a question about the relationship between mathematics and Marxism, and—in particular—dialectical materialism. The dialectical materialism that became codified as the official Soviet understanding of the relation between the sciences and history was largely based on the later works of Friedrich Engels. The question of mathematics was addressed directly in *Anti-Dühring* (1878) and the bizarre but influential *Dialectics of Nature*, an incomplete work published posthumously by the Marx-Engels Institute in Moscow in 1927, and in London with a preface by J. B. S. Haldane in 1940.[136] A short section of *Anti-Dühring*, repackaged as *Socialism: Utopian and Scientific*, went on to become Engels's bestseller.[137] Engels's project was to show that 'nature works dialectically and not metaphysically', and indeed that '[n]ature is the proof of dialectics'.[138]

---

[136] Tristram Hunt, *The Frock-Coated Communist: The Revolutionary Life of Friedrich Engels* (London: Penguin, 2009), 289.

[137] Ibid. 298–300.

[138] Friedrich Engels (tr. Emile Burns), *Anti-Dühring: Herr Eugen Dühring's Revolution in Science* (Moscow: Progress Publishers, 1947), 33.

As its title suggests, *Anti-Dühring* gained its impetus from a critique of Eugen Dühring's philosophy of science. Where Dühring had attempted to apply the principles of philosophy to the modern sciences, Engels insisted that the principles of philosophy must be derived from the sciences. Mathematics cannot stand above or separate from an ever-changing nature, but is rather a part of this flux, evolving with it. Dühring had argued for the 'sovereign validity' of thought, which had an 'unconditional' claim to truth and should not be reduced to the merely human. Engels countered:

> in order that no suspicion may arise that on some celestial body or other twice two makes five, Herr Dühring dare not designate thought as being human, and so he has to sever it from the only real foundation on which we find it, namely, man and nature; and with that he tumbles hopelessly into an ideology which reveals him as the epigone of... Hegel.[139]

The notion that two plus two is four in any *metaphyscial* sense is derided by Engels. Mathematical concepts—like everything else—evolve historically, dialectically. Hegel—who was blamed by Badiou for the 'temporalization of the concept' (that is, historicism)—stands accused here of a different crime: idealism. Engels wanted to show not only that mathematics was subject to dynamic historical forces, but that these historical forces were material ones.

In *Dialectics of Nature*, Engels asserts that three fundamental dialectical laws (extracted from Hegelian idealism but given a material basis here) govern both nature and history. These are: 'the law of transformation of quality into quantity', 'the law of the interpenetration of opposites', and 'the law of the negation of the negation'. The book—composed partly of finished chapters and partly of notes and fragments—assembles a variety of phenomena mainly in the natural sciences which Engels uses tendentiously to exemplify these laws. Engels sets out to show that even the fundamental axioms of mathematics are not fixed but subject to historical development and change, and that it is essentially a descriptive science anchored in the observation of material reality. Which is to say it is both historical and material. Engels attempts to prove that two plus two does not always equal four—that this is historically determined and a matter of convention—by highlighting the differences between different numeral systems. To be sure, he reasons, within the decimal system 2 + 2 = 4. But:

> All numerical laws depend upon and are determined by the system adopted. In dyadic and triadic systems 2 multiplied by 2 does not equal 4,

---

[139] Ibid. 51.

but = 100 or = 11. In all systems with an odd basic number, the difference between odd and even numbers falls to the ground, e.g., in the system based on 5, 5 = 10, 10 = 20, 15 = 30.[140]

It is hard not to see Engels's deployment of different numeral systems on either side of the '=' sign as mere sophistry. If Engels was not aiming to prove that maths was subject to the historical dialectic, he might have expressed himself differently. He might have written that within the binary (or 'dyadic') system, the decimal 2 + 2 = 4 is *expressed* as 10 + 10 = 100. It is simply a mistake to read this as 'ten plus ten equals a hundred', which Engels seems to want us to do. Engels's argument offers no fundamental challenge to the idea that 2 + 2 = 4 (which is not to say that no such challenges exist).

Engels's materialist dialectic view of science, as promulgated by Plekhanov and absorbed by Lenin, took on a central position in the ideology of the Soviet Union, and indeed in the Communist International in general. Stalin himself wrote the chapter on 'dialectical and historical materialism' in that most widely disseminated textbook of Stalinism, *History of the Communist Party of the Soviet Union (Bolsheviks)—Short Course* (1938), and he quotes extensively from both *Anti-Dühring* and the *Dialectics of Nature*.[141] The institutionalization of Engels's ideas as the official scientific outlook of the Soviet state had wide repercussions for the international Communist movement. Tristram Hunt recalls a conversation with Eric Hobsbawm in which the Communist historian remembered 'scientists of the 1930s earnestly hoping that their bench work would fit within Engels's template'.[142] The story of Lysenko and the disastrous effects of a party line on scientific knowledge are well known (although mathematics was in the slightly anomalous position of being allowed some limited independence in the Soviet Union, as I will explain). But the Communist—and in particular the Stalinist—attempt to make mathematics dialectical at least in theory provoked a number of interesting reactions in Britain and Western Europe.

In J. B. S. Haldane's introduction to the 1940 edition of *Dialectics of Nature*, he agreed that dialectics 'can be applied to problems of "pure" science as well as to the social relations of science', and approved of

[140] Friedrich Engels (tr. Clemens Dutt), *Dialectics of Nature* (London: Wellred, 2007), 263.

[141] *History of the Communist Party of the Soviet Union (Bolsheviks)—Short Course*, ed. A Commission of the Central Committee of the CPSU (New York: International Publishers, 1939), 105–31; Robert Service, *A History of Modern Russia: From Nicholas II to Putin* (London: Penguin, 2003), 237–8.

[142] Hunt, *The Frock-Coated Communist*, 293.

the contemporary application of this idea in the Soviet Union.[143] He conceded, though, that the science on which Engels based his remarks was by now out of date: some of the book's weaknesses could be explained due to the historical juncture at which it was written. On the face of it, many of the contradictions that Engels had pointed to within mathematics had been solved in the intervening period. But Haldane proposed that the dialectical conflicts within mathematics had in a sense moved from its everyday practice to its ontological foundations: 'Not only has every effort to deduce all mathematics from a set of axioms, and rules for applying them, failed, but Gödel has proved that they must fail.'[144] Gödel's 'incompleteness theorem' of 1931 seemed to show that the problem of finding stable axiomatic foundations for arithmetic was effectively unsolvable. No system can prove its own consistency, Gödel postulated. The foundational crisis had produced a new contradiction that looked set to be a permanent one. Nevertheless, the strongest criticisms that Haldane ventured in a warmly appreciative preface are reserved for Engels's treatment of mathematics. Responding to a comment that occurs in the manuscript notes for *Anti-Dühring* (which appeared in this edition of the *Dialectics of Nature*, but not during Engels's lifetime) Haldane wrote:

> [Engels] supported the view, quite commonly held in the nineteenth century, that we find truths such as mathematical axioms self-evident because our ancestors have been convinced of their validity, while they would not appear self-evident to a Bushman or Australian black. Now this view is almost certainly incorrect, and Engels presumably saw the fallacy, and did not have it printed.[145]

For Haldane, as for Winston Smith in *Nineteen Eighty-Four*, two plus two is four whether you are a nineteenth-century German industrialist, an Australian aborigine, or the citizen of a country that adopts the slogan '2 + 2 = 5'. Yet even while conceding the transhistorical validity of arithmetical propositions, Haldane hoped to keep the fundamental argument of *Dialectics of Nature*—so central to Soviet science—intact. Haldane wanted the freedom to say that two plus two is four, but did not counterpose this with totalitarian power as Orwell did in *Nineteen Eighty-Four*.

In France, Georges Bataille and Raymond Queneau, working from a trenchantly anti-Stalinist position, drew out the consequences of Engels's failure to assimilate mathematics to the dialectical materialist outlook. In the period from 1931 to 1934, Bataille contributed a number of articles to

[143] J. B. S. Haldane, 'Introduction', in Friedrich Engels (tr. Clemens Dutt), *Dialectics of Nature* (London: Lawrence & Wishart, 1940).
[144] Ibid.   [145] Ibid.

the anti-Stalinist Marxist journal *La Critique Sociale*. One of these articles, 'The Critique of the Foundations of the Hegelian Dialectic', addresses Engels's writings about mathematics, and a section of this was written by Raymond Queneau because of his superior grasp of mathematics. Bataille quotes from Engels's 1885 preface to the second edition of *Anti-Dühring*, where Engels concedes that his project is perhaps incomplete and that his attempts to apply the historical dialectic to natural phenomena were 'only of relative validity'.[146] As Bataille notes, 'This declaration means nothing less than the renunciation of the hope of founding in nature the general law of which class struggle would only have been a particular case'.[147] They also argued that Engels had overstated the contradictions of mathematics by playing around somewhat mischievously with its language: 'Mathematical symbolism, translated into everyday language, can lead to contradictions; but these are, one might say, contradictions without reality, pseudocontradictions.'[148] Bataille wished to retain the idea of a materialist dialectic that shapes the course of human history, but to deny that it has any application in the natural sciences: 'The dialectic does not express the nature of mathematics; it applies to the agent and not to the object of scientific activity.'[149]

The political implications of this are profound, and emphasized again by Alain Badiou, this time in the preface to *Being and Event*. Badiou's attempt to reinstate mathematics as the driving force of philosophy, via the assertion that 'mathematics *is* ontology' forms a contrast with the 'absolute weakness' of the Marxist 'isomorphy between the dialectic of nature and the dialectic of history'. Badiou dilates on the intellectual poverty of Engels's quest:

> This (Hegelian) isomorphy was, of course, still-born. When one still battles today, alongside Prigogine and within atomic physics, searching for dialectical corpuscles, one is no more than a survivor of a battle which never seriously took place save under the brutal injunctions of the Stalinist state.[150]

The vital political importance of maintaining the independence of mathematics and the pure sciences from either theoretical absorption into a 'dialectical materialism' or political subjection by the state is thus asserted by both Bataille and Badiou, in the face of Engels and Stalin. In neither

---

[146] Engels, *Anti-Dühring*, 20.
[147] Georges Bataille, 'The Critique of the Foundations of the Hegelian Dialectic', in Allan Stoekl (ed. and tr.), *Visions of Excess: Selected Writings, 1927–1939* (Manchester: Manchester University Press, 1985), 108.
[148] Ibid. 111.   [149] Ibid.
[150] Alain Badiou (tr. Oliver Feltman), *Being and Event* (London: Continuum, pbk. 2007), 4.

case did the attempt to accord a deeper intellectual respect to mathematics mean a turn towards rigid rationalism.

Bolshevizing Mathematics

These Europe-wide debates were reflected by the fate of mathematics within the Soviet Union and within the Communist party. The leading figures of the Moscow Mathematical Society, Dimitri Egorov and Nikolai Luzin, were close to Florensky and like him saw mathematics as a realm of autonomy and free will with profound religious significance. Egorov was an opponent of any attempts to bring mathematics in line with dialectical materialism, much less the Five-Year-Plan. As president of the Moscow Mathematical Society, he remained an elder of the Church, and also refused to join the Union of Scientific Workers.[151] Facing criticism for this truculence, in 1930 Egorov told a meeting of the society that 'nothing else but the binding of a uniform *Weltanschaung* on scientists is genuine wrecking'.[152] Egorov was arrested in September 1930, for crimes including 'mixing mathematics and religion', and sent to prison exile near Kazan.[153] Florensky, who insisted on giving his scientific papers dressed in his priest's cassock even in the high Stalinist period, was arrested in 1933, sent the following year to the brutal prison camp of Solovki only 100 kilometres from the Arctic Circle, and shot as a counter-revolutionary in 1937.[154]

All this confirms what we might have expected about the extent of academic freedom for mathematicians in the Soviet Union. But the Soviet Union excelled in mathematics. Before the First World War Dimitri Egorov was the only Russian mathematician well known in Western Europe. But, as Graham and Kantor point out, '[b]y the end of the 1920s there was a constellation of such mathematicians. And by 1930 Moscow had become one of the two or three most concentrated focal points of mathematical talent anywhere on the globe.'[155] There was no Lysenko figure in mathematics: in the Soviet Union the field was characterized by conflict between the Bolshevizers and those who sought to pursue a pure mathematics unconstrained by dialectical materialist orthodoxy. The Czech expatriate Ernst Kol'man was a leading figure among the Stalinizers. Kol'man's line was predictable enough: 'Mathematics...cannot be separated either from the

[151] David Joravsky, *Soviet Marxism and Natural Science, 1917–1932* (London: Routledge & Kegan Paul, 1961), 242.
[152] Ibid. 243.   [153] Graham and Kantor, *Naming Infinity*, 136.
[154] Pyman, *Pavel Florensky*, 166, 180–1.
[155] Graham and Kantor, *Naming Infinity*, 103.

philosophy of dialectical materialism or from the policies of our Party', he wrote.[156] His views were heard and reported in Britain; when he attended the International Congress of the History of Science and Technology in London in 1931 with a delegation of ten Soviet scientists, including Bukharin, and B. Hessen (who read a long and influential paper on 'The Social and Economic Roots of Newton's "Principia"'). J. D. Bernal, J. B. S. Haldane, and other key British scientists were present. Speaking at the conference, Kol'man insisted on 'the Leninist principle that the sciences are not impartial', and moreover stressed the need to 'place mathematics at the service of Socialist construction, and in this way save it from the decay that is inescapable under Capitalism'.[157] This was *not* to be done by pursuing arythmology and discontinuous functions: Kol'man attacked a recent book by Luzin, one of the leading lights of the Moscow Mathematical Society, which had followed the path set by Bugaev and Florensky at the turn of the century. Having described Luzin's areas of interest, Kol'man asks: 'where is there in material nature anything for which such an absolute discontinuity would be adequate?'[158] Such mathematics had lost touch with material reality, and Kol'man condemned it as 'solipsism'.[159] Moreover, the quest for the foundations of mathematics was simply an expression of 'the anxiety of bourgeois mathematicians to separate themselves from matter and dialectics by the veil of formal logic, guiding them directly into the desert of scholasticism'.[160] Mathematicians must 'realise the true connection between concrete and abstract, ... dissociate themselves from the attitude which makes a fetish of mathematics, from the idealist and non-dialectic conception of the relation between mathematics and reality'.[161] Kol'man then described the practical tasks that mathematicians must perform in a planned socialist society.

At the congress, the *Manchester Guardian* reported an 'interesting observation' by David Guest—the British Communist mathematician—who suggested that the 'apparent contradictions' of mathematics 'have ... arisen from the separation of mathematics from social life and the failure of philosophers to remember that pure mathematics, as all other knowledge, is founded on human experience'.[162] Guest had experienced

[156] Quoted Alexander Vucinich, 'Soviet Mathematics and Dialectics in the Stalin Era', *Historia Mathematica*, 27/1 (2000), 55.

[157] Ernst Kol'man, 'The Present Crisis in the Mathematical Sciences and General Outlines for their Reconstruction', in *Science at the Crossroads: Papers Presented at the International Congress of the History of Science and Technology Held in London from June 29th to July 3rd, 1931, by the Delegates of the U.S.S.R.* (London: Kniga, 1931), 15.

[158] Ibid. 3.   [159] Ibid.   [160] Ibid. 11.   [161] Ibid. 8.

[162] Our Scientific Correspondent, 'Science Congress: A Neglected Branch of History—the Soviet Theory', *Manchester Guardian* (6 July 1931), 16.

both extremes of the controversy about the nature of mathematical knowledge, having studied mathematical logic under Wittgenstein at Cambridge, and under the formalist David Hilbert at Göttingen.[163] On his return to Cambridge in 1931, following his experience of the rise of Nazism in Germany, he joined the Communist Party. In 1933 Guest travelled to the Soviet Union where he became a teacher of mathematics and physics at the Anglo-American School in Moscow, learning Russian in order to tackle recent Soviet thinking on mathematics.[164] He was appointed to a lectureship in mathematics at Southampton University, where the professor of mathematics H. S. Ruse remembered him discussing philosophical questions that 'seemed to me interesting but rather academic, but were to him of vital importance because they formed the basis of his political convictions'.[165] Guest was killed fighting in the Spanish Civil War in 1938, and his only book, *A Textbook of Dialectical Materialism* (1939), was published posthumously. It contains only hints of what his Marxist mathematics might have looked like. For Guest, dialectical materialism was engaged in a 'fight on two fronts, against a science of metaphysical absolutes on the one hand, and on the other, the idea that "everything is relative"', positions which he associated with his old teachers Hilbert and Wittgenstein respectively.[166] Guest depicted Wittgenstein wallowing in a 'bog of solipsism, mysticism and sheer contradiction' in an essay first published in Moscow in 1934.[167] Writing in the *Labour Monthly*, Guest described the crisis of the foundations of mathematics, with the competing schools of formalism, logicism, and intuitionism. Unlike Kol'man he did not dismiss this as mere bourgeois anxiety: for him, Brouwer and Weyl's questioning of the law of the excluded middle from the perspective of intuitionism was 'the spirit of dialectics breaking through the hard shell of formal logic'.[168] What was needed now was the application of many minds to the problem of developing a properly Marxist mathematics. His Cambridge friend and Party comrade Maurice Cornforth remembered him saying before he left for Spain: 'Mathematical Philosophy will never be settled under capitalism. It requires the co-operation of a whole group of Marxists, and we

---

[163] Maurice Cornforth, 'Recollections of Cambridge Contemporaries', in C. H. Guest (ed.), *David Guest: A Scientist Fights for Freedom, 1911–1938* (London: Lawrence & Wishart, 1939), 95–6.

[164] Frank Jackson, 'A Soviet Worker', in C. H. Guest, *David Guest*, 114–15.

[165] H. S. Ruse, 'David the Intellectual', in C. H. Guest, *David Guest*, 167.

[166] David Guest, *A Textbook of Dialectical Materialism* (London: Lawrence & Wishart, 1939), 64.

[167] David Guest, 'The Machian Tendency in Modern British Philosophy', in C. H. Guest, *David Guest*, 240.

[168] David Guest, 'Book Review: Mathematics', *Labour Monthly*, 19/10 (1937), 646.

haven't the opportunity to do that now!'[169] Killed at the battle of Ebro, Guest never got that opportunity.

The Hours by the Window

Arthur Koestler also travelled to Spain as a Communist to fight for the republic, but he survived, albeit narrowly. Koestler suffered 102 days of imprisonment in a Fascist prison in Seville, where he was subjected to solitary confinement and driven close to insanity by the nightly spectacle of his fellow prisoners being shot without trial in the square outside his window. Koestler later saw this ordeal as an important stage in his turn away from Communism. Mathematics played an important role in the way Koestler imagined this turn.

As a young man Koestler had been fascinated by mathematics and physics, and in his schooling he pursued these subjects passionately and to the exclusion of more literary ones.[170] Though he never acquired any formal scientific qualifications he retained a voracious interest and in 1930 he was appointed as science editor of the *Vossische Zeitung*, Germany's most influential newspaper, a post that required him to keep abreast of the latest developments across the range of scientific disciplines (including mathematics). His time in the Fascist prison was described in the second part of *Spanish Testament* (1937), and was in turn published in a re-edited form as a standalone book, *Dialogue with Death* (1942).[171] In Franco's prison, mathematics provided a temporary respite from the harsh realities: 'a . . . pill to help him to arrive at a *modus vivendi* with his misery'.[172] Koestler occupied himself by scratching mathematical formulae onto the wall of his cell:

> I busied myself with the equation of a hyperbola again. The walls of this cell were beautifully white and unsullied, and provided an extensive surface upon which to write. A piece of wire from my bedstead . . . served me for pencil.[173]

Spanish Testament is shot through with a fear of imminent death, and with a sense of an unresolvable geopolitical crisis as Europe was falling to Fascism. Here, before Koestler's decisive break with Communism, mathematics appears as a form of blank meditation and escapism. When Koestler returned to these events in *The Invisible Writing* (1952), he

---

[169] Guest quoted by Cornforth, 'Recollections of Cambridge Contemporaries', 101.
[170] Michael Scammell, *Arthur Koestler: The Indispensable Intellectual* (London: Faber & Faber, 2009), 24.
[171] Ibid. 148–9.
[172] Arthur Koestler, *Spanish Testament* (London: Victor Gollancz, 1937), 288.
[173] Ibid. 276.

noted that his earlier attempts to describe his imprisonment had neglected 'internal developments' which he was now in a position to analyse, from a post- and indeed anti-Communist standpoint.[174] In retrospect, the mathematical reveries were more than an escapist distraction. He now remembered a particular mathematical epiphany, 'the hours by the window', which he imbued with political significance. Neither *Spanish Testament* nor *Dialogue with Death* contains any mention of Euclid's proof of the infinitude of prime numbers, but in *The Invisible Writing* it becomes the most important of the proofs that Koestler scratches onto the wall. This proof works as follows: take the hypothetically highest prime number P, and multiply it by every natural number up to P ($1 \times 2 \times 3 \times 4 \times \ldots P$, or P!), and then add one. That will produce prime higher than P or contain a prime factor higher then P. Koestler remarks that 'to whatever astronomical regions we ascend in the scale, we shall always find numbers which are not the product of smaller ones, but are generated by immaculate conception as it were'.[175] For Koestler this provided 'a deep satisfaction that was aesthetic rather than intellectual'. He went on:

> the scribbled symbols on the wall represented one of the rare cases where a meaningful and comprehensive statement about the infinite is arrived at by precise and finite means.... Then I was floating on my back in a river of peace, under bridges of silence. It came from nowhere and flowed nowhere. Then there was no river and no I. The I had ceased to exist.
> It is extremely embarrassing to write down a phrase like that when one... aims at verbal precision and dislikes nebulous gushing.[176]

This spiritual awakening through mathematics 'had started with the rational reflection that finite statements about the infinite were possible'. But it provided 'the groundwork for a change of personality', and a decisive break with 'the concise, rational, materialistic way of thinking which, in thirty-two years of training in mental cleanliness, had become a habit and a necessity like bodily hygiene'.[177] The numbers and symbols with which Koestler gradually covered the walls of his cell were for him a kind of universal, infinite language capable of transcending not only this historical moment, but also the philosophy of dialectical materialism which had seemed hard-wired into his mind. Isherwood and Muggeridge had mocked the rigid determinism of dialectical materialism by likening it to a mathematical formula or a multiplication table. In Koestler's hands,

---

[174] Arthur Koestler, *The Invisible Writing: The Second Volume of an Autobiography: 1932–40* (London: Vintage, 2005), 424.
[175] Ibid. 428.   [176] Ibid. 429.   [177] Ibid. 430–1.

mathematics became a means of *breaking with* a philosophy that had come to seem too narrowly rationalistic.

In his mathematically induced state of nirvana, Koestler realized that he was willing to sacrifice his life for the sake of his prison friends Nicholas and Arturo, not because of any utilitarian calculation, but for mysterious spiritual reasons:

> [I]t struck me as self-evident, in the manner of twice two being four, that we were all responsible for each other—not only in the superficial sense of social responsibility, but because, in some inexplicable manner, we partook of the same substance or identity, like Siamese twins or communicating vessels.[178]

He contrasted this with Communist ethics, whereby 'Nicholas existed merely as a social abstraction, a mathematical unit, obtained by dividing a mass of ten thousand Militiamen by ten thousand'.[179] It seems I have come full circle and that I am talking about utilitarianism again. But the situation is more complex than it was with Shaw or Muggeridge: for Koestler 'twice two is four' is on the side of an intuitive ethics of common human feeling, and against the abstractions of dialectical materialism.

As Strachey argued in 'The Strangled Cry', Koestler's vision is of an excessively rationalistic Communism that failed because it strove to govern with simple arithmetic. In *Darkness at Noon* (1940), Rubashov—a representative of the Bolshevik Old Guard under investigation in the Moscow Trials—is portrayed as a man who had 'held to the rules of logical calculation' and 'burnt the remains of the old, illogical morality from his consciousness with the acid of reason'.[180] In the course of his interrogation by Ivanov (another member of the Old Guard) Rubashov—who now doubts the rectitude of a purely arithmetical ethics—turns to Dostoyevsky's *Crime and Punishment* (1866):

> 'As far as I remember, the problem is, whether the student Raskolnikov has the right to kill the old woman? He is young and talented; he has as it were an unredeemed pledge on life in his pocket; she is old and utterly useless to the world. But the equation does not stand. In the first place, circumstances oblige him to murder a second person; that is the unforeseeable and illogical consequence of an apparently simple and logical action. Secondly, the equation collapses in any case, because Raskolnikov discovers that twice two are not four when mathematical units are human beings...'[181]

In revisiting the Russian debates of the 1860s, Koestler invokes an argument initially designed to ward off the rationalistic nihilism of

---

[178] Ibid. 434.   [179] Ibid. 434–5.
[180] Arthur Koestler, *Darkness at Noon* (London: Vintage, 1994), 205.
[181] Ibid. 126–7.

Chernyshevsky. Ivanov's reply serves to emphasize Koestler's sense that Communism was putting into practice those ideas:

> 'Consider a moment what this humanitarian fog-philosophy would lead to, if we were to take it literally; if we were to stick to the precept that the individual is sacrosanct, and that we must not treat human lives according to the rules of arithmetic. That would mean that a battalion commander may not sacrifice a patrolling party to save the regiment.'[182]

The 'humanitarian fog-philosophy' that Ivanov derides is throughout the novel associated with what Koestler terms the 'oceanic sense', borrowing the term from Freud's *The Future of an Illusion* (1927) and *Civilisation and its Discontents* (1929). As he contemplates his death, Rubashov suggests that a morality that is both rational and in touch with this 'oceanic sense' may arise. This is linked with the idea of a mathematics that goes beyond a purely Gradgrindian 'two and two are four, and nothing over'. Koestler hoped that, in the distant future, a 'new movement would arise', which could 'teach that the tenet is wrong which says that a man is the product of one million divided by one million'. Instead, the movement would need to

> produce a new kind of arithmetic based on multiplication: on the joining of a million individuals to form a new entity which, no longer an amorphous mass, will develop a consciousness and an individuality of its own, with an 'oceanic feeling' increased a millionfold, in unlimited yet self-contained space.[183]

As in the 'hours by the window', Koestler envisages here that mathematics might itself provide the answer, arriving at the infinite by precise and finite means. Mathematics was a rational language that opened out onto spiritual experience.

Later, in *The Act of Creation* (1964), Koestler set out a historical account of the development of mathematical concepts pointing out (as Engels had done in *Dialectics of Nature*) that 'Australian aborigines have only three number-words in their vocabulary: one, two, and many.' It does not appear that Koestler meant to imply that mathematical axioms were themselves subject to historical variation, but he insisted that 'Progress in the apparently most rational of human pursuits was achieved in a highly irrational manner.'[184] Mathematical and aesthetic insights happened on the same plane.

Actually existing socialism provoked writers and intellectuals into impassioned and often contradictory debates about the politics of number.

---

[182] Ibid. 127.   [183] Ibid. 207.
[184] Arthur Koestler, *The Act of Creation* (London: Hutchinson & Co., 1964), 622, 625.

The examples I have discussed show that the ways of mapping mathematical concepts onto the politics of twentieth-century Russia were many and contradictory. What is perhaps surprising is how often a causal connection was assumed between political allegiance and views about numbers, counting, or even the ontological status of mathematics. Badiou's argument that mathematics' relation to the other branches of knowledge was fundamentally destabilized by the development of historicism in the late eighteenth century offers some insight into why this might be, given that historicism was institutionalized in the Soviet Union in the form of dialectical materialism. But Badiou also seems determined to link his revival of a transhistorical, metaphysical mathematics to his revival of a revolutionary Maoist politics. In Koestler and in Orwell, by contrast, mathematics appears fundamentally as a mode of writing. The act of writing itself is foregrounded by both writers: Koestler in his cell, scratching Euclid's proof onto the wall, and Winston seeking to preserve his inner freedom, the independence of his mind, by writing out arithmetical propositions in his diary. For these writers, at least, mathematics was not a rigid, deterministic utilitarian calculus, imposed by the totalitarian state. It was an 'act of creation' analogous with writing, and potentially equally important in articulating political freedom in the age of totalitarianism.

3

Crime and Punishment

LEGALIZING BOLSHEVISM

After Crime

One of the utopian impulses that drove the Russian Revolution, and the wider Communist movement, was the idea of a comprehensive remaking of legal relations. In the nineteenth century, the legal norms and institutions of bourgeois society were subjected to a materialist critique by Marx and Engels. Engels wrote that law was 'but the ideologised, glorified expression of the existing economic relations': its self-image as an independent and objective arbiter before which all men were equal was purely ideological, as was its claim to act as a check on the executive powers of government.[1] Law was regarded in Marxist theory as functionally subservient to the interests of the bourgeoisie. As Paul Hirst put it, in this tradition, law was taken to serve two functions, first, the 'regulation of relations of possession' which 'gives to existing relations of production the form of right', and second, 'regulation of the struggle between the classes' which 'serves to contain and repress the antagonism of the exploited class within forms of right legitimated by the order of the state'.[2] In simple terms, the first function is the protection of private property, the institution that is the legal cornerstone of capitalism. The second function is to classify revolutionaries—and more broadly those who would seek to challenge or protest the injustices that capitalism produces—as criminals.[3]

The questions of whether a communist society would need laws and legal institutions to enforce them, and if so what forms these would take,

---

[1] Friedrich Engels, *The Housing Question*, in *Selected Works*, i (Moscow: Foreign Languages Publishing House, 1962), 624–5.

[2] Paul Hirst, *On Law and Ideology* (London: Macmillan, 1979), 96.

[3] This second function has led Marxist historians to reverse the logic and reclassify sundry bandits (influentially for Hobsbawm) and pirates (more recently for Linebaugh and Rediker) as latent revolutionaries. See Eric Hobsbawm, *Primitive Rebels* (Manchester: Manchester University Press, 1959), 13; Peter Linebaugh and Marcus Rediker, *The Many Headed Hydra: Sailors, Slaves, Commoners, and the Hidden History of the Revolutionary Atlantic* (Boston: Beacon Press, 2000), 163.

were theoretical ones until 1917. As in other spheres, the immediate aftermath of the revolution was a fertile period of intellectual experimentation as the challenge of building a communist society gave new impetus to legal theory. As Bob Fine has shown, 'extremely rich theoretical discussions on law and the state . . . were held in the early years of the Bolshevik revolution'.[4] The works of Soviet legal theorists including Piotr Stuchka, Nikolai Krylenko, Andrei Vyshinsky, and Evgeny Pashukanis have an enduring interest and influence.[5] British intellectuals were prompted by developments in Russia to challenge and rethink liberal notions of justice and law.

As even staunch Communists acknowledged, however, law and justice was an area where the Soviet Union opened itself to criticism (to put it mildly). The show trials of 1936–8, which saw the Bolshevik Old Guard confessing to extraordinary crimes against the state they had helped to usher into being, were deeply troubling for Communists and fellow travellers, and for anti-Communists they—more than almost anything else—served as a lesson about what authoritarian socialism was capable of. The Moscow Trials themselves provoked a thoroughgoing questioning of the nature of law, and the possibility of justice, in the context of the ideological struggles of the mid-century.

This chapter explores the ways in which British writers and intellectuals engaged with Communist law on a variety of different levels. As with other chapters in this book, it involves multiple dialogues between Communists, anti-Communists, those who changed their minds, and those who cannot be placed squarely in one camp. However, perhaps more so than any other chapter in this book, this one becomes entangled with a too-familiar narrative about mid-century intellectuals who flirted with Communism in the 1930s, became disillusioned, and then fought the ideological battles of the Cold War as anti-Communists after 1945. This is because the Moscow Trials were perceived at the time as a crucial test— perhaps *the* crucial test—of the integrity of left-leaning observers, and only a small minority of sympathizers (some of whom we will meet in this chapter) continued to defend the conduct of the trials after 1945. More often than the ideas I tackle in the other chapters of this book—the future, numbers, farming, and orality, literacy, and religion—questions of justice and law seemed to draw a fundamental dividing line between liberal

---

[4] Bob Fine, *Democracy and the Rule of Law: Liberal Ideals and Marxist Critiques* (Caldwell, NJ: Blackburn Press, 2002), 155.

[5] Dragan Milovanovic, 'Introduction to the Transaction Edition', in Evgeny Bronislavovich Pashukanis (tr. Barbara Einhorn), *The General Theory of Law and Marxism* (New Brunswick, NJ; London: Transaction Publishers, 2002), p. xvi.

societies and Communist ones. As I aim to do throughout this book, I will show how the binaristic logic of Cold War historiography can be retrospectively unpicked. The stark opposition between liberal and totalitarian justice conceals a complex traffic of ideas within and between the legal systems of several countries.

I begin with the category of crime. In 1937, Dudley Collard, a leading Communist-sympathizing lawyer, member of the Haldane Society of socialist lawyers and leader of the Communist Party Legal Group, 'told how the words "crime" and "criminal" had been taken out of the Soviet vocabulary, and the Penal Code based on curative and educative principles'.[6] Pashukanis pointed out that guidelines for criminal law promulgated in 1919, and then the penal code of 1922, did without the concept of guilt, and the 'Principles of Penal Legislature of the Union' also eliminated the term 'punishment'. Even Pashukanis was a little more circumspect than Collard, acknowledging the mainly 'demonstrative' function of an 'alteration in terminology'.[7] But both understood the Russian Revolution as something that would (in due course) abolish crime and punishment. Marx's writings had posited a revolution that would do away with both private property and the ascendancy of the bourgeois class. If these were successfully abolished, and Marx's critique of law was correct, law would have no remaining function, and crime no meaningful definition.

Anti-Communists in the mid-century were quick to seize on what they perceived as a weakness in Marxist doctrine. It proved relatively easy to create a straw man out of the Marxist sociology of crime. G. K. Chesterton quipped: 'the Socialists used to say that "under Socialism" nobody would lose his temper or quarrel with his mother-in-law'.[8] Everybody knows— Chesterton's joke assumed—that losing one's temper and quarrelling with one's mother-in-law are facts of life that are neither subject to historical variation nor capable of amelioration. Koestler opened up a similar line of attack in 'The Yogi and the Commissar' (1942, collected 1945), mocking the idea that 'all the pests of humanity, including constipation and the Oedipus complex, can and will be cured by Revolution ... [and] that this end justifies the use of all means, including violence, ruse, treachery and poison'.[9] Koestler pointed to the way in which the goal of

[6] *Daily Worker*, 29 Nov. 1937, clipping held at The National Archives, Kew (KV 2/2159).
[7] Evgeny Bronislavovich Pashukanis (tr. Barbara Einhorn) *The General Theory of Law and Marxism* (New Brunswick, NJ; London: Transaction Publishers, 2002), 185.
[8] G. K. Chesterton, 'Notes of the Week', *G.K.'s Weekly*, 4/101 (19 Feb. 1927), 242.
[9] Arthur Koestler, 'The Yogi and the Commissar', in *The Yogi and the Commissar and Other Essays* (London: Jonathan Cape, 1945), 9.

eliminating violence in the future actually legitimized violence in the past and present.

Koestler's mocking suggestion that the Oedipus complex would be one of the things cured by the revolution points to a key tension between social and psychological accounts of the origins of crime. Freud had addressed this in *Civilisation and its Discontents* (1930). 'The communists think they have found the way to redeem mankind from evil', he wrote. He then sketched out an ironic vision of a Communist utopia that was beyond criminality:

> When private property is abolished, when goods are held in common and enjoyed by all, ill will and enmity among human beings will cease. Because all needs will be satisfied, no one will have any reason to see another person as his enemy; everyone will be glad to undertake whatever work is necessary.[10]

Freud did not attempt to adjudicate on whether Communism could turn out to be economically advantageous. He focused his scepticism on its apparent claim to be able to do away with aggressive impulses, and therefore with a legal system whose function is to sublimate the desire for retribution by administering justice:

> I can recognize the psychological presumption behind it as a baseless illusion. With the abolition of private property the human love of aggression is robbed of one of its tools, a strong one no doubt, but certainly not the strongest. No change has been made in the disparities of power and influence that aggression exploits in pursuit of its ends, or in its nature. Aggression was not created by property; it prevailed with almost no restriction in primitive times, when property was very scanty. It already manifests itself in the nursery, where property has hardly given up its original anal form.[11]

For Freud, criminal and aggressive traits were not caused by capitalist property relations, nor could they be eliminated by the abolition of private property. He went on to say that, even if sexual rivalry—a more important 'instrument' of aggression than property—could be eliminated by the complete abolition of the family in some future Communist society, aggression and criminality would not disappear. The question would be what new form these aggressive impulses would take.

Some British intellectuals wondered whether the implicit claim of Marxism, that the abolition of private property would result in the abolition of aggression and criminality, was in itself dangerous. Bertrand Russell was in principle receptive to the ideas of Marxism—'I believe that

[10] Sigmund Freud (tr. David McLintock), *Civilisation and its Discontents* (London: Penguin Books, 2004), 63.
[11] Freud, *Civilisation and its Discontents*, 63.

Communism is necessary to the world',[12] he wrote in *The Practice and Theory of Bolshevism* (1920)—but worried that its lack of respect for the rule of law would lead to anarchy. As he argued in the same book, 'abandonment of law, when it becomes widespread, lets loose the wild beast, and gives a free rein to the primitive lusts and egoisms which civilisation in some degree curbs'.[13] He went on:

> The universal class-war foreshadowed by the Third International, following upon the loosening of restraints produced by the late war, and combined with a deliberate inculcation of disrespect for law and constitutional government, might, and I believe would, produce a state of affairs in which it would be habitual to murder men for a crust of bread, and in which women would only be safe while armed men protected them.[14]

Written in 1920, Russell's analysis reflects the chaos of the Civil War that was then raging in Russia. But it also articulates a more general concern about how a state professing Marxism could deal with questions of law and order. Any revolutionary movement by definition has decided to use illegal means of seizing power. But Marxism—at least in theory—professed to be opposed not simply to Tsarist law or bourgeois law, but to law as such. In all sorts of ways, Russell was more friendly to the Russian Revolution than were either Chesterton or Freud, but his fears go further here. The Marxist critique of law does not merely point to a delicious irony (Chesterton) or reveal socialists' naivety about the sexual origins of aggression (Freud). Such a critique of law opens the door to the end not just of capitalism but of civilization itself, as Russell was at pains to point out: 'Civilization is not so stable that it cannot be broken up; and a condition of lawless violence is not one out of which any good thing is likely to emerge.'[15]

Beyond Punishment

In the mid-century, the theoretical problems of Marxism became entangled with the practical issues facing the Soviet government as it consolidated its power and established a legal framework. The Moscow Trials provoked the highest-profile debate around these questions (and I will discuss these later in this chapter) but before these dramatic events, there was already a fairly substantial literature documenting the everyday functioning of the Soviet legal system. The basic starting point of Chesterton, Freud, and Russell was that crime had not (at least not yet)

---

[12] Bertrand Russell, *The Practice and Theory of Bolshevism* (Rockville, MD: Arc Manor, 2008), 7.
[13] Ibid. 83.   [14] Ibid. 83–4.   [15] Ibid. 84.

disappeared in the Soviet Union. Moreover—despite Collard's zealous assertion that 'crime' had disappeared as a concept there—its continued existence was recognized by the Communist government, which did not abolish law as such but replaced Tsarist legal norms and institutions with new ones. Kingsley Martin noted, during a tour of a Soviet prison, that '[t]heir notion was to abolish prisons altogether'. However, he went on, 'I cannot say I was altogether convinced by this..., for Russian railway stations are haunted by thieves, and every traveller is warned to keep his window shut lest a practiced hand snatches away his bag or overcoat.'[16] Pickpocketing, a crime that ought to be fairly easily explained in terms of relations of property and class, must be added to constipation, the Oedipus complex, and arguing with one's mother-in-law, in the growing list of eternal woes that cannot be eradicated by abolishing private property. Martin, like Chesterton, viewed Communist claims that the revolution will eliminate crime with detached irony: we all know, they both signal to their readers, that revolutions never change much when it comes to petty human vices.

While Martin was wryly sceptical of the notion that crime would simply disappear when full Communism was proclaimed, he was much impressed with practicalities of the Soviet approach to the punishment of criminals, given that they stubbornly continued to exist. He and Low were shown around Bolshevo, a model prison camp outside Moscow that was designed and maintained to show off Soviet correctional methods to Western tourists. Visitors to Bolshevo were almost invariably impressed. In *Political Pilgrims*, Paul Hollander describes a visit to Bolshevo by the Polish socialist Jerzy Gliksman, who went on an Intourist tour in 1935. Gliksman reported—with a note of scepticism absent from Martin's account—that '[e]verything was spotlessly clean', that the food was 'tasty and nourishing', and that the inmates insisted—even when no guard was present—that '[e]verything was ideal, nothing could be better'. Among his companions on the tour, Gliksman noted an elderly English woman moved to 'tears of appreciation and joy', while a French film director whispered to him: 'How beautiful the world could be!'[17] Martin was similarly enthused to find

a thriving little town, which builds its own houses and entertainment halls, which farms its own stock and grows its own food, and which all revolves

[16] David Low and Kingsley Martin, *Low's Russian Sketchbook* (London: Victor Gollancz, 1932), 60.
[17] Jerzy Gliksman qtd. in Paul Hollander, *Political Pilgrims: Western Intellectuals in Search of the Good Society*, 4th edn (London; New Brunswick, NJ: Transaction Publishers, 1998), 155.

around a central factory devoted to the production of all manner of sports goods.[18]

A clean and well-funded forced labour camp is still a forced labour camp. But Martin argued that:

> It is really a mistake to call Bolshevo a prison. It is a colony centred round a factory, which is placed farther away from the temptations of a city than an ordinary factory, and which operates under special restrictions, because the operatives have at some time or other been thieves.[19]

Martin then extends the contrast with the British penal system by noting that—especially during the slump—released prisoners in Britain 'become recidivists, because, having once been to prison, they can find no work and are driven to crime again'.[20] Sympathetic observers often shared Martin's view that the Soviet Union had effectively repurposed the prison as a mechanism for reform rather than punishment. D. N. Pritt—a prominent Communist-sympathizing barrister—wrote that '[t]he Russians apply fully and logically the theory that imprisonment must be reformatory, and not in the smallest degree punitive'.[21] Pritt went on to argue of Soviet prisons that 'everything that Russia has recently done is what English reformers have preached for years with unflagging courage; and their courage will be rewarded, no doubt, when the favourable conditions that have helped reform in Russia are present with us'.[22]

A scathing view of Soviet penal policy was set out in 1931 by the Duchess of Atholl, Katherine Stewart-Murray, a Scottish Unionist MP and prominent critic of the Soviet regime. Her book *The Conscription of a People* (1931) focused on the practice of forced labour, which she under-stood as the central facet not only of the Soviet legal system but also of Stalinist economic policy. Though undoubtedly a Tory—indeed she was, in 1924, the first woman to serve in a Conservative government—she was independent-minded and consistent in her defence of the liberal principles which she applied in her analysis of the Soviet regime's use of forced labour. At a time when many of her Conservative colleagues were pursuing a policy of appeasement, she argued that Nazi propaganda was more ubiquitous in Britain than Communist, and that Hitler's imperial ambitions presented a greater threat to national security than those of Stalin.[23]

---

[18] Low and Martin, *Low's Russian Sketchbook*, 62.   [19] Ibid.   [20] Ibid. 65.
[21] D. N. Pritt, 'The Russian Legal System', in Margaret Cole (ed.), *Twelve Studies in Soviet Russia* (London: Victor Gollancz, 1933), 161.
[22] Ibid. 175.
[23] Katherine Atholl, 'Under Which Heel?', *Saturday Review of Politics, Literature, Science and Art* (8 Aug. 1936), 165.

She resigned her seat in 1939 to fight a by-election over the question of appeasement and in opposition to the National Government's policy towards the Spanish Civil War, losing to the Conservative candidate.[24] Her anti-Fascism and her position on Spain led her to became known as the 'Red Duchess', though the implication that she was in any way sympathetic to Communism was farfetched.[25] For Stewart-Murray, the Soviet Union's 'treatment of political prisoners in the penal camps stands out as a dark stain on the brighter page which the twentieth century is gradually writing in the unhappy tale of prison administration'.[26] It seemed to undermine a general feeling that progress was being made in the field of prisoners' rights. But for her the problem went far beyond the question of how prisoners were treated once convicted. She perceived also an erosion of even any pretence at a distinction between political and judicial power, which seemed offensive to the sacred liberal principle of the rule of law. And finally—in case all moral arguments against the Communists' use of forced labour were to prove ineffective—the Duchess argued that toleration of Soviet forced labour was contrary to British economic interests. It drove down the cost of production, giving Soviet exports an unfair edge, and led to the 'dumping' of cheap commodities on the British market. This had the effect of undercutting domestic producers in Britain and exacerbating unemployment and all the social ills associated with it. She urged the British Government to follow Germany, France, and Italy in taking protectionist 'steps to protect their workers' by imposing tariffs on imports from the Soviet Union.[27]

In *The Conscription of a People*, the legal, economic, and political consequences of forced labour policies were seen as intimately related. Indeed, Stewart-Murray's principal charge against the Soviet system was that it destroyed the barriers between these domains, at great cost. Here was a country where economic imperatives forced sentencing decisions, political disagreement could be redefined as crime, and legal norms about the burden of proof and the presumption of innocence were radically weakened or erased. Her reasoning was set out as follows:

> The desire for increased national output, combined with a pressing criminal problem, produced in 1924 a 'Correctional Labour Code,' requiring a

---

[24] Ross McKibbin, *Parties and People: England 1914–1951* (Oxford: OUP, 2010), 109n.

[25] An interesting account of the 'red duchess' and her anti-Franco activities can be found in Gavin Bowd, 'Scotland for Franco: Charles Saroléa v. the Red Duchess', *Journal of Scottish Historical Studies*, 31/2 (2011), 195–219.

[26] Duchess of Atholl, *The Conscription of a People* (London: Phillip Allan, 1931), 80.

[27] Ibid. 188.

widespread use of prison labour on a commercial basis. The Code required
the 'maximum development' of 'correctional labour' in 'places of detention,'
and frankly proclaimed that both 'loss of freedom and compulsory labour
without detention under guard,' are designed generally to prevent the
commotion of crimes by 'untrustworthy elements of society,' a wording
which suggests that persons might be sentenced on mere suspicion.[28]

Stewart-Murray painted a picture of a Soviet Union in which the law had
broken down as separate sphere, and where consequently the people had
no defence against the political and economic decisions of the executive.

The Duchess of Atholl's analysis suggested that one symptom of the
erosion of the distinctions between economics, politics, and law was
the dispersal of judicial authority in non-judicial bodies. For example,
she noted that, according to a decree of 26 March 1928, 'Persons might be
sentenced to compulsory labour without detention under guard either by
a Court "or by an order of an administrative organ"'.[29] She draws out the
implications of this decree:

> In view of the power given to 'administrative organs' to pronounce sentence
> of compulsory labour, the scheme offered unlimited opportunities of utilis-
> ing for the benefit of Russia's economic development the labour of any
> persons who had shown themselves to be, or might be supposed to be, ill-
> affected to the Government.[30]

For Stewart-Murray, the short phrase 'or by order of an administrative
organ' opened the door to legal decisions being made that would deprive
individuals of their liberty without a trial. She later highlighted regulations
issued by the Supreme Economic Council that recognized 'the manager of
a factory as sole head of the undertaking with power to inflict disciplinary
punishments on workers and all salaried employees'.[31] The power to
impose sentences of forced labour was being delegated to bosses.

For the Duchess of Atholl, this meant that the executive arm of the
Soviet state had seized control of the law and used it for nothing less than
'the enslavement of the Russian people',[32] in the name of increased
economic output. The Correctional Labour Code of 1924, she argued,
showed 'a long-cherished intention on the part of the Soviet Government
to utilise on an ever-expanding commercial basis the labour of persons
supposed to be disaffected to its rule'.[33] And she went on to illustrate how
this worked in practice, showing how Soviet courts were put under
pressure—judges themselves being threatened with forced labour if they
did not comply—to issue more sentences of forced labour in order to fill

---

[28] Ibid. 17.   [29] Ibid. 27.   [30] Ibid. 29.   [31] Ibid. 82.
[32] Ibid. 179.   [33] Ibid. 19.

gaps in the labour market and enable the ambitious production targets of the Five-Year-Plan to be met. 'No clearer indication could be given of the complete subordination of Soviet "justice" to the Soviet Government', she wrote.[34]

Staging Justice

The debate about Soviet penal reform prompted commentators to reflect on its implications for *British* prisons. The same is true for the Soviet judicial system and its courts, which prompted debates about British justice.[35] Kingsley Martin described a visit to a magistrate's court that he visited, run along very different lines to those in England. The magistrate—not himself a trained lawyer—was flanked by two factory workers who acted as 'assessors' (called 'co-judges' elsewhere in the literature), 'who in effect play the part of a jury', and whose votes carried the same weight as that of the presiding magistrate.[36] Before the court was a dispute about a horse and cart in which the plaintiff and the defendant both represented themselves (though Martin emphasized that they had the right to counsel). The case was amicably resolved in less than half an hour, and Martin praised the efficiency and ease of the proceedings. He did, however, notice a different atmosphere when class enemies were before the court:

> At another court some kulaks were being tried, and there, though there was the same care in eliciting evidence, and I think an impartial effort to discover the facts, the atmosphere of the court was definitely hostile to the accused men. The courts, Communists will explain to you, are certainly biased against capitalists. They behave, you are told, just as courts in other countries do in dealing with Communists.[37]

Martin combined the acknowledgement that the courts are 'biased' with the insistence that they were 'impartial' in their effort to determine the facts. There is perhaps here a certain residue of the Marxist critique of law, insofar as Martin responded to the allegation of bias by countering that English courts were also biased by virtue of their role in upholding capitalist property relations, and biased against Communists in particular.

---

[34] Ibid. 30.
[35] John Quigley has argued that 'Lenin's repudiation of tsarist law had worldwide implications' and that the Bolsheviks 'espoused legal concepts that challenged the foundations of Western society'. John Quigley, *Soviet Legal Innovation and the Law of the Western World* (Cambridge: CUP, 2007), 1. Quigley describes the ways in which 'the West' inoculated itself against Communism as it 'absorbed many of the ideas it found threatening' in Soviet law (p. xiv).
[36] Low and Martin, *Low's Russian Sketchbook*, 56.   [37] Ibid. 59.

Martin was no legal expert, and perhaps it showed. He was ready to accept that the Soviet courts were biased in favour of one class over another, merely asserting that 'I have never heard anyone dispute that the Soviet legal system provides a speedy and on the whole honest form of legal procedure'.[38] More expert views of the Soviet legal system were available, however. D. N. Pritt was a prominent lawyer who was appointed King's Counsel in 1927, and was elected as Labour MP for Hammersmith North in 1935. He had become interested in Communism in 1932 when he was part of a Fabian Research Bureau delegation to the USSR, and, as he described it in his autobiography in 1965, had a political awakening: 'Here was a Socialist State, something that we ought to build for ourselves, in our own way; we could do it better and more easily.'[39] His infatuation with Soviet Communism eventually led to his expulsion from the Labour Party in 1940 after he vigorously and publicly defended both the Nazi-Soviet Pact and Soviet policy in the Russo-Finnish war in his book, *Light on Moscow* (1940).[40] Remarkably, he successfully defended his seat as an independent in 1945, defeating the Labour candidate. Though he does not seem to have joined the Party, he was a Communist in all but name.[41] A note in his MI5 file, based on information from Walter Krivitsky, claimed that Pritt was 'one of the chief recruiting agents for Soviet underground organisations in the United Kingdom' and that he would 'do everything possible to assist the Soviet Union in the event of a war with Britain'.[42] Pritt's report, based on his 1932 visit to the USSR with the Fabian Research Bureau, was published the following year under the title 'The Russian Legal System'. In contrast to Martin's blithe description of the procedures of Soviet courtrooms, Pritt noted that 'there is much in the Russian legal system to shock the conventional English lawyer or even the layman'.[43] He thereby acknowledged that there was substantial work to be done if English lawyers were to be convinced of the merits of Soviet justice, both on points of procedure and of principle.

[38] Ibid.

[39] D. N. Pritt, *From Right to Left* (London: Lawrence & Wishart 1965), 38–9.

[40] D. N. Pritt, *Light on Moscow: Soviet Policy Analysed, with a New Chapter on Finland* (Harmondsworth: Penguin, 1940).

[41] Kevin Morgan, 'Pritt, Denis Nowell (1887–1972)', *Oxford Dictionary of National Biography* (Oxford: OUP, 2004); online edn, May 2009, <http://www.oxforddnb.com/view/article/31570> [accessed July 2016].

[42] 'Extract from information given by Walter J. Krivitsky dated Jan/Feb 1940', The National Archives, Kew (KV 2/1062).

[43] D. N. Pritt, 'The Russian Legal System', in Margaret Cole (ed.), *Twelve Studies in Soviet Russia* (London: Victor Gollancz, 1933), 167.

Pritt described the Soviet court's use of 'co-judges', which Kingsley Martin had called 'assessors'. Compared to Martin's, Pritt's account is better informed by his historical understanding of the British legal system in comparison with other European models. He acknowledged that the system of co-judges was one aspect of the Soviet system likely to seem alien to English lawyers. Where Martin suggested an analogy between the two legal systems, explaining that the lay co-judges 'in effect play the part of a jury', Pritt contrasted the system with the workings of the jury trial, arguing that it was:

> the fruit of a compromise between the desire, on the one hand, to staff the courts with judges of the best possible professional qualifications, and the sense, on the other hand, of the importance of maintaining the popular or proletarian atmosphere of the court—of securing, in a word, that men shall truly be tried by their peers.

For Pritt, it was not enough for courts merely to follow procedures and reach a fair decision. Equally important was the need to gain popular assent for those decisions. The structure of English courts also reflected this dual purpose: the judge supplied the legal professionalism and the jury provided the popular legitimacy. Yet Pritt noted that there was a substantial disagreement 'between the view that a jury is a desirable instrument of "popularity" and the view that it is not'. In contrast, 'on the best judgement one can form', the Soviet system 'appears to be the happiest possible instance of successful compromise':

> It wastes little time; it cannot result, like so many jury trials, in a disagreement; and it renders it impossible either to secure a verdict by mere appeal to jury prejudice, or to advance with any confidence a technical argument likely to appeal to a professional lawyer but certain to antagonise anyone who is more than half a layman.[44]

Pritt sought to use this comparative approach to provoke English readers out of their complacent assumption that the jury trial was some kind of absolute or natural form of justice.

Pritt's work implied that the question of how a court can command the legitimacy of popular assent, and—more—claim the mantle of a 'popular justice', was in part a question of theatre. The relationship between theatre and justice was explored powerfully—and also under the influence of Marxism and Leninism—by Bertolt Brecht. Brecht's *Die Maßnahme* (1930) is a *Lehrstück* or short didactic play, variously translated as *The Decision*, *The Measures Taken*, or *The Punitive Measure*, and it played an

---

[44] Ibid. 168–9.

important role in subsequent debates about Communist justice. The play uses avant-garde techniques and a highly artificial formal device to engage the central questions of Marxist ethics. In the play, the four agitators—who have been disseminating Communist propaganda in China—describe to a 'control chorus' how and why they killed a fellow activist—the Young Comrade—and threw his body into a lime pit. In describing their actions, they stage particular scenes, taking on different roles. These operate as plays-within-the-play, and the control chorus are both the audience in a theatrical performance and a jury called upon to reach a verdict on the killing of the Young Comrade. The four agitators agree that 'We shall accept your verdict'.[45] The plays-within-the-play also constitute a trial-within-the-trial: the four agitators make a judgement on the Young Comrade and sentence him to death, and in turn are judged both by the control chorus and the audience, from which they seek the legitimacy of 'popular justice'. Brecht's play drew a clear parallel between the theatre and the courtroom, and between the judge or jury and the audience of the play.

The Young Comrade is killed because his actions—motivated by his empathetic, moral responses to the suffering he witnesses—are holding back the cause of the revolution. He is so moved by the sufferings of the striking workers that he wants to begin the revolution immediately, when defeat is certain, rather than accept further suffering in the present while waiting for the proletariat to be organized into a class-conscious revolutionary force. This attitude is portrayed as an individualistic bourgeois moralism. Asked by the agitators to 'recall comrade Lenin's classic advice', he replies:

> the classics are crap, and I am going to rip them apart; for man, real live man,
> is crying out, and his misery rips through the limitations of their teachings.
> That is why I shall launch the operation instantly and at once.[46]

The didactic purpose of the play is to help the audience to see the futility of the Young Comrade's compassion, and to understand the necessity of subordinating individual 'bourgeois' morality to the interests of the revolution. In the end the Young Comrade agrees that it is best if he is killed, as he risks betraying the others. And the four agitators are absolved from the moral opprobrium and the legal sanctions that would follow from killing a man (perhaps especially a comrade) because they did it in the name of the revolution. As they acknowledge:

---

[45] Bertolt Brecht (tr. John Willett), *The Decision*, in *Collected Plays: Three* (London: Methuen, 1997), 63.
[46] Ibid. 81, 82.

... It is
A terrible thing to kill.
But not only others would we kill, but ourselves too if need be
Since only force can alter this
Murderous world, as
Every living creature knows.
It is still, we said
Not given to us to kill. Only on our
Indomitable will to alter the world could we base
This decision.[47]

The norms of bourgeois justice—and indeed morality—are thus subordinated to the needs of the revolution, and the audience is encouraged to follow the judgement of the control chorus and endorse the murder of the Young Comrade. When it comes to the question of norms, there are at least two ways of reading the play. One could argue that 'comrade Lenin's classic advice' has become the basis for a new set of norms, by which it is possible for the control chorus to determine what constitutes a legitimate use of violence. Or, alternatively, one could argue that the appeal to popular justice—to the control chorus and the audience—is an escape from normative justice itself. According to this second reading, the decision is made not with reference to a particular body of normative law, but is as it were a spontaneous product of the theatrical spectacle—the trial—itself. Justice is what can compel the sympathetic assent of the audience.

Die Maßnahme does not deal with an established Communist state, but with the Party in a state of illegality. Under these circumstances, the question of whether or not the Young Comrade has committed a crime is by definition immaterial: in this play the Party is itself a criminal organization. One must surely draw an absolute distinction between judgements made by a small band of outlaws and those arrived at by legal institutions backed by the legitimizing power of the state. Nevertheless, the reception of *Die Maßnahme* has largely been shaped by the context of the Moscow Trials and Soviet justice more generally. For many commentators, the play was a kind of apology in advance for the 'great terror' of the second half of the 1930s. It became particularly important for Marxist literary critics who wanted to distance themselves from the Soviet version of Communism. For Raymond Williams, the play did not represent 'any dialectical transformation of goodness into its opposite' but instead 'a willing rejection of goodness as it is immediately known'.[48] Theodor Adorno argued that '[t]he wild roar of *The Measures*

[47] Ibid. 87.
[48] Raymond Williams, *Drama from Ibsen to Brecht* (New York: OUP, 1969), 195.

Taken drowns out the noise of the disaster that has overtaken the cause, which Brecht convulsively tries to proclaim as salvation'.[49] It is a key text for thinking about the theatricality of law and Communist law in particular, and it had a direct impact (demonstrably) on Arthur Koestler and (arguably) on Stephen Spender, as they wrote about Communist justice.

By fusing the functions of the judge and the jury in the control chorus, Brecht's play reflected what Pritt had written about the Soviet justice system. A genuinely popular justice, both implied, is inherently informal in its workings and openly partisan in its decision-making. Soviet Marxism had from early on been highly critical of the jury trial. Bukharin and Preobrazhensky's *The ABC of Communism*—a key work of early Bolshevik theory written during the Civil War in 1919 and first published in translation in England in 1922—explicitly denounced the jury system:

> When the masses have been sufficiently brought to heel by capital, so that they are duly submissive and regard the laws of the bourgeois State as their own laws, the workers are permitted to a certain extent to be their own judges, just as they are allowed to vote exploiters and their henchmen into parliament. Thus originated trial by jury, thanks to which legal decisions made in the interests of capital can masquerade as decisions made by the 'whole people'.[50]

Pritt did not go so far as Bukharin and Preobrazhensky in dismissing the jury system out of hand. Any modern court relies for its legitimacy on the creation of what he called an 'atmosphere' and a sense 'that men shall truly be tried by their peers'. The benefit of a close look at Soviet law, for Pritt, was that it helped to show that the procedures of English justice are themselves only compromises between competing priorities, and a contingent product of a particular social and political situation. The comparison tended to imply that the English court system was excessively tied up in a professional and technical legal discourse that was inaccessible to the people on whom it passed sentence. But on the other hand, the mechanism it relied on to balance this—the twelve-person jury of non-experts—left it vulnerable to a kind of populist rhetorical manipulation.[51] In his later work *Law, Class and Society* (1970–2) Pritt

---

[49] Theodor Adorno (tr. Francis McDonagh), 'Commitment', in Ernst Bloch et al., *Aesthetics and Politics* (London: Verso, 1980), 187. Theodore Ziolkowski is unusual in seeing the play as a demonstration of Brecht's 'shrewd understanding of the implications of totalitarian law': Ziolokowski, *The Mirror of Justice: Literary Reflections on Legal Crises* (Princeton: Princeton University Press, 1997), 253.

[50] Nikolai Bukharin and E. Preobrazhensky (tr. Eden and Cedar Paul), *The ABC of Communism* (Harmondsworth: Penguin Books, 1969), 271.

[51] Such a critique of the dangers of the jury trial was not unheard of even among more conventionally liberal English jurists. A. V. Dicey, discussed briefly later, wrote that 'Trial

argued that the jury system performed the role of giving popular legitimacy to the decisions of the court, which nevertheless almost invariably worked to protect the interests of the ruling class. To this end, the ruling class had 'adroitly persuaded much of the public to regard the jury as the "palladium of British justice", guaranteeing that "no man shall be convicted of a crime save by the verdict of his peers" '. But it had also found a way to 'manage the jury system [so] that it can be confident of securing the verdicts it wants in cases important to the maintenance of its class strength'.[52] For example, Pritt noted, the selection process favoured middle-class jurists. The jury, for Pritt, performed a powerful role as an aspect of the spectacle of justice, making the public feel as if it were making the judgements itself. The Soviet system, in Pritt's view, struck a happier compromise: 'A professional judge and two co-judges sit at a small table, and deal with the prosecution, the accused, the advocates, the litigants, with as little formality as a group of English peasants arguing politics in a village inn.'[53]

This question of whether a system of co-judges or of jury trial is preferable was for Pritt largely a matter of how courts balanced popular legitimacy with consistent and professional legal decision-making. In this regard, significant differences existed between the court systems of Western European capitalist countries: variation and innovation in this area should not be dismissed out of hand, he urged. He was more radical in his assessment of 'the relation of the courts to the Executive', which he acknowledged 'is fundamentally different in Russia to what it is in England'. He explained:

> The Russian courts are a mere branch of the Executive, being technically a completely subordinate part of the Ministry of Justice, whereas in England they are theoretically wholly independent. This difference, vital in theory, is probably of little importance in practice. It is no doubt true that the Russian courts reflect the outlook and philosophy of the present Russian Government; but the courts of every country, however independent theoretically, reflect equally truly the outlook of the class from which the judges and the executive are drawn.[54]

---

by jury is open to much criticism; a distinguished French thinker may be right in holding that the habit of submitting difficult problems of fact to the decision of twelve men of not more than average education and intelligence will in the near future be considered an absurdity as patent as ordeal by battle.' A. V. Dicey, *Introduction to the Study of the Law of the Constitution,* 7th edn (London: Macmillan, 1915), 389.

[52] D. N. Pritt *Law, Class and Society,* ii. *The Apparatus of the Law* (London: Lawrence & Wishart, 1971), 83. The scare quotes are Pritt's.

[53] D. N. Pritt, 'The Russian Legal System', 171.   [54] Ibid. 166–7.

The theoretical distinction between an independent judiciary and one that is employed by the Ministry of Justice is not significant in practice, Pritt claimed, since the English bench largely upholds the values of the ruling class and the government. But Pritt was more aware than Martin of the jurisprudential significance of the fact that the Soviet courts acted as an arm of the executive. A. V. Dicey, the Victorian jurist, influentially theorized the rule of law as the fundamental principle of the English constitution. 'The judges', he wrote, 'are invested with the means of hampering or supervising the whole administrative action of the government, and of at once putting a veto upon any proceeding not authorised by the letter of the law'.[55] Dicey sought to demonstrate that this was not some merely theoretical power, giving examples where the power of the executive was checked by the courts. He made a contrast with France, where the notion of *droit administratif* gave 'special protection or privileges to the servants of the state', and so was 'foreign to the fundamental assumptions of our English common law, and especially to what we have termed the rule of law'.[56] Pritt's legal training and practice meant that he had a rigorous grounding in these basic constitutional ideas. It is therefore all the more surprising that, when he came to make recommendations for the reform of English justice, he argued that

> [t]he judges under the new régime should be appointed from year to year by the Executive; they should not necessarily be practicing advocates, but should possess a knowledge of law, sociology, criminology, and political economy, tested by examination; they should be Civil Servants under a Ministry of Justice.[57]

While one might have anticipated, in other words, that he would place a greater value on the independence of the judiciary in a practical as well as a theoretical sense, he also knew very well that other states counting themselves as modern liberal democracies enshrined such principles as the *droit administratif* in their constitutions. His treatment of the question of judicial independence seems to suggest that Pritt worked with a spectrum of different legal arrangements in mind, rather than a binary division between liberal and totalitarian justice. But where Dicey had often made the English common law system the ideal to which other judicial systems were (in general) unfavourably compared, Pritt on the contrary saw the short history of Soviet justice as a salutary lesson for English jurisprudence.

Pritt's notion that Soviet justice could act as a corrective to English law was shared by Harold Laski, whose pamphlet *Law and Justice in*

---

[55] Dicey, *Introduction to Constitution* p.218.   [56] Ibid. 324–5.
[57] Pritt, 'The Russian Legal System', 174.

Soviet Russia (1935) was published by the Hogarth Press, and who acknowledged his debt to Pritt. Though he lacked Pritt's grasp of the technical detail, Laski had a stronger grounding in Marxist philosophy and a greater propensity to theorize. 'Compared with our own', Laski argued that the Soviet legal system 'lacks settled form, dignity, procedural rigour. But', he went on, 'I believe that there are definitely many features in which it brings law more substantially into relation with justice than anything the Common Law system has so far been able to attain'.[58] The informality that Martin and Pritt had praised here promises to produce a more direct form of justice, precisely because it abjures the excesses of legal formalism. This was made manifest, for Laski, in the most informal legal forum of all, the 'comrades' court', where minor grievances could be decided on and fines levied by an impromptu tribunal whose officials were elected on the spot by fellow workers. The Duchess of Atholl was pointedly critical of the comrades' courts. She argued that, although they were limited in their jurisdiction to 'small matters', these were nevertheless alarmingly deemed to include infractions such as 'the inculcation by adults of alcoholic habits in children'. They meted out justice without reference to the established courts of the USSR (so that their decisions could not be appealed in a higher court), and 'left the powers of managers in relation to the enforcement of output undisturbed, while offering to the workers a possibility of greater laxity in matters of personal conduct'. The comrades' courts were thus symptomatic of the blurring of the boundaries between judicial authority and other forms of power that she diagnosed.[59] Laski saw this as a positive effect, arguing that comrades' courts 'introduce what may be termed justice without law into all the relations of social life'.[60] The phrase runs entirely against the English liberal tradition, described by Dicey and embodied in the Duchess of Atholl's critique, whereby the freedom of the individual from arbitrary persecution by the government was guaranteed by the rule of law. It moves closer to the form of justice promoted by Brecht's *Die Maßnahme*, relying on the spontaneous judgement of one's comrades.

'JUSTICE WITHOUT LAW'

Darkness at Noon

Arthur Koestler devoted several pages of *The Invisible Writing* (1954) to an analysis of *Die Maßnahme*, which he had seen in Berlin and which he

---

[58] Harold Laski, *Law and Justice in the Soviet Union* (London: Hogarth Press, 1935), 10.
[59] Atholl, *Conscription*, 108–9.   [60] Laski, *Law and Justice*, 38.

called '[t]he climax of Brecht's literary career, and at the same time the most revealing work of art in the entire Communist literature . . . the perfect apotheosis of inhumanity'.[61] Koestler made a direct link between the morality of Brecht's play and the show trials:

> The play reads like a glorification of the anti-Christ. Perhaps the most uncanny scene is the young comrade's confession, and his acquiescence in his own liquidation. Written in 1931 [sic], it seems to be a prophetic forecast of the Moscow show trials that were to start five years later. The young comrade stands in reality for the old bolshevik guard, the generation of the civil war, who had to be thrown in the lime pit because they had retained some vestiges of humanity; and above all, because they were old-fashioned revolutionaries 'whose heart beat for the revolution', and who put the interest of the coolies before those of the 'controlchorus'.[62]

The logic of Brecht's play, which, Koestler thought, so aptly crystallized the whole Communist attitude to justice, also animates *Darkness at Noon* (1940), Koestler's most sustained engagement with the problems of Soviet justice.

Unlike the texts encountered in this chapter so far, *Darkness at Noon* focused not on the everyday practice of the Soviet courts, but on the large political show trials of 1936–8, and it is to these that I now turn. The three main trials, which attracted much debate and discussion across the political spectrum in Britain, were the Zinoviev trial of 1936, the Radek trial in 1937, and the Bukharin trial of 1938 (the trials tend to be known by the name of their most prominent victim, but there were in each case multiple defendants). What follows is not intended as a contribution to the history of the trials themselves, but as an exploration of how those trials were experienced and imagined by contemporaries in Britain. Koestler's reading of *Die Maßnahme* is a good place to begin this exploration. In proposing a direct lineage from Brecht's play to the Moscow Trials, Koestler poses a key question for any critical analysis of Soviet justice. How far was the attitude to political violence in Brecht's play echoed by that in the trials themselves? And to what extent was Marx's critique of bourgeois justice at the root of both? Writing in *Marxism and Morality* (1985), Steven Lukes asked 'whether the theory constructed by Marx and Engels, and developed by their successors, can in any respect and to any degree account for the moral disasters of Marxism in practice'.[63] Koestler's novel tends to a similar conclusion to that reached by Lukes: 'the theory

---

[61] Arthur Koestler, *The Invisible Writing: The Second Volume of an Autobiography, 1932–40* (London: Vintage, 2005), 51.

[62] Ibid. 53.

[63] Stephen Lukes, *Marxism and Morality* (Oxford: Clarendon, 1985), xi.

of the founders was blind and deaf to, and silent about, certain ranges of moral questions—roughly, those concerning justice and rights, which set constraints on how people are to be treated in the here and now, and in the immediate future'.[64] And for Koestler it was this blind spot within Marxist theory that both dictated the political morality of *Die Maßnahme* and made the Moscow Trials a logical outcome of the Russian Revolution.

In *Darkness at Noon*, the necessity that a well-intentioned individual Party member can and should be publicly sacrificed for the good of the revolution—the theme of *Die Maßnahme*—is a central concern, and the main character Rubashov is both a perpetrator and a victim of this form of Communist justice. The novel describes Rubashov's time in prison as a senior Bolshevik facing trumped up charges of conspiracy to murder No. 1 (the Stalin figure in the novel). It also includes many extended passages where Rubashov remembers his time in the Party, and in particular his role in the demise of three comrades: Richard, Little Loewy, and Arlova. The justifications for his role in the liquidation of these Communists closely mirror Brecht's play, but Rubashov's reminiscences are shot through with doubt. Take for example Richard's liquidation. Rubashov has been sent to a town in southern Germany in 1933, during the first months of the Nazi terror, to meet with this 19-year-old leader of the local Party cell. This cell has been torn apart by recent events, and Richard is a stammering wreck. The meeting takes place in a picture gallery, where Rubashov can see a *Last Judgement* as well as a *Pietà*, the image of the dead Christ obstructed by Richard's head. Rubashov has come to pass judgement on Richard, the kind of summary judgement that the Young Comrade receives at the hands of the four agitators in *Die Maßnahme*. Richard's crime is that he has distributed locally produced propaganda, which acknowledged the defeats suffered by the Party and advocated a rethinking of policy, instead of the centrally produced pamphlets that kept to the line, emphasizing 'phrases about our unbroken will to victory'. Richard protests that 'one must tell the people the truth, as they know it already, in any case'. Rubashov corrects him:

> 'It is impossible to form policy with passion and despair. The Party's course is sharply defined, like a narrow path in the mountains. The slightest false step, right or left, takes one down the precipice. The air is thin; he who becomes dizzy is lost'[65]

The need to suppress 'passion and despair', and to follow the Party line at the expense of individual conscience, reverberates with Brecht's play. And

---

[64] Ibid., xxi.   [65] Koestler, *Darkness at Noon*, 39–41.

just like the interrogation of the Young Comrade in *Die Maßnahme*, this meeting in a provincial museum becomes an improvised court in which Rubashov makes his judgement:

> Rubashov listened in silence. He wanted to hear whether the young man had any more to say, before he himself pronounced the decisive sentence. Whatever Richard said, it could not now change that sentence in any way; but yet he waited.[66]

Though Rubashov does not himself execute Richard, the memory of this judgement haunts him in his prison cell, along with the fates of other Party members in whose demise he had played a part: Little Loewy and Arlova (Rubashov's erstwhile lover and secretary whom he had 'sacrificed . . . because his own existence was more valuable to the revolution').[67]

These reminiscences are always filtered through Rubashov's knowledge that he will soon be on the receiving end of Soviet justice, and the interplay between his memories of passing judgement and the present reality of being judged enables him to empathize both with those he condemned to death, and with those who will in due course condemn him:

> The old compulsion to think through the minds of others had again taken hold of him; he sat in Ivanov's place and saw himself through Ivanov's eyes, in the position of the accused, as once he had seen Richard and little Loewy. He saw this degraded Rubashov, the shadow of the former companion, and he understood the mixture of tenderness and contempt with which Ivanov treated him.[68]

Rubashov understands all too well that there is only one possible outcome for him: 'He knew [Arlova's] fate. Also Richard's. Also Little Loewy's. Also his own.'[69] The temporal sequence no longer matters: future events, with the logic of Soviet justice, can be known with the same certainty as past ones.

Koestler's account of Communist justice, tracing a direct line from Marx through Brecht to the Moscow Trials, was echoed on a more theoretical level in the post-war period by Hannah Arendt. In *The Origins of Totalitarianism* (1951), Arendt argued that 'the monstrous, yet seemingly unanswerable claim of totalitarian rule' was the notion that it could 'do away with petty legality' in favour of a higher justice. As a result, Arendt claimed,

> [t]otalitarian lawfulness, defying legality and pretending to establish the direct reign of justice on earth, executes the law of History or of Nature

---

[66] Ibid. 42.   [67] Ibid. 104.   [68] Ibid. 91.   [69] Ibid. 75.

without translating it into standards of right or wrong for individual behaviour. It applies the law directly to mankind without bothering with the behaviour of men.[70]

Arendt's argument about justice contains the essence of the totalitarian thesis, drawing a strong analogy between Communism and Nazism. The Marxist 'law of History' performs the same function as the racist and eugenicist 'law of Nature' in Nazi thinking, overriding individual legal and ethical judgements in the name of the destiny of a race or class. Arendt thus follows Koestler in suggesting that the Marxist critique of *Recht* is not incidental but fundamental to the politics of Stalinism. Admitting frankly that it existed to further the ends of the proletarian revolution— legitimized by the 'law of History' itself—Communist justice could act 'directly'. The ambition of the comrades' courts to put 'justice without law into all the relations of social life' was seen as a benevolent development by Laski.[71] He drew a strong distinction between this diffusion of an informal, popular justice, and the state's treatment of political crimes. But Arendt's analysis, like Koestler's novel, encourages us to see the two things as profoundly connected, tending to dislodge the formal procedures of a normative body of law from its central constitutional role, and rely instead on a non-normative, 'higher' form of justice.

Rubashov's thoughts in his cell frequently anticipate the Arendtian critique of totalitarianism. He casts 'the movement' as a version of Arendt's 'law of History':

> For the movement was without scruples; she rolled towards her goal unconcernedly and deposed the corpses of the drowned in the windings of her course. Her course had many twists and windings; such was the law of her being. And whosoever could not follow her crooked course was washed on to the bank, for such was her law. The motives of the individual did not matter to her, neither did she care what went on in his head and his heart. The Party knew only one crime: to swerve from the course laid out; and only one punishment: death. Death was no mystery in the movement; there was nothing exalted about it: it was the logical solution to political divergences.[72]

Once the Party line becomes identified with the 'law of History', any divergence from it becomes criminal. And actions committed in its name cannot be judged by any other standard of justice.

The symmetry that Rubashov notes between the judgements he passed on Richard, Little Loewy, and Arlova, and those which will shortly be

---

[70] Hannah Arendt, *The Origins of Totalitarianism* (New York: Schocken Books, 2004), 595.
[71] Laski, *Law and Justice*, 38.   [72] Koestler, *Darkness at Noon*, 65.

enacted on him, tends to support Arendt's description of totalitarian justice. It matters little whether actual crimes have been committed, if someone can be shown to have 'swerve[d] from the course laid out'. This is essential to Koestler's understanding of why the Bolshevik Old Guard publicly admitted to such extraordinary crimes. Rubashov's initial self-denunciation—before he is convinced that admitting to actual acts of treason that he did not commit is just the necessary public counterpart to his private doubts about the direction of the revolution—suggests that the real crime is to place legal considerations over political ones:

> I have lent my ear to the laments of the sacrificed, and thus become deaf to the arguments which proved the necessity to sacrifice them. I plead guilty to having rated the question of guilt and innocence higher than that of utility and harmfulness.[73]

During his interrogation under the lights by Gletkin, Rubashov comes to share the view that the details of any crimes actually committed are less important than intention: 'whether the entire confession had been artificially pumped into him, or only parts of it, now seemed to Rubashov of merely legal interest; it made no difference to his guilt'.[74] In Arendt's terms, the novel describes a totalitarian separation of the 'merely legal' question of whether or not Rubashov actually committed a crime (according to 'standards of right or wrong for individual behaviour'), from a notion of 'guilt' which is defined not in relation to a body of normative law but according to the usefulness of a given actor to the underlying historical project of which the law is now understood to be an expression.

The function of the inquisition in *Darkness at Noon* is not, therefore, to determine what happened and whether it was legal, but to establish Rubashov's attitude to the revolution and then to extract whatever confession seems necessary for the trial to serve its public didactic function. This is explicitly underlined by Rubashov's first interrogator, and fellow veteran of the Party's Old Guard, Ivanov:

> 'You have now repeatedly said "you"—meaning State and Party, as opposed to "I"—that is, Nicolas Salmonovich Rubashov. For the public, one needs, of course, a trial and legal justification. For us, what I have just said should be enough.'[75]

The trial is the place where a 'legal justification' must be set out for the benefit of the public, but not primarily in order to confer popular legitimacy on the decision. Referring to show trials in the post-war Communist bloc, which he sees as evolving directly from the Moscow

---

[73] Ibid. 153.   [74] Ibid. 166.   [75] Ibid. 70.

Trials, Tony Judt argued that they 'were not about justice'. Instead, they must be understood as a form of

> public pedagogy-by-example . . . whose purpose was to illustrate and exem-
> plify the structures of authority in the Soviet system. They told the public
> who was right, who wrong; they placed blame for policy failures; they
> assigned credit for loyalty and subservience; they even wrote a script, an
> approved vocabulary for use in discussion of public affairs.[76]

Indeed, as Vyshinsky—the state prosecutor in the Moscow Trials, and a key Soviet legal theorist—put it in his 1936 *Soviet Manual of Criminal Investigation*, the public tribunals served the primary function of 'mobilisation of proletarian public opinion'.[77] In Koestler's novel, after Rubashov has agreed to do what the Party asks of him and confess to a murderous conspiracy, Gletkin says that his task now is 'to gild the Right, to blacken the Wrong . . . to make the masses understand that opposition is a crime'.[78] Rubashov will step out for his final performance at his public trial with his guilt firmly established: the purpose of the spectacle is purely didactic.

The presentation of the trial itself in *Darkness at Noon* is striking, given the importance given to the public and pedagogical status of this event. Rubashov's interrogations, first by Ivanov and then by Gletkin, are reported in great detail by a third person narrator, mostly from Rubashov's perspective but with occasional deviations, notably to report a private conversation between Ivanov and Gletkin about the progress of the inquisition. In general, overwhelmingly, the novel reports what Rubashov sees, hears, and thinks. The trial itself, however—potentially the dramatic climax of the novel—is conveyed in an oddly detached, third-hand manner. Rather than reporting Rubashov's public confession and cross-examination directly, the narrator describes Vasily, the old porter in Rubashov's apartment block, hearing about the trial as his daughter Vera reads a report from the newspaper. The trial has had its desired effect on Vera, who reasons 'He says himself that he is a traitor. If it weren't true, he wouldn't say so himself.' She declares Rubashov 'disgusting'. But her father Vasily is less convinced: 'Don't imagine that you understand', he

---

[76] Tony Judt, *Postwar: A History of Europe since 1945* (London: Vintage, 2010), 187.
[77] Qtd. ibid.
[78] Koestler, *Darkness at Noon*, 190. It is not uncommon to find Brecht advocating a similar role for the theatre. The Young Comrade's 'confession' is made in the knowledge that, as one of the agitators says, 'even if he does not agree he must vanish, and vanish entirely', but it is crucial for the didactic effect of the play that he accepts the argument that he, and his conscience, must be extinguished 'For the sake of Communism'. Brecht, *The Decision*, 88.

tells her, 'God knows what was in his mind when he said that. The Party has taught you all to be cunning, and whoever becomes too cunning loses all decency.'[79] Vasily's adherence to 'decency' points the reader back to a discussion Rubashov had on that subject with the 'genuine and authentic counterrevolutionar[y]' in the cell next to his.[80] Tapping in code on the adjoining wall, Rubashov insists: 'WE HAVE REPLACED DECENCY BY REASON'.[81] The 'decency' that Vasily holds on to is in some senses too vague to define—though it is no accident that he invokes 'God' at the beginning of this speech. As Vera reads him sections from Rubashov's confession, Vasily quotes lines from the Bible—the cock crying thrice for Peter's betrayal, and 'Let your communication be Yea, yea; nay, nay; for whatever is more than these cometh of evil.'[82] Vasily's need for a set of inflexibly normative ethical commands—the very opposite of the 'direct' form of totalitarian justice, described by Arendt—does not spring from a lingering respect for bourgeois legalism, but from a Christian ethics.

For Arendt, totalitarianism consists in following 'the law of History... without translating it into standards of right or wrong for individual behaviour'. *Darkness at Noon* seems to call for a return to deontological ethics, but the form this takes is more often that of Christian ethics rather than bourgeois legalism. As Rubashov contemplates: 'Perhaps it did not suit man to be completely freed from old bonds, from the steadying brakes of "Thou shalt not" and "Thou mayst not", and to be allowed to tear along straight towards the goal.' He thinks that the Party has been 'sailing without ethical ballast', but again it is the language of the Old Testament—'Thou shalt not'—that provides the link to a stable ethical universe.[83] In the end, Rubashov finds himself yearning for a world in which 'standards of right and wrong for individual behaviour' have a renewed importance, and perhaps in which the totalitarian subordination of legal and ethical norms to the 'law of History' is reversed.

Arendt's and Koestler's analyses of totalitarian justice shared in common the idea that ends had priority over means in the Soviet Union. This is often summed up in the slogan 'you can't make an omelet without breaking eggs'. Arendt analysed and rejected this slogan in an essay called 'The Ex-Communists' (1953): 'The breaking of eggs in action never leads to anything more interesting than the breaking of eggs. The result is identical with the activity itself: it is a breaking, not an omelet.'[84] What

---

[79] Koestler, *Darkness at Noon*, 196–8.   [80] Ibid. 28.   [81] Ibid. 141.
[82] Ibid. 198.   [83] Ibid. 205–6.
[84] Hannah Arendt, 'The Ex-Communists', in *Essays in Understanding, 1930–1954: Formation, Exile and Totalitarianism,* ed. Jerome Kohn (New Yor: Schocken Books, 1994), 397.

is required, Arendt's essay implies, is a properly enforced set of legal norms prohibiting the breaking of eggs. However, the essay also argued that men like Koestler continued to occupy a totalitarian mindset:

> Like the Communists, the ex-Communists see the whole texture of our time in terms of one great dichotomy ending in a final battle. There is no plurality of forces in the world; there are only two. These two are not the opposition of freedom against tyranny (or however one might want to formulate it in traditional terms), but of one faith against another.[85]

This is an interesting passage given that Arendt has often been thought of as someone whose work helped to harden the polarizations of the Cold War. She was, after all, one of the authors of the totalitarian thesis that (in certain hands) crudely pitted liberal-democracy against a totalitarian other that was homogeneously both Nazi and Communist. Frances Stonor Saunders implies that Arendt, like many in the New York *Partisan Review* crowd, knew very well that the publications she was writing for were funded by the CIA, and also that Arendt was connected to the Information Research Department, an anti-Communist propaganda unit of the British state.[86] There can be no doubt that Arendt was an anti-Communist. But in 'The Ex-Communists' she warns against a certain form of anti-Communism, of which Koestler was a key representative, partly by pointing to a 'plurality of forces' rather than a Manichaean separation between Western societies governed by the rule of law, and totalitarian states characterized by unchecked executive power. She concludes the essay by arguing that the ex-Communists 'make of democracy a "cause" in the strict ideological sense' which 'contradicts the rules and laws by which we live and let live'.[87] In *The Origins of Totalitarianism*, Arendt had argued that the Stalinist 'law of history' or Nazi 'law of nature' see a form of 'higher justice' rising above 'petty legality'. Here, Arendt suggests that liberal democracy itself—treated as an end rather than a means—could become that kind of 'cause'.

Norms: Between Pashukanis and Vyshinsky

At the heart of *Darkness at Noon*, and other representations of Soviet justice, is the question of the nature and desirability of legal norms. A slew

---

[85] Ibid. 393. Koestler is not named in the essay; Whittaker Chambers is Arendt's starting point, but it is clear that she means to generalize about a tendency of which Koestler was a prominent representative.

[86] Frances Stonor Saunders, *Who Paid the Piper? The CIA and the Cultural Cold War* (London: Granta, 1999), 111.

[87] Arendt, 'The Ex-Communists', 400.

of publications in the 1970s and 1980s pointed to what they saw as an important deficiency or blind spot in Marxist theory. Marxist critics such as Norman Geras and Stephen Lukes set out to explore what they saw as a paradox in Marxist ethics. On the one hand, as Lukes put it, Marx (and Marxists) dismissed morality, justice, and law as 'a form of ideology, and thus social in origin, illusory in content, and serving class interests'. But on the other hand 'no one can fail to notice that Marx's and marxist writings abound in moral judgements, implicit and explicit'.[88] It is difficult, in other words, to read Marx's angry denunciations of capitalism without the feeling that they are driven by a normative morality, however much he sought to disavow the latter. Brecht's play participated in the same paradox: the right of the Young Comrade to a fair trial, the prohibition on murder, etc. are pushed aside as mere bourgeois sentimentalism. But the desirability of the revolution to which such ethical qualms must be subordinated was itself urged in moral terms. The control chorus says at one point: 'How much meanness would you not commit if the aim is / To stamp out meanness?'[89] The theoretical problem for Marxism—and the practical problem for jurists working in a Communist state—is, where does the ambition to stamp out meanness come from, and where does the definition of 'meanness' come from, if not from a normative justice that purports to rise above mere ideology?

The paradox of the Marxist conception of justice was given practical form in revolutionary Russia, a polity that was founded to some extent on Marx's critique of legal norms. Martin Malia once quipped that '[t]he problem with Soviet legal history is that there's not enough of it'.[90] From 1918 Lenin insisted on the dictatorship of the proletariat's 'unlimited power above all law'.[91] Petr Stuchka, the first president of the USSR's supreme court, said in 1927 that 'Communism means not the victory of

---

[88] Lukes, *Marxism and Morality*, 3. Norman Geras made a similar point: 'Disowning, when he is not actively ridiculing, any attachment to ideals or values, he is nevertheless quite free in making critical normative judgements, author of a discourse that is replete with the signs of an intense moral commitment' (p. 265). Geras argues that Marx's relativizing statements about normative justice are incompatible with the main thrust of his critique of capitalism: 'Marx did think capitalism was unjust but he did not think he thought so' (p. 245). Norman Geras, 'The Controversy about Marx and Justice', in Alex Callinicos (ed.), *Marxist Theory* (Oxford: OUP, 1989), 211–67.

[89] Brecht, *The Decision*, 79.

[90] Malia qtd. Benjamin Nathans, 'Soviet Rights-Talk in the Post-Stalin Era', in Stefan-Ludwig Hoffmann (ed.), *Human Rights in the Twentieth Century* (Cambridge: CUP, 2010), 166.

[91] Martin Malia, *The Soviet Tragedy: A History of Socialism in Russia, 1917–1991* (New York: Free Press, 1994), 118.

socialist law, but the victory of socialism over any law, since with the abolition of classes and their antagonistic interests, law will die out altogether.'[92] These questions were addressed on a theoretical level by Evgeny Pashukanis, a prominent legal theorist of the early Soviet period who took up important political and academic positions in 1924–30. Despite the fact that his theories were plainly incompatible with the emerging Stalinist conception of the state, he also made some headway in Stalin's administration, being appointed Vice-Commissar of Justice as late as 1936 (he disappeared in 1937).[93] Pashukanis played an important role as a representative of Soviet legal thinking on the world stage, and was frequently interviewed by foreign visitors to the Soviet Union. So although his major work, *The General Theory of Law and Marxism* (1924), was not translated into English until 1951, Pashukanis's British contemporaries came into contact with his ideas. He was responsible for inviting Harold Laski to give a lecture series in Moscow in 1935 (the visit that produced Laski's *Law and Justice in Soviet Russia*) and acted as a respondent during these public lectures.[94]

Pashukanis held that law and juridical institutions were specific to capitalist society, and that their sole function was the protection of bourgeois property rights. Criminal law functions to mediate between the competing interests of individuals, and in its form it mirrored the conditions of commodity exchange. Indeed, the modern form of bourgeois law was a result of a historical process by which '[v]engeance is transformed from a purely biological phenomenon into a juridical institution', and moreover 'self-defence ceases to be purely self-defence and becomes a form of exchange'.[95] Crimes are thus weighed with 'equivalent' punishments, just as commodities are traded with those of equivalent exchange-value. In a fully Communist society, no longer founded on the basis of commodity exchange, there would be no legal norms or

---

[92] Stuchka qtd. in Nathans, 'Soviet Rights-Talk', 167.

[93] Dragan Milovanovic, 'Introduction to the Transaction Edition', in Evgeny Bronislavovich Pashukanis (tr. Barbara Einhorn), *The General Theory of Law and Marxism* (New Brunswick, NJ; London: Transaction Publishers, 2002), vii–x.

[94] Our Correspondent, 'Soviet Lawyer Dismissed: More "Wrecking" Violent Attacks on Professor', *Manchester Guardian* (16 Apr. 1937), 15; Our Moscow Correspondent, 'Professor Laski in Moscow, "Dogmatic Certitude of the Communist Mind", an Astonishingly Candid Discussion', *Manchester Guardian* (22 June 1934), 6.

[95] Evgeny Bronislavovich Pashukanis (tr. Barbara Einhorn), *The General Theory of Law and Marxism* (New Brunswick, NJ; London: Transaction Publishers, 2002), 170, 176. There is a useful summary of the debate between Pashukanis and Vyshinsky in Hans Kelsen, *The Communist Theory of Law* (Aalen: Scientia Verlag, 1976). Kelsen was himself a leading legal theorist from the normative, neo-Kantian school.

institutions as Pashukanis defines them. Pashukanis was quite insistent that a notion of 'socialist law' or 'communist law' was oxymoronic: 'The withering away of the categories of bourgeois law will, under these conditions, mean the withering away of law altogether, that is to say the disappearance of the juridical factor from social relations.'[96] Pashukanis did allow for the existence of 'technical regulation' in a Communist society, which could be applied without the oversight of juridical institutions because unlike laws this did not mediate between competing interests. As Paul Hirst has argued, however, technical regulation applied in the service of '[m]obilization towards socialist construction' would involve 'inspection of individual conduct and its adjustment to a norm', even if that were done without formal legal institutions. In fact, Hirst contended, '[i]f Pashukanis's conception were put into operation, medical and psychiatric knowledge would be deployed by state agencies to serve the definition and enforcement of socialist "normality"'.[97] The attempt to theorize a society not regulated by legal or ethical norms ultimately runs up against its own normative assumptions about the nature of the good society. Consequently, these norms end up needing to be enforced directly, without the mediation of legal institutions.

In practice Soviet society did not transcend law as Pashukanis thought it would. Benjamin Nathans has argued convincingly that, right from the beginning, in the 1918 Constitution of Soviet Russia, 'Soviet law harnessed rights to the explicit goal of inverting (rather than abolishing) received patterns of class domination'.[98] This could initially be rationalized by Soviet jurists, including Pashukanis, as a relic of bourgeois law, a temporary measure necessary during the transition to full communism.[99] Soviet legal theory had to adapt to a new reality from 1936, however, when Stalin announced that the revolution had been successfully completed and the 'elimination of the exploitation of man by man' was formalized in article IV of the Stalin Constitution of that year, which Samuel Moyn has labelled 'the most full-blown declaration of rights yet propounded in world history'.[100] Such a proclamation of rights was not compatible with the Marxist critique of *Recht*. It was no longer viable to claim that legal institutions were on their way to withering away, since full Communism had now been declared and the new task became one of

---

[96] Pashukanis, *General Theory*, 61.
[97] Paul Q. Hirst, *Law, Socialism and Democracy* (London: Allen & Unwin, 1986), 48.
[98] Nathans, 'Soviet Rights-Talk', 169.   [99] Pashukanis, *General Theory*, 61–3.
[100] Samuel Moyn, *The Last Utopia: Human Rights in History* (Cambridge, MA: Belknap Press of Harvard University Press, 2010), 70. Needless to say, in practice these rights were frequently not defended. There is then the further irony that, as Moyn noted, 'human rights became almost immediately associated with anticommunism', 71.

explaining and celebrating the existence of a 'Communist justice' that Pashukanis had viewed as oxymoronic. Pashukanis himself became a victim of the purges in 1937.[101]

Andrey Vyshinsky, one of Stalin's key henchmen and the Soviet state prosecutor during the purges, was an even more well-known figure in Western Europe, who became the most prominent theorist of Communist justice after Pashukanis, denouncing him and his followers as 'provocateurs and traitors'.[102] Vyshinsky was unequivocal in insisting, against Pashukanis, that a system of legal norms supported by juridical institutions *was* a vitally important element of socialist society: 'The soviet theory of law and state must afford a system of soviet socialist principles which explain and are a condition of the socialist content of soviet juridic disciplines and juridic institutes.'[103] The point was to establish a new body of normative law with genuinely socialist content. Vyshinsky wrote in 1938 that 'law is, of course, a political category. At the foundation of soviet law lie the political and economic interests of workers and peasants.'[104] In effect, while the names of Marx and Engels were still proclaimed by Soviet jurists, the Marxist critique of law was tacitly abandoned in order that a normative system of Communist law, explicitly based on defending the interests of the worker-state against its enemies, could be put in place.

Laski's enthusiasm for 'justice without law' might imply that he was inclined to a non-normative anti-legalism such as that of Pashukanis. He praised Pashukanis's 'high quality' work as an example of the strong 'philosophic and historical research' in Soviet legal studies, 'especially on the comparative side'. 'But', he continued, 'I think its value is definitely limited by the need for a mechanical conformity to Communist formulae'. Soviet jurists seeking to apply the Marxist critique of law to the realities of the Soviet state tended to 'start out with their conclusions implicit in their premises' and were thus prone to ignore the fact that—for Laski—'the materialist analysis' can be 'but a partial explanation' of the complex functioning of the law.[105] By contrast Laski averred that '[n]o experience I had in Russia was more impressive than a discussion with Mr. Vishinsky', whom he praised as 'a man whose passion was for law reform'.[106] Where he had criticized Pashukanis for a lofty and academic

[101] Milovanovic, 'Introduction', p. x.
[102] Vyshinsky, qtd. in Kelsen, *The Communist Theory of Law*, 116.
[103] Vyshinsky, quoted ibid. 121.
[104] Vyshinsky, quoted in Ziolkowski, *Mirror of Justice*, 253.
[105] Laski, *Law and Justice*, 32–3.   [106] Ibid. 24.

approach, he applauded Vyshinsky's focus on the 'actual experience of the law in action' and claimed that '[h]e brought to the study of the law in operation an energy which we have not seen in this country since the days of Jeremy Bentham'.[107] The force of the comparison with Bentham is to suggest that, while Vyshinsky had a passion for reform, he was not proposing to do away with law as anti-Communists might have feared from the rhetoric of Pashukanis: far from it.

In the end, like Vyshinsky, Laski saw law as a necessary political tool that was inherently normative. He explained the basis of the Soviet legal system by reference to Lenin's maxim that 'Law is a political measure, law is politics':

> No one can examine the foundations of legal doctrine in Russia without the sense of the completeness with which this conception has permeated the whole fabric of the law. Behind all of it is the relentless purpose of consolidating the dictatorship of the proletariat. In every phase of the law, property, contract, tort, crime, its end is the threefold one of crushing counter-revolutionary resistance, of freeing the workers from the impact of what are regarded as capitalist habits, and of building up a social outlook able to work the principles of the communist society.

Laski then compared this partisan and overtly politicized notion of law to the English common law system:

> In all this there is nothing, I think, at which an English student of law need be surprised. The Soviet system of law does what the English system does; it puts the supreme coercive power of the State behind the fundamental premises of the regime of which it is the expression.[108]

Both legal systems, then, upheld the ideology and the attitude to property of their respective regimes. But while Soviet law made this explicit, English law concealed it behind the rhetoric of impartiality and equality before the law. Moreover—given that in both countries law played the role of a socially coercive mechanism, backed up by violence, that aimed to protect or bring into being a particular kind of society—there seemed to be no escaping law's partiality. Ultimately the choice was a political one, between capitalist norms enforced violently by law, and socialist norms enforced violently by law. Laski preferred the latter, and set aside the Marxist critique of *Recht* as so much idle theorizing. The Pashukanis option—the idea that laws and legal institutions would wither away imminently, in the Soviet Union—had disappeared from view.

---

[107] Ibid.   [108] Ibid. 39.

TRIAL AND COUNTER-TRIAL

The Reichstag Fire Trial

Emerging from these debates is a central concern with the trial, both as the forum for the negotiation and enforcement of legal norms and as a site where the theatrical aspects of popular justice become clear. This became a pressing issue for Communists during the Reichstag Fire Trial in Leipzig in 1933, during which the Nazi authorities sought to blame Communists for the arson, and used it as a pretext for the suppression of the Communist Party. Five men were put on trial: Ernst Torgler (the leader of the Communist group in the Reichstag), three Bulgarian Communists including Georgi Dimitrov (leader of the Comintern from 1934–43), and a mentally deficient Dutch tramp, Marinus Van Der Lubbe, who was found near the scene. The Reichstag Fire Trial in Leipzig, and the so-called 'counter-trial' (or 'Reichstag Fire Enquiry') in London, organized by the 'World Committee for the Relief of the Victims of German Fascism', were formative for several of the key protagonists of this chapter. D. N. Pritt was chairman of the Reichstag Fire Enquiry and claimed in his 1965 autobiography to be 'among the first in Britain—outside the Communist Party—to oppose Fascism'. He cited the Reichstag Fire as a 'milestone in my political development', and 'perhaps the most important event between 1917 and 1939'.[109] Arthur Koestler was a 'minor participant', working in Paris for the 'Western Propaganda Chief of the Comintern' Willy Muenzenberg, the chief orchestrator of the counter-trial. Like Pritt, Koestler gave the episode immense significance, describing a 'great propaganda battle between Berlin and Moscow' that held 'Europe spellbound', and arguing that '[h]ad the world understood at the time the stratagems and bluffs involved, it could have saved itself much suffering'.[110] All the men, except Van Der Lubbe, were acquitted, and the findings of the counter-trial—along with the bestselling *Brown Book of the Hitler Terror and the Burning of the Reichstag* (1933), produced by Muenzenberg—played an important role in that acquittal.[111]

Dimitrov's dramatic defiance of Goering from the dock was seen by Communists as a seminal moment in the anti-Fascist struggle. John

---

[109] D. N. Pritt, *From Right to Left* (London: Lawrence & Wishart, 1965), 41–2.
[110] Koestler, *The Invisible Writing*, 237.
[111] The *Brown Book* included the first reporting on Nazi concentration camps, the persecution of the Jews, and other aspects of the Nazi terror, as well as suggesting that the Nazis were responsible for the fire. Koestler wrote that it 'probably had the strongest political impact of any pamphlet since Tom Paine's *Common Sense*'. *The Invisible Writing*, 243. See also Anson Rabinbach, 'Staging Antifascism: *The Brown Book of the Reichstag Fire and the Hitler Terror*', *New German Critique*, 103/35/1 (Spring 2008), 97–126.

Cornford's Spanish Civil War poem 'Full Moon at Tierz: Before the Storming of Huesca' sees Dimitrov's bravery as a pivotal moment of Communist empowerment:

> Three years ago Dimitrov fought alone
> And we stood taller when we won.
> But now the Leipzig dragon's teeth
> Sprout strong and handsome against death,
> And here an army fights where there was one.[112]

Cornford imagined the Communist army that fought for the Spanish republic springing from the teeth of Dimitrov, the 'Leipzig dragon', as in the myth of Cadmus. In Cornford's vision, one man's defiance in the face of his Nazi accusers became the seed for an anti-Fascist army. Such a view of Dimitrov's heroism was widespread on the left. Ralph Fox, in *The Novel and the People* (1937), saw Dimitrov in a similarly heroic light: 'Few would disagree with the view that in our time there is one example of moral grandeur and courage worthy to stand beside the greatest in our human history, the defence of Dimitrov against the fascist court in Leipzig… Indeed, this story of the Reichstag arson is an epic of our time which demands that the artist should give it life.'[113] For Fox, Dimitrov's trial was the great unwritten novel of the 1930s.[114]

D.N. Pritt's later reflections on the Reichstag Fire Enquiry (or counter-trial) celebrated his role in 'a heavy blow for the Nazis, and a triumph for anti-Fascists, particularly for the Communist Party'.[115] For Pritt, the Leipzig trial itself was a 'great propaganda operation' on the part of the Nazis, who saw it as an opportunity to 'deal heavy blow

---

[112] John Cornford, 'Full Moon at Tierz: Before the Storming of Huesca', in *Understand the Weapon Understand the Wound: Selected Writings of John Cornford*, ed. John Galassi (Manchester: Carcanet New Press, 1976), 38–9.

[113] Ralph Fox, *The Novel and the People* (London: Lawrence & Wishart, 1979), 121.

[114] Tantalizingly, there is some evidence that Montagu Slater and Rajani Palme Dutt wrote a play about Dimitrov, but the manuscript, if one exists, has proved impossible to trace. Andy Croft mentions this play in his bibliography 'The Communist Party in Literature', <http://www.letterpressproject.co.uk/media/file/THE_COMMUNIST_PARTY_IN_LITERATURE_by.pdf> [accessed Oct. 2016]. My email correspondence with Andy Croft suggested that a performance of the play at Canning Town Public Hall on 22 June 1953 was advertised in the *Daily Worker* on that day. The evening was organized by the London District Committee; Johnnie Gollan was advertised to speak. Meanwhile Keith Williams alludes in passing to 'Montagu Slater's documentary play on the South Wales mine sit ins *A New Way to Win* (1936), as well as a whole host of agit-prop scripts on issues like Nazi re-armament (*Dr Krupps*) and the Reichstag Fire Trial (*For Dimitrov*)', in *British Writers and the Media, 1930–45* (Basingstoke: Palgrave Macmillan, 1996), 155. I have been unable to locate this script, which is not held in the Montagu Slater papers at Nottingham University.

[115] Pritt, *From Right to Left*, 48.

against Communism everywhere', and 'give some pretext for the terror and dictatorship which they had exercised since the fire, and for new and even more brutal measures in the future'.[116] He began his description of the events by citing Dimitrov's definition of Fascism as 'the open terrorist dictatorship of the most reactionary, most chauvinistic and most imperialist elements of finance capital'.[117] Such a view—that Fascism is essentially continuous with capitalism and not some radical deviation from it—would in principle play into a Marxist critique that does not distinguish between liberal and totalitarian forms of justice, seeing all law as a means, ultimately backed up by violence, of enforcing the power of the ruling class. Yet Pritt's characterization of the counter-trial focuses on 'ascertaining and publishing the true facts': for Pritt this was not the clash of two rival propaganda machines, but a conflict between truth and justice on the one hand and the outrageous fabrications of the Nazis on the other.[118] Still, Pritt was a KC steeped in English law and could hardly fail to recognize that the proceedings in London were irregular. He initially had doubts about whether to be involved at all:

> I had been brought up in the strict traditions of the English Bar, with its extreme respect for Courts (even foreign Courts!); it was a strange idea for British lawyers that individual lawyers, having no jurisdiction or authority, should assume the functions of a Court and pass 'judgement on a foreign government, or members of it, or indeed on anybody, especially in respect of matters actually pending before a regular court.[119]

The mock trial, Pritt was all too aware, had no jurisdiction, and no capacity to compel assent. Moreover, especially insofar as it put on the airs of official justice, it undermined the 'regular court', and therefore the rule of law, in Germany. Pritt nevertheless agreed to chair the enquiry, in the hope that it would lead to 'a very early and very convincing exposure of the wicked and unscrupulous character of the Nazis, and of the utterly false and dishonest basis on which their electoral victory was founded'.[120] The counter-trial presented to Pritt the possibility of an international justice that could rise above the separate jurisdictions of individual nation states. In his 1934 foreword to the *Second Brown Book*—which collected the findings of the counter-trial—Pritt argued that the 'world-wide campaign in the interests of the four innocent men . . . indicates not merely a sentiment but a power which transcends national boundaries'.[121]

---

[116] Ibid. 49–50.   [117] Ibid. 41.   [118] Ibid. 51.   [119] Ibid. 53.
[120] Ibid.
[121] D. N. Pritt, 'Foreword', in World Committee for the Relief of the Victims of German Fascism, *The Reichstag Fire Trial: The Second Brown Book of the Hitler Terror* (London: John Lane the Bodley Head, 1934), p. ix.

Koestler also understood that a 'public shadow-trial of this kind was a novelty for the West', and completely at odds with legal convention. Practically, he noted, this created the bizarre situation where much of the Leipzig court's time was 'spent in frantic efforts to refute the accusations of the *Brown Book* and the findings of the Counter Trial', even to the extent that the *Brown Book* came to be referred to as the 'sixth defendant'. The fact that a Supreme Court should concentrate so much effort on 'refuting accusations by a third, extraneous party' made this, Koestler thought, 'a unique event in criminal history'.[122] Still, he did recognize one significant precedent for the counter-trial: 'Muenzenberg had struck on the idea when, in search of a new propaganda stunt, he had remembered the "secret courts" of Russian revolutionaries in Czarist days.'[123] Koestler thus pointed to the irony whereby the counter-trial presented itself as the extension of liberal justice and judicial independence to Fascist Germany, but was Communist in origin and modelled on the informal justice meted out by revolutionary courts operating (like the tribunal in *Die Maßnahme*) in a state of illegality, without jurisdiction or popular legitimacy.

Pritt felt that it was essential, if the counter-trial was to succeed as propaganda, to emphasize a strong contrast between the totalitarian spectacle in Leipzig and the sober, judicial proceedings in London:

> As it was important to convince Western liberal opinion, I and most of my colleagues thought it necessary to hold the enquiry in the calmest and quietest atmosphere possible, with a procedure substantially *equivalent to that of an English Court*, and to make no appeal to the emotions, or dramatic denunciation of the Nazis—indeed, no condemnation of the Nazis at all until the evidence had been heard and a solid basis for reasoned condemnation established.
>
> It would have been easy to make such a denunciation, and it would have been very effective in some circles; but it would not have influenced the public opinion we wished to win, which would best be impressed by our elucidating the true facts by reliable evidence.[124]

The adherence to the procedural and atmospheric norms of English justice was vital to the theatrical effect: an understated, modern theatre was what was required, where extravagant and melodramatic gestures were banned. When H. G. Wells—who attended the first day of the hearing—wrote to Pritt to tell him that 'he had never attended a duller show in his life', Pritt replied that he 'could not have paid a more welcome compliment to our

---

[122] Koestler, *The Invisible Writing*, 244–5.   [123] Ibid. 244.
[124] Pritt, *From Right to Left*, 54–5 (my emphasis).

success in holding the hearing in a sober and judicial atmosphere'.[125] When high-ranking Comintern official Otto Katz wrote to Pritt to suggest that the Inquiry Commission continue its work to campaign for the release of the acquitted men and identify the real culprits, Pritt declined to participate. His revealing response—a copy of which is held in his MI5 file—stressed that the Commission and the Secretariat had 'done good work, and achieved much' but that 'if they now enter into the general field of controversy they will in my opinion greatly weaken the effect and value of the work they have done, in that they will give to critics in Germany and elsewhere ground for saying that they are a mere propaganda organisation and not a truly judicial body at all'.[126]

Koestler—who of course, unlike Pritt, had disavowed all sympathy for Communism and the Soviet Union—went further in condemning the counter-trial which, though it may have reached a just conclusion, was essentially to be understood as a vehicle for Soviet propaganda. The 'World Committee for the Relief of the Victims of German Fascism' where Koestler was working, monitoring the British press and public opinion, sending out press releases about the counter-trial, was quite simply 'the Comintern's propaganda headquarters in Paris, camouflaged'. The Leipzig trial and the London counter-trial were *both* examples of totalitarian propaganda:

> the world was not yet accustomed to the stage-effects, the fantastic swindles and cloak-and-dagger methods of totalitarian propaganda. And in this case there was not one producer of the show, as later in the Moscow trials but two, who played out their tricks against each other like rival medicine men before the assembled tribe.[127]

The sober tone that the enquiry adopted was a masterpiece of Communist propaganda, Koestler felt, winning over liberal opinion with a theatrical display of seriousness and an almost pedantic adherence to procedural norms. And Koestler felt it was astonishingly successful: 'The world thought that it was witnessing a classic struggle between truth and falsehood, guilt and innocence.'[128]

---

[125] Ibid. 57–8.
[126] D. N. Pritt to Otto Katz, 31 Jan. 1934, The National Archives, Kew (KV 2/1062).
[127] Koestler, *The Invisible Writing*, 242.
[128] Ibid. 237. The use of the 'mock trial' to pass judgement on the new totalitarian states was catching on. On 7 Mar. 1934 the American Jewish Congress staged a 'mock trial of Adolf Hitler' in Madison Square Garden, New York City, finding Hitler guilty of 'high crimes against civilisation' before a live audience of 20,000, with more tuning in to a live radio broadcast. As Louis Anthes writes, 'its organisers deployed the spectacle of legal formality', though in reality the result was never in doubt. Among those giving evidence in New York was Arthur Garfield-Hays, the American representative on the Reichstag Fire

Writing the Moscow Trials

If Pritt emerged from the counter-trial as a symbolic champion of liberal justice over its totalitarian distortions, this was somewhat ironic given that, as we have seen, his legal thinking was fundamentally influenced by his study of Soviet law in 1932, and the scepticism towards bourgeois legal norms that this helped to foster. The irony intensifies when we consider the role that Pritt subsequently played as an observer at the Zinoviev Trial in 1936, becoming the most prominent public defender of the proceedings. *The Daily Worker* (the leading Communist paper) reported on a meeting held by the Friends of the Soviet Union at Conway Hall, where Pritt had spoken in defence of the trial. The headline, 'Critics of Moscow Trial Crushed by Lawyer Eye-Witness', set the tone for the report. Pritt claimed in his speech that the defendants 'did not appear terrorised or otherwise intimidated', that they were not denied counsel but chose to refuse it, that the prosecution was not—contrary to reports—wholly reliant on confessions, and that there was not 'a tittle of evidence' to support claims that the confessions were obtained 'by terror'.[129] The *Manchester Guardian* reported Trotsky himself intervening to condemn Pritt's involvement, arguing that he 'was invited by Stalin to the trials and was furnished with all sorts of privileged information'. Pritt told the *Guardian* the following day that he had never communicated with Stalin and had not been invited, but '[l]ike hundreds of other Englishmen, including several M.P.s, I went to Moscow for my holiday last summer, and while I was there the trial of Zinovieff came on'.[130]

Pritt's pamphlets *The Zinoviev Trial* (1936) and (with Pat Sloan) *The Moscow Trial was Fair* (1936) made the case more fully, seeking to

---

Enquiry Commission that Pritt chaired. Louis Anthes, 'Publicly Deliberative Drama: The 1934 Mock Trial of Adolf Hitler for "Crimes against Civilization"', *American Journal of Legal History*, 42/4 (Oct. 1998), 391. The Reichstag Fire remained an important Cold War flashpoint after the war. Fritz Tobias's *The Reichstag Fire* (London: Secker & Warburg, 1963) became a canonical account, and in the UK received the endorsement of A. J. P. Taylor. It dismissed the Enquiry Commission as Communist propaganda. More recently, legal historians Michael E. Tigar and John Mage praised 'the exemplary role played by two lawyers of the Anglo-American legal tradition'—Pritt and Arthur Garfield-Hays—who 'would be acknowledged today in the legal community as among the leading U.S. and U.K. lawyers of the first half of the twentieth century'. Michael E. Tigar and John Mage, 'The Reichstag Fire Trial, 1933–2008: The Production of Law and History', *Monthly Review*, 60/10 (Mar. 2009),<http://monthlyreview.org/2009/03/01/the-reichstag-fire-trial-1933-2008-the-production-of-law-and-history> [accessed Oct. 2016].

[129] 'Critics of Moscow Trial Crushed by Lawyer Eye-Witness', *Daily Worker*, 1 Oct. 1936, The National Archives, Kew (KV 2/1062).

[130] Cuttings from the *Manchester Guardian*, 11 Feb. 1937 and 12 Feb. 1937. The National Archives, Kew (KV 2/1062).

reassure supporters of the Popular Front he had helped to establish that they had nothing to fear from the Soviet Union.[131] He stressed that the crimes were admitted by the accused, who were 'possessed of physical and moral courage well adapted to protect them from confessing under pressure', and whose 'free-and-easy' demeanour was striking.[132] While the first demand of Muenzenberg's campaign against the Reichstag Fire Trial was 'Free choice of counsel for the accused', and Pritt himself had unsuccessfully put himself forward to defend Dimitrov, here he insisted that Zinoviev and the other defendants renounced their right to counsel voluntarily.[133] Pritt's defence of the proceedings often turned around the idea that they conformed in key respects to the norms of English justice. He noted that the prosecution witnesses were examined by the prisoners 'with the same freedom as would have been the case in England', for example. Where the proceedings did deviate from these norms, Pritt implied that they improved upon them:

> The most striking novelty, perhaps, to an English lawyer, was the easy way in which first one and then another prisoner would intervene in the course of the examination of one of their co-defendants, without any objection from the Court or from the prosecutor, so that one got the impression of a quick and vivid debate between four people, the prosecutor and three prisoners, all talking together, if not actually at the same moment—a method which, whilst impossible with a jury, is certainly conducive to clearing up disputes of fact with some rapidity.[134]

The importance of informality in Pritt's understanding of Soviet justice in his 1932 paper has been established, but it is at odds with his approach to the Reichstag Fire Trial, which involved holding the judicial practices of a corrupt foreign power accountable to the norms of the English courts.

Pritt embodied a form of double dealing that is also present in other Communist legal thinking. Dudley Collard—a Communist lawyer who like Pritt was an observer at the Zinoviev Trial—condemned Nazi justice in a similar way, for example at a meeting of the Relief Committee for the Victims of Fascism, held at Essex Hall in November 1937. Special Branch

---

[131] D. N. Pritt, *The Zinoviev Trial* (London: Victor Gollancz, 1936), D. N. Pritt, *The Moscow Trial was Fair, with Additional Material on the Personalities and Background of the Trial by Pat Sloane* (London: Russia Today, 1936).

[132] Pritt, *The Moscow Trial was Fair*, 6.

[133] World Committee for the Relief of the Victims of German Fascism, *The Reichstag Fire Trial*, 87; Pritt, *The Moscow Trial was Fair*, 6.

[134] Pritt, *The Moscow Trial was Fair*, 6.

sent a spy to the meeting, who summarized Collard's speech for his MI5 file:

> He said that the law of this country had been built up on certain principles for the past hundred years. These principles were such as the equality of man, the independence of Judges and lawyers, and the principle that no man could be tried twice for the same offence. Such principles were the basis of the law in most European countries, but in Fascist countries there had been a gradual drifting away from these principles....
>
> He then read through the code formulated under National Socialism upon which German law was based, and pointed out how the general principles of law were being violated. A political offender in Germany, for instance, could be imprisoned indefinitely as a 'protective measure'. It was also clear that under this case certain pronouncements of the Fuhrer could be accepted as law.[135]

Like Pritt in the Reichstag Fire Enquiry, Collard's strategy when it came to the 'general principles of law' in Nazi Germany was to reassert the liberal norms of English justice.

As with Pritt, Collard took a different tack when asked to account for the conduct of Soviet justice. Special Branch had observed another public appearance by Collard a few months earlier, at a meeting of the Marylebone Left Book Club that focused on 'The Moscow Trial'. Collard noted a widespread 'feeling of suspicion for other countries whose legal systems were not similar to our own', which was 'exemplified in the case of the Moscow trial, upon which the majority of British people looked askance'. Collard thought if people had been present at the trial itself, they would take a different view. He praised both the judge and Vyshisky, the state prosecutor, who 'far from thundering at the accused, as had been stated in the *Daily Express*, had treated them with the utmost politeness, and in addition, had been brilliant in his prosecution of them'.[136] Where he had been willing to draw on the settled traditions of the English Common Law tradition in making his criticisms of Nazi justice, when it came to the Moscow trial he urged his listeners to be open to 'legal systems...not similar to our own'.

Collard continued to act as a public defender of the trials. In 1937, he attended the trial of Radek and others (the so called 'Trial of the Seventeen'), and like Pritt he drew on his legal knowledge and credentials to reassure wavering members of the British Left that the trials were legitimate. These justifications could be found in Collard's book *Soviet*

---

[135] 'Special Report', dated 22 Nov. 1937, The National Archives, Kew (KV 2/2159).
[136] 'Special Report', dated 28 Apr. 1937, The National Archives, Kew (KV 2/2159).

Justice and the Trial of Radek and Others (1937), published by Gollancz with a preface by Pritt, and were cited approvingly in the *Daily Worker*.[137] Collard also made the case in hostile papers. The *Daily Herald* had been one of the left-wing newspapers to criticize the trials frankly. On the day that the verdict was passed on Radek and the other defendants, the *Herald* noted in a leader that Communism was 'hideously scarred by the trial', whether you believed the confessions or thought the whole trial was a frame-up. After all, if the confessions were true, '[i]t must be an intense and repressive dictatorship which drives the Old Bolshevik Opposition into treason, assassination and Fascism'. If the confessions were faked, 'it must be a brutal and vindictive dictatorship which executes or imprisons Old Bolsheviks because they disagree with Stalin'.[138] But the *Herald* also published an account of the proceedings by Collard, stressing that he was the 'only English barrister attending the trial'. Collard in turn asserted that he was 'following it independently and studying it from a legal, rather than a political, viewpoint'. He reminded readers that 'Soviet court procedure resembles that of most Continental countries in form and differs widely from that in Britain', which he hoped would reassure them that there was nothing extraordinary in conducting the initial investigation in private. He reserved special praise for Vyshinsky, who treated the prisoners 'with remarkable restraint and courtesy'.[139] As Peter Deli describes, Collard also participated in a controversy in the pages of the *New Statesman and Nation*, where an editorial by Kingsley Martin followed the *Herald*'s line, suggesting that the reputation of Communism was damaged by the trials whether the confessions were fake or not.[140] Collard's response led to an ongoing controversy in the letters pages.

There was no left-wing consensus about the rights and wrongs of the Moscow Trials.[141] Few onlookers were completely convinced by the conduct of the trials and many were strident in their criticisms of the proceedings. In his pamphlet *The Witchcraft Trial in Moscow* (1936),

[137] Dudley Collard, *Soviet Justice and the Trial of Radek and Others* (London: Victor Gollancz, 1937); 'Soviet Trial Is Fair Says British Lawyer in Moscow', *Daily Worker* (Friday 27 Jan. 1937), 8.

[138] 'Moscow Sentences' (leader), *Daily Herald* (30 Jan. 1937), 8.

[139] 'British Lawyer's Moscow Trial Story—"Frame-Up Out Of Question"', *Daily Herald* (28 Jan. 1937), 1–2.

[140] Peter Deli, 'The Image of the Russian Purges in the *Daily Herald* and the *New Statesman*', *Journal of Contemporary History*, 20/2 (Apr. 1985), 272.

[141] Bill Jones perhaps went too far in implying that the left was duped, wholesale, by the trials in Bill Jones, *The Russia Complex: The British Labour Party and the Soviet Union* (Manchester: Manchester University Press, 1977), 23–4. Paul Corthorn is more measured in an article that explores a wide-ranging and contentious debate in the left-wing press. Paul Corthorn 'Labour, the Left, and the Stalinist Purges of the Late 1930s', *Historical Journal*, 48/1 (Mar. 2005), 202.

the Austrian socialist Friedrich Adler considered the legitimacy of the Zinoviev Trial and its conclusions based only on the published record of the proceedings. Adler dedicated several pages to countering D. N. Pritt's defence of the trial. He first conceded that what Pritt had to say counted as 'noteworthy' because of the 'invaluable service' he had performed in the Reichstag Fire Counter-Trial, where he 'rightly earned the thanks of all anti-Fascists'.[142] But now Adler drew a direct parallel between the Reichstag Fire Trial and the Moscow Trials:

> Pritt actually knows better than many others what efforts were made by the friends of Dimitrov and the other Communist defendants in the Reichstag Fire Trial to secure the admission of foreign lawyers and particularly the admission of Pritt. He himself took a prominent part in these efforts!
>
> Unfortunately, Pritt was not admitted as counsel to the Reichstag Fire Trial in Leipzig and so the expedient of the counter-trial was necessary. We are convinced that if Pritt could emancipate himself from his function as the defender of Vyshinsky he would already be obliged in light of what is known regarding the false confessions in the Moscow Trial to express the same judgement as he pronounced at the end of the counter trial in London with regard to the Reichstag Fire Trial in Leipzig namely that:
>
> 'The proceedings were an offence to the most primitive conceptions of humanity and justice.'[143]

Adler turned Pritt's own rhetoric against him. The principles of liberal justice may have been used to further the Communist cause, but Adler's pamphlet shows that these principles had a life of their own. Adler noted important inconsistencies in the published testimony. He pointed out, for example, that Hotel Bristol in Copenhagen, where—according to the testimony of multiple defendants—Holzman was supposed to have met Trotsky's son in 1932, was in fact pulled down in 1917.[144] Facts like this fed an international Trotskyist campaign against the trials. Soon enough, the Reichstag Fire counter-trial in which Pritt had been so instrumental spawned an imitator that sought to show the failings of the trial Pritt was now defending. This was held in Mexico in 1937, chaired by John Dewey, and it came to be known as the Dewey Commission.[145] It was initiated by

---

[142] Adler, *The Witchcraft Trial in Moscow* (London: Labour party Publications Dept, 1936), 18.

[143] Ibid. 24–5.   [144] Ibid. 14.

[145] A full transcript of the proceedings was published as Preliminary Commission of Inquiry into the Charges Made Against Leon Trotsky in the *Moscow Trials: The Case of Leon Trotsky: Report of Hearings on the Charges Made Against him in the Moscow Trials* (New York: Harper & Bros., 1937).

the American Committee for the Defence of Leon Trotsky and so it struggled to lay claim to the kind of judicial independence that Adler wanted to see.

In February 1946, during the Nuremberg Trials, the findings of the Dewey Commission were cited in an open letter published in *Forward* and signed by Orwell, Koestler, Wells, and others. The defendants in the Moscow Trials of 1936–7 had been found guilty of collaborating with senior Nazis who were now under arrest and interrogation and their papers were in Allied possession, the authors of the letter wrote. Surely, then, it should be possible to use the Nuremberg proceedings to establish once and for all whether or not the confessions heard in the Moscow Trials were true? Urging the prosecutors (among other things) to interrogate Rudolph Hess as to whether his alleged meeting with Trotsky ever took place, the writers of the letter saw an opportunity for 'an investigation aimed at the establishment of historical truth and bearing upon the political integrity of figures and tendencies of international standing'.[146] The possibility of a justice across international borders had undergone an interesting test in the Reichstag Fire counter-trial, a Communist-sponsored attempt to expose the politicization of the German courts. Ironically, the same tactic was then used to turn left-wing opinion against the Soviet Union.

Trial of a Judge

Harry Pollitt, General Secretary of the Communist Party of Great Britain, felt that the widespread discussion of the trials was stopping the Labour intelligentsia from engaging in the Spanish Civil War: '[t]his question has played a very big part here and comes up every day.... the position is exceptionally difficult', he wrote to Page Arnott in 1937.[147] Earlier that year, in the *Daily Worker*, Pollitt struck a defensive tone when he referred to the mounting pressure for a counter-trial: 'The impudent demand for an impartial international court of inquiry is made by people whose lives and activities have been conspicuous for their opposition to revolution.' Pollitt drew on legal convention to assert the sovereignty of the Soviet legal system:

> There isn't a legal man of standing in Britain, whether Liberal, Tory or Labour, who doesn't admit the competence and fairness of the Soviet Court,

---

[146] John Baird et al., 'Letter to the Editor of *Forward*', 16 Mar. 1946, in George Orwell, *The Collected Essays, Journalism and Letters of George Orwell*, iv. *In Front of Your Nose*, ed. Sonia Orwell and Ian Angus (London: Secker & Warburg, 1968), 115.

[147] Qtd. Corthorn, 'Labour, the Left, and the Stalinist Purges', 200.

and who doesn't look upon the demand for an international court as a piece of impertinence and unwarranted interference with the sovereignty of the Soviet Courts of Justice.[148]

This was a total retreat from the idealistic vision of a justice without borders that had been mobilized as Communist propaganda at the time of the Dimitrov Trial.

Pollitt saw the publication of Stephen Spender's *Forward from Liberalism* (1937) as an event with the potential to bring wavering liberal intellectuals back onside, and so help the recruitment drive for Spain. But even in *Forward from Liberalism*, Spender expressed concerns about the 'savage reprisals which followed the murder of Kirov' (many victims of the trials were accused of complicity in a conspiracy to murder Kirov). Spender noted rather ambivalently that '[i]f criticism in Russia is not to become a pernicious disease, it must be legalized'.[149] With a view to recruiting Spender into the CPGB, Pollitt invited him to a meeting, where he took him to task for these criticisms: 'He seemed to think that they were very lucky to have had such nice trials', wrote Spender later.[150] Nevertheless, the high tide of Spender's identification with the Communist Party came a few weeks after the meeting with Pollitt, in an article that appeared in the *Daily Worker* on 19 February 1937, titled 'I Join the Communist Party'. Here Spender sought to 'remove the misapprehensions for which I am alone responsible in my attitude to the Soviet trial', arguing that negative coverage in the 'capitalist Press' was a result of a 'gigantic plot against the Soviet Government'.[151] Spender's liberal friends, Isaiah Berlin in particular, were disappointed by the article.[152]

Writing in his autobiography *World within World* (1951), Spender looked back on his youthful idealism: 'In politics,' he wrote, 'I wished for a social revolution which would achieve justice without introducing new injustices into the methods used to make the revolution.'[153] At least in retrospect, it appeared to Spender first that *justice* was a primary consideration, and secondly that the moral compromises explored by Brecht—the sacrifice of bourgeois legal norms to the ends of political revolution—would be impossible for him to make.

---

[148] 'Harry Pollitt Trounces the Critics of the Moscow Trial', *Daily Worker* (Sat. 30 Jan. 1937), 3.

[149] Stephen Spender, *Forward from Liberalism* (London: Victor Gollancz, 1937), 288.

[150] Stephen Spender, *World within World* (London: Faber & Faber, 1977), 211.

[151] Stephen Spender, 'I Join the Communist Party', *Daily Worker* (19 Feb. 1937).

[152] John Sutherland, *Stephen Spender: The Authorised Biography* (London: Penguin, 2005), 214.

[153] Spender, *World within World*, 31–2.

Much interesting and provocative moral wrangling came during Spender's period of 'aberration', as he described it in *World within World*. In *Forward from Liberalism*, Spender argued that the left should be prepared for a temporary suspension of the constitutional guarantees of liberal democracy, making way for a 'transitional . . . dictatorship against capitalism . . . during a period of reorganization'.[154] Yet if the book allowed for an interruption in the continuous traditions of liberal justice, it did not abandon the concept. Spender stated that:

> by political freedom in a liberal democracy I mean the right to vote, the right to speak freely, rights of assembly, equality before the law, freedom from imprisonment without trial, or arrest without warrant; these freedoms all point to the freedom of an equal and classless society in which they will be fulfilled in every man's life, and not remain abstractions for the poor and legal instruments of ascendency for the rich.[155]

The book is addressed to liberals, and it advises them to hitch their wagon to Communism and accept temporary dictatorship with the ultimate goal of extending liberal protections to the whole of society. Elements of the Marxist critique of justice are there—the talk of 'legal instruments of ascendancy for the rich', for example—but there is also the insistence that (after the transitional period) Communist society will be regulated by normative rights dictated by absolute ideals of justice, and implicitly that it will *need* to be regulated. As I have discussed, the classic Marxist theory of justice, elaborated in the early-Soviet period by Pashukanis, was hostile to any notion that rights and juridical institutions would be required once the class antagonisms of capitalism had been dispensed with. In the Communist future advocated in *Forward from Liberalism*, Lukes's conditions of *Recht* will still apply: Spender does not follow the Vyshinsky line in projecting a socialist basis for law, and envisages a Communist society in which political decisions are subject to the rule of law.

The Moscow Trials, the publication of *Forward from Liberalism* and the incarceration of Spender's lover Tony Hyndman at the hands of the Communists in Spain formed the backdrop to the completion of Spender's verse drama, *Trial of a Judge* (1938). The play's plot derives from the Potempa murders in Germany in 1932, where five Nazis had beaten a Polish Communist to death. They were sentenced to death, but after a campaign by Hitler (who wrote to express his 'unbounded loyalty' to the convicted men) the death sentence was commuted to life imprisonment, and the men were released after the Nazis came to power in 1933.[156] This

---

[154] Spender, *Forward from Liberalism*, 23.   [155] Ibid. 136–7.
[156] Ian Kershaw, *Hitler: A Biography* (New York: W. W. Norton & Co., 2008), 236–8.

was a plain example of political expediency trumping legal formalities. But the play also clearly channels Spender's thinking about the Moscow Trials and the Reichstag Fire Trial, dramatizing the challenges to a liberal version of 'absolute justice' from both Communism and Fascism.

The play's tragic hero is the Judge who convicts Petra's murderers and comes under political pressure from Fascist protestors and the weak-willed representatives of the liberal state to reprieve them. Shortly afterwards, he pronounces another death sentence on three Communists who have discharged a firearm while defending themselves, after carrying a gun has been made punishable by death. Although the law has been followed, the Judge feels that the law is unfair, and his conscience bids him to reprieve the Communists while punishing the Fascists. The Judge is then tried according to the 'people's justice' in an improvised court run by the Fascists, and killed.[157] During this 'trial' scene, the Second Black Prisoner—now part of the 'court'—demands the death penalty, before rounding on the Communists who have been imprisoned alongside the Judge: 'Wait till we get you out of this Court, you scum, dead or alive, it will all be the same in twenty-four hours. Lamp posts, sewers, knives, quick-lime.'[158] In precisely what combination these four things will be used to bring about a painful death is not clear. But it does seem likely that the 'quick-lime' is a reference to the lime pit in Brecht's *Die Maßnahme*, which Spender—a long-time admirer of Brecht—likely saw when he was in Berlin in the early 1930s.

Trial of a Judge revisits the central moral problem of *Die Maßnahme*. Spender's play is a profound meditation on the changing forms of justice as liberalism faced an existential crisis. By taking Nazi justice as its starting point, and putting it into relation with versions of liberal and Communist justice, Spender further complicates the problem. For John Lehmann, the play's theme was 'the hopelessness of being a 'Liberal' when society's decay is being ruthlessly exploited by Fascism'.[159] The Judge's experiences highlight some of the problems of disinterested justice which become particularly acute in the specific context of the rise of Nazism, where both the legislature and the judiciary sought to hold off a revolution by conceding ground to Nazi demands. The Judge is opposed to the death penalty, and in the soliloquy that opens the play, where he has just sentenced Petra's murderers to death, he muses that:

---

[157] Stephen Spender, *Trial of a Judge: A Tragic Statement in Five Acts* (London: Faber & Faber, 1938), 74.

[158] Ibid. 73.

[159] John Lehmann qtd. in Hugh David, *Stephen Spender: A Portrait with Background* (London: Heinemann, 1992), 212.

Every word was true. Not one word
Does my conscience take back.
Yet to call murder murder is a kind of killing.[160]

The Judge's personal beliefs about the rights and wrongs of the death penalty do not determine the verdict or the sentence, but the law as it is means that the correct verdict leads to executions. He speaks for, in his own words: 'the survival of a vision / Within the human memory / Of absolute justice accepted by consent'.[161] The tension between the Judge's willingness to 'consent' to the rule of law, and his feeling that the law on this point is wrong, is a standard feature of liberal justice.

The Judge's impartiality meets with a sterner test, however, when he passes the death sentence on some Communists for the relatively minor crime of carrying a gun, again following the law exactly. The Judge is struck here by an injustice, and by an awareness that the legislation that he is required to apply in a disinterested manner may be unjust:

> Now, suddenly, a new law is passed, making it illegal to carry firearms: so that when a street fight takes place in which some of these young people are attacked by Black Troops—or even by the police—I am asked to sentence them to the same death penalty I passed on Petra's murderers. Yet this morning's case was a very different one from the planned bestiality of Petra's murder.[162]

It seems to Spender's judge that this law deviates drastically from the standards of what he calls 'absolute justice', and as such the 'consent' to the rule of law is in danger.

Spender's play juxtaposes two cases and two verdicts with different political significances. When the Judge comes under political pressure to reprieve the Black Prisoners, impartial justice would seem to serve the political ends of the Popular Front, uniting liberals and Communists against the Fascist murderers. The government itself does not accept the rule of law, and is willing to bend or break laws in order to placate the Fascist mob. Hummeldorf, the Home Secretary, argues that the Black Prisoners must be reprieved in order to prevent them becoming martyrs and triggering a Fascist revolution. 'I always say that we can waive all rules / As long as we still rule those waving waves!', he says.[163] And he admonishes the Judge: '[y]ou seem to forget that the law is intended to protect the State from enemies and not to fulfil an abstract idea of justice'.[164] Given the Judge's strong desire to reprieve the Communists,

---

[160] Spender, *Trial*, 13. [161] Ibid. 30. [162] Ibid. 38. [163] Ibid. 44.
[164] Ibid. 42.

he offers a tradeoff, proposing that both sets of criminals be reprieved, appeasing the outraged Fascist mob on the one hand and his conscience on the other. Hummeldorf tells him that this too will be politically unacceptable: 'Let me tell you that, within a month, to be a communist will be an offence punishable with the executioner's axe.'[165] Political necessity demands that the Fascists be reprieved, while the Communists are executed for their more minor crime. Only in this way, Hummeldorf argues—only by breaking with the principle of the rule of law—can the liberal order be maintained. The Reds are contemptuous of the Judge's seeming vacillation, yet they can also be sarcastic about his supposed impartiality. As Petra's brother, a Communist, says:

> I tell you, this impartial judge
> Weaker than his own justice, shall smile
> And pardon Petra's murderers.[166]

The brother is digging sarcastically here at the hypocrisy of bourgeois justice: the problem in this case is that this justice cannot live up to its own standards, by which there would be no reprieve (as the judge himself acknowledges) for Petra's killers. While the play turns around the parallel between these two crimes, the situation is asymmetrical: the law is systematically biased against Communists. Yet in the case of the convicted Communists, the situation plays out differently: here, the Communists (including Petra's brother, fiancée, and mother) ask that the Judge set aside his impartial application of the law, and reprieve the Communists.

Following the reprieve of the Black Prisoners, there is a scene in which two mobs, the Red Chorus and the Black Chorus, confront each other in the street, armed with guns. The Judge comes out onto the balcony and says:

> Do not put away your revolvers.
> If you wish, shoot, I may not protest.
> For I come to announce not my own resignation
> But the resignation of the law.[167]

The Judge suggests that the reprieve the Black Prisoners will lead to a breakdown of the rule of law, allowing vigilante justice and creating a dangerous situation where blood is repaid with blood.

> The precedent
> Licenses their acts to flourish like a tree
> Spreading murder which grows branches
> Above that soil where the law is buried.[168]

---

[165] Ibid. 44.   [166] Ibid. 23.   [167] Ibid. 57.   [168] Ibid.

The Judge himself had complained of the restrictions that the law imposed on him—he had to sentence the Communists (with whose actions he sympathized) to death when the law demanded it. But though the law, which was capable of outrageous unfairness, is buried, the Judge is still powerless to reprieve the Communists. He explains to Petra's brother:

> The same accomplished fact
> As freed Petra's murderers, sealed your friends' death
> And set a dam across my mouth
> Beyond which no Judgement may flow.[169]

The role that an independent and impartial justice must play, of adjudicating between persons viewed as equal before the law, has no place in the world of Spender's play. As one of the Black Prisoners says: 'When liberal justice whines of violence / Power flies to those with the right of might'.[170] The only thing, implicitly, that Liberal justice can do to stop Fascism is to take sides: to accept that law is simply the violent, coercive instrument of politics and stop pretending to be impartial.

In *Trial of a Judge*, impartial justice comes under attack from both Nazis and Communists. The difference between the two is that while the Red Chorus see 'justice' as part of the ideological superstructure of bourgeois society, the Black Chorus take the racist view that bourgeois justice is a specifically Jewish conspiracy. For example, at the beginning of the 'trial' in Act 4:

THIRD BLACK PRISONER: Heads will roll. Blood must flow.

FIRST BLACK PRISONER: Your Lordship, we find all the prisoners guilty.

SECOND BLACK PRISONER: Discretion, my friend, discretion. You and I, who are in the confidence of the government, we know they're guilty, but we don't say so till we've tried them.

FIRST BLACK PRISONER: Steady, steady, steady. In my opinion, that's a very tendentious thing to say . . . the sort of bastard impartial thing a Jew might say. Guilty! Of course they're guilty!

For the Fascists, the formal procedures of justice are simply a performance designed to conceal the exercise of naked power. The Second Black Prisoner urges 'discretion' in the same way that Pritt had urged that the Reichstag counter-trial must do everything to *appear* like a legitimate court, even though it had no actual jurisdiction. Moreover, according to the First Black Prisoner, the need so to disguise the operations of pure power is a piece of Jewish deception.

---

[169] Ibid. 58.   [170] Ibid. 29.

The Judge stands for the rule of law, and the tragedy of the play is that he fails. This failure is encouraged by Hummeldorf, the liberal statesman who compromised with Fascism to avoid a violent confrontation with it, who is willing to use totalitarian methods to protect the liberal state. He tells the Judge, as he tries to convince him to reprieve the Black Prisoners:

> Abstract justice is nonsense. This is war.
> So kill, kill, kill.[171]

But the play shows—perhaps despite itself—that the Communist critique of justice is fraught with the same danger. Petra's wife, one of the play's Communists, ends the play with this speech:

> But I comfort myself that his dream has come true.
> How he would love to have seen
> The soldiers march towards the boundaries,
> Our men's faces in uniforms all one face,
> The face of those who enter a wood
> Whose branches bleed and skies hail lead.
> And the aerial vultures fly
> Over the deserts which were cities.
> Kill! Kill! Kill! Kill!'[172]

The words exactly mirror those of Hummeldorf earlier in the play—only with the addition of exclamation marks and an additional 'Kill!'. The repetition of this phrase signals an equivalence between Nazi and Communist conceptions of law and plays into the idea of a binary opposition between liberal and totalitarian legal systems.

While the play documented the demise of the Judge—and with him the liberal justice that he represented—unlike *Die Maßnahme* it did not celebrate Communist justice as an alternative. Indeed, as its reception among the Communists seems to suggest, it mourned the passing of 'absolute justice' and seemed to long for its reinstatement. Louis MacNeice's analysis in his autobiography suggested that Spender's play had reached this conclusion despite its author's intentions:

> The intended moral of the play was that liberalism today was weak and wrong, communism was strong and right. But this moral was sabotaged by S.'s unconscious integrity; the Liberal Judge, his example of what-not-to-be, walked away with one's sympathy.[173]

---

[171] Ibid. 43.   [172] Ibid. 115.
[173] Louis MacNeice, *The Strings are False: An Unfinished Autobiography* (London: Faber & Faber, 1996), 167.

MacNeice goes on to describe an 'exhilarating evening' at 'a meeting arranged by the Group Theatre to discuss the play'. A 'squad' of Comrades 'turned up to reprove S. for his heresies'. One elderly comrade pointed out that

> S. could not have meant it, there must have been a mistake, but the writing seemed to imply an acceptance of Abstract Justice, a thing which we know is non-existent. S. deliberately towered into blasphemy. Abstract Justice, he said, of course he meant it; and what was more it existed.[174]

This conviction seems to me to run throughout Spender's work, and forms a crucial context for understanding his engagement with Marxism and his turn to anti-Communism.

Those writers who engaged with the Russian Revolution through the lens of law ran up against profound moral questions. To face up to the Moscow Trials often involved the uncomfortable acknowledgement that justice had a performative dimension, even at home. Rising up in condemnation of the trials led former Marxists to question the grounds on which such a condemnation could be made. 'Justice', when mobilized across national borders, seemed to summon moral and legal absolutes that the Marxist critique of *Recht* had taught them to treat with scepticism, as merely the expression of bourgeois class interests. Yet questions about how to leverage a Marxist critique of *Recht* into a practical programme for government—as in the Pashukanis-Vyshinsky debate, which resonated in Britain—made manifest the problems of an anti-normative approach to ethics and law. Many liberals fell back on ideas of 'absolute justice'—none more vigorously than the ex-Communists who Arendt feared could become totalitarian in their anti-Communism. But (as Geras and Lukes insisted) Marxism also frequently invoked powerful ethical and even legal norms—albeit implicitly, in the force of its denunciations of capitalist exploitation, and in the face of the critique of law that was more explicitly articulated in Marx's own work and in the tradition he inaugurated. In grappling with Soviet law, in theory and in practice, the British intellectuals whose work I have explored in this chapter highlight ongoing tensions and overlaps between attempts to relativize ethical and legal norms and ideas of 'absolute' justice, whether liberal or Marxist in origin.

---

[174] Ibid. 168.

4

Homestead versus Kolschoz

SOCIALISM AND THE SOIL

Rural-Intellectual Radicalism

Ezra Pound's anti-Communism had at its heart the question of land. In Canto 103, he made a striking opposition: 'Homestead versus Kolschoz / Rome versus Babylon'.[1] In so doing he called for an agricultural anti-Communism, a way of opposing the kolkhoz or collective farm that was for him the cornerstone of Bolshevik ideology. For Pound, the homestead was an element of his American heritage that was being trampled both by monopoly capitalism and by the Babylon of Soviet-style Communism. He wrote, in a note to *Strike* magazine in October 1955: 'We ask "The Voice of America" if they are making full use of this idea in the fight against Communism in China. Bolshevism started off as an attack against loan-capital and quickly shifted into an attack against the homestead.'[2] Anti-Communism had been intellectually stymied because it felt the need to defend 'loan capital' against the Bolshevik critique, and loan capital (partly for anti-Semitic reasons) was indefensible in Pound's view. The homestead—connected to a vision of small tenant farmers working the land on a subsistence basis—offered for Pound a positive, peasant-orientated model that could be opposed to the heavily industrialized Soviet kolkhoz, or collective farm. Pound's views on this issue have tended to be understood in terms of his position in a 'tradition of monetary radicals and cranks', as well as through his own Fascism.[3] Pound felt that his voice was not being heard and that, despite his advocacy, the homestead was not being used in anti-Communist campaigns. He

---

[1] Ezra Pound, *The Cantos of Ezra Pound* (New York: New Directions Books, 1996), 752. Where Pound transliterates as 'kolschoz', I will for the sake of consistency use 'kolkhoz' except when I am quoting him directly.

[2] Ezra Pound, quoted in Carroll Franklin Terrell, *A Companion to the Cantos of Ezra Pound* (Berkeley-Los Angeles: University of California Press, 1984), 664.

[3] Meghnad Desai, *The Route of All Evil: The Political Economy of Ezra Pound* (London: Faber & Faber, 2006).

complained in a 1954 letter to Olivia Rosetti Agresti of the 'Dulness of anti communist propaganda, which fails to set HOMESTEAD against kolschoz.'[4] Tyrus Miller has diagnosed a particular variant on anti-Communism that is embodied in E. E. Cummings's *Eimi*—a modernist travelogue describing a journey in the Soviet Union—which is fundamentally concerned with 'anti-Communism's insufficiency and failure to emerge'.[5] Pound—a passionate admirer of *Eimi*—frequently voiced a similar frustration, while also offering a possible solution.[6] If anti-Communism had conventionally been seen as a 'negative, second order ideology' with no positive content, Pound offers the homestead as a way of articulating a positive anti-Communism, less infected by dullness than existing models.[7] Communism, for Pound, could only be defeated with a positive programme that asserted that 'civilisation is from the podere, the homestead'.[8]

This chapter explores the political and intellectual background of Pound's striking opposition, and argues that anti-Communism—broadly conceived—often *did* put forward various versions of smallholding as an alternative to Soviet agricultural collectivism. This was not some arid technical debate about land tenure, however: it struck to the heart of writers' emotional connections to the soil, and their thinking about food and its production. I will argue that Pound's articulation of the binary 'homestead versus kolschoz' is a late and distinctly American twist on a theme which had animated English socialism in the nineteenth century. Left-leaning intellectuals' relationship to the land was challenged and disrupted by the progress of the Russian Revolution, which in certain respects seemed to invert assumptions about how a just society would produce its food, just as it launched an attack on the peasant smallholder, often a heroic figure for British radicals and socialists.

Pound's binary could be translated into British terms as 'Cottage Economy or Collective Farm'. The first term—associated with Romantic, individualistic, anarchistic, and medievalist forms of socialism—was arguably the prominent way of imagining socialist agriculture in England

---

[4] Ezra Pound to Olivia Rosetti, 5 Apr. 1954, in *'I Cease Not to Yowl': Ezra Pound's Letters to Olivia Rosetti,* ed. Demetres P. Tryphonopolous and Leon Surette (Urbana, IL: University of Illinois Press, 1998), 145.

[5] Tyrus Miller, 'Comrade Kemminkz in Hell: E. E. Cummings's *Eimi* and Anti-Communism', *Literature and History,* 24/2 (2015). 25.

[6] Pound's love of *Eimi* is well documented in *Pound/Cummings: The Correspondence of Ezra Pound and E. E. Cummings,* ed. Barry Hearn (Ann Arbor: University of Michigan Press, 1996), *passim,* see in particular 'Introduction', 3.

[7] Benjamin Kohlmann and Matthew Taunton, 'Introduction: Literatures of Anti-Communism', *Literature and History,* 24/2 (2015), 6.

[8] Pound, *I Cease Not to Yowl,* 145.

during the nineteenth century. The phrase originated in the title of William Cobbett's *Cottage Economy* (1822) and Cobbett—with his mixture of radicalism and conservatism—embodied many of the characteristics and contradictions of the later tradition. *Cottage Economy* was a manual of practical advice for labourers, showing them how to produce their own food, but it also stressed the practical and moral benefits of smallholding. Cobbett wrote that

> from a very small piece of ground, a large part of the food of a considerable family may be raised, the very act of raising it will be the best possible foundation of *education* of the children of the labourer; . . . it will teach them a great number of useful things . . . and give them the best chance of leading happy lives.[9]

Viewed in the context of Cobbett's wider critique of industrialism, this can be seen to form part of a recognizably radical tradition. Cobbett aimed to create (or, as he saw it, to restore) a class of free peasant proprietors capable of feeding themselves on a subsistence basis. In *owning* their three acres and a cow, the family of peasant smallholders would achieve independence as well as freedom from hunger—and a range of moral benefits. It was this independence that Pound valued in his celebrations of the homestead. For advocates of the cottage economy, the emphasis is usually on the *quality* of the food and the moral benefits of growing it in this way, rather than the statistical measurement of outputs that tends to preoccupy advocates of collective farming.

The kolkhoz or collective farm—associated with bureaucratic, utilitarian, statist socialism and above all with the USSR—was largely a theoretical construct until the advent of the Bolshevik Revolution. In theory they were owned by the people, and in practice administered by the state. In contrast to the reversion to primitive techniques recommended by Cobbett, William Morris, and Edward Carpenter, advocates of collective farming gloried in new technology, tractors, and efficiency, and instead of small plots, collective farms were to be vast. Industrialized farming techniques would increase yields and reduce labour time. The rhetorical justification for collective farming usually emphasized the *quantity*, rather than quality, of food (commonly imagined as 'grain') produced. The increasing dominance of the collective farm in the socialist imagination, especially following agricultural collectivization in the USSR, was an affront to the cottage economy tradition, but it also played into a pre-existing

---

[9] William Cobbett, *Cottage Economy; Containing Information Relative to the Brewing of Beer, Making of Bread, Keeping of Cows, Pigs, Bees, Ewes, Goats, Poultry, Etc* (London: C. Clement, 1822), 8–9.

debate within nineteenth-century socialism. Perry Anderson has argued that the history of socialism can be seen as a conflict between the aesthetic, Romantic socialism of William Morris and the 'crassly neo-Benthamite utopia of mechanized industrial regimentation' of Edward Bellamy's *Looking Backward*.[10] Anna Vaninskaya makes a similar distinction, linking George Orwell to Morris as part of a Romantic socialist tradition that 'opposes a utopian vision of decentralized democratic community to the evils of rationalist utilitarianism, bureaucracy, and industrial regimentation'.[11] Such are the origins of the opposition between the (Romantic) cottage economy and the (utilitarian) collective farm.

In *The Country and the City* (1973), Raymond Williams explored a history of thinking about a 'golden age' of the rural economy, with a complex and often contradictory politics. He described 'a precarious but persistent rural-intellectual radicalism' that is 'genuinely and actively hostile to industrialism and capitalism; opposed to commercialism and to the exploitation of environment; attached to country ways and feelings, the literature and the lore'.[12] Given that this British tradition of 'rural-intellectual radicalism' is based on an idealized vision of the medieval past—summoning a vision of 'a "natural" subsistence agriculture'—Williams rightly emphasized that the very existence of an independent, land-owning yeomanry in the medieval period is 'doubtful and subject to many exceptions', and moreover that, even where it did exist, 'the social order in which this agriculture was practised was as hard and brutal as anything later experienced'.[13]

Such rural nostalgia relied on certain delusions about the historical past, then, but how pervasive was it? The extent to which purely backward-looking ideas of a rural past form the central strand of 'Englishness' has been much debated since the publication of Martin Weiner's *English Culture and the Decline of the Industrial Spirit 1850–1950* (1981).[14] Since one of the implications of the present chapter is that evocations of a rural 'Merrie England' played an important role in articulating cultural (and agricultural) resistance to Bolshevism, it will be prudent to pause briefly to consider how central this nostalgic and rural 'Englishness'

---

[10] Perry Anderson, *Arguments within English Marxism* (London: Verso Editions, NLB, 1980), 169.

[11] Anna Vaninskaya, 'Janus-Faced Fictions: Socialism as Utopia and Dystopia in Willam Morris and George Orwell', *Utopian Studies*, 14/2 (2003), 84.

[12] Raymond Williams, *The Country and the City* (New York: OUP, 1973), 36.

[13] Ibid. 37.

[14] Martin Weiner, *English Culture and the Decline of the Industrial Spirit 1850–1950* (Cambridge: CUP, 1981). Weiner's arguments were taken up e.g. in Robert Colls and Philip Dodd (eds), *Englishness: Politics and Culture 1880–1920* (London: Croom Helm, 1986).

actually was. Peter Mandler has argued that, while one can find examples of nostalgic, 'back to the land' thinking both in the late Victorian period and between the wars, these were not representative, and moreover—far from being, to adapt E. P. Thompson's phrase, a 'peculiarity of the English'—'a nostalgic interest in the countryside actually had less place in England than elsewhere in Europe'.[15] Surveying some of the evidence often adduced in favour of the thesis that 'Englishness' was characterized by a bucolic Romanticism, Mandler concludes that '[w]orks like these were . . . not uncontroversial appeals to a consensual "Englishness" but were rather angry and fiercely partisan, immediately recognisable to contemporary readers as bearing a specific aesthetic and political charge'. Such a 'political charge' is implicit in Williams's notion of a 'rural-intellectual radicalism', and it is essential to the argument of the present chapter that this was not part of some hegemonic 'Englishness' but an urgent and insurrectionary critique of capitalism. However, when Mandler goes on to say that advocates of a bucolic Merrie England 'came from tiny romantic minorities' in their respective political traditions, 'railing against their philistine masters', he underrates the importance of rural-intellectual radicalism within the mainstream of English socialism in the nineteenth century.[16] The cottage economy was also more international than the 'Englishness' thesis implies, and advocates frequently had recourse to other national traditions of land tenure, not least the American homestead and the Italian podere: apart from Pound, Mussolini's Fascism was hailed by Chesterton, A. J. Penty, and others as a practical programme for the revival of peasant proprietorship that the English should aim to emulate as a means of resisting Bolshevism.

If the cottage economy tradition generally relied on a historically inaccurate picture of the peasant past, how far did this colour its political programme as a purely nostalgic or reactionary one? For Williams, 'the moment comes when any critique of the present must choose its bearings, between past and future'.[17] Williams saw socialism as the only rightful successor to capitalism, but also acknowledged that certain versions of socialism (implicitly the Soviet variety) merely 'offer to complete the capitalist enterprise'. Seeming to muse on the legacy of Soviet agricultural policy for the socialist project in Britain, Williams wrote:

> We hear again and again this brisk, impatient and as it is said realistic response: to the productive efficiency, the newly liberated forces, of the

---

[15] Peter Mandler, 'Against "Englishness": English Culture and the Limits to Rural Nostalgia, 1850–1940', *Transactions of the Royal Historical Society*, 7 (1997), 157.
[16] Ibid. 168.   [17] Williams, *The Country and the City*, 36.

capitalist breakthrough; a simultaneous damnation and idealisation of capitalism, in its specific forms of urban and industrial development; an unreflecting celebration of mastery—power, yield, production, man's mastery of nature—as if the exploitation of natural resources could be separated from the accompanying exploitation of men.[18]

The prioritization of 'yield' over more qualitative considerations, however romantic these may sound—rural community, connection with the soil, and the rhythm of the seasons—seems to have encapsulated for Williams the inhumanity of that socialism which takes its cues from the Soviet experiment. Even so, Williams ascribed a rather limited role to what he calls an 'old, sad, retrospective radicalism' that, in the face of a militantly industrializing Soviet Communism, 'seems to bear and to embody a human concern'.[19] This chapter seeks to go further than Williams did in recovering the cottage economy ideal from the realm of pure reactionary nostalgia: as I hope to show, it was not only a retrospective fantasy about a medieval past, but also a vital tool for critics of Soviet agricultural policy, and one that offered a utopian, future-oriented alternative to collectivism. Indeed, in the terms I set out in Chapter 1, the cottage economy was one way in which a vision of a post-capitalist but decisively non-Bolshevik future could still be articulated after 1917.

From Tolstoy to Free Trade

English socialism in the nineteenth century produced nuanced positions on agricultural land tenure: forms of collectivism and even campaigns for the unilateral nationalization of all farmland were tempered—or indeed often motivated—by the cottage economy ideal. The land must be nationalized, socialists like Morris and Robert Blatchford (author of *Merrie England* (1893)) argued, in order that a free yeomanry, wrenched from the land during the agricultural revolution, might be restored to the land. Russia already played a role in such debates because of the influence of Tolstoyanism. Tolstoy's teachings were based on non-violence, a Christian anarchism that entirely refused the authority of the state, and a return to a simple life based on subsistence agriculture. This was taken up by

---

[18] Ibid. 37. One can see why members of the New Left, who sought to reactivate what was progressive in the English radical tradition in contradistinction to the Soviet version of socialism, were sometimes drawn to the figures of the Soviet Right Opposition such as Bukharin, who advocated a conciliatory approach to the peasantry. Connectedly, it is worth noting that, in this context at least, Williams's arguments are even more hostile to Trotskyism (whose historic role had been to advocate an *accelerated* programme of agricultural industrialization and collectivization) than they are to Stalinism.

[19] Ibid. 37.

British intellectuals including John Kenworthy and John Bruce Wallace, and in groups including the Croydon Brotherhood Church and its colony in Purleigh, Essex.[20] The reception of these ideas in Britain, as Charlotte Alston has argued, was partly conditioned by the existence there of 'a strong tradition of back-to-the-land utopian communities'.[21] Indeed, Tolstoy's peasant-orientated, back-to-the-land philosophy was so central to the international perception of Russian radicalism that it fundamentally shaped the way the events of 1917 were initially understood. As James Meek put it: 'Nobody knew who the Bolsheviks were; everyone knew Tolstoy. Many foreign commentators visualised the Bolsheviks as holy vegetarians, sternly gentle, with long beards, smocks and baggy trousers.'[22] By now, the Bolsheviks tend to be seen as militantly urban, identified with the industrial working class, and touting a programme of rapid industrialization entirely at odds with the rural radicalism of William Morris or Tolstoy—but this may not have been immediately apparent to contemporaries. Still, as Michael Denner has argued, Tolstoyans themselves countenanced ways of working with the Bolsheviks to achieve their ends.[23] Vladimir Chertkov, Tolstoy's literary executor and a leading figure in the international Tolstoyan movement, published a pamphlet that defended the revolutionaries in the face of British intervention on the side of the Whites in the Civil War: perhaps utopian Tolstoyan agrarian communities could find ways of getting on board with the Bolshevik programme?[24]

Such a reconciliation between rural radicalism and the Bolshevik ambition to collectivize agriculture was never viable. The realities of Soviet agricultural policy—which, as Sheila Fitzpatrick affirms, tended towards 'large-scale, mechanized agricultural unit[s] producing for the state in the same way as large commercial farms produced for the market in a capitalist system'—altered the terms of the British debate.[25] It was increasingly apparent that all the peasant-oriented socialisms of the nineteenth

---

[20] Charlotte Alston, 'Britain and the International Tolstoyan Movement, 1890–1910', in Rebecca Beasley and Philip Ross Bullock (eds), *Russia in Britain 1880–1940: From Melodrama to Modernism* (Oxford: OUP, 2013), 53–70.

[21] Ibid. 63.

[22] James Meek, 'Some Wild Creature', *London Review of Book*, 32/16 (22 July 2010), 3–8, <http://www.lrb.co.uk/v32/n14/james-meek/some-wild-creature> [accessed 26 May 2016].

[23] Michael Denner, 'The "Proletarian Lord": Leo Tolstoy's Image during the Revolutionary Period', in Donna Tussing Orwin (ed.), *Anniversary Essays on Tolstoy* (Cambridge: CUP, 2010), 219–44.

[24] Vladimir Cherrtkov and Pavel Birukov, *Save Russia: A Remarkable Appeal to England by Tolstoy's Literary Editor in a Letter to his English Friends* (London: C. W. Daniel, 1919).

[25] Sheila Fitzpatrick, *Stalin's Peasants: Resistance and Survival in the Russian Village After Collectivization* (New York and Oxford: OUP, 1994), 39.

century—from Morris in Britain to Tolstoy in Russia—were inherently incompatible with Bolshevism. As the Russian Revolution progressed, the choice became a starker one between peasant smallholding on the one hand and Communist large-scale industrialized farming on the other: 'Homestead versus Kolschoz'. The free yeoman, the peasant smallholder—so important to nineteenth-century British socialists—was increasingly seen as an intrinsically anti-Communist figure.

The status of the peasant in radical and revolutionary movements was a key question in Russia before 1917. Russia's reputed 'backwardness' was—as I argued in a different context in Chapter 1—crucial to its international position, and above all this was understood as an agricultural backwardness. The agricultural revolution that was supposed to have torn the yeomanry from the land in Britain had not occurred in Russia. The system of land tenure in the nineteenth century was essentially feudal, with serfdom abolished as late as 1861. Many among the Russian intelligentsia had idealized the peasantry in the 1870s, but the Russian Marxism that emerged as a distinct force in the 1880s was distinctly anti-peasant in orientation. Russian Marxism was—in contrast to English Marxism—'an ideology of modernization as well as an ideology of revolution'.[26] English Marxism (from William Morris to E. P. Thompson) tended to be sceptical of modernization—capitalist progress—and often sought to restore the best elements of the pre-capitalist past.

There were other reasons for British observers to be sceptical about the expansion of the state into the production, distribution, and regulation of the food supply, along the lines suggested by the Bolshevik Revolution. Since the abolition of the Corn Laws in 1846 conventional wisdom dictated that the best system, from the point of view of feeding the poor, was free trade, because it ensured the availability of cheap imported food.[27] The Labour Party itself was staunchly pro-free trade throughout the 1920s, and when it started to argue for a more interventionist state the example of Soviet Russia was a key reference point.[28] But by then a deeper shift had already taken place. The Great War that helped to precipitate the Bolshevik Revolution in Russia saw a massive expansion of the British state, as a percentage of GDP and in terms of its powers, mass conscription being the most keenly felt.[29] A state that had sent its young men to die in France was increasingly seen as having a reciprocal responsibility

[26] Ibid. 25–6.
[27] Frank Trentmann, *Free Trade Nation: Commerce, Consumption, and Civil Society in Modern Britain* (Oxford: OUP, 2008), 213–14.
[28] Ibid. 311, 343.
[29] Roger Middleton, 'The Size and Scope of the Public Sector', in *The Boundaries of the State in Modern Britain* (Cambridge: CUP, 1996), 93, 96.

towards its citizens: calls for state provision of healthcare, housing, and unemployment benefit were starting to be heard.[30] In terms of food, a new feeling that the state had a vital role to play in managing and regulating its supply was an important feature of the inter-war period. The claim that free trade could alleviate poverty was based on the supply of cheap imported food, but after the war the emphasis of the popular debate increasingly moved from the price of food to its healthiness: from quantitative considerations to qualitative ones. Frank Trentmann writes:

> Talk of 'necessaries', so vital to the public appeal of Free Trade in the Victorian and Edwardian period, now moved away from a liberal defence of markets and cheapness to a more social-democratic focus on public health. To be a citizen meant to have access to 'essential' food, which states should provide at fair prices. Cheapness, in other words, no longer prevented malnutrition.[31]

Milk was a key commodity in this shift. Governmental intervention began with the Milk and Dairies Order in 1901, which established minimum levels of butterfat and non-fat solids below which milk was considered to be adulterated and unfit for sale. Legislation gathered momentum after the Great War, in the context of a wave of infant mortality caused by infected milk in hospitals which resulted in public pressure for the state to regulate the supply.[32] This was part of a movement which tended to emphasize that '[w]hat mattered now was not so much what food cost as what was in it': the state had a new role to play in ensuring the quality of food.[33] The Milk Control Board was established in 1918, and 'the state was on the point of taking over the entire wholesale milk trade'.[34] In Britain, the increased socialization of the food supply was all about guaranteeing the *quality* of produce, and as such it drew on native traditions of English socialism as much as it reminded many of the Soviet experiment.

The Fabian Society—the inheritor of the nineteenth-century tradition of utilitarian socialism—had in the Edwardian period been preparing the ground for the increased intervention of the state into the control of the food supply. For Fabians, the regulation of various foodstuffs would not be enough to guarantee their safety; public ownership was what was required. F. Lawson Dodd's Fabian Tract *Municipal Milk and Public Health* (1905) drew a comparison with the regulation and then

---

[30] On housing, see Matthew Taunton, *Fictions of the City: Class, Culture and Mass Housing in London and Paris* (Basingstoke: Palgrave Macmillan, 2009).

[31] Trentmann, *Free Trade Nation*, 214.

[32] Edith Holt Whetham, *The Agrarian History of England and Wales* (Cambridge: CUP), viii. *1914–39* (Cambridge: CUP, 1978), 25.

[33] Trentmann, *Free Trade Nation*, 220.   [34] Ibid. 203.

nationalization of the water supply: 'mere external interference was insufficient, and hence a movement became general towards investing the ownership as well as the control of the water supplies of the country in the hands of the community'.[35] Dodd's proposals were explicitly opposed to the free-trade orthodoxy: '[i]t is only necessary to convince the public that it can no longer afford to drink dirty and expensive milk in order to support its adherence to a worn-out and obsolete economic theory'.[36] Hubert Bland's 1905 tract on the state feeding of school children is another example of Edwardian Fabianism calling for the expansion of the state to take control of its citizens' diets, arguing that 'all children, destitute or not, should be fed, and fed without charge, at the expense of the State or Municipality'.[37] This enthusiasm for the socialization of the food supply helps to explain how Fabians who seemed relatively moderate in the Edwardian period—such as Shaw and the Webbs—could become apologists for Stalin's collectivization drive in the 1930s.

THREE ACRES AND A COW

Municipal Milk

G. K. Chesterton resisted Fabian moves towards state ownership and state control in the Edwardian period, and later made this resistance the main plank of his critique of the Communist collectivization of agriculture. Chesterton and his circle seem to have dwelt on milk in particular, perhaps because of its evocative qualities as a substance that plays a key role in binding an infant to its mother. If the state was taking control of the nation's milk, was it in some ways taking over responsibilities that properly belonged to parents, and so endangering the institution of the family? In *Tales of the Long Bow* (1925) Chesterton imagined an agrarian revolution in England driven by the cottage economy ideal, seeking to 'establish a yeomanry'.[38] *Tales*—sometimes somewhat confusingly referred to as a short story collection, despite its continuous narrative and consistent cast of characters—can be read as a rewriting of William Morris's *News from Nowhere* (1890) for the age of actually existing socialism. The utopia that begins to emerge in the course of the novel was conceived as a definite

[35] F. Lawson Dodd, *Municipal Milk and Public Health* (London: Fabian Society, 1905), 3.
[36] Ibid. 18.
[37] Hubert Bland, *'After Bread, Education': A Plan for the State Feeding of School Children*, Fabian Tract No. 120 (London: Fabian Society, 1905), 9.
[38] G. K. Chesterton, *Tales of the Long Bow* (London: Darwen Finlayson, 1962), 125.

alternative not only to the plutocratic capitalism that held sway in the contemporary English countryside as Chesterton saw it, but also to Bolshevik calls for state-led agricultural collectivism. The story revolves around the League of the Long Bow—a 'strange organization [that] originated in certain wild bets or foolish practical jokes indulged in by a small group of eccentrics'[39]—who, with the aid of an American millionaire, initiate a rural revolution in order to deliver the ownership of the agricultural land not to the municipal or state authorities, but directly into the hands of independent peasant smallholders. The motto of this book is 'Three Acres and a Cow', and the politics of milk production play a role in its engagement with debates about agriculture.[40] Towards the end of the book, one of the Leaguers—given the suitably revolutionary name of Robert Owen Hood—reads out a history of the revolution to his confreres:

> 'The recent success of the agrarian protest', remarked Hood in authoritative tones, 'is doubtless to be attributed largely to the economic advantage belonging to an agrarian population. It can feed the town or refuse to feed the town; and this question appeared quite early in the politics of the peasantry that had arisen in the western counties. Nobody will forget the scene at Paddington Station in the first days of the rebellion. Men who had grown used to seeing on innumerable mornings the innumerable ranks and rows of great milk-cans, looking leaden in a grey and greasy light, found themselves faced with a blank, in which those neglected things shone in the memory like stolen silver.'[41]

Habit has led Chesterton's city dwellers to assume passively that their milk will arrive at Paddington every morning. This assumption represented for Chesterton a total dissociation from the soil, and therefore from the means by which these benighted metropolitans might produce their own livelihoods, as Cobbett had dictated. The dairy farmers, in thus being taken for granted, are alienated from the product of their labour, which materializes with predictable regularity, miles from its place of production, hygienically in cans. Chesterton's book satirizes the well-meaning but irreducibly statist approach to public health summed up in a Fabian pamphlet like Dodd's *Municipal Milk and Public Health*. As the plutocratic government attempts to shore up its power, it is Sir Horace Hunter—a 'celebrated hygienist'—who is 'put in charge of the highly hygienic problem of the milk supply'.[42] As well as being a progressive medical man, Dr Hunter is one of the landowners who become involved in a conspiracy to nationalize the land. But whereas the Bolsheviks sought to do this in the name of

[39] Ibid. 177.   [40] Ibid. 178.   [41] Ibid. 173.   [42] Ibid.

the people and under the slogan of 'bread, peace and land', here nationalization is mooted as a means of staying the progress of the agrarian revolution. In the terms of this novel, neither Fabian-style municipal regulation nor Bolshevik-style collectivization in any way constrain Hunter's power. In fact, they have the potential to become the instruments of that power. Only peasant smallholding—the cottage economy—offers a viable means of breaking the monopoly on food production, which is intimately linked to the monopoly on political power.

Chesterton was only half of what George Bernard Shaw called the 'Chesterbelloc': 'a very amusing pantomime elephant, the front legs being that very exceptional and unEnglish individual Hilaire Belloc, and the hind legs that extravagant freak of French nature, G. K. Chesterton'.[43] Indeed, Chesterton's political ideas were very close to those of his friend Belloc. Like Chesterton, Belloc used the milk trade as an example to illustrate 'one of the stock arguments of Communism', in a series of articles on 'The Restoration of Property', published in the *English Review* in 1933:

> Your Fabian bewailed the state of affairs in which two small men, each with the goodwill of a milk walk, overlapped. He pointed out that the expenses of distribution would be vastly reduced by one system controlling the whole mass of small milk walks as they existed not so long ago. He has lived to see the thing come about, in this country at least; for the small man in the milk trade has almost disappeared. A huge monopoly has swallowed him up.[44]

Belloc was concerned to defend the small distributor, as much as the small producer, against large monopolies. Whether monopolies were owned by the state or by capitalists, for Belloc the effect was the same. Belloc saw Communism not just as something that is 'over there' in Russia, but as a real tendency within British life and one, moreover, that 'moves along the same lines as Capitalism'.[45] Both Communism and capitalism would entail giving over the control of the milk trade to a 'huge monopoly', destroying the 'small men' and *independence* that three acres and a cow might give them.

For Chesterton and his circle, then, Bolshevik collectivization policies served to underline the intensely authoritarian potential of seemingly innocuous Fabian arguments about public health that had been gathering momentum since the Edwardian period. The Communist government

[43] George Bernard Shaw, 'Chesterton and Belloc', *The New Age* (15 Feb. 1908), 309.
[44] Hilaire Belloc, 'The Restoration of Property: II. THE HANDICAP AGAINST Restoration', *English Review*, 56/2 (Feb. 1933), 174.
[45] Ibid. 170.

was itself unabashed about referring to the grain requisitions of the Civil War period as part of a 'food dictatorship'.[46] '[F]ood is a weapon' was Litvinov's mantra, as Harold Henry Fisher noted in a 1927 analysis of the famines of 1919–23—a Bolshevik slogan that was frequently quoted by anti-Communists to exemplify the cruelty of the Communist approach to agriculture.[47] Revd Ronald Knox was another close ally of Chesterton's and a prolific Roman Catholic intellectual who played a key role in Chesterton's conversion to Catholicism.[48] Knox also contemplated the nationalization of the milk supply in a futuristic fiction that implicitly linked the establishment of the Milk Board in Britain to agricultural collectivization in Soviet Russia. He contributed a mock-up of a hypothetical edition of *The Times* under the title 'If the General Strike had Succeeded' in a volume of counterfactual history called *If it had Happened Otherwise* (1932). His contribution included various stories about and reflections on the establishment of a Communist state in Britain, including two letters to the editor on the 'Milk Pool in Hyde Park'. Knox's imagined Communist government has developed a system of storing milk in a huge pool in Hyde Park, to the extent where, as one aggrieved correspondent puts it, 'several suburbs entirely depend on it for their daily supply'. This state-owned milk supply is 'a weapon' with which the Government 'can threaten, if its authority should at any time be defied, to starve London into obedience'.[49] The echo of Litvinov seems highly pertinent here. Well-meaning Fabian proposals—that milk must be nationalized for health reasons—are linked to a highly authoritarian 'food dictatorship'.

Distributism versus Kolkhoz

The critique of Bolshevism set out by Chesterton, Belloc, and Knox was closely focused on the problem of property. Chesterton was not content simply to oppose the latest developments in Russia, however: like Pound, he hoped that smallholding could supply anti-Communism with the positive programme it seemed to lack. In 1926 he started his own political party, the Distributist League, which stood for the establishment of a system of free peasant proprietorship. At the inaugural meeting of the

[46] S. A. Smith, *The Russian Revolution: A Very Short Introduction* (Oxford: OUP, 2002), 77.

[47] Harold Henry Fisher, *The Famine in Soviet Russia, 1919–1923: The Operations of the American Relief Administration.* (New York: Macmillan, 1927), 62.

[48] Ian Ker, *G. K. Chesterton: A Biography* (Oxford: OUP, 2011), 466.

[49] Roland Knox, 'If the General Strike had Succeeded', in *If it had Happened Otherwise* (London: Sidgwick & Jackson, 1972 [1932]), 285.

Distributist League, Chesterton explained its programme by adapting a maxim of Francis Bacon's: 'Property is like muck, it is good only if it be spread.'[50] Indeed, the central tenets of Distributism were the defence of small property and the rehabilitation of peasant smallholding, a radical egalitarianism coupled with a fierce opposition both to socialist collectivism and to monopoly capitalism.[51] Remember that in 1954 Ezra Pound could be found complaining of the 'Dulness of anti communist propaganda, which fails to set HOMESTEAD against kolschoz':[52] in fact the Distributist League—a small organization, although one with a prominent and eloquent spokesman and president in Chesterton—did exactly that. It might have been called the Homestead League, or even the Cottage Economy Party. Chesterton was a devoted reader of Cobbett, advocating in his book *William Cobbett* (1925) 'the revival of the things that Cobbett wished to revive . . . such as liberty, England, the family, the honour of the yeoman, and so on'.[53] Chesterton established his own weekly magazine— *G. K.'s Weekly*—to promote these ideas, stating in his first editorial (under the heading 'The First Principle') that '[t]his paper exists to demand that we fight Bolshevism with something more than plutocracy'.[54] This reads like an answer to Pound's question, but one can also find in Chesterton's writing from this period a frustration with the mainstream of anti-Communism that echoes Pound: 'we are Anti-Bolshevist and also Anti-Anti-Bolshevist; that is, quite opposed on principle to most prominent Anti-Bolshevists', he wrote.[55] The main current of anti-Bolshevism that Chesterton wished to distance himself from was explicitly pro-capitalist, while Distributism mobilized the cottage economy ideal as a corrective to capitalism as well as Bolshevism.

Chesterton only started to call this approach 'Distributism' at a relatively late stage of his career, but its core tenets—egalitarianism, the

---

[50] G. K. Chesterton qtd. in Margaret Canovan, *G. K. Chesterton: Radical Populist* (London; New York: Harcourt Brace Jovanovic, 1977), 89.

[51] Canovan, *G.K. Chesterton: Radical Populist*, 18. 'The basic position of Distributism', as Morag Shiach explains, 'was that property should be divided up among the largest possible number of people, since the ownership of property is a basic right and its concentration the greatest possible threat to liberty.' Morag Shiach, *Modernism, Labour and Selfhood in British Literature and Culture* (Cambridge: CUP, 2004), 224.

[52] Ezra Pound to Olivia Rosetti, 5 Apr. 1954, in *I Cease Not to Yowl* 145.

[53] G. K. Chesterton, *William Cobbett* (London: Hodder & Stoughton, 1925), 5. Chesterton had also contributed an introduction to a new edition of Cobbett's *Cottage Economy* in 1916, G. K. Chesterton, 'Introduction', in William Cobbett, *Cottage Economy* (London: Douglas Pepler, 1916), i–vi.

[54] G. K. Chesterton, 'The First Principle', *G.K.'s Weekly*, 1/1 (21 Mar. 1925), 3.

[55] G. K. Chesterton, 'The Anti-Anti-Bolshevist', *G.K.'s Weekly*, 1/23 (22 Aug. 1925), 510.

advocacy of peasant smallholding, and the dual resistance to collectivism and monopoly capitalism—were present in his work from early on. Chesterton's career helps to demonstrate the changing relationship between the cottage economy ideal and the word 'socialism'. In the 1890s, Chesterton became a passionate convert to socialism after reading Blatchford's *Merrie England*.[56] When he continued to promote the cottage economy ideal after 1917—like a number of Catholic intellectuals including Belloc and Knox—this alienated him from the socialist (and in particular the Bolshevik-sympathizing) left. As he put it in *Eugenics and Other Evils* (1922), 'At one time I agreed with Socialism, because it was simple. Now I disagree with Socialism, because it is too simple.'[57] Chesterton continued in his admiration of that key figure in nineteenth-century English socialism, William Morris, but after the rise of Stalin it became oddly incongruous (in Chesterton's eyes) that Morris should have described himself as a socialist. Perhaps Morris was culpably naive about the likely consequences of nationalizing the land: at any rate, Chesterton argued, it was impossible to imagine that Morris 'would have tolerated for ten seconds the vast industrial materialism of the Five-Year Plan'.[58] It would be disingenuous to argue that it was only the Bolshevik Revolution that put Chesterton off socialism, however. His essay 'Why I am Not a Socialist' was published in the progressive journal *The New Age* (edited by A. R. Orage) in 1908, as part of a fascinating series of essays to which Belloc, George Bernard Shaw, and H. G. Wells also contributed. Belloc and Chesterton—still widely viewed as progressives, and still regular contributors so such modernist magazines as *The New Age*—were concerned to differentiate their approach from the 'socialism' of their Fabian interlocutors. Here, Chesterton identified that word not with Morris but with the Fabian Society, which—as we have seen—was already advocating statist socialism. Chesterton argued that, in a true democracy, the people would 'crush Socialism with one hand and landlordism with the other'. He went on:

> They will destroy landlordism, not because it is property, but because it is the negation of property. It is the negation of property that the Duke of Westminster should own whole streets and squares of London . . . If ever the actual poor move to destroy this evil, they will do it with the object not only

[56] William Oddie, *Chesterton and the Romance of Orthodoxy: The Making of GKC, 1874–1908* (Oxford: OUP, 2008), 130.

[57] G. K. Chesterton, *Eugenics and Other Evils* (London: Cassell & Co., 1922), 159.

[58] G. K. Chesterton, *As I was Saying: A Book of Essays* (London: Methuen & Co., 1936), 128.

of giving every man private property, but very specially private property; they will probably exaggerate in that direction; for in that direction is the whole humour and poetry of their own lives.[59]

British responses to the Bolshevik Revolution—Chesterton's in particular— were shaped by this pre-existing fissure within the progressive intelligentsia around the question of property. In 1908, the essential basis of Chesterton's political philosophy sprang from the precept that 'an Englishman's house is his castle'.[60] It was in the shadow of the Bolshevik Revolution that Chesterton in a sense weaponized this political philosophy, calling it 'Distributism' and establishing the League in order to supply a positive answer to the Bolshevism which—he at least thought— had monopolized the British left as much as it sought to monopolize the land.

As an 'Anti-Bolshevist' and also an 'Anti-Anti-Bolshevist', Chesterton's stance confused some of his interlocutors. When, in a 1934 BBC radio broadcast, Chesterton damned Burke's response to the French Revolution but at the same time described Bolshevism as 'unlimited sweating', Shaw enquired: 'if so fearless a commentator, professing as a Distributist to be on the Left of Communism, can out-Burke Burke thus, whom in England can Stalin trust?'[61] Shaw's question admits a certain level of confusion about what now constituted 'Left' and 'Right'. It is symptomatic of a shifting conception of the right–left dichotomy, an example of what Lakoff and Johnson influentially called 'metaphors we live by' in a 1980 book of that name.[62] Marcel Gauchet's article 'Right and Left' traced the history of this spatial metaphor for political identity in France, from the revolution into recent time. Somewhat in the spirit of Lakoff and Johnson, he bemoaned the fact that little consideration had been given to the terms 'right and left', attributing this failure to the fact that '[t]hinkers are never keen to reflect on that which enables them to think'. For Gauchet, the French 'produced a simplifying symbolism whose widespread applicability suggests that it contains some secret of modern politics and citizenship'. By considering this term in a *longue durée*, Gauchet showed how the ground was prepared for the Age of Extremes, the post-1917 landscape. 'The dramatic polarization of Communism and Fascism ultimately

---

[59] G. K. Chesterton, 'Why I am Not a Socialist', *The New Age* 2/10 (1908), 190.

[60] Ibid. 190.

[61] George Bernard Shaw et al., *Stalin-Wells Talk: The Verbatim Record and a Discussion by G. Bernard Shaw, H. G. Wells, J. M. Keynes, Ernst Toller and Others* (London: New Statesman and Nation, 1934), 27.

[62] George Lakoff and Mark Johnson, *Metaphors we Live by* (Chicago: Chicago University Press, 2008).

reactivated the structural factors that had helped to root the right-left dichotomy in the heart of French political life', he wrote.[63] The underlying metaphor of a political spectrum from left to right, on which any person or text could be positioned, shaped the understanding of the Russian Revolution in Britain as much as it did in France. But the spectrum metaphor—one that we still live by—has definite limits, as Shaw's confused reasoning seems to illustrate. Distributism was profoundly egalitarian in its attitude to personal possession: more so than Communism. Egalitarianism is a key tenet of the left, so Distributism must be to the left of Communism. Yet Chesterton defined Bolshevism as 'unlimited sweating'. Sympathy with Bolshevism (and its policy of pursuing agricultural collectivization at the expense of 'kulaks' or peasant proprietors) seemed to Shaw to sit on the left of the spectrum. However, it is not simply that Chesterton was a crank: much of what we think of as the 'left-wing' thought of nineteenth-century Britain was explicitly pro-peasant and opposed to the industrialization of agriculture. The metaphor of the 'right and left' has the effect of clustering together views on a wide range of social, political, economic, and other issues. The Soviet government could be seen to be pursuing a wide range of policies that could not traditionally be thought of as 'left', and indeed it defined its own 'Left Opposition' as a group—led by Trotsky—who wanted to accelerate the process of agricultural collectivization (where the 'Right Opposition' sought to continue the conciliatory attitudes to the peasantry that had prevailed during the NEP period). The Russian Revolution had a disruptive effect on the 'right and left' metaphor, and in time gave rise to new and widespread understandings of what it meant to be on the left. This affected the debates covered in the other chapters of this book, but it is perhaps nowhere more evident than in discussions about agriculture and land tenure.

If food and farming were the starting points for a Distributist critique of Bolshevik theories of property, then that critique was extended into other domains in fascinating ways. By way of example, I will now briefly show how such arguments were extended, first to debates about the city, and secondly to the question of free speech. Critics of Distributism (such as George Bernard Shaw) frequently asked how a cottage economy approach—which seemed to have obvious application for rural, agricultural land—could be applied in cities and towns.[64] Collectivism came

[63] Gauchet, 'Right and Left', in Pierre Nora and Lawrence D. Kritzman (eds), *Realms of Memory: The Construction of the French Past* (New York: Columbia University Press, 1996), 274.

[64] This question is discussed in a debate between Shaw and Chesterton, published as G. K. Chesterton, and G. B. Shaw, *Do we Agree?* (London: Cecil Palmer, 1928), 43–4. A fuller exploration of the relationship between Distributism and the city can be found

naturally to cities and towns, since they depended heavily on shared infrastructure: roads, railways, sewers, electricity, gas, water supplies, etc. Moreover, since they did not on the whole produce food, they were reliant on the countryside producing large agricultural surpluses, and therefore being farmed on a more efficient basis than the subsistence allowed by 'Three Acres and a Cow'. In his *Principles of Political Economy* (1848) J. S. Mill expressed a general preference for free enterprise and private ownership, but he nevertheless argued that 'practical monopolies' (or 'natural monopolies') such as transport systems and utilities were best owned and managed by the state in the interests of society in general: the complexity of modern urban life necessitated a certain degree of state collectivism.

Chesterton's contributions to the debate about the Distributist city were inconsistent. At one moment he seemed to argue that cities must cease to exist: 'we hope to change England from a nation of machine-miners, clerks and carriers to a nation of farmers and craftsmen'.[65] Elsewhere he seemed to reverse this view: 'at no time did I say that we must make the whole community a community of agricultural peasants. It is absurd.'[66] Perhaps Distributism could develop a model of private property that could mitigate the city's perceived overdependence on networked infrastructure and its tendency towards natural monopoly? But that this dependence was a bad thing was never in doubt. The Chestertonian critique of collectivism was leveraged into a general condemnation of metropolitan man's dependence on urban infrastructure in 'The Paradise of Human Fishes' (1925), a short story that appeared in *G. K.'s Weekly*, the first in a series called 'Utopias Unlimited'. The story was unsigned, but it is reasonable to presume that it was Chesterton's work. In the story, Mr Peter Paul Smith of Brompton, West London, has a dream in which he goes deep-sea diving in the Atlantic. He finds at the bottom of the ocean a city of 75,000 inhabitants called Gubbins City. On arrival he meets a native who explains the origins of the city to him in an American accent:

> You must be about the only guy that don't know how Old Man Gubbins bought all the bottom of the Atlantic dirt cheap, because all the other boobs thought it was only dirt with nothing to it. He's planted his factories here; and I tell you, Sir, this is going to be the new civilization.

in Matthew Taunton, 'Distributism and the City', in Matthew Beaumont and Matthew Ingleby (eds), *Chesterton, London and Modernity* (London: Bloomsbury, 2013), 203–27.

[65] G. K. Chesterton, 'What we're Getting at', *G. K.'s Weekly*, 5/107 (2 Apr. 1927), 320.
[66] Chesterton and Shaw, *Do we Agree?*, 45.

Smith is not convinced, and his response immediately recalls the state of dependency in which city-dwellers find themselves in *Tales of the Long Bow*. 'What an awful life', Smith says, 'to live and die breathing air that's only pumped down to you by the favour of somebody miles away.'[67] The problem with Gubbins City, in this story, is that it makes you dependent on Old Man Gubbins for your air. 'Of course in our situation', the resident explains, 'we have to do pretty much as we're told by the headquarters on land; and the old man likes to keep his finger on the string.' The force of the story is that this is not unique to Gubbins City—that really any city, by virtue of its size and its necessary dependence on infrastructural natural monopolies, is reliant on the favour of some distant person or authority. When Smith challenges him, the native of Gubbins City responds:

> Are there many brooks in Brompton? . . . or have you a well in your front garden, or do you go out and drink the rain? No, you have all your water pumped to you by the favour of somebody miles away. I don't see there's much difference between us. You are surrounded by air and have water pumped to you. We are surrounded by water and have air pumped to us. But we should both die if anything went wrong.

This goes to the heart of the problem of the city as Chesterton saw it. The sheer scale of the modern metropolis puts it out of the grasp of the 'ordinary man'—a common touchstone in Chesterton's political writing. London, Chesterton's story says, is analogous to Gubbins City in this respect: it makes its citizens dependent for their livelihood on 'the favour of somebody miles away'. Smith is appalled to see that the inhabitants of Gubbins City are attached to their air supply by a tube to their diving helmets, 'like marionettes'. But again his interlocutor draws a parallel with London: 'I fancy you people are hung on wires, too; telephone wires; telegraph wires; all sorts of wires.'[68] The effect of the story is to make us aware of the networked infrastructure upon which metropolitan man has become dependent, and to alert us to the dangers of this dependence. Intriguingly, in certain places Distributists did hint that there might be ways to achieve their ends in an urban environment without simply replacing the cities with subsistence farms. Belloc, for example, commented that 'much of the centralized mechanical production of our time could be decentralized through the now widely distributed use of

---

[67] G. K. Chesterton, 'The Paradise of Human Fishes', *G.K.'s Weekly*, 1/2 (28 Mar. 1925), 16.
[68] Ibid. 16, 17.

electrical power'.[69] Here, there emerges at least the possibility that Distributism might not simply hark back to an imaginary version of the Middle Ages, but look forward to a future in which the judicious and decentralized application of modern technology has helped to produce a genuinely egalitarian distribution of property and power.

The question of property and tenure also underpins Chesterton's account of freedom of the press. This had long been a left-wing cause, yet—like cottage economists—free speech advocates suddenly found themselves at odds with the global voice of the left. Communist sympathizers jumped to the defence of the controls the Soviet government exerted over publishing. Stephen Spender, for example, wrote in 1937 that '[h]aving discovered what is essential to freedom, the Soviet state quite rightly insists that this shall not be disputed; no one is "free" to preach against freedom, to uphold private enterprise or exploitation of man by man. Freedom is not a joke, to be turned against people who believe in it.'[70] In his second editorial in *G. K.'s Weekly*, titled 'The Real Bolshevist Peril', Chesterton made a strong link between the Bolshevik attitude to property and the problem of free speech:

> The tradition of true opposition is part of the tradition of property and liberty; it is a tradition of the West. It can only be tolerated where other rights are allowed to strike root besides the royal or senatorial power. Those rights must be protected by a morality which even a strong central government will hesitate to defy. In other words, there can only be criticism where there are sub-units of property and sub-loyalties of the family and the guild. There can only be a critic of the state where a religious sense of right protects his claim to his own pen or his own printing press. It is absurd to suppose that he could borrow the royal pen to advocate regicide or use the government printing-presses to expose the government. The whole point of Socialism, the whole case for Socialism, is that the State is directly responsible for everything. Everything is staked on the State's justice; it is putting all the eggs in one basket. Many of them will be rotten eggs; but you will not even be allowed to use them at political elections.[71]

This argument, linking the state-ownership of the printing presses to the absence of liberal freedom expression, was echoed later by Arthur Koestler: '[t]he State monopoly in publishing', he wrote, 'is in the long run a more decisive feature of the Communist régime than the concentration camps

[69] H. Belloc, 'The Restoration of Property: IV', *English Review*, 57(1) (July 1933), 27.
[70] Stephen Spender, *Forward from Liberalism* (London: Gollancz, 1937), 275.
[71] G. K. Chesterton, 'The Real Bolshevik Peril', *G.K.'s Weekly*, 1/2 (28 Mar. 1925), 3.

and even the one-Party system'.[72] If Chesterton's analysis always began with the question of land tenure, it proceeded analogically, making the principle of 'Three Acres and a Cow' apply to the tools of the writer's trade, and connecting freedom of conscience to private property. Ironically, Chesterton was working at a time that saw the 'censorship of huge numbers of books' in Britain, making it—as Rachel Potter argues—'one of the most highly controlled periods in the history of literary expression'.[73] Chesterton seems to have steered clear of much direct confrontation with censorship. But to those writers in Britain who experienced censorship at the hands of private printers, editors— and the wider networks of censorship that Potter describes—it must have seemed that, while private property in printing presses might well be a necessary condition for free expression, it was by no means a sufficient one.

Conservative Land Nationalization

Where Burke had argued against revolutionary change in general, Chesterton explicitly advocated an English Revolution at home as a way to *avoid* the creeping progress of socialism, which as he saw it was merely the culmination of the monopolistic tendencies of Edwardian capitalism. As he wrote in *What's Wrong with the World* (1910): 'We can now only avoid Socialism by a change as vast as Socialism. If we are to save property, we must distribute property, almost as sternly and sweepingly as did the French Revolution. If we are to preserve the family we must revolutionise the nation.'[74] His passion for the French Revolution was real: had it not produced a country of peasant proprietors? Neither was he opposed in principle to a revolution in Russia. He was no friend to the Tsars, and his response to the Russian Revolution of 1905 was enthusiastic. As he wrote in 1907: 'there is a Revolution of some kind going on in Russia; and that ought to be enough to make any healthy man happy. Revolution is certainly the divine part of man.'[75] The land reforms that followed the 1905 Revolution were plainly to Chesterton's taste, and he later professed himself an admirer of Pyotr Stolypin's 'policy of peasant proprietorship'.[76]

---

[72] Arthur Koestler, *The Invisible Writing: The Second Volume of an Autobiography: 1932–40* (London: Vintage, 2005), 79.

[73] Rachel Potter, *Modernist Literature* (Edinburgh: Edinburgh University Press, 2012), 113. See also Rachel Potter, *Obscene Modernism: Literary Censorship and Experiment 1900–1940* (Oxford: OUP, 2013).

[74] G. K. Chesterton, *What's Wrong with the World* (London: Cassell & Co., 1910), 275.

[75] Chesterton quoted in Oddie, *Chesterton and the Romance of Orthodoxy*, 372.

[76] G. K. Chesterton, *The Appetite of Tyranny* (Kila, MT: Kessinger, 2004), 19.

Chesterton, then, was more than capable of celebrating revolutions on foreign soil, when they chimed with his other aims. Distributism was the form that Chesterton's English Revolution would have to take.

It is telling, then, that in his novel of the English Revolution, *Tales of the Long Bow*, socialism—particularly in its Bolshevik form—is cast as a reactionary ideology that the capitalist government might use to hold off the agrarian revolution and arrest the spread of smallholding. The capitalist landowners Lord Normantowers, Sir Horace Hunter, and Mr R. Low are terrified by the peasant uprising and they turn to the Prime Minister, the Earl of Eden, to protect their class interests. They are initially outraged and disturbed by his proposal:

> 'The time has come,' said the Prime Minister, 'to Nationalize the Land.'
>
> Sir Horace Hunter rose from his chair, opened his mouth, shut it, and sat down again, all with what he himself might have called a reflex action.
>
> 'But that is Socialism!' cried Lord Normantowers, his eyes standing out of his head.
>
> 'True Socialism, don't you think?' mused the Prime Minister. 'Better call it True Socialism; just the sort of thing to be remembered at elections. Theirs is Socialism, and ours is True Socialism.'
>
> 'Do you really mean, my lord,' cried Hunter in a heat of sincerity stronger than the snobbery of a lifetime, 'that you are going to support the Bolshies?'
>
> 'No,' said Eden, with the smile of a sphinx. 'I mean the Bolshies are going to support me. Idiots!'[77]

The Prime Minister believes that the nationalization of the land can be deployed as a socialistic gesture to get the 'Bolshies' onside, while also upholding the hegemony of the ruling elite. True enough, he acknowledges, '[a]ll our fine old English castles and manors, the homes of the gentry . . . they will become public property, like post offices'.[78] Yet, when Normantowers protests that his castle will be seized, the Prime Minister is able to reassure him:

> 'It comes under the department of Castle and Abbey Estates in Section Four,' said Lord Eden, referring to the paper before him. 'By the provisions of the new Bill the public control in such cases will be vested in the Lord-Lieutenant of the County. In the particular case of your castle—let me see—why, yes, of course, you are Lord Lieutenant of that county.'
>
> Little Lord Normantowers was staring, with his stiff hair all standing on end; but a new look was dawning in his shrewd though small-featured face.[79]

[77] Chesterton, *Tales*, 150–1.   [78] Ibid. 151.   [79] Ibid. 152.

The socialist state that the Prime Minister proposes to bring into being will pay landowners compensation for the loss of their estates, and it will then appoint them as the handsomely salaried managers of those same estates. 'Can't you see you'll get twice as much as before?' the Prime Minister reassures his friends, 'First you'll be compensated for losing your castle, and then you'll be paid for keeping it.' Bolshevik socialism is thus represented as the continuation of monopoly capitalism in a new guise: 'Look how easily we remained in the saddle, in spite of democratic elections; how we managed to dominate the Commons as well as the Lords. It'll be the same with what they call Socialism. We shall still be there; only we shall be called bureaucrats instead of aristocrats.'[80]

This story about a Conservative Prime Minister's strategic embrace of 'True Socialism' is a sort of morality tale about Bolshevism told from the top down: its implication that state control of the means of production is simply equivalent to private capitalist control is illustrated by the irony that the bureaucrats are actually the landowners from the old regime. This was a tendency that Chesterton elsewhere identified in his own contemporary Britain. In a undated and—as far as I have been able to determine—unpublished 'open letter' that sets out a rather singular analysis of the General Strike of 1926, he wrote that 'the rich have, in a sense, become socialists; but only on the condition that they also be slave-owners'.[81] In these strikes, Chesterton asserted, the interests of the capitalist mine-owners were best-served by state intervention and 'Socialist' arguments about the 'comfort and convenience of the whole nation'. Meanwhile, the workers' position was weakened because they had 'to fight mainly with the remains of rather rhetorical Socialism & dreams, as yet somewhat dim, of the old liberty of the medieval guilds & charters'.[82] Chesterton was emphatically on the side of the workers, but he argued that their only route to victory was to free themselves from the remains of a socialism which played into the hands of the mine-owners, and to focus instead on bringing those dreams of the 'old liberty of the medieval guilds & charters' into sharper focus.

In *Tales of the Long Bow*, the Distributist revolution—grounded in 'the old liberty of the medieval guilds and charters'—wins out over the corrupt socialism that the plutocratic government attempts to impose. Having taken possession of their farms, the new peasantry have 'struck their roots

---

[80] Ibid. 153.

[81] G. K. Chesterton, 'Open Letter: The Set-Back to English Socialism' (manuscript, n.d.), G.K. Chesterton collection, Harry Ransom Center, University of Texas (Box 1 Folder 1), p. 3.

[82] Ibid. 2, 5.

very deep', and therefore resist the scheme of 'Land Nationalization'.[83] The metaphor of 'striking root' resonates with Chesterton's editorial on free speech, where private property is seen as the sole mechanism by which other independent interests might be 'allowed to strike root besides the royal or senatorial power'. Allowing a free and independent peasantry to take root in the soil creates an essential counterweight to centralized governmental power. Chesterton's narrator links this peasant resistance to events in Russia: 'the Government, which had already adopted a policy commonly called Socialist from motives that were in fact very conservative, found itself confronted with the same peasant resistance as brought the Bolshevist Government in Russia to a standstill.'[84] Indeed, in Russia in 1925, during the NEP period, agricultural collectivization had effectively been put on hold: the peasants had stolidly resisted the grain requisitions of the Civil War period. The peasant proprietor had won a temporary victory, and in that victory Chesterton saw hope that in England, too, the peasant smallholder might prevail against the general trend by which land ownership was being consolidated into the hands of an elite.

Distributism constitutes a small but significant chapter in history of attempts to create a 'third way' that was neither capitalist nor socialist, and which attempted to exist outside the 'left and right' metaphor for political position. But even when one tries to think outside of this metaphor, it is difficult to escape the uncomfortable tendencies that emerged out of this attempt to articulate a positive anti-Communist programme. Chesterton started to see Mussolini's Fascism as the best political means to achieve his objectives. Moreover, he was not alone among cottage economy advocates: increasingly, Fascism become a home for those who wanted to 'set HOMESTEAD against kolschoz'.[85] A. J. Penty, for example, followed a trajectory from disciple of Morris in the Edwardian period, through guild socialism, and finally to the belief that the 'Regulative Guild State' he desired had come into being in Mussolini's Italy.[86] Again the constant was the belief in 'a local life... rooted in local traditions', a revival of 'the corporate life of the Middle Ages'.[87] The attempt to articulate a positive alternative to Bolshevik collectivism, that was nevertheless anti-capitalist, sent many advocates of the cottage economy on a path to Fascism.

[83] Chesterton, *Tales*, 178.   [84] Ibid. 290.
[85] Ezra Pound to Olivia Rosetti, 5 Apr. 1954, in *I Cease Not to Yowl*, 145.
[86] Philip Conford, *The Origins of the Organic Movement* (Edinburgh: Floris Books, 2001), 154.
[87] Arthur Joseph Penty, *Means and Ends* (London: Faber & Faber, 1932), 55, 67.

PROCESSING THE TERROR FAMINE

Denial

While the Distributist League conducted its largely theoretical debate about property and agriculture, other writers and intellectuals responded in more detail to actual conditions in the Russian countryside. In the years 1932–4, one of the worst famines in human history swept the USSR. Estimates as to the death toll vary.[88] And yet, despite the appearance of first-hand reports by Malcolm Muggeridge and Gareth Jones in the *Manchester Guardian* and further coverage across the print media, a significant portion of the British intelligentsia ignored it or questioned the reliability of the reports, which inevitably reflected badly on the Communist government.[89] The scepticism towards the famine, and the widespread public ignorance about one of the most catastrophic occurrences of state-sponsored mass murder in the twentieth century, led Robert Conquest to ask—in the first synoptic history of what he christened 'the terror-famine'—'how is it possible that these events are not fully registered in our public consciousness?'[90] Conquest went on to point out that Stalin and his henchmen had concealed and distorted the facts, and that they were 'abetted by many Westerners' in doing so.[91] From the standpoint of the present, and with the benefit of the historical work of Conquest and others, the fact of the famine takes on a significance that only a few Western commentators were willing to attribute it in the 1930s. Inevitably, albeit anachronistically, it appears to us now as the salient fact about the Soviet Union during the first Five-Year-Plan.

Denial of the famine was not some far-left deviation, nor was it restricted to Communists. Foremost among the deniers of the famine were the leading Fabians Beatrice and Sidney Webb. In *Soviet Communism: A New Civilization* (1935), they attributed all talk of a manmade famine to 'persons hostile to the Soviet Union'.[92] 'What the Soviet Government was faced with', they wrote, 'was, in fact, not a famine but

---

[88] The various sources relating to the famine are well sifted in Dana G. Dalrymple, 'The Soviet Famine of 1932–4', *Soviet Studies*, 15/3 (1964), 250–84.

[89] Muggeridge's reports appeared in the *Manchester Guardian* on the 25, 27, and 28 Mar. 1933. There is a useful archive of Jones's writings on Russia at <http://www.garethjones.org/soviet_articles/soviet_articles.htm.>

[90] Robert Conquest, *The Harvest of Sorrow: Soviet Collectivisation and the Terror Famine* (New York: OUP, 1986), 5.

[91] Ibid. 5.

[92] Sidney Webb and Beatrice Webb, *Soviet Communism* (London: Longmans, Green & Co., 1944), 258.

a widespread general strike of the peasantry, in resistance to the policy of collectivization, fomented and encouraged by the disloyal elements of the population.'[93] This was entirely in line with Soviet propaganda, and it missed the role of the state in setting and brutally enforcing grain quotas. Still, peasant resistance to these quotas was not simply a myth. As Fitzpatrick put it, '[t]he famine of 1933 was the consequence of an irresistible force (the state's demand for set quotas of grain) meeting an immovable object (the peasants' stubborn passive resistance to these demands)'.[94] This was not merely the resistance of peasant smallholders who wanted to farm at subsistence levels out of some misplaced preference. It was the resistance of starving people who did not wish to relinquish what little grain they had, often—as Muggeridge noted in the *Manchester Guardian*—for it to be exported to Western Europe.[95] In *Winter in Moscow* (1934), a harrowing novel about Western journalists in Russia at the time of the famine, Muggeridge tells the story of a peasant family whose last bag of flour is requisitioned. The delirious mother kills her children and puts their bodies in sacks, before surrendering them as grain and killing the man sent to collect them.[96] Muggeridge's narrator notes that 'Bolshevism, like an enormous stomach, threw out digestive juices and assimilated the affair',[97] and goes on to describe how these events are reported in the Soviet press as '[s]ymptomatic of new tactics of kulak elements'.[98]

The Webbs argued that the Soviet government attempted 'so drastic . . . so hazardous an experiment' because 'there was no other course open to them'.[99] But—even though they seemed aware of at least some of the consequences of collectivization—they stood full square behind it. Playing into the 'Homestead versus Kolschoz' binary with which the present chapter has been working, the Webbs' endorsement of the collective farm comes with a critique of smallholding. Here, they reflect on the task facing the Communist authorities:

> To convert, within less than a decade, even two thirds of a population of 120 millions of peasantry steeped in ignorance, suspicion and obstinacy, accustomed for centuries to individual cultivation of the little holdings that they now deemed their own, with all the cunning and greed that such a system develops, into public-spirited cooperators working on a prescribed plan for a

---

[93] Ibid. 265.   [94] Fitzpatrick, *Stalin's Peasants*, 5.

[95] Malcolm ['A Correspondent'] Muggeridge, 'The Soviet and the Peasantry: An Observer's Notes. I. Famine in North Caucasus. Whole Villages Exiled', *Manchester Guardian* (1933), 13–14.

[96] Malcolm Muggeridge, *Winter in Moscow* (London: Eyre & Spottiswoode, 1934), 57–61.

[97] Ibid. 62.   [98] Ibid. 63.   [99] Webb and Webb, *Soviet Communism*, .235.

common product to be equitably shared among themselves, might well have
been deemed hopelessly impracticable.[100]

What is at stake here is not merely the 'backwardness' of the Russian
peasant, but the whole principle of smallholding. The Webbs collapsed
the distinction between peasant capitalism (along the lines promoted by
Stolypin's land reforms after the 1905 revolution, and by NEP in the
1920s) and the attachment to the medieval *mir*. Both were seen as versions
of the cottage economy, which was indicted with encouraging 'cunning
and greed', while the collective farm was promoted as the cure.[101] The
Fabian commitment to the principle of collective ownership of agricultural land predated the Bolshevik Revolution: perhaps the only way of
holding on to the ideal in the period of actually existing collective farming
was to insist that it was working, and blame any setbacks on kulaks, or
peasants' selfish addiction to subsistence farming.

There were some on the British left who—forgetting traditional suspi-
cions about industrialism in general—enthusiastically celebrated Soviet
farming precisely as a modern, industrialized alternative to subsistence
agriculture. If it bore similarities to American capitalist ranch farming, so
much the better: this was the most modern and efficient arrangement and
would no doubt yield more 'grain'. Joan Beauchamp, for example, a
suffragette and co-founder of the Communist Party of Great Britain,
compared the collective farms with American ranches in her book *Agriculture in Soviet Russia* (1931). She noted approvingly that the director of
the Verblud (a state farm) 'spent a year in Canada and the U.S.A. studying
large-scale farming methods'.[102] Moving onto the Gigant, 'the largest farm
in the world' at 450,000 acres, she praised the way it was 'completely
mechanised as far as the actual cultivation is concerned'.[103] She continued:
'The director of Gigant told me that he considered himself the richest man
in the world, for "his" farm is four times the size of the biggest farm in
America.'[104] What is surprising is that a British socialist, traditionally so
critical of Fordist industrialism, could find this appealing. Neither was
Beauchamp overly concerned that the director of the Gigant could be so
overtly compared with a capitalist landowner. The possessive 'his' may

---

[100] Ibid. 245.
[101] This was an attitude shared by many Western proponents of Soviet-style collectivization. The American enthusiasts N. Buchwald and R. Bishop marvelled at the progress
made since 1929, when 'the vast majority of the Soviet peasants were individual small-scale
farmers' and complained that 'even now many backward peasants are prejudiced against
collective large-scale farming'. N. Buchwald and R. Bishop, *From Peasant to Collective
Farmer* (London: Martin Lawrence, 1933), 13.
[102] Joan Beauchamp, *Agriculture in Soviet Russia* (London: Victor Gollancz, 1931), 14.
[103] Ibid. 18–19.   [104] Ibid. 20.

appear in scare quotes here, but in other respects his status and attitude seem merely to confirm Chesterton's idea that land nationalization perpetuated the concentration of land in the hands of a plutocratic elite.

Animal Farming

George Orwell developed a critique of collectivization that drew on the spirit of Merrie England and the cottage economy to create a place for a socialist agriculture that was emphatically different from the Stalinist collective farm. Orwell's thinking about farming was linked to his hatred of industrialized food, which he rarely missed an opportunity to pillory. In *Coming up for Air* (1939), for example, George Bowling bites into a fishy-tasting frankfurter, and sees it as part of a modern trend towards 'making sausages out of fish, and fish... out of something different'. In *Keep the Aspidistra Flying* (1936), Gordon Comstock complains about the advertisements opposite the bookshop he works in 'exhorting you to rot your guts with this or that synthetic garbage'. He lists a series of patent products: 'QT Sauce, Tru-weet Breakfast Crisps ("Kiddies clamour for their Breakfast Crisps"), Kangaroo Burgundy, Vitamalt Chocolate, Bovex'.[105] The spectre of 'Bovex'—a fictional beef extract, meant to evoke Bovril or Oxo—returns to haunt Gordon later in the novel, when the company publishes a series of 'Bovex Ballads', sickly slabs of advertising doggerel that offend his poetic sensibilities as much as Bovex turns his stomach.[106] Losing out on good-quality food was for Orwell one of the worst effects of poverty, and he argued in *The Road to Wigan Pier* (1937) that the 'cheap luxuries' of the industrial age were palliatives forced on the poor as a replacement for the wholesome food they really needed.[107]

Because food was a social and political issue for Orwell, he was profoundly concerned with the ways in which it was produced, and obsessed with the practicalities and the economics of farming. In much of his early work, we find the impetus to understand capitalist agriculture from the perspective of the worker. During his down and out phase, Orwell went hop-picking, recording his experiences in his diary and in an article for the *New Statesman and Nation,* and fictionalizing them in his novel, *A Clergyman's Daughter* (1935). As in much of Orwell's reportage writing, his focus was on the appalling conditions suffered by the workers. He pointed out in his *New Statesman* article that '[t]he spiny stems cut the palms of

---

[105] George Orwell, *Keep the Aspidistra Flying* (London: Secker & Warburg, 1998), 4.
[106] Ibid. 257.
[107] George Orwell, *The Road to Wigan Pier* (London: Secker & Warburg, 1998), 83.

one's hands to pieces' and 'as far as wages go, no worse employment exists'.[108] In *A Clergyman's Daughter*, Dorothy experiences the tough living conditions of the hop-pickers, spending her nights sleeping a hut, sharing a pile of filthy straw with an indeterminable number of fellow pickers.[109]

In the case of the hop farms, Orwell was presented with a system of capitalist agriculture based on large-scale farms worked by itinerant labourers paid by the bushel. In his diary he describes the lives of Barrett and George,

> good specimens of the itinerant agricultural labourer. For years past they had worked on a regular round: Lambing in early spring, then pea-picking, strawberries, various other fruits, hops, "spud-grabbing", turnips and sugar beet. They were seldom out of work for more than a week or two, yet even this was enough to swallow up anything they could earn.[110]

Unlike coal mining or factory work, which brought workers together in a physical space and created (as Marx pointed out) a sense of community, a potential for organization and an awareness of shared grievance, Orwell stressed that the nomadic life of the agricultural labourer was too dispersed and chaotic for any of these to apply. 'Altogether the farmers have the hop-pickers in a cleft stick, and always will have until there is a pickers' union. It is not much use to try and form a union, though, for about half the pickers are women and gypsies, and are too stupid to see the advantages of it.'[111] What was more, as Dorothy observes in *A Clergyman's Daughter*, the farmers had little choice about how much they could pay their workers, since 'the price of hops is now so low that no farmer could afford to pay his pickers a living wage'.[112] Landowners and workers alike were at the mercy of the market. Perhaps the models of socialist organization that apply in a mine or a factory—starting with trade unions—cannot simply be applied to the farm. Which begs the question, an important one for Orwell: what would a socialist farm look like?

Orwell's *Animal Farm: A Fairy Story* (1945) is generally read as an entirely allegorical text, as if the farm merely stood for something else: the Soviet Union. Such a reading could be thought to be endorsed by the novel's subtitle, and by the unignorable correspondences between Napoleon and Stalin, Snowball and Trotsky, and so on. Still, at the risk

---

[108] George Orwell, 'Hop Picking', *New Statesman and Nation* (17 Oct. 1931), in *A Kind of Compulsion: 1903–1936,* ed. Peter Davison (London: Secker & Warburg, 1998), 233.
[109] George Orwell, *A Clergyman's Daughter* (London: Secker & Warburg, 1998), 107–8.
[110] Orwell, *A Kind of Compulsion,* 224.   [111] Ibid. 223.
[112] Orwell, *A Clergyman's Daughter,* 118.

of appearing rather literal-minded, I would like to propose that *Animal Farm* is also about farming. Old Major (who in a way stands for Marx or Lenin) decries the situation on Manor Farm—a capitalist enterprise— where 'nearly the whole produce of our labour is stolen from us by human beings'.[113] The political philosophy of animalism, which he then elaborates, is essentially a means for the animals to keep the products of their labour for themselves, and the pigs on the farm lead a revolution that is meant to bring this to pass. But in practice, the promised abundance is always deferred, as the pigs exhort the other animals to renewed hardships as they work to bring into being a radiant future. Napoleon—the pig who represents Stalin in the story—tries to conceal the food shortage: sheep are instructed to remark within hearing of a human visitor that their rations have been increased. Empty bins are filled with sand and topped with grain to give the impression of abundance to neighbouring farmers.[114] This evokes the Potemkin villages created by Stalin's regime to give the impression of opulence to capitalist visitors, or the propagandistic statistics on grain production that—as Orwell complained—Gollancz reproduced for the edification of the Left Book Club.[115] The clash between the Soviet state and the peasantry is represented by the hens who refuse to yield up their eggs for sale off the farm at a time of famine. Napoleon says that they 'should welcome this sacrifice as their own special contribution towards the building of the windmill' (clearly standing for the high-profile industrial projects of the various Five-Year-Plans, such as the Dnieper Dam and Magnitogorsk).[116] But the hens protest by laying their eggs from the rafters, causing them to smash on the floor. Napoleon orders that their food ration be stopped completely, and after nine hens have starved to death they relent, and their eggs are taken and sold. The rebellious hens are later slaughtered.[117]

As well as targeting the brutal coercion that Stalin's regime used in what Muggeridge termed a 'war between the government and the peasants', Orwell's satirical presentation of these events raises questions about whether the state has any right to exert control over the food supply.[118] Under both capitalism and Soviet Communism—in Manor Farm and Animal Farm alike—farmers are forced to produce a large surplus that is 'taken away' to feed the urban population. Whether the prices are set by a

---

[113] George Orwell, *Animal Farm: A Fairy Story* (London: Secker & Warburg, 1987), 4.
[114] Ibid. 50.
[115] George Orwell, review of N. De Basily, *Russia under Soviet Rule* in *New English Weekly* (12 Jan. 1939), repr. in *Facing Unpleasant Facts*, 316.
[116] Orwell, *Animal Farm*, 43.   [117] Ibid. 51, 56.
[118] Malcolm Muggeridge, 'The Soviet's War on the Peasants', *Fortnightly Review*, 33 (1933), 558.

cartel of supermarkets or by the state, the net effect is that farmers have to surrender a large proportion of their produce, and except for very large landowners who in any case do not work the land themselves, they rarely end up rich. The central contention of Orwell's satire is that the pigs take over from the humans—the Communist state exploits the peasantry in exactly the same way as capitalist landowners or the old Tsarist autocracy did. Neither achieves the implicit—though surely unattainable—goal of allowing farmers to eat all they produce.

The idea that the Soviet farm was a version of the large capitalist farm had a certain currency in the period. *The Economist* noted that '[t]he present *Sovhos* [state farm] is a big mechanised estate run on commercial lines similar to those on which big estates are conducted in the U.S.A. and other capitalist countries'.[119] For those like Muggeridge and Orwell who were critical of collective farming but were on the left, the comparison of the state farm with capitalist agriculture was an important rhetorical strategy. As Muggeridge wrote, the Bolsheviks' 'dreams and plans were essentially urban; proletarian Big Business; Marx-Ford Bourneville'.[120] In Orwell's *Nineteen EightyFour*, Winston Smith encounters a similar argument in Emmanuel Goldstein's *Theory and Practice of Oligarchical Collectivism* (a fictional critique of Ingsoc meant to represent Trotsky's writings):

> It had long been realized that the only secure basis for oligarchy is collectivism. Wealth and privilege are most easily defended when they are possessed jointly. The so-called 'abolition of private property' which took place in the middle years of the century meant, in effect, the concentration of property in far fewer hands than before: but with this difference, that the new owners were a group instead of a mass of individuals. Individually, no member of the Party owns anything, except petty personal belongings. Collectively, the Party owns everything in Oceania, because it controls everything, and disposes of the products as it thinks fit. In the years following the Revolution it was able to step into this commanding position almost unopposed, because the whole process was represented as an act of collectivization.[121]

Goldstein's analysis essentially repeats Chesterton's earlier theory that land nationalization might be forced on the people by a plutocratic elite, for its own benefit. And like Chesterton, leftists who saw the dangers of collectivization often wanted to reassert a kind of connection with the soil that the collective farms had destroyed. Muggeridge explained that Soviet

---

[119] Unsigned, 'Reconstruction in Russia. IV. Revolution by Tractor', *The Economist*, 110/4506 (4 Jan. 1930), 7.

[120] Muggeridge, 'The Soviet's War on the Peasants', 558.

[121] George Orwell, *Nineteen Eighty-Four* (London: Secker & Warburg, 1997), 214–15.

agricultural policy was 'inconceivable and horrible to anyone having even a remote connection with earth, with the seasons, with the labour of sowing and the joy of harvest; plausible enough in some stuffy café or committee room'.[122]

Orwell's opposition to the kolkhoz did not arise only because—unlike Shaw and the Webbs—he acknowledged the existence of a catastrophic, man-made famine.[123] It had at its root a smallholder's temperamental distrust for industrialized farming, and the suspicion that the metropolitan intelligentsia were disconnected from the soil and from the material basis of food production. Indeed he connected the two phenomena when he wrote in his review of Maurice Hindus's *Green Worlds* that 'most of the "romantics" who have rhapsodized over the collective farms are people who would not know a Rhode Island Red if they saw one'.[124] The Rhode Island Red is a popular breed of domestic chicken that Orwell himself kept.[125] Indeed, Orwell gained an extensive practical knowledge of the problems that faced the small yeomanry, spending many years patiently trying to establish himself as a subsistence farmer. These efforts are recorded in minute detail in his domestic diaries, made available in the *Collected Works*. Here is a typical entry:

> Much cooler & occasional showers. Mr H. finished cutting the hay & collected it today. Sowed turnips & planted out a row of mixed greens from the seed bed. Both broody hens with chickens laid today, & one (the youngest) had three other eggs hidden at the back of the coop.
>
> 14 eggs + 3 in coop.[126]

In this diary he makes frequent reference to the *Smallholder* magazine, to which he seems to have been a subscriber.

It is important to register that Orwell was often highly critical of those popular advocates of the cottage economy as a political project, who—like Chesterton, Belloc and Roland Knox (who wrote about the milk pool in Hyde Park, and whom Orwell mocked)—were Catholics or Fascists.[127] He wrote mockingly, in a review of Chesterton's book on

---

[122] Muggeridge, 'The Soviet's War on the Peasants', 561.

[123] Review of Eugene Lyons, *Assignment in Utopia*, in *Facing Unpleasant Facts*, 159.

[124] Review of Maurice Hindus, *Green Worlds*, in *Time and Tide* (21 Oct. 1939), in *Facing Unpleasant Facts*, 412–13.

[125] George Orwell, 'Domestic Diary', in *Facing Unpleasant Facts*, 456.

[126] George Orwell, 'Domestic Diary', dated 28.6.39, in *Facing Unpleasant Facts*, 442.

[127] For Orwell's attitude to Chesterton and two contemporary Roman Catholic newspaper columnists, 'Beachcomber' and 'Timothy Shy', who derived their political ideas from Chesterton, see 'As I Please' 30, *Tribune*, 23 June 1944, in George Orwell, *I Have Tried to Tell the Truth: 1943–44*, ed. Peter Davison (London: Secker & Warburg, 1998), 261–3. Orwell did give some credit to the man who had given him his first work as a professional

Dickens, of 'the mythical Middle Ages beloved of Roman Catholics, when peasants were boozy but monogamous, and there was no serfdom and no Holy Inquisition'.[128] But while he distanced himself from such medievalism, Orwell argued that there was a need 'to try & keep alive the older version of Socialism' in the face of Soviet Communism, 'even when it doesn't seem strategically opportune'.[129] Throughout his political writing we can find suggestions that the 'older version of socialism' he sought to keep alive involved a connection with the soil that Soviet tractor farming had ignored. No doubt thinking back to his experiences on the Kentish hop farm, Orwell wrote in November 1939 of

> the enormous gulf that lies between any kind of independent farmer and a hired labourer. The truth is that the natural human love of the soil raises a very difficult problem—not completely solved even in Soviet Russia— because no merely economic improvement does away with the difference between owning one's own land and cultivating someone else's.[130]

Orwell seems to imply that the 'independent farmer'—a figure intrinsically resistant to Soviet collectivism—may have a role to play in addressing the problems of the hop farms and of capitalist agriculture in general.

Such questions are addressed more programmatically in *The Lion and the Unicorn* (1941), where Orwell set out a six-point plan for 'socialism in Britain'. Collectivism had a central role to play, and this was no Distributist utopia. Orwell's first demand was for the 'Nationalization of land, mines, railways, banks and major industries'.[131] He wrote elsewhere that socialism was 'centralised ownership of the means of production, plus political democracy'.[132] But when Orwell got onto the practicalities of collectivism, it seemed that peasant smallholding—of the type condemned by Shaw, the Webbs, and others as 'backward'—would be a feature of the socialist future. He wrote:

---

writer, in *G.K.'s Weekly*: 'Chesterton's vision of life was false in some ways, and he was hampered by enormous ignorance, but at least he had courage. He was ready to attack the rich and powerful, and he damaged his career by doing so.' (p. 263).

[128] Orwell, *A Kind of Compulsion*, 326.

[129] Orwell to Naomi Mitchison, 17 June 1938, in *Facing Unpleasant Facts*.

[130] George Orwell, review of *Teamsman* by Crichton Porteous, a book about a man bought up in Manchester 'with good prospects in the cotton trade' who goes back to the land and works as a farmer. *Facing Unpleasant Facts*, 414–15.

[131] George Orwell, *The Lion and the Unicorn: Socialism and the English Genius*, in *A Patriot After All: 1940–41*, ed. Peter Davison (London: Secker & Warburg, 1998), 422.

[132] George Orwell, 'Will Freedom Die with Capitalism', *The Left News* (Apr. 1941), in *A Patriot After All*, 458–64.

Nationalization of agricultural land implies cutting out the landlord and the tithe-drawer, but not necessarily interfering with the farmer. . . . With certain kinds of petty trading, and even the small-scale ownership of land, the State will probably not interfere at all. It would be a mistake to start by victimizing the smallholder class, for instance. These people are necessary, on the whole they are competent, and the amount of work they do depends on the feeling that they are 'their own masters'. But the State will certainly impose an upward limit to the ownership of land (probably fifteen acres at the very most), and will never permit any ownership of land in town areas.[133]

Orwell's thinking about farming culminated in this distinction between the needs of the country and the needs of the city. Wholesale collectivization, Orwell argued, would suit the city, and industries like coal mining, very well. But he was more cautious when it came to the countryside. In seeking to hang on to 'the older form of Socialism' in the face of the seemingly pervasive Soviet variety, Orwell was also trying to hang on to an older form of agriculture. Upholding the importance of the independent, smallholding farmer, Orwell drew on the tradition of the cottage economy, resisting the Fabian endorsement of the Soviet collective farm. In effect, Orwell was a collectivist in the city and a Distributist in the country.

COMMUNIST PASTORAL

Mediating the Collective Farm

The English publisher and writer John Rodker could be said to have played a small but important role in mediating the realities of the collective farm for a British audience. A chapter by Ian Patterson gives us the fullest picture we have of Rodker's career as an advocate for Soviet culture, above all during the period in which he acted as a literary agent for PresLit, placing translations of Soviet literature with British publishers and magazines. Rodker, Patterson argues, 'played a central, complex and unacknowledged role in the Soviet Union's self-presentation in Britain'.[134] He was not a Communist, and his primary interest in the Soviet Union was cultural. In his long and complex engagement with Soviet culture, Rodker placed considerable emphasis on questions of food

---

[133] Orwell, *The Lion and the Unicorn*, 423.
[134] Ian Patterson, 'The Translation of Soviet Literature: John Rodker and PresLit', in Rebecca Beasley and Philip Bullock (eds), *Russia in Britain 1880–1940: From Melodrama to Modernism* (Oxford: OUP, 2013), 195.

and farming. He had visited the Soviet Union in the summer of 1933 and recorded his impressions in a fascinating series of unpublished articles, now held in his archive at the Harry Ransom Center, University of Texas. Many of these touch on questions of agriculture and food, and yet it is difficult to pin Rodker down to a single way of seeing the collective farm, or to align him with the broad camps I have described. Alongside views that appear to be in line with Soviet propaganda, we find some unusual and fascinating deviations. As Patterson notes, the article called simply 'Harvest in the U.S.S.R.' '[u]ncharacteristically . . . reads . . . like straight propaganda'.[135] It was turned down by Gerald Barry's *Week-End Review* (which would merge with the *New Statesman* next year). In the article, Rodker found it 'strange' that British newspapers were carrying reports that 'the peasants are reduced to eating grass and seeds and bark, when it is not each other: and this at a moment when barns and grain elevators are full to overflowing, and when for the first time in years, there is a free market in bread'.[136] Rodker contrasts the bumper harvest made possible by collectivization with 'what [the peasants] could have got by their own unaided efforts, on their own miserable strips of land'. Collectivization had shaken the Russian peasantry out of its 'notoriously conservative attitude to change'. The celebration of the collective farm comes with the by now conventional denigration of the social and psychological effects of smallholding. So far, Rodker's analysis is not so different from the propaganda of the Webbs.

Yet even in 'Harvest in the U.S.S.R.', there is a hint of another, more independent agenda that is more fully developed in the other Russian articles and plays out across Rodker's career. The arresting opening sentence of the article is: 'The general attitude towards the bounties of nature is, in the Soviet Union, so opposed to that which prevails elsewhere that the two worlds seem hardly compatible.'[137] The explanation Rodker goes on to give is that in the Soviet Union harvest figures are a matter of national, popular interest, even among the urban population, whereas in Western Europe—where there was a crisis of overproduction and low prices—the discussion centred on how best 'to limit wheat growing areas, to plough cotton back into the earth, to cast millions of sacks of coffee into the sea'.[138] Commentators such as G. T. Wrench saw the fully mechanized collective farm as something that alienated Russians from a proper relation with the soil but Rodker—at least in this article—found there a

---

[135] Ibid. 193.
[136] John Rodker, 'Harvest in the U.S.S.R.' Rodker Papers, Harry Ransom Center, University of Texas at Austin. Box 37 Folder 2, 2.
[137] Ibid. 1.   [138] Ibid.

healthier 'attitude towards the bounties of nature', even as he compared the collectivization drive's commitment of manpower, machinery, and newspaper correspondents to the mass mobilization of the Great War.

In 'Russian Impressions I' it is clearer that Rodker was aware of a famine, though doubtless not of its scale: 'the queues for paraffin, bread and tobacco, sometimes a couple of hundred yards in length, all tell their tale', he notes.[139] 'Every Russian will tell you the past year has been an extremely difficult one.'[140] Rodker's essays are more effective, though, when they turn away from the official line about the efficiency of agricultural production to explore the experiences of buying and consuming food. The best of Rodker's Russian sketches is 'Five Plates of Soup'. More of a prose poem than an essay, it adopts a breathless, paratactic and sometimes ungrammatical style. Much like the tradition of 'presentist' writing about the Soviet Union that I described in Chapter 1, typified by the work of Dorothy Richardson, its goal is to submit to experience rather than engaging in a political analysis. In this case this entails a turn from thinking about the production of food, to its consumption:

> Yes, I confess it, I was impressed by Russia, something tremendous is being built up there, the factories of course; but also there was that pub. in Moscow, a drinking shop really, with the navvies, the factory hands, the clerks and journalists, and even may be the directors of enormous enterprises, even a Commissar maybe, all sitting round the american-cloth-topped tables with litres of beer or noggins of vodka, chewing bits of salt herring helped down by squat juicy Russian cucumbers drawn from the pocket; and no side, no class distinction of any kind anywhere, or so it seemed, and no man different from another except for his clothes, and the waiter as good as the next man.[141]

This description appears as a kind of hurried list, but the effect of the parataxis is to produce a non-hierarchical sentence to match Rodker's claims about the experience of Soviet reality. But if it involves an embrace of Soviet reality as it is, the sketch also deliberately refuses to corroborate the official government line on the abundance of the harvest (quite unlike 'Harvest in the U.S.S.R.'). There is a humorous, mock-heroic aspect to Rodker's description of an evening meal and a dispute over the bill:

> [T]here [in Russia] as elsewhere there is soup and soup. But not of the factory soup do I sing now, all cabbage and water, tepid, unappetising (but

---

[139] John Rodker, 'Russian Impressions I', Rodker Papers Harry Ransom Center University of Texas at Austin. Box 37 Folder 2, p. 1.

[140] Ibid. 1.

[141] Rodker, 'Five Plates of Soup', Rodker Papers Harry Ransom Center University of Texas at Austin. Box 37 Folder 2, 1.

oh, how lackadaisical the appetite we brought to it) yet cheap considering its 35 kopecks, say twopence at the outside. No, I sing the glorious hotel-soup, boiling hot, on a plate like a cart-wheel, with its quarter of cabbage, its meat-chunk, its fat-freckles gold-winking, so sadly absent from the soup mentioned earlier, and its traces of vegetables unprocurable elsewhere, and the luscious piroghi, or maybe bliny or even welsh-rarebit, though cold, that always went with it, a soup most excellent and always perfection, outclassing by far bortch aristocratic or creme farinaceous. Thus was our diet, thus our sustenance, drawn from our lunch tickets, and uplifted forth went we, out among the muscovite, and bade three eat with us ere the next dawning.[142]

This comical tone is maintained through an epic battle with a 'comrade-manager' who insists that, since soup is not served after 8 pm, they must pay a heavy surcharge. 'You'd have trouble paying that lot for soup in London in any capitalist hang-out, we told him.'[143] When the hotel manager emerges, to insist that the rules be followed, he is described as a 'tartar-dictator'.[144] The manager's petty tyranny is magnified to absurd proportions, with the effect that it tends to undermine Rodker's initial description of a Russia in which there was 'no class distinction of any kind anywhere', and where 'the waiter [was] as good as the next man'.

The end of the story provides a comic climax, as Rodker's narrator rhetorically escalates his complaint in a parody of the bureaucratic language of the Soviet state: 'But who passed the decree, how was it made operative, what cook's soviet promulgated it, and when and by whom was it ratified? No soup after 8?'[145] Rodker's story pokes fun at the assumption that Communist politics could or should solve every problem that might be encountered: '2/6 for soup, well, I ask you? What sort of a revolution do you call that?'[146] It is a sketch, in a sense, about the limits of politics, and it implies that fears about a total state monopoly on food were misplaced. Even in a socialist command economy where private property has been abolished, the state in the end does not administer the soup: waiters do. Food, for Rodker, becomes a site for thinking about the continuities between pre-revolutionary and post-revolutionary society, and between socialist Russia and capitalist Britain. As Rodker put it a few years later in a letter to Ezra Pound: 'generally speaking, from an economic point of view—and a biological one—I dont [sic] see [the USSR] as very different from anywhere else'.[147]

What finally emerges from Rodker's essays is an attempt to set aside Soviet politics and grasp Russian *culture* instead. Patterson argues convincingly

---

[142] Ibid. 2.   [143] Ibid. 3.   [144] Ibid.   [145] Ibid.   [146] Ibid. 4.
[147] John Rodker to Ezra Pound, 29 June 1936, Rodker Papers, Harry Ransom Center, University of Texas at Austin, Box 39, Folder 9, p. 1.

that Rodker was constitutionally apolitical and that his 'primary interests were cultural'.[148] His aspiration to grasp Soviet culture and downplay the importance of Soviet politics became an increasingly important trope for Anglo-Soviet alliance in wartime. As Jim Aulich has pointed out, there was a concerted policy in British war propaganda to refer to 'Russia' rather than 'The Soviet Union', with the aim of separating the positive image of the war ally that it was seeking to promote from any association with Communist politics.[149]

The Cultural Turn

During the war, no doubt responding to the new appetite for Soviet culture in Britain, Rodker edited a collection of Russian stories under the title *Soviet Anthology*, published by Jonathan Cape in 1943. Some of these stories were set on collective farms, and the selection itself is revealing about the kind of contact Rodker wanted to establish between British readers and Soviet agriculture.

Rodker's motivations in compiling his *Soviet Anthology* can be traced in his correspondence with the two men who translated the bulk of the stories, Harry Stevens (working under the pseudonym 'Stephen Garry') and Alec Brown. These letters need to be read in the context of the new political relationship between Britain and Russia, since the two countries were by now allies in the war against Hitler. That Jonathan Cape—not a specialist socialist publisher like Gollancz, for example—was interested in such a work was perhaps testament to the renewed public appetite for Soviet culture in the context of this wartime alliance. Stevens wrote in June 1942 suggesting a list of stories that he might translate, 'with an idea to variety of interest: from civil war days to collective farming and reconstruction'. The two stories that deal most explicitly with the life of the collective farm are Piotr Pavlenko's 'A Night Talk' (titled 'Nightpiece' in the published *Anthology*) and Venyamin Kaverin's 'Thomas the Ostrich'. If Rodker's 'Harvest in the U.S.S.R.' on the whole inhabits the standard tropes and distortions of Soviet propaganda about the collectivization drive, these stories and the editorial discussions around them suggest quite a different approach. In his list of potential stories, Stevens summarizes 'Thomas the Ostrich' in these terms: 'A boy's love of machines and contempt for animals, and how his ride on an ostrich

---

[148] Patterson, 'The Translation of Soviet Literature', 191.
[149] Jim Aulich, 'Stealing the Thunder: The Soviet Union and Graphic Propaganda on the Home Front during the Second World War', *Visual Culture in Britain*, 13/3 (2012), 363n.

saved a collective farm'. Making the case for the story's inclusion in the collection, Stevens goes on: '"Thomas the Ostrich"... is really rather good, with a touch of humour'.[150]

The quality of humour is indeed essential to Kaverin's story and to the perspective on Soviet collective farming that Rodker and his translators now sought to project to British readers in wartime. That this was a deliberate aim of the anthology is suggested in a later letter. Stevens writes: 'I'm glad you like "Thomas": with Kataev and the other he will give a rather different impression of Soviet literature from that conveyed by previous anthologies!'[151] 'Thomas the Ostrich' (which was first published in Russian in 1930, in the midst of the collectivization drive) does seem to have captured the imagination, and Rodker granted permission for the BBC to broadcast a dramatization on its Senior English programme on 23 February 1945.[152]

When the story begins, the narrator has persuaded two (somewhat reluctant) other members of the kolkhoz to 'rest for a couple of hours or so from the clanking of tractors', since almost all the grain has been harvested, and pay a visit to the Zoological Gardens at nearby Askania-Nova.[153] The story thus establishes an opposition between the completely mechanized life of the collective farm where men work with machines rather than horses and donkeys, and a more pastoral setting at the zoological gardens where animals no longer work and men gawp at them on their days off. This opposition is deepened when, after becoming separated from his companions, the narrator befriends a boy 'between ten and twelve years old' called Piotka who is employed to care for animals at the zoo.[154] The irony and humour of the story rests in Piotka's over-enthusiastic embrace of the ideology of collectivization. For example, Piotka has a habit of quantifying the power of particular models of tractor—the caterpillar, the 'Monarch', the 'International'—in relation to the animals he reluctantly tends: 'Caterpillars are as strong as devils. I've worked it all out. If one bison is equal to three and a half horses, a caterpillar tractor is equal to seventeen and one-seventh bisons. Seventeen and one-seventh! Why, that's a whole herd!'[155] Piotka then happily

---

[150] Harry Stevens to John Rodker, 31 Mar. 1942, Harry Ransom Center, Rodker Papers Box 12 Folder 3, p. 1.

[151] Stevens to Rodker, 28 July 1942, Harry Ransom Center, Rodker Papers Box 12 Folder 3, p. 1.

[152] The letters pertaining to this broadcast are S. McGrath to G. Wren Howard, 29 Nov. 1944; Dahlia Fraser to Rodker, 30 Nov. 1944; Rodker to Jonathan Cape, 1 Dec. 1944, Harry Ransom Center, Rodker Papers Box 12 Folder 3.

[153] Venyamin Kaverin, 'Thomas the Ostrich', tr. Stephen Garry, in John Rodker (ed.), *Soviet Anthology* (London: Jonathan Cape, 1943), 76.

[154] Ibid. 78.   [155] Ibid. 79.

converts this into a different currency: 'it is equal to eighty full-grown African ostriches. Now that's talking! There's power for you!'[156] His tractor obsession is combined with an explicit disdain for animals, who—as his calculations repeatedly reveal—can scarcely measure up against the sheer power of modern agricultural machinery:

> 'Why, Piotka, you don't seem to like animals very much,' I said, recalling how harshly he had treated the young ostriches.
> He shrugged his shoulders with the utmost contempt.
> 'And why should I like them?' he asked. 'They're all weak. What's the strongest animal of all? The elephant. And how many elephants could the "Monarch" tractor drag away?'[157]

The humour for which Rodker and Stevens seemed to value the story is unmistakably partly laughter at the po-faced celebrations of tractor-power which were a familiar aspect of Soviet propaganda. It is certainly a 'boy meets tractor' story, but it can produce a 'rather different impression of Soviet literature' because it is also aware of the conventions of the genre and able to laugh at them.

The tractor's omnipotence is comically undermined in the story's exciting and absurd conclusion. A fire sweeps across the collective farm, and the workers try to manage the blaze while contacting the fire brigade. But the phone lines are down, none of the cars are working, and, as one worker pointedly notes: 'we've got no horses'.[158] Piotka at this point takes the initiative, and summons Thomas the ostrich: one animal with which he has, almost despite himself, formed a bond. Straddling the ostrich as if it were a horse, Piotka makes the twenty-five-mile journey to Central Village to summon the fire brigade, and saves the collective farm from total destruction. The central opposition between animals and machines is then revisited in the story's conclusion:

> 'Well, Piotka,' I said, 'you were telling me yesterday that animals were just good for nothing, that none of them had any strength. But if it hadn't been for your Thomas the whole of the steppe from Askania right to the sea of Azov might have gone up in flame.'
> We all gazed at the ostrich. It shifted from foot to foot, cocked its head on one side, and blinked, blinked.
> 'Maybe,' said Piotka, as he poured his tea into a soup basin. He crumbled some bread and onion into the tea, thrust the basin under the ostrich's nose, graciously tickled it around its neck and sat down again.

---

[156] Ibid. 80.   [157] Ibid. 82.   [158] Ibid. 86.

'Maybe,' he repeated. 'But after all, it was only by chance that all the machines happened to be out. And if we'd even had one old Tin Lizzie here . . .'

He suddenly broke off and screwed up one eye. He began to whisper, wriggling his fingers, then bit his lip and screwed up his other eye as he reckoned:

'Say a Ford has got twelve and a half horse-power, and an ostrich has go three-quarters horse-power exactly. Well you reckon up for yourselves how much faster I'd have driven to Central Village. Sixteen and one-eighth times as fast . . .'

'But this time you're wrong,' I said. 'It's sixteen and two thirds.'[159]

Events have taken a turn that might well have lead Piotka to reassess his constant preference for tractors over animals. Indeed, the narrator is quick to derive this moral and he suggests it, somewhat tongue in cheek, to Piotka. Piotka resolutely refuses to learn the lesson of his own heroic actions, however, and continues to look forward to a future in which the ever-increasing power and efficiency of machines make animals like Thomas obsolete, even as he affectionately tickles the ostrich around the neck.

The humour of 'Thomas the Ostrich' thus seems somewhat subversive in the context of Soviet policy on the collectivization and mechanization of agriculture. The *Anthology* also included four stories by Mikhail Zoschenko, who was to become the victim of a high-profile cultural purge initiated by A. A. Zhandov in 1946, that became known as the Soviet Literary Controversy and was widely debated in left-leaning literary journals in Britain.[160] There is some evidence, should one wish to adduce it, that Rodker might have been seeking to bring dissident voices from the Soviet Union to an Anglophone readership. However, the other collective farm story that Stevens translated for the anthology— 'Nightpiece', by Piotr Pavlenko—takes a much more conventional line. The protagonist, Kharlai, is an old man who works in the apiary on the collective farm, but retains a romantic attachment to the farm he used to run. He has been called out of the apiary to help with the harvest, and asks a young woman in the fields 'I suppose . . . you've reaped and harvested your own land in your time?'[161] His own 'narrow strip of land' had become part of the vast collective farm and is 'not to be found amid all the stretch of many

---

[159] Ibid. 92.

[160] Ben Harker, 'Politics and Letters: The "Soviet Literary Controversy" in Britain', *Literature and History*, 24/2 (2015). 41–56.

[161] Piotr Pavlenko, 'Nightpiece' (tr. Stephen Garry), in John Rodker (ed.), *Soviet Anthology* (London: Jonathan Cape, 1943), 103.

acres of drowsy grain'.[162] As the memory of his own land gnaws at him, he takes a ride on a combine harvester to search for it, and eventually locates it:

> The combine was now driving all over his life. Here—how well he still remembered it!—they had fought with stakes over a question of the field boundaries; there, by a little bush, his elder daughter had been born; farther on, close to the road, the wheat had once caught fire; and somewhere near by a wandering pilgrim had died in 1917 after telling of the end of the war. Now grain, level, thick, a single flood, was growing all over those memories.[163]

The rooted life of the traditional peasantry—working along the lines of what the English tradition called a 'cottage economy'—permits an organic and personal connection with a particular piece of land, which becomes layered with personal and historical memories. In the collective farm, all this is flattened and homogenized in the name of industrially produced 'grain'. But if this story opens up the possibility of such a critique, it is also quick to shut it down again. After this experience, Kharlai sits down with a watchman and a stableman and they stay up all night talking. The discussion takes the form of a self-criticism in which they discuss 'the almost forgotten past . . . their terrible, ignorant way of life, and their many mistakes, . . . condemning their failure to recognise the new great reality'.[164] The narrator goes on: 'These men, whose lives had been filled to overflowing with innumerable labours, deprivations and failures, now wanted to see not themselves, but stronger, finer, and more reliable people working under the Soviet regime.'[165] Kharlai in the end recognizes that his attachment to his 'narrow strip of land', and his belief that when the combine harvester is 'driving all over his life' when it crosses his land, are so many romantic relics of a past age, inimical to the bold new life of the Soviet Union. It is an interesting story in its own right, and the extent to which it dramatizes the psychological and social effects of collectivization should not be underestimated. But in the end, unlike 'Thomas the Ostrich', the story is not interested in putting an ironic distance between the reader and the ideology of Stalin's collectivization drive. The stern seriousness with which the younger generation of Communists go about their work on the farm is admired by the old men at the centre of the story, who are only sorry that, despite their best efforts, their physical and mental limitations prevent them from being of the utmost service to the Soviet regime.

---

[162] Ibid. 105–6.   [163] Ibid. 106.   [164] Ibid. 107–8.   [165] Ibid. 108.

The two stories present very different perspectives on collectivization. To suggest that Rodker was seeking out writers who were challenging Soviet propaganda on the countryside in order to promote a somewhat dissident point of view would be an oversimplification. The ideological and aesthetic variety on offer in the *Soviet Anthology* seems to have been part of the point. As Stevens wrote to Rodker:

> As for there being no clear line: does it really matter? Let it just be a book of short stories, with no ideological aim, and no 'line' whatever, but just a book to swim on the current and show that 'lines' in Russia as everywhere else are being steadily, and now rapidly obliterated![166]

So this was to be a book of Soviet stories 'with no ideological aim'. Both of the collective farm stories have contrasting but clear didactic, political meanings, yet the desired effect of the *Anthology* was to subordinate a political understanding of the Soviet Union to a cultural one. Such an understanding was substantially complicated when it came to considerations of Soviet agriculture, but Rodker's efforts in this area opened up an interesting territory. As much as the politics and the economics of food and farming may have changed under Stalin's rule, Rodker sought to redirect attention to the everyday, where could still be found a resilience and humour that was worthy of celebration despite the disasters of Stalin's agricultural policies.

English and Russian Journeys

J. B. Priestley had become a popular voice during the Second World War as a significant radio personality who gave patriotic addresses on the BBC. As a lifelong socialist—though never a member of the Communist Party—the wartime alliance offered him hopes of a progressive partnership between Britain and the Soviet Union that would last into the postwar period. He said in 1942:

> The British people have the most tremendous enthusiasm for the Russians and the Russian war effort. I have done a good deal of talking at the big war factories, and it has always been my experience that any reference to Russia immediately starts these audiences cheering. The enthusiasm is not political. Very few of these people are Communists, or even Socialists. But the heroic effort of the Red Army and the tremendous support given to that Army by the whole Russian people are things that the people here understand and sympathise with, and so there has been developed this colossal enthusiasm which has led to a very general keen interest in the Soviet Union throughout

---

[166] Stevens to Rodker, 28 July 1942.

this country, and I believe that this can easily result in a very real and lasting friendship between the British and Russian peoples, a friendship that may play a very great part in the future organisation of world affairs.[167]

With a view to sustaining Anglo-Soviet amity after the end of the war, Priestley paid a visit to the country where he was already a celebrity: *An Inspector Calls* received its first performance there in 1945, and his work was widely known and discussed. His account of his travels, *Russian Journey* (1946), can be thought of as a post-war sequel to his successful and popular *English Journey* (1934). This pamphlet was published by the Society for Cultural Relations with the USSR, an organization that—as Emily Lygo has shown—claimed to be 'non-political' and 'neutral in its attitude towards the USSR' but in its 'publications and events put forward representation of the USSR that was almost exclusively positive'.[168] The emphasis on an apolitical celebration of 'Russian' culture was arguably, for the SCR at least, a way of disguising a more explicitly political affiliation. *Russian Journey* is upbeat about most aspects of Soviet life, but Priestley was aware of the tradition of Communist travelogues, and the often-heard criticism that the authors of those books were duped by the Communist authorities. He admitted upfront that he travelled as a guest of VOKS and that he and his wife were 'most generously treated'. But he emphasized too that 'we did not spend all our time hedged around by interpreters, detectives and dictaphones, that we saw what we wanted to see and often made last-minute choices and so paid unexpected visits, and that if we wanted to be alone (and my wife knew enough Russian to enable us to talk to people) then we were left alone'.[169] Of course, there are two ways of reading the phrase 'we saw what we wanted to see', and no doubt like many sympathetic visitors, the Priestleys 'toured their own ardent preconceptions', in Patrick Wright's phrase.[170]

Witnessing first-hand what had happened to Soviet agriculture was a priority for Priestley. 'From the first I made up my mind that whatever else I saw in the Soviet Union I would certainly insist on seeing some Collective Farms'.[171] Though he insisted at several points that 'I do not pretend to know much about agriculture', he clearly saw the kolkhoz as

[167] J. B. Priestley, speaking on 'Answering You: J. B. Priestley, Leslie Howard, Geoffrey Crowther and George Strauss', *The Listener*, 690 (2 Apr. 1942), 439.

[168] Emily Lygo, 'Promoting Soviet Culture in Britain: The History of the Society for Cultural Relations between the Peoples of the British Commonwealth and the USSR, 1924–45', *Modern Language Review*, 108/2 (Apr. 2013), 577.

[169] J. B. Priestley, *Russian Journey* (London: Writers Group of the Society for Cultural Relations with the USSR, 1946), 3, 4.

[170] Patrick Wright, *Iron Curtain: From Stage to Cold War* (Oxford: OUP, 2007), 261.

[171] Priestley, *Russian Journey*, 8.

fundamentally important in any assessment of the successes and failures of Communism in practice. He gave three reasons for this importance:

> I wanted to see if Socialism could work on the land, if only because so many people tell one that it cannot. Then again, I remembered the grim story of the abolition of the Kulaks, the rich peasant farmers who refused to join the experiment. Finally, I was curious to learn what this 'collectivisation' meant when it was applied to farming.[172]

Priestley clearly followed the official Party line in his belief that the 'grim story' of the collectivization drive was caused by 'rich peasant farmers', which in fact scarcely existed after 1917. But his instincts about the fundamental importance of the countryside in assessing the outcomes of the Bolshevik Revolution align with many of the other texts discussed in this chapter.

Priestley was overwhelmingly positive about his experiences on a wide variety of collective farms. He insisted that he was 'no agricultural expert' before going on to: 'But I do know something about human nature, and I left the last of all those Collective Farms convinced that the psychological gains had been very considerable.' The emphasis on the 'psychological gains' is a telling echo of Cobbett's earlier insistence on the benefits of beekeeping and home brewing, though the context has changed completely. Indeed, the gains are a result of a system in which 'Several hundred people combine to run a large farm instead of scratching away at little farms': again it seems that the kolkhoz must be understood as the opposite of the cottage economy.[173] As if to hammer home the point, Priestley set out an explicit critique of the cottage economy tradition:

> Many of my literary colleagues, although they have never been seen in the fields early on a winter morning, are always telling us of the value and virtues of a sturdy peasantry, rooted in the soil. Unfortunately, as the war showed in more than one country, there are peasant vices as well as peasant virtues: notably, narrowness of outlook, a hard meanness, a constant sour greed.

With Chesterton, Belloc, and their descendants firmly in his sights, Priestley distanced himself from the cottage economy tradition in order to embrace Soviet tractor farming, and a 'mechanised battalion of farm workers'.[174]

And yet, *Summer Day's Dream* (1949)—a play first performed only three years after the publication of *Russian Journey*—seems to push in a wholly different direction, revelling in its utopian cottage economy setting. Set in 1975, in the aftermath of a nuclear war, England's great

---

[172] Ibid.   [173] Ibid. 9.   [174] Ibid. 11, 9.

industrial cities have been destroyed and the country has been returned to small-scale, subsistence farming. The globalized industrial economy still exists, and is effectively managed and shared by three superpowers: the USA, India, and the Soviet Union. Britain's discovery of a new economy based on subsistence farming and barter—which in some respects resembles the Distributist utopia sketched out by Chesterton and Belloc—is a happy accident resulting from its nuclear annihilation. The play is set in what had been a 'fine old country mansion' but, with the gentry gone, is now 'really a farmhouse'.[175] When Irina Shetsova—who 'represents the Synthetic Products department of the Soviet Foreign Trade Commission'[176]—asks 'is it a Capitalist or Socialist system', she is told that '[i]t isn't a system at all, as far as I can see. We just get along as best we can. We aren't bothering with systems.'[177]

The play's central character is Stephen Dawlish, an old man who had been a powerful industrialist before the nuclear war, but now celebrates the physical and moral benefits of subsistence farming:

STEPHEN (*after a pause*): When are you picking up the potatoes?
FRED: Next week. I thought we might all take it easy a bit the rest of this week—after the hay.
STEPHEN: Certainly. Take it easy. I spent more than half my life, when I ought to have been enjoying myself, arguing and planning and running around like a maniac, all to sell a lot of things to people I didn't know so that I could buy a lot of things I never had time to use. Sheer lunacy. And it took nothing less than an atom bomb to blow me out of it.[178]

The play dramatizes a visit to the farm by three representatives of the three great global powers who have arrived in this part of the South Downs with a view to building a huge industrial installation to extract chalk and use it to make a synthetic substance called 'Mixture B'.[179] When their helicopter fails, and given that the most advanced form of transportation now available in England is a horse, they find themselves stranded and are welcomed into Stephen Dawlish's home. They get to know his family, and learn something of the benefits of an apparently more primitive way of life.

Priestley stages an explicit dialogue between the cottage economy and Soviet Communism. On her arrival, Irina Shetsova is openly scornful of the England she discovers: 'I do not like this place, or these people. Now

[175] J. B. Priestley, *Summer Day's Dream*, in *The Plays of J. B. Priestley*, iii (London: Heinemann, 1950), 416.
[176] Ibid. 414. [177] Ibid. 433. [178] Ibid. 410. [179] Ibid. 426.

that they no longer have world power, these people, they lose themselves in a decadent romanticism.'[180] It is the familiar attitude of the Bolshevik collectivizer to the 'backward' politics of the smallholding peasantry. But Priestley engages the audience's sympathy firmly on the side of the new English yeomanry. Stephen's grandson Chris falls quickly in love with the beautiful but stern Irina, and it is his task to win over this frosty Russian utilitarian with his brand of bucolic Romanticism:

> You are the most beautiful woman I have ever seen—and yet nothing I do or say touches you at all. As if a man tried to pluck the flower of the world and found it was made of steel and ice. It's blue midsummer here, and you stare at me out of a Siberian winter.[181]

Her sexual frigidity is also related to her portrayal as a dogmatically doctrinal Communist. Chris attempts to woo her with some lines from *The Tempest* and she responds with a Marxist analysis, stating that 'This Caliban is portrayed as a victim of British Imperialism'. Chris responds that 'It's like looking at a cheap little textbook bound in silver and gold.' As beautiful as he finds her, Chris implies that her mental habits are completely overrun by Marxist doctrine.

Over the course of the play, however, Irina softens under the influence of Chris's love and the simple pleasures of subsistence agriculture. The quality of the food the Dawlishes grow is repeatedly remarked upon, and Irina comments specifically on the 'wonderful milk'.[182] She is also moved by the sheer contact with the natural world which her life as a Soviet official denies her:

> MARGARET: I saw you walking about by yourself, looking at the flowers. Probably some of them are strange to you.
> IRINA: Yes, they are. And I should like to know their names. I was born and brought up in Moscow, where my father was an engineer. But the brother of my mother—my—my—
> MARGARET (prompting her): Uncle—
> IRINA: Yes, my uncle—was the director of a kolkos—collective farm—in the Ukraine and nearly every year, in summer, when I was young I would stay with him. And now I have been remembering all that.
> MARGARET: Yet that is quite different, isn't it?
> IRINA: Quite different. Yet when I was alone in your garden, hearing so many birds sing, looking at so many flowers, I began to remember those times when I was younger—and deep inside

---

[180] Ibid. 423.   [181] Ibid. 422.   [182] Ibid. 434.

I felt something—something—oh—it is difficult for me to describe. My English has not been used to describe such feelings, but only for official and trade discussions and negotiation. And now—when I do not want to discuss and negotiate—when I talk in a beautiful wild garden in the evening—and I feel so many things at once—so happy—so sad—so much strange aliveness inside—I have no words in English—only in Russian, which no one here can understand. (She ends rather wistfully.)[183]

That reference to the kolkhoz is somewhat ambivalent. On the one hand, Irina's absorption in the life of the Dawlishes' farm calls to mind memories of her childhood experiences on her uncle's collective farm. But she is also quick to agree that that the kolkhoz was 'quite different'. Indeed, the difference seems to have been underlined in the previous scene, where Stephen had been explaining to the American visitor, Franklyn Heimer, how good life without tractors can be:

STEPHEN: We don't have tractors either. We prefer animals, horses chiefly. That was a horse in the cart we sent for you and your companions. They're pleasant creatures, and very useful. Unlike tractors, they learn our ways, they reproduce themselves, they help to manure the soil, and now we haven't to work in factories to produce goods for export to pay for the petrol we used to have to import. It's more fun and much healthier looking after horses than working in a factory. And I've tried both.

HEIMER: Sure thing—but—hell! Horses are so slow.

STEPHEN: In this part of the world, Mr. Heimer, nature is slow too. So we're all slow together.[184]

The contrast Stephen draws between tractors and animals works in exactly the opposite way to the comparison drawn by Piotka in Kaverin's 'Thomas the Ostrich'. And while Stephen is undoubtedly depicted as a sentimental old man, his attachment to his smallholding is not undercut by irony in the way that Piotka's love of tractors was. It is hard to square this with the Priestley of *Russian Journey*, who had marvelled at the fact that 'before the war the Soviet Union had enough tractors to plough up all the cultivated land in Britain in less than two days'.[185] It only shows that Priestley felt the appeal of the collective farm *as well as* the cottage economy. Neither one had a monopoly on the future.

Over the course of the play, Irina is converted to the cottage economy ideal to the extent that she intervenes to save the Dawlishes'

---

[183] Ibid. 432.   [184] Ibid. 415.   [185] Ibid. 9.

farm from the incursions of the three powers (although not to the extent that she decides to stay there with her lover Chris). This idyll is no doubt partly a nostalgic reversion to an imagined past. As well as celebrating his freedom from tractor farming, Stephen also revels in the lack of modern telecommunications technology: not only the 'T.V.-com' but telephones:

> I was in industry once, Mr. Heimer, and I can remember how I used to be surrounded by batteries of telephones all ringing and buzzing all day and then when I'd rush home to try to rest, the things would start, ringing and buzzing there. I didn't like it then. Now, looking back on it, I'd call it just plain hell.

When asked 'how do you talk to people?' Stephen drily replies 'We just go up to them—open our mouths—and start talking'.[186] The story embodies an aversion to a life led 'hung on wires' that recalls Chesterton and Belloc's critique of networked infrastructure. The resemblance goes deeper. When Irina quizzes Fred—a sort of labourer who has a share in the farm—about how things are run, she, as a representative of Soviet Communism, is keen to know 'Is the cultural life organised from a centre?'. And Fred's response echoes the arguments of Distributism: 'No. We don't have anything organised from centres. When all the centres were blown to bits, we decided we wouldn't bother with centres any more. Seems to work all right.'[187] But is Priestley's play reducible to simple nostalgic medievalism, or does it open out onto an alternative, non-Bolshevik future? What happens if we, following Williams, ask it to 'choose its bearings, between past and future'?[188] There is at least a case to be made that the play is not *only* nostalgic: the vision it counterposes to the industrialized tractor farm is something more than a fantasy of England's past. Stephen's dislike for tractors and telephones does not extend to technology as such. Noticing that the Dawlishes still rely on electric light, Heimer challenges Stephen:

> HEIMER: Well, Mr. Dawlish, I see you don't turn up your nose at electricity—
>
> STEPHEN (*turning, shouting angrily*): Mr. Heimer, we don't turn up our noses at anything that's really useful, pleasant, and won't make slaves out of us.
>
> . . .
>
> STEPHEN (*as he attends to beer*): We make this supply of electricity locally, with a couple of wind vanes up on the down. I had a hand in it so I know all about it. It's a sketchy, weak supply but it does what we want it to do. Now—try that—(*Hands him his beer.*)[189]

---

[186] Ibid. 414.   [187] Ibid. 433.   [188] Williams, *The Country and the City*, 36.
[189] Priestley, *Summer Day's Dream*, 435.

It seems that while many modern technologies tend towards a 'natural monopoly', this is not always the case. Electricity can be decentralized in its production as well as its consumption. Although the Dawlishes' 'sketchy, weak supply' hardly catapults them into an electrified radiant future, Priestley does show an interest in thinking through the technological possibilities of a post-infrastructural age.

In many ways, the pastoral fantasy of *Summer Day's Dream* seems to be quite simply at odds with the favourable account of Soviet collectivization in *Russian Journey*. Yet even in *Russian Journey*, with its forthright criticism of the cottage economy tradition, Priestley acknowledged that there are peasant virtues as well as vices: 'the problem is how to keep the virtues while dropping the vices'. And he concluded that the collective farms—far from destroying the rooted peasant communities as Chesterton and others proclaimed—'have begun to solve that psychological and social problem'. Rather than abolishing the peasants, in a sense they were perfecting them. He goes on to explain:

> These Collective workers are honest-to-goodness folk of the soil, with most of the old earthy good qualities, which shone in their broad smiling faces. But the old peasant weaknesses, I felt, were vanishing. Their outlook was broadening, the sour greed had gone, and though they were hard enough in their resistance to the invaders, whom they fought stubbornly to the last ditch, they were no longer grasping and mean, indifferent to anything but what profit they could wrest out of the land. They were citizens and not serfs of the soil. They welcomed education instead of bitterly opposing it. They were keeping the best of their charming old customs but ridding themselves of bigotry, superstition and prejudice.[190]

Priestley's work in the second half of the 1940s involved a dramatic exploration of the tension between the cottage economy and the collective farm. Unlike Chesterton and Belloc, he was not promoting the cottage economy as an anti-Communist alternative to the collective farm, or in Pound's terms attempting to 'set HOMESTEAD against kolschoz'.[191] Priestley seemed to hold both possibilities in view, just as he sought a cultural rapprochement between the peoples of Russia and England.

Merrie Russia

There were other sympathetic accounts of Soviet collective farming that sought, as Priestley had done, to produce a kind of accommodation with the cottage economy tradition. Intriguingly, such accounts sometimes

[190] Priestley, *Russian Journey*, 12.
[191] Ezra Pound to Olivia Rosetti, 5 Apr. 1954, in *I Cease Not to Yowl*, 145.

stressed the *continuities* in Russian agriculture, from the small-scale strip farming organized around the *mir*, to the state and collective farms established during Stalin's collectivization drive. Margaret Cole, for example, argued that Russia

> benefitted from a communal village association which preserved in Russian agricultural life a tradition of collective responsibility which had been lost in England since the last Labourers' Revolt ended in the graves at Micheldever. This tradition, passing through many vicissitudes, has proved the basis for the collective farm and rural soviet organisation which is so strongly established today.[192]

The reference to Micheldever is striking. This Hampshire parish had been a hotbed of activity during the Swing Riots in 1830. These rural uprisings saw peasants, smallholders, and agricultural labourers rise up against the landlords in a spate of rick-burning, machine-breaking, cattle-maiming, and various infringements of the game laws.[193] The Swing Riots are frequently associated with William Cobbett, who stood trial for inciting the rebellion (though on this occasion he was acquitted). Hobsbawm and Rudé note that William Winkworth, one of the leaders of the disturbances around Micheldever, read Cobbett's *Political Register* aloud to 'a small party of Hampshire bumpkins' on Saturday nights.[194] The uprising was rapidly suppressed: across the country 277 individuals were sentenced to death (although only five were eventually hanged) and more were deported to Australia.[195] By the 'graves at Micheldever' Margaret Cole presumably refers to those of the hanged men, whose demise was described by her husband, G. D. H. Cole, in his 1924 biography of Cobbett:

> Henry Cook, a ploughboy of nineteen, who had seriously damaged Mr. Bingham-Baring's hat with a blow, and had been one of a mob who went round 'extorting money,' had no confessions to make, and was duly hanged. It was worse than treason to knock off the hat of a Baring. Cook was buried at Micheldever amid the solemn mourning of the whole parish. His name was often in Cobbett's mouth later—the hardest taunt he could fling at the Whig butchers.[196]

G. D. H. Cole was a key figure in the Guild Socialism that Raymond Williams turns to at the end of *Culture and Society*, describing it as a

[192] Margaret Cole, *Our Soviet Ally: Essays* (London: Routledge & Sons, 1943), 6.
[193] The story of the Swing Riots was influentially set out in 1969 in Eric Hobsbawm and George Rudé, *Captain Swing*, new edn (London: Phoenix Press, 2001).
[194] Hobsbawm and Rudé, *Captain Swing*, 246.
[195] Carl J. Griffin, 'Affecting Violence: Language, Gesture and Performance in Early Nineteenth-Century English Popular Protest', *Historical Geography*, 36 (2008), 143.
[196] G. D. H. Cole, *The Life of William Cobbett* (Abingdon: Routledge, 2011), 360.

'creative and indispensable' element of British culture, a valuable resource in Williams's quest to dissociate his version of Marxism from the Soviet Communism. Margaret Cole's attempt to see in the Soviet collective farm a revival of the spirit that had been crushed during the suppression of the agrarian protests of 1830 suggests a number of incongruities. We have seen how Chesterton used Cobbett's idea of the cottage economy as a kind of bulwark against Soviet collectivization. But for Cole, the goals of a Cobbett-inspired agrarian movement—crushed by the landlords in Britain—have finally been realized in Stalin's collectivization drive. That collectivization drive, as we have seen, was associated with rapid mechanization and industrialization: but Swing was a rebellion against the introduction of new technologies into agriculture, and 'remains the biggest single episode of machine-breaking in British history'.[197] Cole is writing from a pro-Soviet, Fabian perspective, yet she could describe the kolkhoz as if it was a continuation of the medieval peasant farming that had died first in England. The Russian peasant was not imagined as holding back the progress of socialism—on the contrary, his backwardness was to be celebrated as the foundation for the socialist organization of the countryside.

Joan Beauchamp was keen to show how the Russian collective farm could outdo the American ranch in terms of efficiency and output. Her book, *Agriculture in Soviet Russia*, is an overt celebration of what Williams decried as an inhuman emphasis on 'power, yield, production, man's mastery over nature'. But, in a bizarre twist, like Cole she also wanted to understand the collective farm as a fulfilment of the dreams of Merrie England that had captivated English socialists in the nineteenth century. She wrote:

My train arrived at Ubokaya, a village which used to be in the Ukraine but is now included in the Northern Caucasus, at 9.30 in the morning just in time to catch a glimpse of a curious and interesting ceremony. The collective farms of the district had already gathered their harvest and were bringing their grain to the railway. An avenue had been made of brilliant red banners with such legends as 'A Present to the Soviets from the Collective Farms,' 'Socialised Grain for the People,' 'The Five Year Plan in Four Years' and other slogans. Down the avenue under the banners came an endless procession of wagons each drawn by two bullocks, beautifully garlanded and well groomed for the occasion. The wagons were piled high with sacks of grain and attended by women and children in gay frocks and festive decorations. Trains, alas, do not wait on ceremony, and I was reluctantly forced to leave

---

[197] Carl J. Griffin, 'Swing, Swing Redivivus, or Something After Swing? On the Death Throes of a Protest Movement, December 1830–December 1833', *International Review of Social History*, 54/3 (Dec. 2009), 460.

these village rejoicings, but I felt that at last I had seen something not unlike the legendary 'Harvest Homes' of Merrie England, which have now in my native Somersetshire dwindled into the dull and formal Harvest Festival of the village church.[198]

It would be relatively easy to dismiss Beauchamp as another 'useful idiot' duped by a Potemkin display of opulence—a visitor to Animal Farm impressed by barrels that seem to be overflowing with the fruits of a bountiful harvest, never suspecting that beneath a thin layer of grain there was only sand. There would be some truth to this. However, Beauchamp is no longer trading in the official utilitarian language of efficiency and output: this is the Romantic rhetoric of Merrie England in full swing. The Russian countryside has become a kind of fantasy space where the contradictions between Romantic socialism and utilitarian socialism, between Merrie England and the Five-Year-Plan, and between the cottage economy and the collective farm can be resolved. The desire to resolve the contradictions between these traditions was a strong one.

During the years in which Soviet agriculture underwent its rapid and violent collectivization, a series of debates that had their roots deep in English history were freshly politicized. Many on the left accepted that the new face of socialist farming and socialist food must follow the Bolsheviks in embracing centralized state control, collective (or national) rather than individual ownership, and a high degree of industrial mechanization. But—despite Pound's complaint that the 'homestead' had never established itself as an alternative to the kolkhoz in anti-Communist propaganda—there were those, such as Chesterton and Belloc, who mobilized Cobbett and the cottage economy tradition against Soviet collectivization. This was not just to fall back on a bucolic and Romantic 'Englishness': it was a pointed and polemical intervention that sought to describe an alternative post-capitalist future. In response to this effort, or less consciously as a way of making the collective farm palatable to a certain kind of reader, thinkers such as J. B. Priestley, Joan Beauchamp, and Margaret Cole sought in various ways an accommodation between the kolkhoz and the cottage economy, or even a dialectical synthesis of the two. In all these cases, this involved a misrepresentation of the realities of collectivization, and a degree of complicity in the covering up of Stalin's crimes.

Raymond Williams's *The Country and the City* should perhaps be read in light of these debates. Williams sought to lend legitimacy, or at least sympathy, to those voices who complained that industrial modernity had

---

[198] Beauchamp, *Agriculture in Soviet Russia*, 9–10.

destroyed the stable rhythms of subsistence agriculture, and torn the peasantry from the soil. One of the heroes of Williams's book is the Scottish Communist writer, Lewis Grassic Gibbon. Williams contrasts Grassic Gibbon with D. H. Lawrence, whose work is seen as a powerful but fundamentally conservative response to the incursion of industrial modernity into the countryside. In Grassic Gibbon, by contrast: 'More historically and more convincingly, the radical independence of the small farmers, the craftsmen and the labourers is seen as transitional to the militancy of the industrial workers.'[199] Unlike in the Soviet Union, where Stalin had set the interests of the urban working class against that of the backward peasantry, in Grassic Gibbon's *Scots Quair* trilogy Williams finds the possibility of an alliance between those two classes. In the story of Chris Guthrie's passage from the agrarian past to the urban future, and her son's political radicalization, Grassic Gibbon suggests a way in which the agrarian radicalism of Cobbett and the Micheldever rebels might develop into a modern socialism that is rooted in peasant concerns but not constrained by them.

---

[199] Williams, *The Country and the City*, 270.

5

The Compensations of Illiteracy

THE SPELL OF WRITING

The Opium of the People

Travelling in the Soviet Union in 1926, the English businessman Denys Trefusis recorded his experiences in a grandiloquently titled though unpublished manuscript, 'The Stones of Emptiness'.[1] Trefusis was a fluent speaker of Russian and a frequent visitor between 1908 and 1928. He had links with the Russian aristocracy and the post-revolutionary émigré community, and counted among his friends one of the richest men in Russia at the time of the revolution, the Oxford graduate and homosexual Prince Yusupov, notorious for murdering Rasputin in 1916.[2] There could be little doubt that Trefusis's sympathies lay with the displaced and dispossessed Russian aristocracy, and his contempt for the Bolsheviks and for the Communism they preached is evident throughout 'The Stones of Emptiness'. Describing his arrival in Red Square, he recounts the following anecdote:

> At the entrance to the other side of the square is a shrine which was held to be the most sacred in Moscow by the faithful. In the old days no one ever thought of passing this shrine without crossing himself, and even now a large number of people—particularly the elderly—continue the same practice. Let into a wall in the street beside this Holy of Holies is a plaque of Gothic design with the following words written in large letters:-
> 'RELIGIA OPIUM DLA NARODA.'

---

[1] Trefusis had a precarious and antagonistic link to the modernist intelligentsia through his marriage to Violet Trefusis (née Keppell) whose affair with Vita Sackville West was memorialized in Virginia Woolf's *Orlando: A Biography* (1928). He had promised never to have sex with his wife as a condition of their marriage, a union forced on Violet by her mother Alice Keppel (mistress to Edward VII). The whole affair became notorious in 1920 when Trefusis and Harold Nicholson (husband of Vita Sackville-West) flew to France to interrupt their wives' elopement. Diana Souhami, *Mrs Keppel and her Daughter* (London: Flamingo, 1997), 123–334.

[2] Online Finding Aid, Rare Book & Manuscript Library, Columbia University (http://www.columbia.edu/cu/libraries/inside/projects/findingaids/scans/pdfs/ldpd_bak_4078440.pdf).

'Religion is opium for the people.' When this plaque was first set up many of the illiterate devout stopped before it and, mistaking the inscription for some text from the Gospel, crossed themselves and bowed down before it. They are wiser now.[3]

The scene operates as a parable about the failure of the revolution to emancipate the people. Observant, illiterate Russian peasants genuflect before an atheistic Marxist slogan in the mistaken belief that it is biblical. They are still enslaved, just as reliant on these new masters, to whom the monopoly on the written word has simply been transferred. The anecdote dramatizes the mystical power of writing, even—perhaps especially—for the illiterate.

In this chapter I argue that the link Trefusis makes between questions of orality and literacy and those of religion and politics are not merely fortuitous, and in fact point to an important constellation of interlinked concerns nourished by the Russian Revolution. The tension between the illiterate peasantry and the metropolitan intelligentsia was also, for British observers, a clash between Orthodox Christianity and Marxist atheism. Trefusis clearly wanted to understand the Bolshevik Revolution in a religious frame, and the title of his text is drawn from Isaiah, cited in the epigraph:

It shall be an habitation of dragons, and a court for owls

And He shall stretch out upon it the line of confusion, and the stones of emptiness

(Isaiah XXXIV)

The epigraph and title work to situate Trefusis's account of the progress of revolution in the context of Isaiah's prophecy of God's judgement against the nations. In this passage, Isaiah depicts Edom—an enemy of Israel— laid waste, its human population annihilated and the land become 'burning pitch', overgrown with thorns and inhabited by vultures and owls. Trefusis suggests that the crushing realities of Soviet economics—the only solution to which would involve the Bolshevik leaders in 'a complete renunciation of their bastard notions of Communism'[4]—are sent by a vengeful God. So, when the peasants kneel before Marx's slogan, they are sanctifying words which aim to tear apart the very conditions of their worship. The words command the reverence they intend to destroy. The irony crystallizes much of what is at stake in the specifically Russian articulation of politics and religion.

---

[3] Denys Trefusis, 'The Stones of Emptiness: A Picture of Soviet Russia' (typescript, 1926), Rare Book & Manuscript Library, Columbia University, 16.

[4] Ibid. 173.

Trefusis's anecdote bears comparison with a famous story recounted in Claude Lévi-Strauss's *Tristes Tropiques* (1955), in the chapter called 'A Writing Lesson'. Both Lévi-Strauss's discussion and the subsequent controversy about it help to shed light on the whole question of orality and literacy as it relates to Russia and its revolution. Lévi-Strauss describes conducting research among the Nambikwara, an Amazonian tribe who had no knowledge of writing and who Walter Ong would therefore have designated as living in a condition of 'primary orality'. I argued in Chapter 1 that Russia was frequently understood as a primitive or 'cold' society in Lévi-Strauss's terms, and throughout his work, cold, primitive societies are associated with orality and illiteracy. In the course of 'The Writing Lesson', Lévi-Strauss decides to distribute pens and paper among the illiterate Nambikwara, and after a few days he notices that they are drawing wavy lines on the pieces of paper, imitating the anthropologist's note taking but producing only meaningless scribbles. The leader of the tribe, however, grasps something of what writing is for even if he cannot himself decipher it. He then begins to play an elaborate game in which he pretends to the rest of the tribe that he can understand the anthropologist's writing, and there develops, as Lévi-Strauss puts it, an 'unspoken agreement between us that his scribblings had a meaning that I did my best to decipher'. The leader of the tribe, without actually learning to write, 'allied himself with the white man, as equal with equal, and could now share in his secrets'.[5]

In a sleepless night, Lévi-Strauss begins to process these events, and tries to draw from them a general lesson about the function of writing in society. The leader's use of writing as a means of gaining power over the rest of the tribe becomes emblematic of writing's inherent tendency to 'distribute . . . individuals into a hierarchy of castes and classes'. Indeed, Lévi-Strauss continues, 'the primary function of writing, as a means of communication, is to facilitate the enslavement of other human beings'. Against the Kantian notion of an Enlightenment that emerges through the public exercise of reason (fundamentally through writing and in print), Lévi-Strauss asserts that '[t]he use of writing for disinterested ends, and with a view to satisfactions of the mind in the fields either of science or the arts, is a secondary result of its invention—and may even be no more than a way of reinforcing, justifying, or dissimulating its primary function'.[6]

Lévi-Strauss's claim that the 'primary function' of writing is the consolidation of social hierarchy is prefigured by Trefusis's encounter with the

---

[5] Claude Lévi-Strauss (tr. John Russell), *Tristes Tropiques* (New York: Criterion Books, 1961), 289.
[6] Ibid. 292.

Russian peasantry. Marx's atheism aimed to break the spell of a religion that held the people in its thrall. But, so it appears here, it was not religion that had enslaved the people but writing. The Russian peasantry under Communism remain under the spell of a writing whose content proves to be less important than the medium itself and the structure of domination it apparently upholds. The medium is the message. As much as the Communist authorities purported to be driving out a medieval form of ideological control—and as brutal as they were in their purges against the Orthodox priesthood—they had in fact replicated it. The final section of this chapter explores the important role played by the icon, and iconoclasm, in this debate. The important point for now is that, as much as the Church it replaced, the Soviet state seemed (in Trefusis's view) to lean on the power that the written word gives to those who master it. The Bolshevik authorities were like the Nambikwara leader: the source of their power was not any understanding of the message (of Marxist philosophy in this case) but a grasp of the power of the medium itself. At least at first: Trefusis concludes his account of this phenomenon with the sentence 'They are wiser now', and implicitly we understand that the peasants are no longer kneeling uncomprehendingly before Marx's words. What good this wisdom has done them, Trefusis does not specify. Nevertheless, as we shall see, everywhere in the writings of visitors to the Soviet Union we find the idea that, in spite of Marxism-Leninism's professions of a dogmatic and violent atheism, the Soviet state had shaped itself to imitate the Church that it was often understood to replace.

Lévi-Strauss's writing lesson remains famous today in part because Derrida uses it in *Of Grammatology*, where he subjects the assumptions that Lévi-Strauss brings to the episode to a biting critique. Derrida adopts several lines of attack, some of which I find more convincing than others—there is not space to resurrect this now rather hoary debate here, but it is worth drawing out one aspect of Derrida's argument. Derrida diagnoses a tendency to what he calls 'phonocentrism' in Lévi-Strauss's work, by which he means the tendency to value speech above writing, orality over literacy. He then attempts to extend this diagnosis, suggesting that the main currents of Western thought as a whole have tended to be phonocentric. The debate about Russia as an oral society goes to show that this latter claim at least is dubious. I discuss in this chapter many canonical thinkers who were as sceptical as Derrida (for different reasons) about the tendency to idealize oral societies. There was no hegemony of phonocentric thought but a vigorous debate about the nature and reality of orality, newly politicized by the advent of the Bolshevik Revolution. In *On Voice in Poetry* (2015), David Nowell Smith has argued convincingly that the critique of phonocentrism, 'according to which voice is the privileged "philosopheme" of Western metaphysics', is largely an effect of bad translations of Derrida, who was in fact much more interested in and receptive to voice than his Anglophone reception might lead us to believe. For Nowell Smith, 'the cardinal sin of "phonocentrism" has led, in Anglophone literary studies at least, to a prohibition on the term "voice" for wellnigh four decades, and with it, the impoverishment of our thought'.[7] I am less interested in determining where Derrida himself stands than I am in this general prohibition on voice, which has given us a distorted picture of literary history. Placed in the context of debates about the Russian Revolution, where the political stakes of the argument become clear, the ban on 'voice'—the intense Derridean scepticism towards the very notion of 'oral culture'—appears as a Cold War ideology, an elaborate and coded way of endorsing liberal pluralism as distinct from the cultural assumptions of Communism.

Derrida's critique nevertheless helps to pinpoint a value-laden celebration of oral culture as a lost culture of presence that—while by no means hegemonic—forms a recognizable strand in the way in which writers have thought about primitive cultures. Derrida writes that '[t]he ideal profoundly underlying this philosophy of writing is...the image of a community immediately present to itself, without differance, a community of speech where all the members are within earshot'.[8] One can certainly find examples of writers—particularly Russophiles in the pre-revolutionary period—who thought about rural Russia in exactly this way, as a culture in which people were more present to one another because there was no writing to get in the way. Indeed, the pervasiveness of conflicting published reports about the nature of the USSR tended to demonstrate that the printed materials purporting to describe Russia as it was amounted to a tissue of propaganda. The need to talk face to face with real Russians was a driving force that sent many intellectuals to Russia, even if (ironically enough) the outcome of their visit was usually another book to add to the pile.

Orality and Russophilia

Stephen Graham's love affair with Russia began with its books—those of Tolstoy and Dostoyevsky in particular. But after his first arrival in Moscow in 1908, he began to see that 'Russia was different from the

---

[7] David Nowell-Smith, *On Voice in Poetry: The Work of Animation* (Basingstoke: Palgrave, 2015), 5, 6.

[8] Jacques Derrida (tr. Gayatri Chakravorty Spivak), *Of Grammatology* (Baltimore; London: Johns Hopkins University Press, 1976), 136.

Russia in books written by Russians... [Dostoyevsky] will never take you into a Russian Church, nor will he reveal the mystery of the ikons or the spell of Russian music'.[9] Graham's biographer Michael Hughes suggests that the 'moment of epiphany' came for Graham when he 'stood hour after hour mesmerized by the sound of chanting in the cathedral church' at Sergiev Posad.[10] Indeed, the experience of sound becomes a counterweight to the silent contemplation of the written text in Graham's work, and this has a distinct political implication. Graham's Russian epiphany was imagined as an immersion in sound and a reawakening of the senses that had been deadened by the excessively rationalistic, individualistic print culture of the West. In *Undiscovered Russia* (1912), books are seen as a hostile imposition that threatens to break up the communal oral culture of the Russian peasant and to destroy his hitherto untainted Christianity. Graham celebrates the Russian peasantry in the following terms: 'The moujiks are sociable and brotherly; they do things together, sing together, pray together, live together. They like meeting together in public places, in churches and markets.'[11] This 'sociability' involves above all membership of a religious community that has not fallen under the spell of individualism. In *The Rise of the Novel* (1957), Ian Watt described the emergence in the seventeenth century of the modern idea of 'a whole society mainly governed by the idea of every individual's intrinsic independence... from other individuals': *Robinson Crusoe* (1719) would have been unimaginable without this pretext. And Watt went on to argue that the primary historical causes of the rise of individualism are 'modern industrial capitalism and the spread of Protestantism, especially in its Calvinist or Puritan forms'.[12] For Stephen Graham, the Russian peasantry was a social formation that had resisted or simply bypassed the influences both of the Protestant Reformation and of modern industrial capitalism.

Like Watt, Graham links the high literacy that could produce *Robinson Crusoe* with Protestant individualism:

Carlyle once observed that the book had now become the church. Men entered into books as formerly they entered churches. This is profoundly true, but it is not a truth of which to be necessarily proud. The book has been a great separating influence. It has taken us away alone. It has refused to be shared with others. It has taken us from our parents, our wives, our

---

[9] Stephen Graham, 'Wondrful Scene' (MS) qtd. Michael Hughes, *Beyond Holy Russia: The Life and Times of Stephen Graham* (Cambridge: Open Book Publishers, 2014), 32.
[10] Ibid. 32–3.
[11] Stephen Graham, *Undiscovered Russia* (New York: John Lane, 1912), 279.
[12] Ian Watt, *The Rise of the Novel: Studies in Defoe, Richardson and Fielding* (London: Pimlico, 2000), 60. Watt himself had borrowed these ideas from R. H. Tawney, *Religion and the Rise of Capitalism: A Historical Study* (London: John Murray, 1926).

husbands, our friends. It has given us riches, and not necessarily given the
same riches to others. It has distinguished us; it has individualised us. It has
created differences between ourselves and our fellow-men. Hence our pride,
our suspicion, our distrust.[13]

And he goes on to claim that the Russian peasantry retains its sociability
because it is relatively untouched by the influence of the printed word:

> In Russia there are no books. The Church supplies the place of all books—I
> am, of course, speaking of the peasantry. Instead of every book being a
> church, the church is the book.
>
> Hence the delight in every tiniest portion of Church ritual; hence the full
> attendance at the churches; hence the delight in the service and in the music.
> Hence the wonderful singing, that is accompanied without organ and
> without books of the score. . . .
>
> Because the peasants have no books to read, they are all forced to read the
> book of Nature. They do not hear the imitation of the nightingale, therefore
> they listen to the nightingale itself. They do not look at 'real life' as depicted
> in novels, therefore they look at real life without the novels.[14]

It is not merely the familiar story about impact of print and literacy on
religious worship—whereby solitary Bible-study displaces communion as
the centre of a religious life—that concerns Graham. As in Watt's account
of seventeenth-century England, the diagnosis spreads to literature, where
the novel is seen both as a result of the rise of an increasingly individualistic sensibility and as a vector for the intensification of that sensibility.
Finally, Graham's rosy picture of the Russian peasantry is linked to a rosy
picture of medieval Britain:

> As I have said before—in Russia you may study conditions of life which were
> once conditions of England. You can see what England has left behind. Here
> in the life of this medieval peasantry is a veracious picture of our own past. It
> is more instructive than any book.[15]

As we found in Chapter 1, pre-revolutionary Russia was often described
as belonging to the past, and in Graham's medievalist vision of Russia,
the orality of its religious practices operates as a rebuke to the post-
Reformation culture in which the book has replaced the Church. Writing,
and the printed book in particular, formed a barrier between the individual and true experience, whereas, as Michael Hughes points out, Russia

---

[13] Graham, *Undiscovered Russia*, 279–80.
[14] Ibid. 280–1. As S. A. Smith notes, 'there was no tradition of Bible reading in [pre-
Revolutionary] Russia except among the Protestant denominations'. S. A. Smith, *The
Russian Revolution: An Empire in Crisis* (Oxford: OUP, 2017), 23.
[15] Graham, *Undiscovered Russia*, 281.

'increasingly appeared to him as a vast sacred space where the fabric of everyday life was shaped by the pervasive presence of the infinite'.[16]

Graham's suspicion of the book and his celebration of the oral culture of the peasantry foregrounds the role of communications technologies—above all, print—in debates about orality and literacy. Lévi-Strauss's post-war distinction between 'hot societies'—literate, Western, progressive—and cold ones—oral, primitive, resisting progressive historical development—were thus substantially prefigured by earlier debates about Russia. Marshall McLuhan's distinction between 'hot media' and 'cold media' developed Lévi-Strauss's thought into the study of communications technologies in a way that echoes Graham's enthusiasms. Hot media, above all print, encouraged one-way communication and suggested a hierarchy between a single author and multiple consumers of the printed word. McLuhan also argued that '[a]s an intensification and extension of the visual function, the phonetic alphabet diminishes the role of the other senses of sound and touch and taste in any literate culture'.[17] Cool media (typical of oral societies but also identified with certain modern technologies, such as telephones and computers) encouraged multi-directional conversations and were intrinsically non-hierarchical. Graham's work prefigures McLuhan's analysis of an overly literate Western culture, cut off from sensuous reality by the predominance of the phonetic alphabet and the printed word, and for him the journey into Russia involved both a sensory immersion in sound and a recovery of a lost orality.

For Graham as for Trefusis, the question of Russian peasant illiteracy cannot be separated from a consideration of religion: because they did not suffer the separating influence of the book, Russian peasants were closer to God and closer to the origins of Christianity. While religion is not connected to orality in this way by atheists Lévi-Strauss and Derrida, for Catholics Marshall McLuhan and his student Walter J. Ong, the effects of print and mass literacy on religion is a major theme. Ong wrote:

> Religion has to do somehow with the invisible, and when the earlier oral-aural world, with its concentration on voice and sound, finally yields to the more markedly visual world incident to script and print, one may be tempted to argue, religion finally must go.[18]

[16] Hughes, *Beyond Holy Russia*, 33.

[17] Marshall McLuhan, *Understanding Media: The Extensions of Man* (London: Abacus, 1973), 94.

[18] Walter J. Ong, *The Presence of the Word: Some Prolegomena for Cultural and Religious History* (New Haven: Yale University Press, 1967), 10.

And of medieval Christianity:

> The Bible was present to people largely in what we can style an oral
> mode.... [T]he culture as a whole assimilated the biblical word not
> verbatim but as oral cultures typically assimilate a message, thematically
> and formulaically, tribally rather than individually, by contrast with
> post-typographic culture.[19]

Ong clearly echoed Graham's earlier claims about a peasant Russia in
which '[t]he Church supplies the place of all books'. The chief 'compensation of illiteracy' that Graham touts in the strikingly tendentious title of
his chapter, and of which the Russian peasant is the chief beneficiary, is
rather literally the *immediacy* of experience: that is to say experience that is
unmediated, pure presence. Graham wrote:

> By far the greatest compensation of all this is that through his illiteracy, the
> peasant is nearer to reality. He does not read about life, he lives; he does not
> read about death, he dies; he does not read about God, he prays. He has his
> own thoughts, and they are not muddled up with other people's thoughts.
> His mind is not a confusion of a thousand disconnected ideas; he reflects in
> his soul the deep beauty of Nature itself.[20]

Graham insisted that the moujiks' experience both of earthly life and of
God was unmediated by text. His writing about Russia is steeped in that
reverence for the 'primitive' that unites Lévi-Strauss with Rousseau in
Derrida's critique. Derrida is able to chide Lévi-Strauss for ignoring his
own evidence about the violence and hierarchization of the Nambikwara,
which existed before they had any contact with writing. Though Graham's
moujiks be poor, his picture of their life is overwhelmingly a positive one,
so one has to look elsewhere than in his books to find evidence of the
brutality that often characterized peasant life under the Tsars, and the role
that various religious rituals played in that brutality. Orlando Figes's
account is particularly vivid in its unpleasantness, pointing to barbaric
practices such as the public deflowering of new brides (by a village elder if
the groom proved impotent), the celebration of domestic violence in
proverbs such as 'the more you beat the old woman, the tastier the
soup will be', and a range of publicly administered violent punishments
including castration, branding, eye-gouging, amputations, hacking to
death with sickles, and the driving of wooden stakes down the throat.[21]
We cannot be sure what Graham saw, what he chose to ignore, and what

[19] Ibid. 269.   [20] Graham, *Undiscovered Russia*, 282–3.
[21] Orlando Figes, *A People's Tragedy: The Russian Revolution, 1891–1924* (London:
Jonathan Cape, 1996), 94–7.

he repressed. Nevertheless, as with later depictions of the peasantry during collectivization discussed in Chapter 4, where Communist-sympathizing visitors proved blind to their suffering even in the midst of a great famine, delusions about Russia seem to persist despite the face-to-face encounter with the evidence. What I am trying to establish here is the way in which a certain structural opposition between orality and literacy tends to shape the ways in which Russia was seen, understood, and depicted by British observers. This binary opposition did not originate with Graham, although as we have seen he goes so far in its celebration of the oral culture of the peasant that his work makes it particularly dramatic.

Low Church Leninism

In British culture this binary opposition between orality and literacy could rarely be thought without being linked to the schism in the Western Church. Russophiles like Graham identified pre-revolutionary Russia with the medieval Christianity that prevailed in Britain before the Protestant Reformation. As such, their stance mirrored Ong's celebration of the orality of Catholicism, and his critique of Protestantism's perceived over-reliance on print: 'the efficacy of the sacraments in Catholic teaching is certainly more readily comprehensible to oral-aural man . . . than it would be to cultures tyrannized over by the alphabet and more particularly by print', he wrote, while 'the extreme Protestant view appears by contrast to be thoroughly in accord with the typographic state of mind'.[22] Looking at Russia helped those Western visitors who shared Graham's High Church orientation to see by contrast the damage that the Reformation, the Renaissance, and the Enlightenment had done to Christianity in Britain, as we have seen. On the other hand, for a writer like Robert Byron who was less inclined to be hostile to the forces of modernity, Enlightenment, and atheism, some of Russia's present *difficulties* (he visited in 1932) could be explained by the absence of a Reformation: 'From the domination of ideas which this [Orthodox] Church exercised from the tenth century on, no Renascence ever delivered Russia.'[23] It became possible, therefore, to read the Bolshevik Revolution as the belated arrival of a Reformation that had passed the Eastern Church by or at least failed with the 'Triumph of Orthodoxy' in the two Iconoclastic Controversies of eighth- and ninth-century Byzantium.

---

[22] Ong, *Presence of the Word*, 279–80.
[23] Robert Byron, *First Russia, Then Tibet: Travels through a Changing World* (London: Tauris Parke Paperbacks, 2011), 28.

The oral culture of the Russian peasantry idealized by Graham could thus be thought of as under threat from an urban and literate Bolshevik culture, which made peasant literacy one of its priorities in the NEP period in particular. Indeed, the connection between literacy and revolution has long been established: as Figes notes, '[t]he three great revolutions of modern European history—the English, the French and the Russian—all took place in societies where the rate of literacy was approaching 50 per cent'.[24] The violent anti-clericalism of the Bolsheviks created a number of striking echoes with Britain during the Reformation. In a symbolic repetition of a common trope the dissolution of the monasteries, the Bolsheviks removed church bells to be melted down, silencing the inclusive auditory world of the Orthodox Church, putting the metal to some more rational, utilitarian use. Graham's writings on post-revolutionary Russia—to which I will return later—tend to argue that the Bolshevik Revolution heralded secularization plain and simple: 'It is absurd to call Communism a religion; no religion can be based on materialism', he claimed.[25] Yet, from the perspective of Protestant Northern Europe at least, the notion of secularization is irreducibly tied up with the Reformation. This entanglement frequently shows itself in Graham's writing on the Revolution, and in British responses to the Revolution more generally. In the specific religious sense, the revolutionaries could be seen as reformers.

Thus, one common variety of Western infatuation with Communism puts it in line with a sort of Low Church asceticism. Bolshevism, in this view, renounced the worldly possessions and luxuries which had in capitalist countries become a fetish. John Maynard Keynes was always baffled by the left's widespread adoption of Marx's *Capital*: 'an obsolete economic textbook which I know to be not only scientifically false but without interest or application to the modern world'.[26] His visit to the Soviet Union in 1925 seemed to confirm that Communism had not delivered economic prosperity. This led him to speculate, later, on the psychological roots of Communism:

> Communism is not a reaction against the failure of the nineteenth century to organise optimal economic output. It is a reaction against its success. It is a protest against the emptiness of economic welfare, an appeal to the ascetic in us all.[27]

[24] Figes, *A People's Tragedy*, 93.

[25] Stephen Graham, *Stalin: An Impartial Study of the Life and Work of Joseph Stalin* (London: Ernest Benn, 1931), 135.

[26] John Maynard Keynes, *A Short View of Russia* (London: Hogarth, 1925), 13–14.

[27] Bernard Shaw, *'talin-Wells Talk: The Verbatim Record and a Discussion* (London: The New Statesman and Nation, 1934), 36.

Perversely, perhaps—because it flew in the face of Communist propaganda about the increased efficiency of a planned economy—Keynes postulated that the appeal of Communism was in its ascetic reaction *against* 'optimal economic output'. Against the corruption and worldliness of Holy Russia and its priestly orders, and against the acquisitive culture of Western capitalism, Keynes's Bolshevism counterposed an austere and disciplined self-denial. In his memoir 'My Early Beliefs', addressed to his friends in the Bloomsbury Group, Keynes again mocked the *'reductio ad absurdum* of Benthamism known as Marxism' and commented that 'We [i.e. liberal Bloomsbury] have completely failed . . . to provide a substitute for these economic bogus-faiths capable of satisfying our successors. But we our-selves have remained . . . altogether immune from the virus, as safe in our citadel of our ultimate faith as the Pope of Rome is.'[28] Keynes realized the power of religion and persistently compared competing economic models with clashing theologies. Soviet Communism is cast here as a dangerously ascetic and puritanical answer to the classical economics of nineteenth-century liberalism. That said, Keynes was far from advocating a retrench-ment in classical economics. His position was delicately poised, acknow-ledging that Communism supplied a genuine need for something like *faith*, and that the failure of classical liberalism to supply that need was as important as its increasingly evident failure to organize 'optimal economic output'. Keynes knew that the third way he went on to propose in his *General Theory of Employment, Interest and Money* (1936) must not only win arguments in universities and policy committees, but also command the faith and reverence of intellectuals, politicians, and voters.

Keynes's picture of Bolshevism as an ascetic Protestant sect was literal-ized in the Communism of Hewlett Johnson, the infamous theologian known as the 'Red Dean' of Canterbury. Johnson played 'an important role in developing public interest in and support for Soviet Communism', and he was certainly the most prominent person in Britain to make the argument that Soviet Communism was the realization of Christian ideals on Earth.[29] Rather than operating as a spiritual replacement for Chris-tianity as Keynes had argued, Johnson's Communism is a renewal of the forces of the Protestant Reformation which are thus organized against the corruption of a Western Christianity that is deemed to operate in com-plicity with capitalism. Indeed, Johnson's career was aptly described by

---

[28] John Maynard Keynes, 'My Early Beliefs', in *The Collected Writings of John Maynard Keynes*, x. *Essays in Biography* (London: Macmillan, 1972), 446.

[29] David Ayers, 'Hewlett Johnson: Britain's Red Dean and the Cold War', in Philip Emil Muehlenbeck (ed.), *Religion and the Cold War: A Global Perspective* (Nashville, TN: Vanderbilt University Press, 2012), 81.

Martin Malia as a manifestation of 'low church Leninism'.[30] Johnson's arguments were made from the pulpit, in many speaking engagements, and in a series of publications, most notably his widely discussed book, *The Socialist Sixth of the World* (1939). Johnson's view of the professed atheism of the revolution was as follows:

> Marx, Lenin and Stalin were anti-religious just because they believed that religion had consistently aligned itself with organized injustice. Outrages were committed on the Church in proportion as the Church had become corrupt and wealthy, neglectful not only of social justice, liberty, education of the masses, and social welfare in general, but actively persecuting those who made these things their concern.[31]

The established Church had become the instrument of political power and the chief defence of the Tsardom: Bolshevism was justified—in Christian terms!—in tearing it down. Had not Christ driven the money changers from the temple? In the essays later collected in *Christians and Communism* (1956), Johnson made a direct analogy between modern Communism and the Diggers and Levellers of the English Civil War. The Digger Gerrard Winstanley is cited there as an authority: against the 'tithing priest' who argues that the phrase 'the poor shall inherit the earth' was meant simply to provide 'Inward satisfaction of mind', Winstanley asserted that 'the Scripture is to be really and materially fulfilled'. Johnson's was a radical puritanism that saw Christ's teachings as a revolutionary doctrine advocating the material equality of man. 'Winstanley would have been at home... with Marx and Engels in 1849', Johnson wrote.[32] For Johnson, the Protestant ethic was closely aligned with the spirit not of capitalism, but of Communism.

ORTHODOX COMMUNISM

Political Religions

Johnson's ascetic, Low Church Leninism was far from the whole story, and it flew in the face of a much more pervasive assumption about the *continuities* between the Orthodox religion and Soviet Communism. For many observers—as Trefusis's example shows—the emerging Communist

---

[30] Martin Malia, *Russia under Western Eyes: From the Bronze Horseman to the Lenin Mausoleum* (Cambridge, MA; London: Belknap Press of Harvard University Press, 1999), 341.
[31] Hewlett Johnson, *The Socialist Sixth of the World* (London: Gollancz, 1939), 357.
[32] Hewlett Johnson, *Christians and Communism* (London: Putnam, 1956), 95–6.

society retained key features of that religion, most notably its orality. Versions of this basic thesis abound in travelogues, fictional depictions of the Soviet Union, and more philosophical essays about Communism. Take this characteristic passage from Robert Byron's travelogue *First Russia, Then Tibet* (1933):

> the new rulers soon discovered ... that this was hardly the moment to dispense with the traditional ally of all government. 'Religion,' they had thundered, 'is the opium of the people.' The practical value of this maxim now became fully apparent to them. Since all pre-existing religions were proscribed by the new philosophy, there was only one course open to them in their need for a popular soporific. This was to erect the philosophy itself into a new religion. And this they had done. They have preserved the jealousy of the God of Israel while dispensing with the God himself, and the external ceremony of the Orthodox church while dispensing with the Church. In place of the single God enthroned in heaven, they have substituted the Mass enthroned on earth; in place of the Church, a hierarchy no less intolerant—YOUTH. It is a different kind of opium; its dreams are less reposeful. But it works.[33]

As Marxists, Byron mused, the Bolsheviks were in an excellent position to understand the social and political function of religion. In power, and not inclined to follow Marx's prophecy to the extent of actually withering away themselves, members of the Communist government found themselves in need of a 'popular soporific' of their own. And atheism could therefore be understood not as an absence of religion but as an alternative religion, which actually adopts the 'jealousy of the God of Israel' and the 'external ceremony of the Orthodox church' because they happen to be to hand, in an act of bricolage. Byron's tone is light and ironic: he seems just as detached from the atheist slogan that the Bolsheviks 'thundered' as he does from the realpolitik by which they hypocritically adapted this very atheism into a hollowed-out version of the religion it sought to destroy. They were not true to the atheism they professed, Byron seemed to say, but the atheism itself—at least in this thundering Marxist form—was in itself suspect. Byron's insistence on the continuities between Bolshevism and the Orthodox religion is a leitmotif in many discussions of the religious significance of the revolution, and it returns with different emphases and different meanings across a wide range of writing on or about Russia and Communism. The purpose of what follows here is to discover the force of the substitutions Byron lists: 'philosophy' for 'religion', 'the jealousy of the God of Israel' for 'God himself', 'the external

---

[33] Byron, *First Russia, Then Tibet*, 35.

ceremony of the Orthodox church' for 'the Church', 'the single God enthroned in heaven' for 'the Mass enthroned on earth', 'YOUTH' for 'the Church', 'a different kind of opium' with 'less reposeful' dreams for 'the opium of the masses'.

The possibility that secular political institutions could operate as an empty vessel into which the nectar of religious ardour could be poured is predicated on the widespread reconceptualization of religion at the turn of the twentieth century of which William James is the avatar. His notion that 'feeling is the deeper source of religion, and that philosophic and theological formulas are secondary products, like translations of a text into another tongue' suggests an amorphous and portable 'feeling' that can adapt to and find satisfaction in a huge variety of institutional and doctrinal configurations.[34] Imagining a portable 'religious feeling' assumes that the institutions and practices of Hinduism and those of Lutheran Protestantism cater to a common set of needs and desires. And if theologically and liturgically very different religions and denominations can satisfy this psychological need, why not the secular apparatus of Party and State? Indeed, Emilio Gentile and Robert Mallett have drawn on functionalist theories of religion suggested by James's contemporaries Emile Durkheim and Gustave Le Bon to show how '[i]n effect, even a party such as the Bolshevik party, which professed atheism and conducted anti-religious campaigns, constitutes a type of political sacralisation'.[35] This modern conception of religion, then, seems to enable the sorts of substitution of secular political institutions for religious ones that Byron and others used to characterize post-revolutionary Russia. The Bolshevik Revolution initiated the era of 'political religions'.

However, where Gentile and Mallett draw together a number of writers, including Bertrand Russell and John Maynard Keynes, to show that the 'sacralising' tendency of Bolshevism was clear already in the 1920s, their focus is firmly on the sociology of religions, which are to be understood as systems of myths and rituals facilitating social cohesion, or as answering a basic human need for belief. A political party or movement or even a government can just as well perform these social functions and supply these needs, according to this argument. But the sociology of religion was designed to articulate general statements that hold true for *all* religions. An account of 'Bolshevism as religion' that is more sensitive

[34] William James, *The Varieties of Religious Experience: A Study in Human Nature* (London: Penguin, 1985), 431.

[35] Emilio Gentile and Robert Mallett, 'The Sacralization of Politics: Definitions, Interpretations and Reflections on the Question of Secular Religion and Totalitarianism', *Totalitarian Movements and Political Religions,* 1/1 (2000), 19.

to the theological and doctrinal divergences within and between religions should provide more nuanced explanations of the roles it played in British cultural and political life. As we have seen in previous chapters, a pre-existing debate is given new political meaning by the advent of the Bolshevik Revolution.

For Hewlett Johnson, as we have seen, the Russian Revolution could be thought of as a belated Reformation within the Eastern Church and welcomed as a rechristianization of Russia. It could serve as a model for reshaping a Western Christendom where the relationship between Church, state, and capitalist monopolies was too cosy. To take a contrasting example, Sidney Webb in a paper from 1933 described Communism as the rise of a 'new world-religion' which would 'naturally deny the existence of all other creeds', and it thus represented a new rival to Christianity to set alongside Islam and Buddhism.[36] Webb explicitly distinguished this emergence of a genuinely new Bolshevik religion from the various reformist movements which constituted 'a distinctive body of practice within one of the existing religions'. He moreover claimed that Communism was 'unconnected... with the various mysticisms which masked the Russia of the nineteenth century'. Webb was willing to grant that Communism was atheist, but pointed out that Buddhism has no deity and that therefore religions need not have one.[37] Both Johnson and Webb are willing to think of Communism as a religion, but these examples testify that it is only when we extend our analysis beyond the binary opposition between secular and religious that we can begin to account for the important differences in the cultural work a 'political religion' can be thought to do.

Phonocentric Communism

The notion that the Russian Revolution perpetuated and indeed propagated the oral culture of Russian Orthodoxy has far-reaching consequences which bear both on the language of Communism and on the question of religion. Ong himself used the Soviet Union as an example of a modern society with a high level of residual orality:

> The clichés in political denunciations in many low-technology, developing cultures—enemy of the people, capitalist war-mongers—that strike high literates as mindless are residual formulary essentials of oral thought processes. One of the many indicators of a high, if subsiding, oral residue in the

---

[36] Sidney Webb, 'On the Emergence of a New World Religion', *International Journal of Ethics*, 43/2 (Jan. 1933), 168.
[37] Ibid. 168, 169, 171.

culture of the Soviet Union is (or was a few years ago, when I encountered it) the insistence on speaking there always of 'the Glorious Revolution of October 26'—the epithetic formula here is obligatory stabilization, as were Homeric epithetic formulas 'wise Nestor' or 'clever Odysseus', or as 'the glorious fourth of July' used to be in the pockets of oral residue common even in the early twentieth-century United States. The Soviet Union still announces each year the official epithets for various loci classici in Soviet history.... Once a formulary expression has crystallized it had best be kept intact. Without a writing system, breaking up thought—that is, analysis—is a high-risk procedure. As Lévi-Strauss has well put it in a summary statement 'the savage [i.e. oral] mind totalizes'.[38]

For Ong the residual orality of Soviet culture is embodied in the officially approved pat phrases used to describe historical events, social classes, and individuals. This is complicated for Ong, who admits that such phrases 'strike high literates as mindless', and wryly hints at a link between orality and totalitarianism by placing a quotation from *The Savage Mind* (1962) in this context, informing us of the 'totalising' tendencies of the oral mind. But Ong's work—while perhaps less bombastic than McLuhan's in this respect—reacts against high literacy and looks forward to a 'secondary orality' that he hopes is coming to replace it. In his description of the linguistic culture of the Soviet Union, the 'clichés in political denunciations' are not condemned because they are oral, but treated in a mildly ironic way as the persistence of an underdeveloped mentality. The residues of oral culture live on in the languages of all advanced nations, but they are particularly noticeable in a 'low technology, developing culture' like the USSR. Given that elsewhere in his work (and especially in that of his mentor Marshall McLuhan) signs of residual or resurgent orality are gleefully welcomed as an antidote to the excessive literacy of the capitalist, Protestant West, this is an intriguingly ambivalent passage.

In the work of some British Communist writers working between the wars, the notion of Communism as a political orientation capable of reviving an oral-aural sociality that had been swept aside by the allied forces of capitalism, mass literacy, and Reformation, was much more stridently celebrated. Ben Harker has argued that this is a significant element in the cultural discourse of the Popular Front, and discussed the work of the English Communist poet Jack Lindsay in these terms. The historical hinge of his argument is the moment at which the Popular Front line succeeded the Comintern's 'class against class' policy, in 1935.

---

[38] Walter J. Ong, *Orality and Literacy: The Technologizing of the Word*, (London: Routledge, 1995), 38–9.

This is important context as it meant a shift in national Communist movements—dictated by Moscow—from the policy of building an international proletarian movement, hostile to national social democratic parties, to foster instead 'nationally grounded popular fronts—alliances of likeminded anti-fascists of various political allegiances—to defend the structures of national bourgeois democracy and resist fascism'.[39] The rapprochement with native left-wing movements was accompanied by a reconsideration by Communists of the specific national conditions of the emergence of capitalism and concomitant movements of radical resistance. In Britain this meant a reassessment of the period of the Reformation and the Renaissance. Part of this reassessment was the Communist critic Christopher Caudwell, who wrote of the Elizabethan stage—clearly anticipating McLuhan and Ong—that it was 'the product of a society passing from collectivity to individuality'.[40] Such an analysis of English literary history (and here it is definitely a question of Englishness rather than Britishness) inspired a set of intellectuals and poets—including Ewan MacColl, A. L. Lloyd, Jack Lindsay, and Edgell Rickword—in a quest for the recovery of a lost, oral culture that embodied the ethos of Communism in a specifically English way. I would like to label this distinctive tendency a phonocentric Communism. A. L. Lloyd became a leading authority on English folksong and a key figure in the folk revival. His pamphlet *The Singing Englishman* (1944) celebrated a Middle Ages in which '[a]ll classes of townspeople and country people were making up folksongs and passing them on', and bemoaned the modern 'regression . . . of folk songs' under pressure from 'the development of railways and the installation of gasmeters . . . the invention of the phonograph and the radio and the daily delivery of newspapers . . . the development of industrial technique and the alteration or disappearance of jobs which formerly were accompanied by singing'.[41] Lloyd's Communist sympathies and his recognizably English take on Marxism are intrinsic to the analysis, which concludes by looking forward to a time when

---

[39] Ben Harker, ' "Communism is English": Edgell Rickword, Jack Lindsay and the Cultural Politics of the Popular Front', *Literature and History,* 20/2 (2011), 18. Harker's essay supplies an excellent corrective to Jed Esty's interesting thesis in *Shrinking Island*, that the late-modernist move away from Britishness and towards a pastoral vision of England was fundamentally a story of imperial decline: there is no doubt some truth in this, but the omission of any discussion of the Popular Front seems, with Harker's work in view, to miss an important political context. See Jed Esty, *A Shrinking Island: Modernism and National Culture in England* (Princeton: Princeton University Press, 2004).

[40] Qtd. Harker, 'Communism is English', 18.

[41] A. L. Lloyd, *The Singing Englishman: An Introduction to Folksong* (London: Workers' Music Association, 1944), 21, 52.

society is so altered that there is no longer any special distinction or variance between the composer and the rest of his fellowmen, till cultured music and popular music have become one and the same. And that is just the sort of thing we can confidently look forward to, if ever we have a society all of a piece, one where men can be what they are, and think and feel and sing as they do, without reference to class or colour or creed.[42]

Communist Britain would revel in a revival of popular folksong, with the hierarchy that the printed book implies between the producer and the consumer of poetry dissolved. Poets, musicians, and singers would no longer exist as a separate, professionalized elite, but everyone would join together in song. This celebration of an oral culture with its roots in the medieval past and destined to be revived in the Communist near future thrives on what Derrida diagnosed as an ideology of 'presence'. As such, though the politics are very different, it recalls Graham's celebration of the Russian peasantry. The Communism that emanated from Moscow but that, in the Popular Front period, enjoined national Communist movements to reconnect with their native traditions, thus provoked the development of a phonocentric politics to match the more explicitly religious phonocentrism I identified in Graham.

With these ambitions in mind, the Popular Front poet Jack Lindsay set out a programme for the revival of oral poetry in 'A Plea for Mass Declamation', a fascinating essay which Harker situates in this context. Lindsay argued that under capitalism poetry had lost its 'socially valuable relation with the speaking voice'. This meant a separation between the consumer and the producer of poetry, resulting in 'a poetry losing its content and reality' in the self-conscious pursuit of form (his target here is the perceived formalism of high modernist poetics, reserved now for the 'elegists of bourgeois decay').[43] Lindsay's diagnosis was a reaction against both capitalism and the technology of print, which he saw as closely related phenomena:

> The invention of printing, of course, had much to do with the deflection of poetry from the living voice. But printing did not arise in a social void. As a spreader of knowledge, it had a concrete good-effect; as a part of the capitalist forces, it intensified the forms of abstraction arising from bourgeois individualism. To analyse the way that these two aspects of the printed book—its uniting and dividing powers—operated, we would need to go into much detail. It is enough here to note how the book helped the severing of poetry from its communal basis.[44]

[42] Ibid. 68.
[43] Jack Lindsay, 'A Plea for Mass Declamation', *Left Review*, 3/9 (Oct. 1937), 516.
[44] Ibid. 511, 512, 516, 512n.

Against the 'dividing powers' of the book, Lindsay sought to develop a Communist poetics of 'mass declamation' that could return poetry to its oral roots. His mass declamation poems 'On Guard for SPAIN!' and 'not english? a reminder for May Day' were published in the *Left Review* and according to Harker 'enjoyed wide circulation during the popular front years'.[45] 'not english?' is an interesting work: while it obviously eschews the astringent difficulty and self-conscious literariness of high-modernist poetry, it does not return to traditional patterns of metre and rhyme that we might associate with the folk revival. In its loose free verse with occasional use of rhyme and anaphora it is rather more reminiscent of the vibrant, exhortatory rhetoric of Whitman (albeit never so good).[46]

The question of individual and collective voices is also addressed in Lindsay's poem 'Lenin—1937'. Here Lenin becomes the focal point around which the diverse voices of the Communist international can coalesce. As in his mass declamation poems, the speaker is a plural 'we':

> In Lenin all the voices were concentrated,
> Returning in action, returning in clarity,
> We acclaim in Lenin
> A brain crystalline with integrity,
> A heart warm as the South of vineyards,
> The brain and heart in perfect harmony.[47]

Lindsay pictures Lenin as an individual capable of encompassing 'all the voices', not subsuming them in a monologue but concentrating them. The second line suggests—somewhat obscurely—a reciprocal dialogue involving the other voices, and Lenin is later acclaimed for his 'sharp ears listening'. Though Lenin possesses a 'crystalline' brain, there is no sign of the excessive rationalism that Lindsay elsewhere associated with print culture, because it is in 'perfect harmony' with a warm heart, connected both to ears and to speaking voice. In his *Short History of Culture* (1939), Lindsay made an almost identical point but this time the voice belonged to the Soviet Union itself: 'that voice, which is now the voice of the working classes and their allies all over the world, the confident voice of the millions of the Soviet Union'.[48]

Lindsay's comrade Edgell Rickword shared many of these concerns. His 'Notes on Culture and the War' appeared in *Poetry and the People* in 1940,

---

[45] Harker, 'Communism is English', 23.
[46] Jack Lindsay, 'Not English?', *Left Review* (3 Oct. 1937), 511–17.
[47] Jack Lindsay, *Collected Poems* (Lake Forest, IL: Cheiron Press, 1981), 325.
[48] Jack Lindsay, *Short History of Culture* (London: Gollancz, 1939), 388.

and commented on the wartime paper shortage. Rickword was inclined to see a silver lining:

> [D]ifficulties create opportunities, and it would be no bad thing if the rationing of paper helped to restore the balance between the written and the spoken word which is now weighted so heavily in favour of the latter. Reading is a solitary act, it is often a means of escape from reality, but speech is necessarily social. So it may be a very good thing for us to be thrown on our resources and unable to stuff our heads with the crudities and sentimentalities of the millionaire Press. Then the natural storytellers and poets will come into their own, making conscious the feelings of their group, be it large or small.[49]

Far from holding back the cause of a people's poetry, the paper shortage—Rickword hoped—would help to spark a renaissance of oral poetry. In so doing it would help bring English culture closer to that of the two Popular Front touchstones, Russia and Spain, whose revolutionary socialism (Rickward implies) drew strength from the illiteracy of the peasantry:

> In Russia and in Spain, where the bulk of the population was a largely illiterate peasantry, oral poetry was a part of everyday life, the ballad singer was the radio and the newspaper of the countryside.[50]

While the USSR is undoubtedly important in these Popular Front texts, Harker is surely right to stress the Englishness of this brand of Communism. (In the post-war period, these ideas of a native, folk communism became an important resource for the New Left as they sought to articulating a version of English socialism *against* Stalin.) Still, the model of Russia, its idealized peasantry, and even its religion continued to play a role. In 1952, Jack Lindsay published a voluminous history of medieval Byzantium, *Byzantium into Europe: The Story of Byzantium as the First Europe (326–1204 AD) and its Further Contribution Till 1453 AD*. As his tendentious title implied, Lindsay was concerned 'to vindicate a great and maligned phase of human development'—the Byzantine state—and to stress its vital importance to the history and development of modern Europe. Byzantium's modern detractors, notably Arnold Toynbee, were guilty of promulgating 'a dogmatic view of the absolute opposition of East and West', and indeed their systematic disparagement of Byzantine politics and cultural achievements was a means to 'rationalise a blind hatred of

[49] Edgell Rickword, 'Notes on Culture and the War', *Poetry and the People*, 19 (July 1940), 7.
[50] Ibid. 8.

the U.S.S.R.'[51] If Lindsay had immersed himself in English history in the Popular Front years, the turn to Byzantium after 1945 is framed as a way of overcoming the divisive rhetoric of the Cold War: 'we are dealing with a European process, a world process, not one of East versus West or West versus East', he writes. Western societies 'must find, as part of their own movement forward into freedom and universality, the way in which they can work harmoniously with the Soviet Union for the realisation and development of their common heritage.'[52] Critics of the Byzantine system had deplored the close links between the Orthodox Church and the state. But Lindsay argued that 'the story of the eastern Church . . . is one long story of violent reactions against this collaboration, and when significant revolt against Church-authority begins in the West it is the *eastern* tradition that is being carried on'.[53] As with Stephen Graham, it is the intransigent folk religion of the peasant that Lindsay wants to celebrate—precisely because it was often deeply hostile to the state. Eastern Christianity could not be conflated with the established Church and its various oppressions— on the contrary it provided a template for resisting such oppressions.

George Bernard Shaw came from a different generation and a different section of the Communist-sympathizing left, but in the 1930s—when he was in his seventies and eighties—his twin obsessions with Stalinism and with linguistic reform were intriguingly combined in a way that reflects the obsessions of Lindsay and his circle. Shaw had long felt that the twenty-six letter Phoenician alphabet used in English was hopelessly inefficient, to the point where he abandoned it and did all of his own writing in shorthand. While this measure was intended to make efficiencies, it meant that someone had laboriously to transcribe and type up everything he wrote (luckily for those like me who lack shorthand, the typed transcripts are almost invariably attached to the shorthand originals in the archive). He freely acknowledged that, as a result of this practice, 'nobody's time is saved but my own'. The Cyrillic alphabet—which had been streamlined by orthographic reforms decreed by the Bolsheviks in 1917 as part of the drive to improve peasant literacy—was held up by Shaw as an example of a script that was more phonetically based and closer to speech. Here is an excerpt from a note on 'Basic & Spelling', transcribed from Shaw's shorthand:

It may seem only a laughing matter that we have to spell the common word 'though' with six letters instead of two as the time lost is only a fraction of a

[51] Jack Lindsay, *Byzantium into Europe: The Story of Byzantium as the First Europe (326–1204 A.D.) and its Further Contribution Till 1453 A.D.* (London: Bodley Head, 1952), 469, 466, 467.
[52] Ibid. 469.   [53] Ibid. 465.

second. But multiply that fraction of a second by the number of times the word has to be written in the British Empire and in North America every hour, every day, every month, every century, and its cost grows from the fraction of a farthing to pounds, tens of pounds, hundreds, thousands, millions, billions of pounds; and the cost of a change becomes unspeakably negligible. The fact that Russia, with its 35 letter alphabet, can spell my name with two letters instead of four, may conceivably make it impossible for us to compete economically in the world with Russia.[54]

The Cyrillic alphabet, then, was a technology every bit as important as the tractor to the efficiency of Stalin's Soviet Union, and as such it was something that Britain should both envy and strive to emulate. As Shaw complained: 'If only the British Government was as intelligent as I am!'[55] Shaw does not link his proposed orthographic reforms to the religious questions I have been discussing, but he does treat the latter separately. It is notable that as well as seeing Soviet Russia as a place where the gap between written and spoken discourse had been narrowed by concerted governmental action, he also saw it as a country which had 'unconsciously and spontaneously established as its system of government an as-close-as-possible reproduction of the hierarchy of the Catholic Church', albeit one that had given 'a genuine democratic basis to the system'.[56] As far as I know, Shaw does not seem to have thought through any connection between these things. Still—no doubt partly because of the widely acknowledged connection between the development of moveable type printing and the Protestant Reformation—the Catholic Church was often thought of as residually oral. If, as Shaw argues, Russian script is closer to speech because it is more fully phonetic, then perhaps the persistent orality that Bolshevik culture shares with Catholicism is the key to the analogy Shaw posits between their social structures. Shaw does not spell this out, but the cluster of ideas to which I have drawn attention seems to make the analysis possible.

Some Anti-Communist Uses of Literacy

Such views were not the preserve of Communists and fellow travellers: their anti-Communist antagonists also picked up on a tendency to orality

---

[54] George Bernard Shaw, 'Basic & Spelling' (typescript), George Bernard Shaw Papers, Harry Ransom Center, University of Texas, Austin, Box 4 Folder 12.
[55] Ibid.
[56] George Bernard Shaw, 'Why Not Give the Intellectuals a Chance', *Nash's Pall Mall Magazine*, 486 (Nov. 1933), 95.

in Communist culture, but instead of celebrating the revival of a communal oral tradition they saw it as a dangerous sign of a mass conformism that threatened to crush independent thought. Arthur Koestler, like Ong, noticed the use of formulaic and habitual speech in the Party. Here he describes the effect on his own speech when he joined the party:

> My vocabulary, grammar, syntax, gradually changed. I learnt to avoid any original form of expression, any individual turn of phrase. Euphony, gradations of emphasis, restraint, nuances of meaning, were suspect. Language, and with it thought, underwent a process of dehydration, and crystallised in the ready-made schemata of Marxist jargon. There were perhaps a dozen or two adjectives whose use was both safe and mandatory, such as: decadent, hypocritical, morbid (for the capitalist bourgeoisie); heroic, disciplined, class-conscious (for the revolutionary proletariat); petit-bourgeois, romantic, sentimental (for humanitarian scruples); opportunist and sectarian (for Right and Left deviations respectively); mechanistic, metaphysical, mystical (for the wrong intellectual approach); dialectical, concrete (for the right approach); flaming (protests); fraternal (greetings); unswerving (loyalty to the Party).'[57]

Somewhat paradoxically, in Koestler's text the high literate philosophy of Marxism is transformed into epithetic formulae as it becomes part of the oral texture of the Communist International. Approved adjectives attach themselves to certain nouns so that 'unswerving loyalty to the Party' becomes an oral tag like 'brave Nestor', 'beautiful princess', or 'sturdy oak' (Ong's other examples). Ong sought a value-neutral way to describe these oral residues, but Koestler takes the position of the high literate, condemning them as clichés and an unwelcome degeneration into primitive orality. The reversion of language to a preliterate state, moreover, results in the dehydration and crystallization of thought.

This position is a fairly familiar one. The sheep in Orwell's *Animal Farm: A Fairy Story* (1945), for example, represent a similar fear that, in Communist culture, easily memorable oral formulae of the 'four legs good, two legs bad' variety will displace the rich analytical complexity of literate language. In his journalism, Orwell consistently remarked on the propensity of Marxist jargon to degenerate into what Ong referred to as 'epithetic formulas'. This concern to defend language from Communist influences also emerged in an earlier text—*The Road to Wigan Pier* (1937):

> [W]e need intelligent propaganda. Less about 'class consciousness', 'expropriation of the expropriators', 'bourgeois ideology', and 'proletarian solidarity', not to mention the sacred sisters, thesis, antithesis, and synthesis; and

---

[57] Arthur Koestler, *The Invisible Writing: The Second Volume of an Autobiography: 1932–40* (London: Vintage, 2005), 32–3.

more about justice, liberty, and the plight of the unemployed. And less about mechanical progress, tractors, the Dnieper dam, and the latest salmon-canning factory in Moscow; that kind of thing is not an integral part of Socialist doctrine, and it drives away many people whom the Socialist cause needs, including most of those who can hold a pen.[58]

Again, it is the recoil of the high literate 'who can hold a pen' from what had become—above all in the Communist Party but also in the left as a whole—a set of ritualistic and predictable clichés.

For Orwell, these Communist clichés were identified closely with the Auden circle, which formed for him a close-knit homosocial coterie that was susceptible to bad ideas and clichés partly because ideas were allowed to circulate among them orally rather being viewed solely through the distancing medium of print. Orwell placed a great value on the detached distance that purely written communications enabled. For this reason he seems almost to have regretted getting to know Spender and to like him—as if 'presence' (as Derrida defined it) involved a necessary and unwelcome suspension of the critical faculties. Spender wrote to Orwell in 1938 (enclosing a copy of *Trial of a Judge*) and enquired why, now that the two had met face to face and become friends, Orwell had withdrawn his previously published savage criticisms of Spender's Communist sympathies. Orwell's reply is fascinating:

> You ask how it is that I attacked you not having met you, & on the other hand changed my mind after meeting you. I don't know that I had ever exactly attacked you, but I had certainly in passing made offensive remarks about 'parlour Bolsheviks such as Auden & Spender' or words to that effect. I was willing to use you as a symbol of the parlour Bolshie because *a.* your verse, what I had read of it, did not mean very much to me, *b.* I looked upon you as a sort of fashionable successful person, also a Communist or Communist sympathiser, & I have been very hostile to the C.P. since about 1935, & *c.* because not having met you I could regard you as a type & also an abstraction. Even if when I met you I had not happened to like you, I should still have been bound to change my attitude, because when you meet anyone in the flesh you realise immediately that he is a human being and not a sort of caricature embodying certain ideas. It is partly for this reason that I don't mix much in literary circles, because I know from experience that once I have met & spoken to anyone I shall never again be able to show any intellectual brutality to him, even when I feel I ought to, like the Labour M.Ps. who get patted on the back by dukes & are lost forever more.[59]

---

[58] George Orwell, *Orwell's England,* ed. Peter Davison (London: Penguin, 2001), 215.
[59] Orwell to Spender, 15 Apr. 1938, in *Facing Unpleasant Facts,* 132.

The face to face contact that admirers of Russian or Soviet orality so valued—from Stephen Graham to Jack Lindsay—is here seen as potentially impairing the powers of disinterested judgement that were essential to a frank and critical exchange of views. 'Intellectual brutality' was arguably one of the things that Graham and Lindsay felt was too prominent in Anglo-Saxon literary culture, and one of the reasons a dose of a more communal and less individualistic culture and politics (however imaginary) was called for. Orwell's 'parlour Bolsheviks' had rather overdosed on personal intimacy and became involved in a sort of participatory act of mass declamation: four legs good, two legs bad. It was Orwell's separation from the warmly communal network of friendships represented by this Communist-leaning group that enabled him to treat their ideas with the 'brutality' he felt they deserved. As soon as he came to know Spender personally he became less able to treat him as 'an abstraction'. The distancing powers of print were, for Orwell, essential to his project of countering Communist influences among the literary left, and presence was a dangerous intoxicant that threatened to blunt his critique.

If Orwell was in many ways wary of the dangers of becoming immersed in an oral culture, he nevertheless grappled earnestly with the question of how complex ideas can be adequately communicated to a working class that retained many oral characteristics. The critique of Soviet propaganda from *The Road to Wigan Pier* that I quoted earlier is not a critique of propaganda or slogans as such: 'we need *intelligent* propaganda' Orwell wrote, but the stock phrases of the Third International sounded merely pretentious. Similar questions go to the heart of Orwell's famous essay, 'Politics and the English Language' (1946). Orwell argues that 'modern writing at its worst . . . consists in gumming together long strips of words which have already been set in order by someone else'.[60] By making Harold Laski one of his examples, Orwell implicates Communist and fellow-travelling intellectuals in general. In *Culture and Society* (1958), Raymond Williams agreed with Orwell's diagnosis but commented acidly that '[t]o overlook this practice in Orwell himself would be ridiculous and harmful'.[61] In his early work Williams underestimates both Orwell and the problem Orwell was seeking to confront. Orwell's arguments about language pull in two directions: first the desire to speak plainly in the dialect of the tribe, and secondly the avoidance of jargon and cliché. While clearly uncomfortable with the Third International's deployment of

---

[60] George Orwell, 'Politics and the English Language', in *Essays* (London: Penguin, 1994), 354.
[61] Raymond Williams, *Culture and Society: Coleridge to Orwell* (London: Hogarth Press, 1993), 288.

mantras, Orwell's is not striving to purge written language of all of its oral residues—that *would* entail a hypocrisy of the kind Williams identifies because of the at times mantric quality of his prose. 'Two and two make five', 'four legs good, two legs bad', 'a boot stamping on a human face forever', 'some animals are more equal than others': these are crafted slogans that have succeeded in becoming part of an anti-Communist oral vernacular. Rather than rejecting slogans, Orwell seeks to replace the technical vocabulary of Marxist sociology with something a tad more familiar, invoking 'justice, liberty, and the plight of the unemployed' instead of 'thesis, antithesis and synthesis'. Orwell's injunction to simplify language is intended to purge it of the intellectual simplifications we know as jargon, but the request for 'intelligent propaganda' nevertheless signifies a desire to mediate between the high literacy of intellectual discourse and the persistent orality of the masses.

Raymond Williams's entry in *Keywords* (2nd edn. 1983) on 'Jargon' turns on exactly this Orwellian dilemma:

> The specialized vocabularies of various sciences and branches of knowledge do not ordinarily attract description as jargon if they remain sufficiently specialized. The problem is usually the entry of such terms into more general talk and writing.[62]

So the specialist terminology of Marxism only attracts hostile criticisms (like Orwell's) when it descends from the rarefied and specialist discourses of sociology and philosophy into the realm of 'general talk', where it can take on life as part of the oral fabric of Party life. Williams seems tacitly to acknowledge Orwell's point that the habitual use of jargon can be obfuscatory, but Williams wants to warn that without technical vocabulary that may sound rebarbatively difficult at first, new thoughts and analyses may not be possible. Ultimately this vocabulary—and here Williams is thinking of the categories of Marxist sociology whose habitual and unthinking application Orwell had decried—must percolate into ordinary speech if it is to play its role in developing class consciousness (to use a jargon term). The two writers are remarkably similar in their aspirations but they disagree over whether Marxism is the right message and the Party (or some democratized version of it) the right medium for its diffusion.

Orwell attacks the propensity of undigested Marxist terminology to become jargon, then, but he also sees problems with simplifying Marxist language into everyday terms. The phrase 'Four legs good, two legs bad' from *Animal Farm* originates when Snowball (Trotsky in the parable)

---

[62] Raymond Williams, *Keywords: A Vocabulary of Culture and Society* (London: Fontana, 1988), 175.

decides that Animalism 'can be reduced to a simple maxim', and uses some rather elaborate creative logic to explain how birds have four legs despite appearances to the contrary. Orwell goes on: 'The birds did not understand Snowball's long words, but they accepted his explanation, and all the humbler animals set to work to learn the new maxim by heart.' We then learn that the sheep take particularly well to the slogan, bleating it 'for hours on end, never growing tired of it'.[63]

In a similar vein, following his abortive attempt to learn how to read, the cart-horse Boxer falls back on some simple oral formulae which are presented as a barrier to independent thought: 'His two slogans, "I will work harder" and "Napoleon is always right", seemed to him a sufficient answer to all problems.'[64] Orwell's parable is about the manipulation of the illiterate masses by a literate elite—a secular clergy with exclusive access to the sacred texts and a populous which is forced to accept their explanations, though they cannot understand them. It thus bears a tangible relation to religious debates to which I have drawn attention. Orwell and Koestler can be grouped together as the inheritors of the spirit of the Reformation, concerned about a wave of Counter-Reformation originating in the Soviet Union and threatening to sweep Europe.

GRAMOPHONE, TELEPHONE, TYPEWRITER, ICON

Stalin's Voice

Anti-Communist ideas about the strong residual orality of Communist culture are the inverted mirror image of Stephen Graham's nostalgic picture of Russian peasant orality. In his account of the early years of Communism in *Russia in Division* (1925), Graham himself insisted that '[t]he Russia that we knew is gone . . . . To the emigrants, to the poets and singers, there is a Russia, but it is a sort of invisible kingdom, something that was, is, and shall be, but a dream, a hope, an ideal homeland.'[65] Later, in *Stalin: An Impartial Study of the Life and Work of Joseph Stalin* (1931), Graham described a land in which the communal village life of the Russian peasantry he so admired had been destroyed. '[P]easant life as we know it was broken up' he wrote. 'Culture is almost dead . . . . The religious side of Russian nature has almost been eclipsed.'[66] In line

[63] George Orwell, *Animal Farm* (London: Penguin, 1989), 22.   [64] Ibid. 21.
[65] Stephen Graham, *Russia in Division* (London: Macmillan, 1925), 3.
[66] Graham, *Stalin*, 114, 135.

with those accounts of the revolution that cast it as a version of the Reformation, Stalin is seen as a silencer of holy noise. Here is Graham's description of the arrival of Stalin in Tsaritsin during the Civil War:

> [I]n a very short while after the arrival of Stalin, invested with power of life and death and all other possible Red authority, the city underwent a complete change. The cafés closed; the dancing stopped; the talkative population forbore to talk in the streets. The church bells ceased ringing. Armed sentries stood at the street-corners; plain-clothes men verified the papers of people who ventured out of doors. The city was changed to an armed camp with the strictest discipline. The Cheka was set up; the pale flag of terror was hoisted over Tsaritsin.[67]

For Graham, as we have already seen, a 'talkative', oral culture is a democratic and polylogic one, where communication is multidirectional and every statement is subject to debate and challenge. The chatter of many voices goes hand in hand here with the 'church bells', symbolic not of the hierarchy of the Orthodox Church or (much less) the Tsardom, but of the anarchic Russian Christianity that Graham had celebrated in *Undiscovered Russia*. Graham paints the rise of Communism, and of Stalin in particular, as the rise of a monologic culture of enforced silence, where the state held a monopoly on sound and voice. This is also clearly seen as a typographic culture (in the terms of McLuhan and Ong): in place of voices, the people have 'papers' which are subject to verification by the state, but never form the basis of a dialogic exchange.

For Graham, Stalin's revolution came to replace the 'talkative', 'sociable and brotherly' polylogic culture of the moujiks with a silence monologically enforced by the Cheka. In *Stalin*, as in his earlier work, Graham was fascinated by questions of communication, and the communications techniques and technologies that Stalin used are constantly at issue. He asserted that Stalin 'had no gift of speech as Trotsky had'.[68] He is described repeating what Lenin said 'with the facility of a parrot'.[69] Elsewhere, we learn that '[h]is speeches are written and he stares at his manuscript while he reads. As an orator he would be ineffective but for the fascination of his personality and his sharp unexpected gestures. The wording is succinct and direct.'[70] Graham also compared these 'discursive and urbane' speeches with his 'sparse and rough' conversation, implying that he was incapable of dialogic oral exchange. The difference between a scripted speech and a spontaneous conversation also underpins the contrast Graham made between Stalin and Lenin:

---

[67] Ibid. 44–5.   [68] Ibid. 42.   [69] Ibid. 72.   [70] Ibid. 121–2.

Stalin . . . made Lenin's books into a Bible of the revolution, a sacred Gospel. In this he went against the spirit of Leninism. For Lenin had been for the democratisation of the revolution. In his opinion, two men's counsels had been better than one. He had always been loath to proscribe any of the comrades. He felt that the Party had to live by its collective wisdom rather than through the guidance of one man. But Stalin, for his own ends converted Bolshevism into a theocracy. His training for priesthood in his adolescence may have helped him when, as it were, he invented Command-ments of Lenin. 'I am the Lord thy God, thou shalt have no other gods but me.'[71]

Despite his protestations to the contrary it seems Graham was willing to think of Stalinist Communism in religious terms, as the replacement of an oral-aural religion of the people with a monologic religion of the sacred text. In short, as a version of the Reformation as Ong understood it. Lenin by no means escaped criticism in Graham's book, but it is notable here that Leninism is presented as a road not taken, a dialogical alternative to Stalinism. This adds special pathos to Graham's description of Lenin's final illness, which is portrayed above all as a failure of speech. The man who might have made Communism into a conversation was reduced to 'a living corpse', who 'babbled incoherently, with saliva trickling down his chin . . . . He could read and understand and hear but he could not say or act.'[72]

Such considerations are also apparent as Graham turns to Stalin's use of modern electronic communications technologies such as the telephone and the telegraph. Graham's book is full of telegrams, which enabled a sort of rapid and silent communication across the vast land mass of the Soviet Union, and Stalin proved particularly capable of manipulating these to his advantage. For example, having consolidated his power in Tsaritsin, which was now under siege by the Whites, Stalin began a purge of the army, killing off and imprisoning many of the troops sent to him by Trotsky. Graham writes:

> Mass executions took place and almost the whole of the military staff sent to the city by Trotsky were placed under arrest and taken to a floating prison on the Volga. Trotsky telegraphed, 'Set these men at liberty at once!' but Stalin countersigned the telegram: 'No attention need be paid to this.'[73]

An utterance in a conversation demands an answer, and where Trotsky seemed to imagine the telegraph as an extension of conversation, placing some duty on the listener, Stalin had a different interpretation and could

---

[71] Ibid. 95–6.   [72] Ibid. 86.   [73] Ibid. 46.

countersign the order, nullifying its effect and infuriating Trotsky. On the other hand, throughout the siege of Tsaritsin Stalin is described as 'keeping in close touch with Lenin, in Moscow, by wireless', using the telegraph to develop a private and intimate bond with Lenin, shutting Trotsky out.[74] In Stalin's later career as general secretary of the Party, the telephone came to play an analogous role, so that Graham writes: '[t]he telephone and the executioner form his measure of law'.[75] As we saw in Chapter 3, as much as the show trials sought to mimic in certain respects the norms of bourgeois public justice, key legal decisions were in effect taken by the executive, and in secret. 'A telephone message from him to the G.P.U. disposes of the freedom, perhaps the life, of any individual in Russia', Graham remarked.[76] For Graham the telephone enabled secret justice by creating a new form of privacy, allowing Stalin to communicate instructions to executioners outside of any public forum (let alone a public court).

For Graham the Russian Revolution was in part a revolution in communication, where the communal oral culture of the peasant was replaced by a culture of silence, of trial by telecommunication, not a democracy of voices but a bureaucracy of papers and documents. It was a transition from the polylogic oral culture of the moujiks to the monologic literate culture of Stalinism, to mirror the 'decay of dialogue' that Ong saw as a result of the modern ascendancy of the printed word over oral-aural culture. Following the development of moveable type, '[s]peech is no longer a medium in which the human mind and sensibility lives', and '[t]hought becomes a private, or even an antisocial enterprise', Ong claimed.[77] Yet the idea of oral culture as dialogic is by no means a matter of consensus. The great Russian theorist of dialogue, Mikhail Bakhtin, took a different view. The Russian peasantry formed for him an extreme case of an oppressively monologic culture:

> [A]n illiterate peasant, miles away from any urban center, naively immersed in an unmoving and for him unshakeable everyday world, nevertheless lived in several language systems: he prayed to God in one language (Church Slavonic), sang songs in another, spoke to his family in a third and, when he began to dictate petitions to the local authorities through a scribe, he tried speaking yet a fourth language (the official-literate language, 'proper' language). All these are *different languages*, even from the point of view of

[74] Ibid. 45.   [75] Ibid. 124.   [76] Ibid. 120.

[77] Walter J. Ong, *Ramus, Method, and the Decay of Dialogue* (Chicago: Chicago University Press, 2004), 291.

abstract socio-dialectological markers. But these languages were not dialogically coordinated in the linguistic consciousness of the peasant; he passed from one to the other without thinking, automatically: each was indisputably in its own place, and the place of each was indisputable. He was not yet able to regard one language (and the verbal world corresponding to it) through the eyes of another language.[78]

Peter Womack notes, in a discussion of this passage, that Bakhtin ascribes to the Russian peasantry a 'special linguistic poverty'. The 'separation from history deprives the Russian peasant of any linguistic consciousness at all' so that he is condemned to 'an endless discursive present, where nothing that is said could imaginably be said differently'. Never regarding one language through the eyes of another, the peasant's 'speech world is devoid of dialogue'. In the preliterate Russian peasantry, Womack glosses, 'Bakhtin sees a primordial desert where the real life of language has not yet begun.'[79] For Bakhtin, it is in high literacy—and above all in the novel— that the dialogical imagination reaches its apotheosis. Studying the novel 'is like studying languages that are not only alive, but still young', because '[o]f all the major genres only the novel is younger than writing and the book: it alone is organically receptive to mute forms of perception, that is, to reading'. Like Koestler and Orwell, Bakhtin saw monologism and orality as linked phenomena, and his celebration of novelistic dialogism is at the expense of other genres (epic and tragedy), 'dead languages' that 'retain their ancient oral and auditory characteristics'.[80]

In his review of Koestler's *Darkness at Noon* (1940), Orwell uses another image for the monological nature of Communist society. Describing Gletkin, one of Rubashov's interrogators, Orwell writes that '[h]e is the "good party man," an almost perfect specimen of the human gramophone'.[81] The 'good party man' is defined by his automatic and mechanized speech, metaphorically linked with a still relatively new technology. The gramophone image had appeared earlier in the intelligentsia's discussions of Communist culture. When H. G. Wells interviewed Stalin for the *New Statesman and Nation* in 1934, for example, John Maynard Keynes's response compared Stalin with a gramophone. This was part of a fascinating exchange with Wells, George Bernard Shaw, and others in the letters pages

---

[78] Mikhail Bakhtin (tr. Caryl Emerson and Michael Holquist), *The Dialogic Imagination* (Austin, TX: Texas University Press, 1981), 295–6.
[79] Peter Womack, *Dialogue* (Abingdon: Routledge, 2011), 146–7.
[80] Bakhtin, *The Dialogic Imagination*, 3.
[81] George Orwell, '*Darkness at Noon*', *New Statesman and Nation* (4 Jan. 1941), in *A Patriot After All*, ed. Peter Davison (London: Secker & Warburg, 1998), 358.

of that magazine.[82] The interview and the resulting exchange of letters were subsequently republished as a pamphlet, called *The Stalin-Wells Talk*, at the behest of the *New Statesman's* editor, Kingsley Martin. All three of the main participants in the debate were concerned with failures of communication and the impossibility of dialogue, and Keynes used the gramophone analogy to explain this:

> My picture of that interview is of a man struggling with a gramophone. The reproduction is excellent, the record is word-perfect. And there is poor Wells feeling that he has his own chance to coax the needle off the record and hear it—vain hope—speak in human tones. . . . [George Bernard Shaw] reproves Wells as a bad listener. But, in fact, Wells's weakness is that he can't bear gramophones. He is enjoying the most interesting interview of his life—and he is stupendously bored. Desperately he struggles. Clumsily he coaxes. But it is no good. To the end the reproduction is excellent and the record word-perfect.[83]

The gramophone seems to Keynes an appropriate analogy for Stalin's voice, on three levels. First, its discourse is predetermined: Wells cannot halt or deflect the course of Stalin's speech which is set in shellac. Secondly, Keynes notes Stalin's inability to produce 'human tones'. Like the gramophone, Stalin has transformed the human voice into something inhuman and mechanical. Thirdly, Stalin shares with the gramophone the limitations of one-way speech: both are incapable of listening, and therefore they cannot participate in a dialogue. Keynes's criticism of Wells, on the other hand, is that 'He has nothing to offer Stalin'—by which Keynes means that Wells can present no alternative economic plan, such as the one Keynes was developing in his *General Theory of Employment, Interest and Money*, published two years later in 1936. 'That is what Stalin might have pointed out, if gramophones could hear', Keynes goes on (Wells later levelled a similar accusation at Shaw—who jumped to the defence of Stalin—labelling him 'practically stone deaf').[84] So the interview is doubly dysfunctional when considered as a piece of dialogue: Stalin was incapable of listening, and Wells had nothing to say.

It might be assumed that the gramophone—because it encourages listening—would form part of the 'secondary orality' that McLuhan and Ong were keen to welcome. However, interestingly enough, McLuhan

[82] See Matthew Taunton, 'Russia and the British Intellectuals: The Significance of the *Stalin-Wells Talk*', in Rebecca Beasley and Phillip Bullock (eds), *Russia in Britain, 1880–1940: Melodrama to Modernism* (Oxford: OUP, 2013), 209–24.

[83] George Bernard Shaw et al., *The Stalin-Wells Talk: The Verbatim Record and a Discussion* (London: New Statesman and Nation, 1934), 30.

[84] Ibid. 33, 37.

saw the gramophone not as a vector of 'secondary orality' at all but as a 'hot' medium in the sense already defined, 'a form of auditory writing' that added fuel to the fire, encouraging an intensification of the effects of print culture rather than allaying them. Far from producing a participatory oral-aural culture, McLuhan suggests that the gramophone 'may well have diminished individual vocal activity, much as the car had reduced pedestrian activity'.[85] Its tendency (at least in its first, mechanical phase, before—McLuhan thinks—it was redeemed by electric media like the tape recorder) was to produce a single unlistening voice in the centre, with listeners positioned as passive, silent consumers.

As this debate about gramophones attests, the *Stalin-Wells Talk* was fundamentally concerned on a thematic and formal level with the possibilities of dialogue, and in that it condensed many of the British left's key concerns about the Soviet Union. Wells's encounter with Stalin was conceived as a foil to his interview with Roosevelt earlier in the same year, and—in the text of the interview itself and in his subsequent reflections on it—the contrast Wells drew between the Roosevelt and the Stalin administrations is the contrast between a dialogic and a monologic style of government. In his *Experiment in Autobiography* (1934) Wells wrote 'the one is a receptive and coordinating brain-centre; the other is a concerted and personal direction.'[86] Wells concluded the interview by gently pressing Stalin about the position of writers in the Soviet Union and suggested that the Soviet Writers' Union might want to affiliate to the PEN club (of which he had recently become president): the 'co-ordinating brain centre' relied on a degree of press freedom not currently available in the USSR (though Wells appears culpably optimistic about Stalin's potential for flexibility on that point).

Alongside its thematic preoccupation with the difficulties of dialogue, the pamphlet is interesting because it attempted to resolve these difficulties on the level of form by staging a dialogue between the USSR and Britain, and also engaging Communist, Trotskyist, and liberal voices from within the British left. Creating dialogues of this kind seems to have been a preoccupation of Kingsley Martin, whose *New Statesman* had hosted the original interview and published the resulting letters, and at whose behest the whole lot was republished in pamphlet form. Martin had previously published *Low's Russian Sketchbook* (1932). The text is by Martin, with pictures by David Low, but Martin includes passages of dialogue

---

[85] McLuhan, *Understanding Media*, 293.
[86] H. G. Wells, *Experiment in Autobiography: Discoveries and Conclusions of a Very Ordinary Brain (since 1866),* 2 vols (London: Faber, 1984), i. 792.

representing his conversations with Low. In the book's chapter about religion, for example, we read:

DL: 'I think perhaps Lenin is becoming a god'.

KM: 'Well, we've not much evidence, but why should not men someday grow out of wanting the supernatural? The present world provides plenty of food for wonder and awe. I think Lenin is becoming a legendary hero rather than a god.'[87]

As editor of the *New Statesman*, in *Low's Russian Sketchbook*, and in his role as publisher of the *Stalin-Wells Talk*, Martin sought to maintain a dialogue with and about the Soviet Union, a multi-faceted conversation in which harsh criticisms could freely be aired and discussed. When Keynes filed a prickly review of *Low's Russian Sketchbook* to the *New Statesman*— arguing that Martin was credulous, 'too full of good will', and that '[w]hen a doubt rises, it is swallowed down if possible'—Martin was furious, but he printed it anyway.[88] There must be no appearance of a cover up. The *New Statesman* must play host at all times to a genuine dialogue, partly to prove that left-wing culture was not as monologic as critics maintained.

Elsewhere in *Low's Russian Sketchbook*, Martin praised Soviet factory newspapers where he found an article titled 'Bring the Guilty to Book', discussing, in the frankest possible manner, everything that is wrong in the factory. This led him to conclude that the press was free enough to play host to a robust and inclusive conversation. 'Both criticism and reply are outspoken, constructive, and, as far as I can gather from a number of enquiries, quite bona fide.'[89] It is possible to surmise that Martin was picking up on the regime's propensity to blame its mid-level bureaucrats: as Fitzpatrick notes, 'the party leaders had little confidence in their own bureaucratic cadres, and constantly bemoaned their lack of education, common sense, and a work ethic'.[90] Bureaucrats and local officials were frequently pilloried in the popular press, and this was encouraged by the regime which presented itself as on the side of the people against the corrupt and incompetent bureaucracy. Indeed, Stalin's use of the telephone—a cool medium par excellence, celebrated by McLuhan for the way it empowers all in two-way communications—performed a

---

[87] David Low and Kingsley Martin, *Low's Russian Sketchbook* (London: Victor Gollancz, 1932), 50.

[88] This exchange of letters can be found in Elizabeth Johnson and Donald Moggridge (eds), *The Collected Writings of John Maynard Keynes*, xxviii. *Social, Political and Literary Writings* (Cambridge: CUP, 2012), 15–18.

[89] Low and Martin, *Low's Russian Sketchbook*, 84, 89.

[90] Sheila Fitzpatrick, *Everyday Stalinism: Ordinary Life in Extraordinary Times: Soviet Russia in the 1930s* (New York; Oxford: OUP, 1999), 29.

similar function. In 1930 when the writer Mikhail Bulgakov wrote to complain about his mistreatment by censorship officials, Stalin telephoned to reassure and encourage him. The medium was the message. Stalin embraced telephony to show the intelligentsia that he was not a gramophone, and that he deplored the inflexible monologism of the bureaucracy as much as they did. In a similar way, the publication of the *Stalin-Wells Talk* touts the openness of Communist culture to dialogue. It does not observe the distinction between oral and written discourse: a spoken interview is transcribed and printed; written responses are treated as spoken interjections (so that Shaw's unreceptivity to the other letters and the original printed interview can be described as 'deafness'). The very title of the *New Statesman and Nation* advertised the merger of the prominent liberal *Nation and Athenaeum* with its younger socialist rival *The New Statesman*. This merger happened in 1931, bringing liberals like Keynes into closer professional contact with socialists like Shaw, and resulting in the appointment of Kingsley Martin from the *Manchester Guardian*. Martin's editorship of the *New Statesman and Nation* embodied a cultural politics which performatively embraced dialogue.[91] But this very openness could be thought to constitute its own metalinguistic monologue, as the idea that the Soviet Union had descended into autocratic demagogy was (despite a great deal of evidence) presented as one opinion among many.

Monologue and the Party Line

Monologism persisted as a concern in the post-war period, and indeed I would argue it became a central Cold War concern, for Communists, anti-Communists, and waverers alike. In *The Golden Notebook* (1962), Doris Lessing placed her narrator and protagonist Anna Wulf at the heart of the intellectual, psychological, and political struggles of British Communism during the 1950s. Benjamin Kohlmann has described the novel as a 'socialist bildungsroman', a genre which often 'signals an attempt to come to terms both with socialism's defeats and with the endeavor to create a space for forms of socialist commitment outside the CP'.[92] The following passage dramatizes the discussions within Anna's party cell in response first to the ructions in Yugoslavia, then to Khrushchev's secret speech to the twentieth Party congress, and finally to the crushing of the

[91] See Adrian Smith, *The New Statesman: Portrait of a Political Weekly* (London: Frank Cass, 1996), 245–50.
[92] Benjamin Kohlmann, 'Toward a History and Theory of the Socialist Bildungsroman', *Novel: A Forum on Fiction*, 48/2 (2015), 181.

Hungarian uprising in 1956. This struggle was clearly intensely felt by Lessing herself, who was radicalized in Southern Rhodesia during the war, and (after moving to London in 1949) was a member of the Communist Party of Great Britain from 1952 (when she visited the Soviet Union as part of a delegation of writers) to 1956. The events which Anna and her comrades grapple with here, in other words, contributed to Lessing's own disillusionment and departure from the Party. This passage comes from the 'Free Women' section, when Anna is describing to Molly the 'disquiet in our circles' as a result of 'this plot and that, and Yugoslavia etc.' Anna focuses on the responses of three male comrades, Tom, Len, and Bob, with whom she corresponds about the crisis:

'Well, I suddenly got letters from all three of them—independently of course, they didn't know, any of them, the others had written. Very stern, they were. Any rumours to the effect that there was any dirty work in Moscow or ever had been or that Father Stalin had ever put a foot wrong were spread by enemies of the working class.'

Molly laughed, but from politeness; the nerve had been touched too often.

'No, that isn't the point. The point is, these letters were interchangeable. Discounting handwriting of course.'

'Quite a lot to discount.'

'To amuse myself, I typed out all these letters—long ones at that, and put them side by side. In phraseology, style, tone, they were identical. You couldn't possibly have said, this letter was written by Tom, that one by Len.'

Molly said resentfully: 'For that notebook or whatever it is you and Tommy have been secret about?'

'No. To find out something. But I haven't finished.'

'Oh all right, I won't press you.'

'Then the Congress and almost instantly I got three more letters. All hysterical, self-accusatory, full of guilt, self-abasement.'

'You typed them out again?'

'Yes, and put them side by side. They might have been written by the same person. Do you see?'

'No. What are you trying to prove?'

'Well, surely the thought follows—what stereotype am I? What anonymous whole am I part of?'

'Does it? It doesn't for me.' Molly was saying: If you choose to make a nonentity of yourself, do, but don't stick that label on me.

... Anna said quickly: '... [T]here was a period of what may be described as confusion, and some left the Party.... Then suddenly, and in the same week... I got three more letters. Purged of doubt, stern and full of purpose. It was the week after Hungary. In other words, the whip had been cracked, and the waverers jumped to heel. Those three letters were identical too—I'm not talking about the actual words, of course,' said Anna impatiently, as Molly looked deliberately sceptical. 'I mean the style, the phrases, the way words were linked together. And those intermediary letters, the hysterical self-abasing letters, might never have been written. In fact I'm sure Tom, Len and Bob have suppressed the memory that they ever wrote them.'[93]

This passage holds written and oral language in a kind of tension. Lessing separates oral discussion between the comrades on one hand from the written texts of the letters on the other. She also plays with the idea of different media forms, as the supposedly personal medium of handwriting is tested against the typewriter.

Heidegger thought of the typewriter as 'the irruption of the mechanism into the realm of the word' which therefore 'withdraws from man the essential rank of the hand'.[94] For Heidegger, handwriting preserves elements of language linked to gesture and embodiment against the standardizing tendency of mechanization. Handwriting—like speech—had gestural possibilities that allowed an utterance to be infused with an individual and expressive meaning above and beyond the merely symbolic function of language as a system of signs. The typewriter flattened out these expressive possibilities. As familiar as this Romantic view of handwriting is, there are reasons to doubt its veracity. It is worth recalling in this context that Elizabeth Eisenstein (drawing on McLuhan and Ong) diagnosed on the contrary a 'new sense of individualism' that emerged 'as a by-product of the new forms of standardisation' in the period of the early printing press and the Reformation. Print culture, for Eisenstein, led to an *intensification* of individuality, not its suppression. Using Montaigne as her reference point, she argued that '[t]he more standardised the type... the more compelling the sense of an idiosyncratic personal self'.[95] When the visual differences that distinguished handwritten manuscripts had been made invisible by the advent of print, there was greater pressure—or should that be greater opportunity?—to individuate oneself by deploying new or otherwise idiosyncratic phrases (that is, by the avoidance of clichés and oral formulae, 'words which have already been set in order by someone else').

---

[93] Doris Lessing, *The Golden Notebook* (London: Harper Perennial, 2007), 63–4.

[94] Martin Heidegger (tr. Andre Schuwer and Richard Rojcewicz), *Parmenides* (Bloomington and Indianapolis: Indiana University Press, 1992), 85.

[95] Elizabeth Eisenstein, *The Printing Revolution in Early Modern Europe*, 2nd edn (Cambridge: CUP, 2005), 62.

Anna Wulf's experiment tests both of these perspectives on type: the individuality that seemed to be preserved in handwriting is shown to be illusory when the words, with their similar constructions and eerily familiar logic, are viewed through the neutral matrix of type. Though her correspondents write freehand, their discourse is structured—even at the level of 'the style, the phrases, the way words were linked together'— by Party norms and the latest Moscow line. Mirroring Ong's observations about the residual orality of Soviet culture, Lessing's text suggests that the possibility of dialogue is always being undermined by the tendency of Communist language to regress into clichés and formulae in exactly the ways Koestler and Orwell were concerned about. Whether or not type-writing or handwriting are in themselves conducive to the expression of 'an idiosyncratic personal self', Party discourse retains (Anna seems to discover) a strong oral residue even when written or typed. Comrades may think that they speak, write, and think autonomously, but their various utterances tend inexorably to form a unison. What is perhaps more striking still is that—after criticisms of Stalin have effectively been licensed by Khrushchev's secret speech—Tom, Len, and Bob's letters sound an identical note: 'hysterical, self-accusatory, full of guilt, self-abasement'.

Interestingly enough, Lessing's preface to *The Golden Notebook*, pub-lished in 1971, nine years after the novel first appeared, described con-temptuously 'the age of compulsive reverence for the written word' in which she lived. She directed readers towards oral storytelling as an antidote to the hegemony of writing: 'the real history of Africa is still in the custody of black storytellers and wise men, black historians, medicine men: it is a verbal history, still kept safe from the white man and his predations'.[96] Lessing was a friend of Jack Lindsay's, and it seems that they shared some similar concerns. If *The Golden Notebook* at some level links the monologism of Party culture to the sorts of habitual oral formulae I have been examining, the dialogism it seeks to put in its place is not a recoil into high literacy but an attempt (mirroring in some senses those made by Orwell and Williams) to build a conduit between orality and literacy. The novel's unique formal arrangement divides Anna's life into four coloured notebooks consisting of an account of her wartime and pre-war experiences in Southern Rhodesia (black), descriptions of her experi-ences in the Communist Party (red), attempts at a novel about another novelist suffering from writers' block called Ella (yellow), and the personal journal containing accounts of Anna's psychiatric treatment, dreams, and emotional recollections (blue). These are all interwoven with a novel,

---

[96] Lessing, *The Golden Notebook*, 18.

'Free Women', and a fifth, titular golden notebook, attempting to synthesize the other four so that Anna can put 'all of myself in one book', appears near the end.[97] The reader is orientated in relation to the novel's various discourses by a seemingly authorial metalanguage which states from which notebook we are reading and sometimes provides context, always from within square brackets.

Meanwhile, the separated discourses that make up the novel also compete to explain each other: for example the golden notebook (not until page 554!) explains 'Free Women' as a novel written by Anna whose first line, 'The two women were alone in the London flat', was suggested by Saul. The assumed hierarchy of discourses is thus disrupted. As Lessing explains in her preface (which in the context of this novel even more than most we must surely treat sceptically as merely another discourse competing for the explanatory authority of metalanguage): 'In the inner Golden Notebook, which is written by both of them, you can no longer distinguish between what is Saul and what is Anna, and between them and the other people in the book.'[98] The displacement of a stable authorial 'I' and the refusal of the novel's constituent parts to resolve into a narrative whole are both mirrored by Anna's final mental breakdown. Benjamin Kohlmann notes that this breakdown is presented as a route to freedom, from the constraints both of the Party itself and of the narrative form of the *Bildungsroman*:

> similar to Anna's collapse, which Lessing held to signal Anna's ultimate liberation from social constraints, the dispersal of narrative coherence in the golden notebook marks the point at which Anna's life story escapes the artificial constraints of narrativization that render life as a steady development from youth to mature adulthood.[99]

For Kohlmann, the open-ended structure of Lessing's novel reflects the socialist *Bildungsroman*'s attempts 'to come to terms both with socialism's defeats and with the endeavor to create a space for forms of socialist commitment outside the CP'.[100]

In a related set of arguments, critics such as Carol Franko, Joanne Frye, and Claire Sprague have read *The Golden Notebook*'s formal complexity as an attempt to stage a form of Bakhtinian dialogism.[101] The novel's

---

[97] Ibid. 519.   [98] Ibid. 8.

[99] Kohlmann, 'Toward a History of the Socialist Bildungsroman', 180.

[100] Ibid. 181.

[101] Carol Franko, 'Authority, Truthtelling, and Parody: Doris Lessing and "The Book"', *Papers on Language and Literature*, 31/3 (Summer 1995), 255, Claire Sprague, 'Multipersonal and Dialogic Modes in *Mrs Dalloway* and *The Golden Notebook*', in Ruth Saxton and Jean Tobin (eds), *Woolf and Lessing: Breaking the Mold* (New York: St Martin's

juxtaposition of multiple irreconcilable voices, refusing to speak in unison, might seem at first glance extravagantly dialogical. However, Bakhtin did not elaborate his theory by reference to narratives like *The Golden Notebook* which ostensibly consist of a compilation of interlocking and overlapping texts. In any case such texts are extraneous to Bakhtin's argument, which concerns not a particular set of playfully dialogic novels, but novelistic discourse as such. The dialogism that Bakhtin finds in Fielding, in Dickens, and above all in Dostoyevsky is the 'internal dialogism of double-voiced prose discourse': in other words, it is the dialogue that is possible *within* conventional realist narrative. Bakhtin is explicitly sceptical of attempts to externalize this dialogism formally, for similar reasons that he deems drama to be a monologic form:

> [T]he internal dialogism of double-voiced prose discourse can never be exhausted thematically..., it can never be developed into the motivation or subject for a manifest dialogue, such as might fully embody, with no residue, the internally dialogic potential embedded in linguistic heteroglossia.[102]

Where the formal properties of a text have been designed to deliver the message 'this text is dialogic', there is a danger that this message itself will become a writerly monologue. The dextrous mediation between different voices is one of the ways in which monological control can display itself. This is the argument that Womack makes about Salman Rushdie's *The Satanic Verses* (1988): it is 'not so much dialogic discourse as the idea of it' that is used to counter the perceived monologism of Islam, so that 'beneath the polychromatic surface there is a single, sustained authorial intention'.[103] Like *The Satanic Verses*, *The Golden Notebook* falls foul of Bakhtin's strictures in its attempts to 'embody' or 'exhaust' the dialogic potential of language, though Lessing does this for what she sees as urgent political reasons. It could be argued moreover that the Cold War structure of feeling, which celebrates the dialogism of ideological diversity and openness to disagreement (typical of liberal capitalism) in contrast to a monological other, has persisted after the fall of the Berlin Wall rather than disappearing, but with Islam replacing Communism in the role of monological other. *The Satanic Verses* could be thought of as a foundational text in that transition.

The section of 'Free Women' quoted earlier, where Party discourse is explicitly at issue, helps us to understand the political valency of Lessing's polyphonic formal strategies. Here, Anna receives several letters from

Press, 1994), 3–14., Joanne Frye, *Living Stories, Telling Lives: Women and the Novel in Contemporary Experience* (Ann Arbor: University of Michigan Press, 1986).

[102] Bakhtin, *The Dialogic Imagination*, 326.   [103] Womack, *Dialogue*, 80.

different authors which converge in their historical narrative, in the interpretation they put on it, and even in their diction and phraseology. *The Golden Notebook*, meanwhile, presents a series of texts with the same author that are fundamentally divergent in narrative, tone, and style. The Party suffers, in Lessing's novel, from the same 'linguistic poverty' that Bakhtin found in the Russian peasantry: Anna Wulf's committed correspondents have a monologic relationship to their own discourse, they are 'not . . . able to regard one language . . . through the eyes of another language'. Whereas Anna and her experiments with the typewriter explicitly do exactly that. Anna's typewriting, which forms part of the 'Free Women' narrative, is in turn seen through the eyes of the other notebooks which emerge as contexts for the production of that novel-within-the-novel. The novel embraces dialogism—the idea of dialogism at least—in pointed and ostentatious contrast to the monologism of Party culture. Moving away from the Party into a more complex set of political identifications—highlighting the position of women, sexuality, the role of the psyche and its relation to 'objective' historical circumstances, etc.—Lessing thus promotes literary dialogism as a fundamental weapon against the oral monologism of 'four legs good, two legs bad'.

Icons and Iconoclasm

The persistence of a Russian peasant orality into the Communist period is a pervasive trope that still fundamentally shapes British understandings, appropriations, and representations of the Russian Revolution. By the time we get to Lessing, the specifically religious context for this is sublimated, and indeed even its Russian aspect is subordinated to the activities of the Communist International. But to draw this chapter to a close I want to focus on a frequently cited example of the continuity between the Orthodox faith and Russian Communism: the icon. The icon operates, in the Western imaginary, as an essential metonym for the Orthodox religion as a whole, and yet it can usefully complicate the rather binaristic model of Catholic orality and Protestant literacy that underpins the work of McLuhan and Ong. Looking East disrupts the narrative in Western Christianity which pits iconoclastic Protestant advocates of the biblical text against the rich and multi-sensory experience of the Catholic liturgy. As Diarmid McCulloch points out, our idea of '*the* Reformation'—Protestantism's challenge to the Western Church—is really only the third of three fundamental attempts to reshape Christian doctrine in relation to the image. The first is the Byzantine iconoclasm in the eighth–ninth century, then the reshaping of the Western Church in the eleventh and twelfth centuries, and only then the sixteenth-century

Protestant Reformation. British observers of the Russian Revolution
tended to translate it into the terms of the last of the three. But, as we
shall see, it is worth considering the very different role that the image
played in the Byzantine iconoclastic controversies whose ultimate result
was the triumph of Orthodoxy, which in turn gave the Russian Church its
distinctive character.

The Bolshevik government's relationship with the icon was complex:
on the one hand, the Communists blamed the old regime and the
Orthodox Church for neglecting Russia's artistic heritage, and used this
as a pretext for nationalizing churches and their contents. Icons could thus
be 'liberated and treated as monuments of Russian artistic achievement', as
John Marks writes, notably celebrated in a major exhibition in Moscow in
1926, which travelled to London's Victoria & Albert Museum in 1929 as
the 'Russian Ikon Exhibition'.[104] On the other hand, as we have seen, the
revolution heralded a large-scale destruction of churches and religious
artefacts. The exhibition and the surrounding state-sponsored celebration
of icons had a 'hidden agenda', Marks argues, namely stimulating a
demand for icons among Western collectors and providing a source of
income.[105] Still, the notion not only that the icon survived the Bolshevik
Revolution but also that it has a persistent power in Communist culture is
everywhere to be found in writings about the Soviet Union in the inter-
war period. When Bertrand Russell travelled to Russia in 1920, with the
country still in the throes of civil war, he wrote about the process by which
icons seamlessly shifted their frame of reference from Christian saints to
secular political figures:

> Lenin and Trotsky already figure in woodcuts as Moses and Aaron, deliverers
> of their people, while the mother and child who illustrate the statistics of the
> maternity exhibition have the grace and beauty of mediæval madonnas.
> Russia is only now emerging from the middle ages, and the Church tradition
> in painting is passing with incredible smoothness into the service of Com-
> munist doctrine.[106]

Russell invoked the medieval in his view of modern Russia. The continuity
of practices of image-making and idolatry across the threshold of modernity

---

[104] John Glen King, *The Rites and Ceremonies of the Greek Church in Russia* (1772), qtd.
in Richard Marks, 'Russian Icons through British Eyes, c.1830–1930', in Anthony Cross
(ed.), *A People Passing Rude: British Responses to Russian Culture* (Cambridge: Open Book
Publishers, 2012), 80–1.

[105] Ibid. 86.

[106] Bertrand Russell, *The Practice and Theory of Bolshevism* (Rockville, MD: Arc Manor,
2008), 31.

is implicitly seen (as in many cases we have already encountered) as an example of Russia's failure to have a Reformation.

Many other observers made similar observations about the icon. Here is Francis Yeats-Brown, writing in the *English Review*:

> I saw in Moscow photographs of the bearded founder of the faith, and pictures of the child Lenin in places where ikons would have been in the old days, while the term 'the General Line of the Party' has acquired a sacrosanct significance; it is the Holy Ghost of the religion whose father is Marx and whose son is Lenin.[107]

Robert Byron took up the same theme:

> In factories and clubs, the icon corner has been replaced by the Lenin or the Marx corner: hideous busts of pseudo-bronze stand on pyramidical pedestals . . . In the separate rooms, less expensive coloured prints replace the erstwhile less expensive icons, forerunners of a new and monotonous hagiography depicting Stalin, Kalinin, Krupskaya, and Budenny. In the large towns, every third shop window teems with these frightful representations, of all sizes to suit all purses, and exhibiting a lack of artistry sickening to behold. On being told the sum formerly derived by the Pechersky Lavra in Kiev from the sale of holy pictures, I was anxious to learn what profit accrued to the present government from the same source. The answer to my inquiry was, that far from there being any profit, the State actually incurred a considerable loss in promoting the distribution of its blessed effigies.[108]

For Byron, the icon is just as pervasive in Soviet culture as it was under the Tsardom, but the economy of the image has been reversed.

Similar concerns were voiced in Aldous Huxley's fascinating essay on 'idolatry', in which he decides that it 'richly deserves its high place in the hierarchy of sins' and that '[o]ur own age has witnessed a huge and violent recrudescence of idolatry'—in other words, the kind of secular Counter-Reformation I have already described. He condemned in general 'the worship of such man-made organisms as the State, the Nation, the Class, the Party', and takes as a specific Russian example the idea that 'the images hung up in public places and in the icon-corner of the home are those, not of saints, but of the local politicians'.[109] The icon-corner, also called the 'red corner', is where the Russian peasants would keep their icons, images of saints and of Christ himself, which in Orthodox theology were thought to carry the direct imprint of the divine. As S. A. Smith puts

---

[107] F. Yeats-Brown, 'Messiahs and Machines', *English Review*, 57/2 (Aug. 1933), 169.

[108] Byron, *First Russia, Then Tibet*, 37.

[109] Aldous Huxley, 'Idolatry', n.d., Huxley Papers, Harry Ransom Center, Box 4 Folder 14.

it, '[a]n icon did not merely depict a person or an event in sacred history, but was a medium that conveyed the numinous presence of that which it depicted'.[110] Icons were understood to exemplify *presence* and not signification. As was remarked by many British visitors to the Soviet Union, instead of abolishing the icon-corner, the effect of the Bolshevik Revolution was that the holy icons were replaced with images of prominent revolutionaries. Bissera Pentcheva, a theorist of the Orthodox icon, has elaborated a theory of what she calls the 'performative icon'. In Pentcheva's reading of Orthodox theology, the icon is not merely a visual representation in the way that Western theology understands depictions of Christ or saints, but operates by activating all five senses to 'trigger an intuition of sacred presence'. As such—and here there are strong echoes of Stephen Graham's descriptions of the religion of the moujiks—icon-worship encourages 'a participatory, sensorial experience of the holy'.[111] This is exactly what McLuhan and Ong wanted to reactivate, and Huxley, Byron, and Russell and other British observers sense it as a specific danger of what they see as the iconophilia of Communist culture. For them, the icon and its secular reconfiguration under Bolshevism appeared as a symbol of a failed Reformation, part of Communism's culpable glorification of the image and preservation of an unaccountable hierarchy reminiscent of the priestly orders of the Catholic Church. The image could be filed with medieval orality, and set against the forces of literacy and modernity.

In his history of Byzantium, Jack Lindsay wanted to understand iconoclasm as a democratizing movement that provided a template for a 'revolt against Church-authority'.[112] He emphasized that 'the support for iconoclasm was very wide indeed', and mocked H. St. L. B. Moss's assertion (in *Byzantium: An Introduction to East Roman Civilization* (1948)) that 'the triumph of the icon-defenders was a victory for popular religion and popular ways of thought'.[113] Lindsay understood the Byzantine iconoclasm as a democratizing and secularizing force, and as a precursor both to the Protestant Reformation and to the Russian Revolution. Yet—as we have seen—in other senses he thought of the Communist Revolution as capable of undoing some of the wrongs done by the Reformation: above

---

[110] S. A. Smith, *The Russian Revolution: An Empire in Crisis, 1890–1928* (Oxford: OUP, 2017), 21.

[111] Bissera V. Pentcheva, 'The Performative Icon', *The Art Bulletin*, 88/4 (Dec. 2006), 651.

[112] Lindsay, *Byzantium into Europe*, 465.

[113] Ibid. 226. H. St. L. B. Moss, 'The History of the Byzantine Empire: An Outline: (a) From A.D. 330 to the Fourth Crusade', in Norman H. Baynes and H. St. L. B. Moss, *Byzantium: An Introduction to East Roman Civilization* (Oxford: OUP, 1961), 16.

all, the turn towards print and the concomitant rise of individualism. The Reformation for Lindsay had a complex legacy: its anti-clerical and iconoclastic energies needed to be harnessed for the present, but its promotion of the printed word in preference to images and sounds was the essence of capitalist individualism. The contradiction emerges from texts written at different times of Lindsay's career and in different contexts, but it is telling. The Orthodox icon cannot easily be classified in terms of the orality and literacy debate, and it poses a distinct problem for the Ongian opposition (itself born out of the specific conditions of the Protestant Reformation) between the written word on the one hand, and sounds and images on the other. Diarmid McCulloch has argued that, while early Protestantism drew inspiration from the Byzantine iconoclasm of the ninth century, it could only do so because it radically misunderstood the terms of the controversy. Byzantine Iconoclasts were not opposed to the elaborate liturgical and oral traditions of the Church as the Protestant Reformers later were. Indeed this is specifically what they advocated as against the icon. The icon, meanwhile, was celebrated by Iconophiles as democratic, 'available to the entire people of God, and not only to those found in church'. Which is to say that it played a similar role in the Byzantine Iconoclastic Controversy as the book was often thought to play in the Protestant Reformation. Iconoclasm stood for 'the monopoly claims of holy noise, in the form of the liturgy of the Byzantine Church', whereas the prevailing iconophilia represented 'the dissident and democratic voice of contemplative silence'. Iconophilia drew on 'a popular movement rooted among laypeople to save images from the consequences of high clericalism and imperial policy'.[114] In McCulloch's understanding of Byzantine Christianity, the icon could neither be grouped with oral liturgy, nor could it be identified with the hierarchical structures of the Church against the people.

For centuries, Russian icons had served as the basis for Anglican homilies on 'the similarity between the burthensome ceremonies of the Greek and Roman church . . . whence every protestant may learn to set a just value on that reformation which is established in his own'.[115] This is an important context for the Anglo-Russian debates about the role of the image and its relationship with oral 'liturgy' that this chapter has explored. Considering the role of the icon prompts us to rethink a binary

---

[114] Diarmid McCulloch, *Silence: A Christian History* (London: Penguin, 2013), 107–8.

[115] John Glen King, *The Rites and Ceremonies of the Greek Church in Russia* (1772), qtd. in Marks, 'Russian Icons', 73. Marks's interesting chapter charts the emergence of a (still relatively niche) appreciation of Russian icons in the nineteenth century, both as objects of religious devotion (predominantly among High Churchmen) and as art objects.

understanding of Christian culture that gives sole priority to the schism in the Western Church. Such a binary model acted as a limitation on much of the writing about orality and literacy in Russia and the Soviet Union that I have considered in this chapter. The Protestant Reformation, or rather its popular association with the forces of literacy over orality, had a formative influence on Cold War culture in Britain. That centuries-old religious and political division furnished a ready-made set of polarities that helped to shape the cultural conflicts that were set in motion by the Russian Revolution.

Conclusion

This book has sought to establish that the cultural effects of the Bolshevik Revolution are broader and more wide-ranging than is commonly assumed. In so doing, it has suggested the revision of a number of conventional literary-historical narratives. One familiar story that *Red Britain* calls into question is that of the 1930s as a 'Red Decade', dominated by the Auden gang and confined to a few short years. This story allowed the radical energies unleashed by the Bolshevik Revolution to be conveniently bracketed off, as the youthful and naive enthusiasm of a group of upper-middle-class, Oxford poets quickly collapsed into profound disillusionment. This narrative feeds a tendency to see the politicization of literature as a temporary, ill-conceived, and ultimately doomed experiment, confined to that decade. To be sure, disillusionment was by no means limited to the Auden circle: they were far from alone in registering the effects of the Moscow Trials, the gulag, famine in the Ukraine, and the Nazi-Soviet Pact—as this book has shown. But rather than seeing these events as the end point of a failed and juvenile romance with Communism, my account sees them as integral to the revolution as it unfolded, and the resistance they provoked as central to the ways in which that revolution helped to shape British culture. In place of a tale of doomed romance about how the British intelligentsia fell in love with Communism and then rejected it, I offer a more open-ended account of how the characteristic modes of a Romantic, humanist English socialism established in the nineteenth century were overlaid with a harder and more utilitarian socialism emanating from Russia, and how the two continue to interact in an as yet unresolved way.

The narrative of the 'Red Decade' also relies on another story about the modernism that is taken to have preceded it. The 1930s generation, this story goes, turned away from an ideology of aesthetic autonomy to experiment with politically engaged literature, and assumed with Orwell that 'all art is propaganda'.[1] This is also often understood as a return to

---

[1] George Orwell, 'Charles Dickens', in *Essays* (London: Penguin, 1994), 67.

realism after the heights of experimental modernism in the 1920s. Recent theorists of 'late modernism' have challenged this account by seeking to extend the period of modernism into the 1930s and then the post-war period, arguing that the turn to a more politicized idiom was shift within modernism rather than the rejection of it.[2] This work has been invaluable in helping us to break down a hard distinction between the politicized literature of the 1930s on the one hand, and an aesthetically autonomous modernism on the other. Yet the selective canon on which this reperiodization frequently relies—giving a particular prominence to the late works of Virginia Woolf and T. S. Eliot, then Samuel Beckett, Djuna Barnes, and Wyndham Lewis—points to some of its limitations. The account of literary culture that I have set out in these pages is not easily integrated into an imperialistic expansion of modernism as a literary historical category (which has been driven by the extraordinary intellectual and institutional successes, over the last twenty years, of modernist studies as the central paradigm for understanding twentieth-century culture). As my reading of Dorothy Richardson's *Pilgrimage* suggests, it may prove productive instead to read the politicized debates of the 1930s and the Cold War—in short, the mid-century—backwards into the 1920s. Taking my cue from recent theorizations of the 'long 1930s', I suggest that, rather than extending modernism as the master narrative of twentieth-century culture, there is something to be gained in extending recent discussions of the characteristic forms and concerns of the mid-century into the 1920s, to 1917, and perhaps beyond.[3]

Part of the effect of suggesting stronger cultural and political continuities between the mid-century, the Bolshevik Revolution, and the years in-between is to encourage an engagement with the cultural legacies of Marxism on a new level. The Frankfurt school analysis of culture remains influential. It has contributed to the theorization of modernist culture as a bid for a depoliticized and ahistorical autonomy with a 'political unconscious'

---

[2] Three influential books that have influentially sought to extrapolate a 'late modernism' are Jed Esty, *A Shrinking Island: Modernism and National Culture in England* (Princeton: Princeton University Press, 2004); Marina MacKay, *Modernism and World War II* (Cambridge: CUP, 2009); and Tyrus Miller, *Late Modernism: Politics, Fiction, and the Arts between the World Wars* (Berkeley, CA: University of California Press, 1999).

[3] See Benjamin Kohlmann and Matthew Taunton, 'Introduction—The Long 1930s', in Taunton and Kohlmann (eds), *A History of 1930s British Literature* (Cambridge: CUP, 2019) and Leo Mellor and Glyn Salton-Cox, 'Introduction', in Mellor and Salton-Cox (eds), *The Long 1930s* (special issue), *Critical Quarterly*, 57/3 (2015), 1–9. The increasing interest in the 'mid-century' as a literary-historical category, of which the Oxford Mid-Century Studies book series is an example, also testifies to a perceived need to place limits on the expansion of modernism. 'Mid-century' offers a more open-ended paradigm that is relatively free from association with a particular set of aesthetic protocols or political commitments.

that renders aesthetic formalism an essential component of Marxist praxis. I have focused instead on the role Marxist and Leninist ideas played in animating that culture—Marxism (and its reception) appear as a part of the object of analysis rather than as a methodological frame through which to view the culture. This is not to say that I have not made use of the resources of Western Marxism, and the cultural emphases of the New Left, in making my arguments. It hardly needs to be said that there is no tradition that has been so productive as Marxism in theorizing literature's position vis-à-vis society, and my work draws heavily on this legacy. But *Red Britain* suggests a definite development out of the New Left's attempts to triangulate culture, society, and economy, moving still further from the economic determinism the New Left deplored in Stalinized Marxism. Raymond Williams's essay 'Base and Superstructure in Marxist Cultural Theory' is indicative of this tendency, both because it rightly sought to move the explanatory force of Marxism beyond a 'fixed and definite spatial relationship', and because it (wrongly, in my view) left intact the fundamental Marxian axiom 'that social being determines consciousness'.[4] While recognizably emerging from the tradition represented by Williams, *Red Britain* suggests that culture and politics are dynamically and dialogically interrelated, and not determined by the mode of production. Consciousness is fully capable of determining social being. British intellectuals came face to face with this when they confronted Stalin's reorganization of the Soviet economy—most brutally obvious in the collectivization of agriculture. Their responses to this were both highly various and themselves suggestive of the limitations of a Marxist aetiology of culture. Hoping to learn from the dynamic engagements with Marxism that it describes, *Red Britain* adopts a still more flexible approach to historical causality than the one Williams proposed, granting no primacy to the economic considerations. Rather, I see the overlapping spheres that go to compose modernity—economics, law, politics, futurology, agriculture, literature, to name a few—as quasi-autonomous, if also structurally linked in a multitude of ways, like the chapters of this book.

---

[4] Raymond Williams, 'Base and Superstructure in Marxist Cultural Theory', *New Left Review*, 82 (1973), 3.

Bibliography

Friedrich Adler, *The Witchcraft Trial in Moscow* (London: Labour Publications Department, 1936).

Theodor Adorno (tr. Francis McDonagh), 'Commitment', in Ernst Bloch et al., *Aesthetics and Politics* (London: Verso, 1980), 177–95.

Charlotte Alston, 'Britain and the International Tolstoyan Movement, 1890–1910', in Rebecca Beasley and Philip Ross Bullock (eds), *Russia in Britain 1880–1940: From Melodrama to Modernism* (Oxford: Oxford University Press, 2013), 53–70.

Perry Anderson, *Arguments within English Marxism* (London: Verso, 1980).

Edna Andrews, *Conversations with Lotman: Cultural Semiotics in Language, Literature, and Cognition* (Toronto: University of Toronto Press, 2003).

Anonymous, 'Extract from information given by Walter J. Krivitsky dated Jan/Feb 1940', The National Archives, Kew (KV 2/1062).

Commission of the Central Committee of the CPSU (ed.), *History of the Communist Party of the Soviet Union (Bolsheviks): Short Course* (New York: International Publishers, 1939).

Anonymous, Online Finding Aid, Rare Book & Manuscript Library, Columbia University <http://www.columbia.edu/cu/libraries/inside/projects/findingaids/scans/pdfs/ldpd_bak_4078440.pdf>.

Anonymous, 'Special Report', dated 22 Nov. 1937, The National Archives, Kew (KV 2/2159).

Anonymous advertisement, 'U.S.S.R.—The New Travel Land', *The New Statesman and Nation,* 3/60 (16 Apr. 1932), 505.

Louis Anthes, 'Publicly Deliberative Drama: The 1934 Mock Trial of Adolf Hitler for "Crimes against Civilization"', *American Journal of Legal History,* 42/4 (Oct. 1998), 391–410.

Hannah Arendt, 'The Ex-Communists', in *Essays in Understanding, 1930–1954: Formation, Exile and Totalitarianism*, ed. Jerome Kohn (New York: Schocken Books, 1994), 391–400.

Hannah Arendt, *On Revolution* (London: Penguin, 1990).

Hannah Arendt, *The Origins of Totalitarianism* (New York: Schocken Books, 2004).

Isaac Asimov, '1984', in *Asimov on Science Fiction* (Garden City, NY: Doubleday, 1981), 275–89.

Isaac Asimov, 'Let's Get Together', *Infinity,* 2/1 (Feb. 1957), 64-80.

Isaac Asimov, 'More Science Fiction from the Soviet Union', in Isaac Asimov, *Asimov on Science Fiction* (Garden City, NY: Doubleday, 1981), 171–7.

Isaac Asimov, 'Science Fiction from the Soviet Union', in Isaac Asimov, *Asimov on Science Fiction* (Garden City, NY: Doubleday, 1981), 164–70.

Duchess of Atholl, *The Conscription of a People* (London: Phillip Allan, 1931).

Katherine Atholl, 'Under Which Heel?', *Saturday Review of Politics, Literature, Science and Art* (8 Aug. 1936), 165.

C. R. Attlee and G. D. H. Cole, 'Introduction', in Margaret I. Cole (ed.), *Twelve Studies in Soviet Russia* (London: Victor Gollancz, 1933), 8–11.

W. H. Auden, *Selected Poems* (London: Faber & Faber, 1979).

Jim Aulich, 'Stealing the Thunder: The Soviet Union and Graphic Propaganda on the Home Front during the Second World War', *Visual Culture in Britain,* 13/3 (2012), 343–66.

David Ayers, 'Hewlett Johnson: Britain's Red Dean and the Cold War', in Philip Emil Muehlenbeck (ed.), *Religion and the Cold War: A Global Perspective* (Nashville, TN: Vanderbilt University Press, 2012), 65–87.

David Ayers, 'John Cournos and the Politics of Russian Literature in The Criterion', *modernism/modernity*, 18/2 (Apr. 2011), 355–69.

Alain Badiou (tr. Oliver Feltman), *Being and Event* (London: Continuum, pbk, 2007).

Alain Badiou (tr. David Macey and Steve Corcoran), *The Communist Hypothesis* (London: Verso, 2010).

Alain Badiou (tr. Robin Mackay), *Number and Numbers* (Cambridge: Polity, 2008).

Alain Badiou, 'Philosophy and Mathematics: Infinity and the End of Romanticism', in *Theoretical Writings*, ed. and tr. Ray Brassier and Alberto Toscano (London; New York: Continuum, 2004), 21–38.

Simon Bainbridge, 'Politics and Poetry', in Pamela Clemit (ed.), *The Cambridge Companion to British Literature of the French Revolution in the 1790s* (Cambridge: Cambridge University Press, 2011), 190–205.

John Baird et al., 'Letter to the Editor of Forward', 16 March 1946, in Sonia Orwell and Ian Angus (eds) *The Collected Essays, Journalism and Letters of George Orwell, iv. In Front of Your Nose* (London: Secker & Warburg, 1968), 115–16.

Mikhail Bakhtin (tr. Caryl Emerson and Michael Holquist), *The Dialogic Imagination* (Austin, TX: Texas University Press, 1981).

Anindita Banerjee, *We Modern People: Science Fiction and the Making of Russian Modernity* (Middletown, CT: Wesleyan University Press, 2012).

Georges Bataille, 'The Critique of the Foundations of the Hegelian Dialectic', in Allan Stoekl (ed. and tr.), *Visions of Excess: Selected Writings, 1927–1939* (Manchester: Manchester University Press, 1985), 105–15.

Rebecca Beasley and Philip Ross Bullock, 'Introduction: Against Influence: On Writing about Russian Culture in Britain', in Rebecca Beasley and Philip Ross Bullock (eds), *Russia in Britain, 1880–1940: From Melodrama to Modernism* (Oxford: Oxford University Press, 2013), 1–18.

Rebecca Beasley and Philip Ross Bullock (eds), *Russia in Britain, 1880–1940: From Melodrama to Modernism* (Oxford: Oxford University Press, 2013).

Joan Beauchamp, *Agriculture in Soviet Russia* (London: Victor Gollancz, 1931).

Matthew Beaumont, *Utopia Ltd: Ideologies of Social Dreaming in England, 1870–1900* (Leiden; Boston: Brill, 2005).

Hilaire Belloc, 'The Restoration of Property: II The Handicap Against Restoration', *English Review*, 56/2 (Feb. 1933), 169–82.

H. Belloc, 'The Restoration of Property: IV', *English Review*, 57(1) (July 1933), 24–36.

Hubert Bland, *'After Bread, Education': A Plan for the State Feeding of School Children, (Fabian Tract No. 120)*, (London: Fabian Society, 1905).

Gavin Bowd, 'Scotland for Franco: Charles Saroléa v. the Red Duchess', *Journal of Scottish Historical Studies*, 31/2 (2011), 195–219.

Brian Boyd, *Vladimir Nabokov: The Russian Years* (Princeton: Princeton University Press, 1990).

Fernand Braudel (tr. Immanuel Wallerstein), 'History and the Social Sciences: The Longue Durée', *Review (Fernand Braudel Center)*, 32/2 (2009), 171–203.

Bertolt Brecht (tr. John Willett), *The Decision* in *Collected Plays: Three* (London: Methuen, 1997), 61–91.

Sascha Bru, 'Avant-Garde Nows: Presentist Reconfigurations of Public Time', *Modernist Cultures*, 8/2 (2013), 272–87.

N. Buchwald and R. Bishop, *From Peasant to Collective Farmer* (London: Martin Lawrence, 1933).

Nikolai Bugaev, 'Les mathématiques et la conception du monde au point de vue de la philosophie scientifique', in Ferdinand Rudio (ed.), *Verhandlungen des Ersten Internationalen Mathematiker- Kongresses in Zürich Vom 9. Bis 11. August 1897* (Leipzig: B. G. Teubner, 1898), 206–23.

Nikolai Bukharin and E. Preobrazhensky (tr. Eden and Cedar Paul), *The ABC of Communism* (Harmondsworth: Penguin Books, 1969).

Robert Byron, *First Russia, Then Tibet: Travels through a Changing World* (London: Tauris Parke Paperbacks, 2011).

Margaret Canovan, *G. K. Chesterton: Radical Populist* (London; New York: Harcourt Brace Jovanovic, 1977).

E. H. Carr, 'Introduction', in Nikolay Gavrilovich Chernyshevsky, *What is to be Done? Tales about New People* (London: Virago, 1982).

David Cesarani, *Arthur Koestler: The Homeless Mind* (London: Heinemann, 1998).

Vladimir Cherrtkov and Pavel Birukov, *Save Russia: A Remarkable Appeal to England by Tolstoy's Literary Editor in a Letter to his English Friends* (London: C. W. Daniel, 1919).

G. K. Chesterton, 'The Anti-Anti-Bolshevist', *G. K.'s Weekly*, 1/23 (22 Aug 1925), 510.

G. K. Chesterton, *The Appetite of Tyranny* (Kila, MT: Kessinger, 2004).

G. K. Chesterton, *As I was Saying: A Book of Essays* (London: Methuen & Co., 1936).

G. K. Chesterton, *Autobiography* (London: Hutchinson, 1969).

G. K. Chesterton, *Eugenics and Other Evils* (London: Cassell & Co., 1922).

G. K. Chesterton, 'The First Principle', *G. K.'s Weekly*, 1/1 (21 Mar. 1925), 3.

G. K. Chesterton, 'Introduction', in William Cobbett, *Cottage Economy* (London: Douglas Pepler, 1916), pp. i–vi.

G. K. Chesterton, *The Napoleon of Notting Hill* (London: Capuchin Classics, 2008).

G. K. Chesterton, 'Notes of the Week', *G. K.'s Weekly*, 4/101 (19 Feb. 1927), 242.

G. K. Chesterton, 'Open Letter: The Set-Back to English Socialism' (manuscript, n.d.), G. K. Chesterton collection, Harry Ransom Center, University of Texas (Box 1 Folder 1).

G. K. Chesterton [?], 'The Paradise of Human Fishes', *G. K.'s Weekly*, 1/2 (28 Mar. 1925), 16–17.

G. K. Chesterton, 'The Real Bolshevik Peril', *G. K.'s Weekly*, 1/2 (28 Mar. 1925), 3.

G. K. Chesterton, *Tales of the Long Bow* (London: Darwen Finlayson, 1962).

G. K. Chesterton, 'Why I am Not a Socialist', *The New Age*, 2/10 (1908), 189–90.

G. K. Chesterton, *What's Wrong with the World* (London: Cassell & Co., 1910).

G. K. Chesterton, 'What we're Getting at', *G. K.'s Weekly*, 5/107 (2 Apr. 1927).

G. K. Chesterton, *William Cobbett* (London: Hodder & Stoughton, 1925).

G. K. Chesterton, and G. B. Shaw, *Do we Agree?* (London: Cecil Palmer, 1928).

William Cobbett, *Cottage Economy; Containing Information Relative to the Brewing of Beer, Making of Bread, Keeping of Cows, Pigs, Bees, Ewes, Goats, Poultry, Etc* (London: C. Clement, 1822).

G. D. H. Cole, *The Life of William Cobbett* (Abingdon: Routledge, 2011).

Margaret Cole, *Our Soviet Ally: Essays* (London: Routledge & Sons, 1943).

Robert Colls and Philip Dodd (eds), *Englishness: Politics and Culture 1880–1920* (London: Croom Helm, 1986).

Dudley Collard, *Soviet Justice and the Trial of Radek and Others* (London: Victor Gollancz, 1937).

Commission of the Central Committee of the CPSU (ed.), *History of the Communist Party of the Soviet Union (Bolsheviks): Short Course* (New York: International Publishers, 1939).

Philip Conford, *The Origins of the Organic Movement* (Edinburgh: Floris Books, 2001).

John Connor, 'Anglo-Soviet Literary Relations in the Long 1930s', in Benjamin Kohlmann and Matthew Taunton (eds), *A History of 1930s British Literature* (Cambridge: Cambridge University Press, 2019), 317–30.

Steven Connor, 'Blissed Out—on Hedonophobia', <http://stevenconnor.com/blissedout>[accessed July 2017].

Steven Connor, *Living by Numbers: In Defence of Quantity* (London: Reaktion, 2016).

Robert Conquest, *The Harvest of Sorrow: Soviet Collectivisation and the Terror Famine* (New York: Oxford University Press, 1986).

John Cornford, 'Full Moon at Tierz: Before the Storming of Huesca', in John Galassi (ed.), *Understand the Weapon Understand the Wound: Selected Writings of John Cornford* (Manchester: Carcanet New Press, 1976), 38–40.

Maurice Cornforth, 'Recollections of Cambridge Contemporaries', in C. H. Guest (ed.), *David Guest: A Scientist Fights for Freedom, 1911–1938* (London: Lawrence & Wishart, 1939), 95–101.

Paul Corthorn, 'Labour, the Left, and the Stalinist Purges of the Late 1930s', *Historical Journal,* 48/1 (Mar. 2005), 179–207.

John Cournos, *London under the Bolsheviks: A Londoner's Dream upon Returning from Petrograd* (London: Russian Liberation Committee, 1919).

Andy Croft, *Red Letter Days: British Fiction of the 1930s* (London: Lawrence & Wishart, 1990).

Andy Croft, 'The Communist Party in Literature', <http://www.letterpressproject. co.uk/media/file/THE_COMMUNIST_PARTY_IN_LITERATURE_by.pdf> [accessed Oct. 2016].

Anthony Cross (ed.), *A People Passing Rude: British Responses to Russian Culture* (Cambridge: Open Book Publishers, 2012).

Dana G Dalrymple, 'The Soviet Famine of 1932–4', *Soviet Studies,* 15/3 (1964), 250–84.

Hugh David, *Stephen Spender: A Portrait with Background* (London: Heinemann, 1992).

C. Day Lewis, *Collected Poems 1929–33* (London: Hogarth Press, 1945).

Peter Deli, 'The Image of the Russian Purges in the Daily Herald and the New Statesman', *Journal of Contemporary History,* 20/2 (Apr. 1985), 261–82.

Michael Denner, 'The "Proletarian Lord": Leo Tolstoy's Image during the Revolutionary Period', in Donna Tussing Orwin (ed.), *Anniversary Essays on Tolstoy* (Cambridge: Cambridge University Press, 2010), 219–44.

Michael Denning, 'The Novelists' International', in Franco Moretti (ed.), *The Novel,* i. *History, Geography and Culture* (Princeton: Princeton University Press, 2006), 703–25.

Jacques Derrida (tr. Gayatri Chakravorty Spivak), *Of Grammatology* (Baltimore, MD; London: Johns Hopkins University Press, 1976).

Jacques Derrida (tr. Robert Harvey), 'Politics and Friendship: An Interview with Jacques Derrida', in E. Ann Kaplan and Michael Spriker (eds), *The Althusserian Legacy* (London and New York: Verso, 1993), 182–231.

Jacques Derrida and Maurizio Ferraris (tr. Giacomo Donis), *A Taste for the Secret* (Cambridge: Polity Press, 2001).

Meghnad Desai, *The Route of All Evil: The Political Economy of Ezra Pound* (London: Faber & Faber, 2006).

Isaac Deutscher, ' "1984": The Mysticism of Cruelty', in *Heretics and Renegades and Other Essays* (London: Hamish Hamilton, 1955), 35–50.

A. V. Dicey, *Introduction to the Study of the Law of the Constitution,* 8th edn (London: Macmillan, 1915).

Charles Dickens, *Hard Times* (Oxford: Oxford University Press, 2003).

Wai Chi Dimock, 'A Theory of Resonance', *PMLA,* 112/5 (Oct. 1997), 1060–71.

F. Lawson Dodd, *Municipal Milk and Public Health* (London: Fabian Society, 1905).

Fyodor Dostoyevsky (tr. Jane Kentish), *Notes from Underground and The Gambler* (Oxford: Oxford University Press, 2008).

David Dwan, 'Orwell's Paradox: Equality in Animal Farm', *ELH* 79/3 (2012), 655–83.

Elizabeth Eisenstein, *The Printing Revolution in Early Modern Europe*, 2nd edn (Cambridge: Cambridge University Press, 2005).

Friedrich Engels (tr. Emile Burns), *Anti-Dühring: Herr Eugen Dühring's Revolution in Science* (Moscow: Progress Publishers, 1947).

Friedrich Engels (tr. Clemens Dutt), *Dialectics of Nature* (London: Wellred, 2007).

Friedrich Engels, *The Housing Question*, in *Selected Works*, i (Moscow: Foreign Languages Publishing House, 1962).

Jed Esty, *A Shrinking Island: Modernism and National Culture in England* (Princeton: Princeton University Press, 2004).

Kerstin Fest, *And All Women Mere Players?: Performance and Identity in Dorothy Richardson, Jean Rhys and Radclyffe Hall* (Vienna: Braumüller, 2008).

Orlando Figes, *A People's Tragedy: The Russian Revolution 1891–1924* (London: Pimlico, 1997).

Bob Fine, *Democracy and the Rule of Law: Liberal Ideals and Marxist Critiques* (Caldwell, NJ: Blackburn Press, 2002).

Harold Henry Fisher, *The Famine in Soviet Russia, 1919–1923: The Operations of the American Relief Administration* (New York: Macmillan, 1927).

Mark Fisher, *Capitalist Realism: Is There No Alternative?* (Ropley: 0 Books, 2009).

Sheila Fitzpatrick, *Everyday Stalinism: Ordinary Life in Extraordinary Times: Soviet Russia in the 1930s* (New York; Oxford: Oxford University Press, 1999).

Sheila Fitzpatrick, *The Russian Revolution*, 3rd edn (Oxford: Oxford University Press, 2008).

Sheila Fitzpatrick, *Stalin's Peasants: Resistance and Survival in the Russian Village after Collectivization* (New York and Oxford: Oxford University Press, 1994).

Michel Foucault, 'What is Enlightenment' (tr. Catherine Porter), in Paul Rabinow (ed.), *The Foucault Reader: An Introduction to Foucault's Thought* (London: Penguin, 1991).

Carol Franko, 'Authority, Truthtelling, and Parody: Doris Lessing and "The Book"', *Papers on Language and Literature*, 31/3 (Summer 1995), 255.

Sigmund Freud (tr. David McLintock), *Civilisation and its Discontents* (London: Penguin Books, 2004).

Joanne Frye, *Living Stories, Telling Lives: Women and the Novel in Contemporary Experience* (Ann Arbor: University of Michigan Press, 1986).

John Galsworthy, *The Forsyte Saga*, 3 vols (London: Penguin, 2001), ii.

Lee Garver, 'The Political Katherine Mansfield', *modernism/modernity*, 8/2 (2001), 225–43.

Marcel Gauchet (tr. Arthur Goldhammer), 'Right and Left', in Pierre Nora and Lawrence D. Kritzman (eds), *Realms of Memory: The Construction of the French Past* (New York: Columbia University Press, 1996), 240–98.

Emilio Gentile and Robert Mallett, 'The Sacralization of Politics: Definitions, Interpretations and Reflections on the Question of Secular Religion and Totalitarianism', *Totalitarian Movements and Political Religions*, 1/1 (2000), 18–55.

Alexander Gerschenkron, *Economic Backwardness in Historical Perspective: A Book of Essays* (Cambridge, MA: Belknap Press of Harvard University Press, 1962).

Michael Glynn, *Vladimir Nabokov: Bergsonian and Russian Formalist Influences in his Novels* (Basingstoke: Palgrave Macmillan, 2007).

Emma Goldman to Bertrand Russell, 9 Feb. 1925, in Emma Goldmann Papers, Tamiment Library, New York University, Box 4 Folder 3.

Victor Gollancz, *My Dear Timothy: An Autobiographical Letter to his Grandson* (London: Victor Gollancz, 1952).

Loren Graham and Jean-Michel Kantor, *Naming Infinity: A True Story of Religious Mysticism and Mathematical Creativity* (Cambridge, MA; London: Belknap Press of Harvard University Press, 2009).

Stephen Graham, *Russia in Division* (London: Macmillan, 1925).

Stephen Graham, *Stalin: An Impartial Study of the Life and Work of Joseph Stalin* (London: Ernest Benn, 1931).

Stephen Graham, *Undiscovered Russia* (New York: John Lane, 1912).

Carl J. Griffin, 'Affecting Violence: Language, Gesture and Performance in Early Nineteenth-Century English Popular Protest', *Historical Geography*, 36 (2008), 139–62.

Carl J. Griffin, 'Swing, Swing Redivivus, or Something After Swing? On the Death Throes of a Protest Movement, December 1830–December 1833', *International Review of Social History*, 54/3 (Dec. 2009), 459–97.

David Guest, *A Textbook of Dialectical Materialism* (London: Lawrence & Wishart, 1939).

David Guest, 'Book Review: Mathematics', *The Labour Monthly*, 19/10 (1937), 644–6.

David Guest, 'The Machian Tendency in Modern British Philosophy', in C. H. Guest (ed.), *David Guest: A Scientist Fights for Freedom, 1911–1938* (London: Lawrence & Wishart, 1939), 219–49.

Ian Hacking, *The Taming of Chance* (Cambridge: Cambridge University Press, 1990).

J. B. S. Haldane, 'Introduction', in Friedrich Engels (tr. Clemens Dutt), *Dialectics of Nature* (London: Lawrence & Wishart, 1940).

T. G. N. Haldane, 'Power and Industrial Developments', in Margaret I. Cole (ed.), *Twelve Studies in Soviet Russia* (London: Victor Gollancz, 1933), 53–74.

Paul Hamilton, 'Introduction', in Paul Hamilton (ed.), *The Oxford Handbook of European Romanticism* (Oxford: Oxford University Press, 2016), 1–12.

Ben Harker, '"Communism is English": Edgell Rickword, Jack Lindsay and the Cultural Politics of the Popular Front', *Literature and History*, 20/2 (2011), 16–34.

Ben Harker, 'Jack Lindsay's Alienation', *History Workshop Journal*, 82/1 (2016), 83–103.

Ben Harker, 'Politics and Letters: The "Soviet Literary Controversy" in Britain', *Literature and History*, 24/2, Special Issue: *Literatures of Anti-Communism*, ed. Benjamin Kohlmann and Matthew Taunton, (2015), 41–56.

François Hartog (tr. Joel Golb), 'The Modern Régime of Historicity in the Face of the Two World Wars', in Berber Bevernage and Chris Lorenz (eds), *Breaking up Time: Negotiating the Borders between Present, Past and Future* (Göttingen: Vandenhoek & Ruprecht, 2013), 124–33.

François Hartog (tr. Saskia Brown), *Regimes of Historicity: Presentism and Experiences of Time* (New York: Columbia University Press, 2015).

Barry Hearn (ed.), *Pound/Cummings: The Correspondence of Ezra Pound and E. E. Cummings* (Ann Arbor: University of Michigan Press, 1996).

Martin Heidegger (tr. Andre Schuwer and Richard Rojcewicz), *Parmenides* (Bloomington and Indianapolis: Indiana University Press, 1992).

Martin Heidegger (tr. W. B. Barton, Jr. and Vera Deutsch), *What is a Thing?* (Chicago: Henry Regnery Co., 1967).

Paul Q. Hirst, *Law, Socialism and Democracy* (London: Allen & Unwin, 1986).

Paul Hirst, *On Law and Ideology* (London: Macmillan, 1979).

Eric Hobsbawm, *Primitive Rebels* (Manchester: Manchester University Press, 1959).

Eric Hobsbawm and George Rudé, *Captain Swing*, new edn (London: Phoenix Press, 2001).

Paul Hollander, *Political Pilgrims: Travels of Western Intellectuals to the Soviet Union, China, and Cuba, 1928–1978* (Oxford: Oxford University Press, 1981).

Paul Hollander, *Political Pilgrims: Western Intellectuals in Search of the Good Society*, 4th edn (London; New Brunswick, NJ: Transaction Publishers, 1998).

Nick Hubble, *The Proletarian Answer to the Modernist Question* (Edinburgh: Edinburgh University Press, 2017).

Michael Hughes, *Beyond Holy Russia: The Life and Times of Stephen Graham* (Cambridge: Open Book Publishers, 2014).

Michael Hughes and Harry Wood, 'Crimson Nightmares: Tales of Invasion and Fears of Revolution in Early Twentieth-Century Britain', *Contemporary British History*, 28/3 (2014), 294–317.

Tristram Hunt, *The Frock-Coated Communist: The Revolutionary Life of Friedrich Engels* (London: Penguin, 2009).

Edmund Husserl (tr. David Carr), *The Crisis of European Sciences and Transcendental Phenomenology: An Introduction to Phenomenological Philosophy* (Evanston, IL: Northwestern University Press, 1970).

Aldous Huxley, 'Idolatry', n.d., Huxley Papers, Harry Ransom Center, Box 4 Folder 14.

Samuel Hynes, *The Edwardian Turn of Mind* (London: Pimlico, 1991).

Stephen Ingle, *The Social and Political Thought of George Orwell: A Reassessment* (London: Routledge, 2005).

Christopher Isherwood, *Lions and Shadows: An Education in the Twenties* (London: Hogarth Press, 1938).

Frank Jackson, 'A Soviet Worker', in C. H. Guest (ed.), *David Guest: A Scientist Fights for Freedom* (London: Lawrence & Wishart, 1939), 113–19.

William James, *The Varieties of Religious Experience: A Study in Human Nature* (London: Penguin, 1985).

Alan Johnson, 'The New Communism: Resurrecting the Utopian Delusion', *World Affairs*, 175/1 (May 2012), 62–70.

Elizabeth Johnson and Donald Moggridge (eds), *The Collected Writings of John Maynard Keynes*, xxviii. *Social, Political and Literary Writings* (Cambridge: Cambridge University Press, 2012).

Hewlett Johnson, *Christians and Communism* (London: Putnam, 1956).

Hewlett Johnson, *The Socialist Sixth of the World* (London: Victor Gollancz, 1939).

Bill Jones, *The Russia Complex: The British Labour Party and the Soviet Union* (Manchester: Manchester University Press, 1977).

David Joravsky, *Soviet Marxism and Natural Science, 1917–1932* (London: Routledge & Kegan Paul, 1961).

Tony Judt, *Postwar: A History of Europe since 1945* (London: Vintage, 2010).

Thomas Karshan, 'Introduction', in Vladimir Nabokov (tr. Anastasia Tolstoy and Thomas Karshan), *The Tragedy of Mister Morn* (London: Penguin, 2012), pp. vii–xxiv.

Thomas Karshan, *Vladimir Nabokov and the Art of Play* (Oxford: Oxford University Press, 2011).

Venyamin Kaverin, 'Thomas the Ostrich' (tr. Stephen Garry), in John Rodker (ed.), *Soviet Anthology* (London: Jonathan Cape, 1943), 76–92.

Hans Kelsen, *The Communist Theory of Law* (Aalen: Scientia Verlag, 1976).

Ian Ker, *G. K. Chesterton: A Biography* (Oxford: Oxford University Press, 2011).

Frank Kermode, *History and Value: The Clarendon Lectures and the Northcliffe Lectures 1987* (Oxford: Clarendon, 1988).

Ian Kershaw, *Hitler: A Biography* (New York: W. W. Norton & Co., 2008).

John Maynard Keynes, 'My Early Beliefs', in *The Collected Writings of John Maynard Keynes*, x. *Essays in Biography* (London: Macmillan, 1972), 433–50.

John Maynard Keynes, *A Short View of Russia* (London: Hogarth, 1925).

Roland Knox, 'If the General Strike had Succeeded', in *If it had Happened Otherwise* (London: Sidgwick & Jackson, 1972 [1932]), 277–89.

Arthur Koestler, *The Act of Creation* (London: Hutchinson & Co., 1964).

Arthur Koestler, *Arrow in the Blue: The First Volume of an Autobiography: 1905–31* (London: Vintage, 2005).

Arthur Koestler, *Darkness at Noon* (London: Vintage, 1994).

Arthur Koestler, *The Invisible Writing: The Second Volume of an Autobiography: 1932–40* (London: Vintage, 2005).

Arthur Koestler, 'Soviet Myth and Reality', in *The Yogi and the Commissar* (New York: Macmillan, 1946).

Arthur Koestler, *Spanish Testament* (London: Victor Gollancz, 1937).

Arthur Koestler, 'The Yogi and the Commissar', in *The Yogi and the Commissar and Other Essays* (London: Jonathan Cape, 1945), 9–20.

Benjamin Kohlmann, *Committed Styles: Modernism, Politics and Left-Wing Literature in the 1930s* (Oxford: Oxford University Press, 2014).

Benjamin Kohlmann (ed.), *Edward Upward and Left-Wing Literary Culture in Britain* (Farnham: Ashgate, 2014).

Benjamin Kohlmann, 'Toward a History and Theory of the Socialist Bildungsroman', *Novel: A Forum on Fiction*, 48/2 (2015), 167–89.

Benjamin Kohlmann and Matthew Taunton, 'Introduction: Literatures of Anti-Communism', *Literature and History*, 24/2, (Special Issue: *Literatures of Anti-Communism*, ed. Benjamin Kohlmann and Matthew Taunton (2015), 5–10.

Benjamin Kohlmann and Matthew Taunton, 'Introduction—The Long 1930s' in Taunton and Kohlmann (eds), *A History of 1930s British Literature* (Cambridge: Cambridge University Press, 2019), 1–14.

Benjamin Kohlmann and Matthew Taunton (eds), *Literatures of Anti-Communism*, special issue, *Literature and History*, 24/5 (Spring 2015).

Ernst Kol'man, 'The Present Crisis in the Mathematical Sciences and General Outlines for their Reconstruction', in *Science at the Crossroads: Papers Presented at the International Congress of the History of Science and Technology Held in London from June 29th to July 3rd, 1931, by the Delegates of the U.S.S.R.* (London: Kniga, 1931).

Reinhardt Koselleck (tr. Keith Tribe), *Futures Past: On the Semantics of Historical Time* (New York: Columbia University Press, 2004).

George Lakoff and Mark Johnson, *Metaphors we Live by* (Chicago: Chicago University Press, 2008).

Harold Laski, *Law and Justice in the Soviet Union* (London: Hogarth Press, 1935).

D. H. Lawrence, 'Democracy', in Edward D. McDonald (ed.), *Phoenix: The Posthumous Papers of D. H. Lawrence* (Harmondsworth: Penguin, 1978), 699–718.

D. H. Lawrence, 'When Wilt Thou Teach the People', in *The Complete Poems of D. H. Lawrence*, ed. Vivian de Sola Pinto and Warren Roberts, 2 vols (New York: Viking Press, 1971), 442–3.

Vladimir Ilich Lenin (tr. Robert Service), *The State and Revolution* (London: Penguin, 1992).

Doris Lessing, *The Golden Notebook* (London: Harper Perennial, 2007).

Michael H. Levenson, *Modernism* (New Haven, CT; London: Yale University Press, 2011).

Claude Lévi-Strauss, *The Savage Mind* (London: Weidenfeld & Nicolson, 1966).

Claude Lévi-Strauss (tr. Monique Layton), *Structural Anthropology*, ii (Chicago: University of Chicago Press, 1983).

Claude Lévi-Strauss (tr. John Russell), *Tristes Tropiques* (New York: Criterion Books, 1961).

Jack Lindsay, *Byzantium into Europe: The Story of Byzantium as the First Europe (326–1204 A.D.) and its Further Contribution Till 1453 A.D.* (London: Bodley Head, 1952).

Jack Lindsay, *Collected Poems* (Lake Forest, IL: Cheiron Press, 1981).

Jack Lindsay, 'A Plea for Mass Declamation', *Left Review*, 3/9 (Oct. 1937), 511–17.

Jack Lindsay, *Short History of Culture* (London: Gollancz, 1939).

Peter Linebaugh and Marcus Rediker, *The Many Headed Hydra: Sailors, Slaves, Commoners, and the Hidden History of the Revolutionary Atlantic* (Boston: Beacon Press, 2000).

A. L. Lloyd, *The Singing Englishman: An Introduction to Folksong* (London: Workers' Music Association, 1944).

David Low and Kingsley Martin, *Low's Russian Sketchbook* (London: Gollancz, 1932).

Roger Luckhurst, *Science Fiction* (Cambridge: Polity, 2005).

Georg Lukács (tr. Arthur Kahn), 'Narrate or Describe?', in *Writer and Critic and Other Essays* (London: Merlin Press, 1970), 110–48.

Stephen Lukes, *Marxism and Morality* (Oxford: Clarendon, 1985).

Rosa Luxembourg, *The Mass Strike* (London: Bookmarks, 1986).

Emily Lygo, 'Promoting Soviet Culture in Britain: The History of the Society for Cultural Relations between the Peoples of the British Commonwealth and the USSR, 1924–1945', *Modern Language Review,* 108/2 (Apr. 2013), 571–96.

Emily Lygo, 'British Cultural Engagement and Exchange with the USSR', *Russian Journal of Communication,* 8/3 (2016), 213–16.

Eugene Lyons, *Assignment in Utopia* (London: George G. Harrap & Co., 1938).

Diarmid McCulloch, *Silence: A Christian History* (London: Penguin, 2013).

Marina MacKay, *Modernism and World War II* (Cambridge: Cambridge University Press, 2009).

Ross McKibbin, *Parties and People: England 1914–1951* (Oxford: Oxford University Press, 2010).

Marshall McLuhan, *Understanding Media: The Extensions of Man* (London: Abacus, 1973).

Louis MacNeice, *The Strings are False: An Unfinished Autobiography* (London: Faber & Faber, 1996).

Isobel Maddison, 'Trespassers will be Prosecuted: Dorothy Richardson among the Fabians', *Literature and History,* 19/2 (Autumn 2010), 52–68.

Peter Mandler, 'Against "Englishness": English Culture and the Limits to Rural Nostalgia, 1850–1940', *Transactions of the Royal Historical Society,* 7 (1997), 155–75.

Martin Malia, *Russia under Western Eyes: From the Bronze Horseman to the Lenin Mausoleum* (Cambridge, MA; London: Belknap Press of Harvard University Press, 1999).

Martin Malia, *The Soviet Tragedy: A History of Socialism in Russia, 1917–1991* (New York: Free Press, 1994).

Richard Marks, 'Russian Icons through British Eyes, c.1830–1930', in Anthony Cross (ed.), *A People Passing Rude: British Responses to Russian Culture* (Cambridge: Open Book Publishers, 2012), 69–88.

Karl Marx (tr. Ben Fowkes), *Capital: A Critique of Political Economy* (Penguin Books, 1976), i.

Karl Marx and Friedrich Engels, *The Communist Manifesto* (Harmondsworth: Penguin Books, 1967).

Karl Marx and Friedrich Engels (tr. W. Lough), *The German Ideology* (London: Lawrence & Wishart, 1970).

Elizabeth Maslen, '"The Menacing Shapes of our Fever": Looking Back at Auden's "Spain"', in Stephen M. Hart (ed.). *¡No Pasarán!: Art, Literature and the Spanish Civil War* (London: Tamesis Books, 1988), 65–82.

Leo Mellor and Glyn Salton-Cox, 'Introduction', in Mellor and Salton-Cox (eds), *The Long 1930s* (special issue), *Critical Quarterly,* 57/3 (2015), 1–9.

James Meek, 'Some Wild Creature', *London Review of Books,* 32/16 (22 July 2010), 3–8, <http://www.lrb.co.uk/v32/n14/james-meek/some-wild-creature> [accessed May 2016].

Roger Middleton, 'The Size and Scope of the Public Sector', in *The Boundaries of the State in Modern Britain* (Cambridge: Cambridge University Press, 1996).

Tyrus Miller, 'Comrade Kemminkz in Hell: E. E. Cummings's Eimi and Anti-Communism', in Benjamin Kohlmann and Matthew Taunton (eds), *Literatures of Anti-Communism* (special issue), *Literature and History,* 24/1 (2015), 11–26.

Tyrus Miller, *Late Modernism: Politics, Fiction, and the Arts between the World Wars* (Berkeley, CA: University of California Press, 1999).

Dragan Milovanovic, 'Introduction to the Transaction Edition', in Evgeny Bronislavovich Pashukanis (tr. Barbara Einhorn), *The General Theory of Law and Marxism* (New Brunswick, NJ; London: Transaction Publishers, 2002).

Kevin Morgan, 'Pritt, Denis Nowell (1887–1972)', *Oxford Dictionary of National Biography* (Oxford: Oxford University Press, 2004); online edn, May 2009 <http://www.oxforddnb.com/view/article/31570> [accessed July 2016].

William Morris, *News from Nowhere or an Epoch of Rest, Being Some Chapters from a Utopian Romance* (Oxford: Oxford University Press, 2003).

Samuel Moyn, *The Last Utopia: Human Rights in History* (Cambridge, MA: Belknap Press of Harvard University Press, 2010).

Malcolm Muggeridge ['A Correspondent'], 'The Soviet and the Peasantry: An Observer's Notes. I. Famine in North Caucasus. Whole Villages Exiled', *Manchester Guardian* (25 Mar. 1933), 13–14.

Malcolm Muggeridge, 'The Soviet's War on the Peasants', *Fortnightly Review,* 33 (1933), 558–64.

Malcolm Muggeridge, 'To the Friends of the Soviet Union', *English Review,* 58/1 (Jan. 1934), 44–55.

Malcolm Muggeridge, *Winter in Moscow* (London: Eyre & Spottiswoode, 1934).

Vladimir Nabokov, *Bend Sinister* (London: Penguin, 2010).

Vladimir Nabokov, 'The Creative Writer', *NEMLA Bulletin* (Jan. 1942), 21–9.

Vladimir Nabokov (tr. Michael Scammell and Dmitri Nabokov in collaboration with Vladimir Nabokov), *The Gift* (London: Penguin, 2001).

Vladimir Nabokov, *Nikolai Gogol* (New York: New Directions, 1961).

Sara Nadal-Melsió, 'Georg Lukács: Magus Realismus?', *Diacritics,* 34/2 (2004), 62–84.

Benjamin Nathans, 'Soviet Rights-Talk in the Post-Stalin Era', in Stefan-Ludwig Hoffmann (ed.), *Human Rights in the Twentieth Century* (Cambridge: Cambridge University Press, 2010), 166–90.

Friedrich Nietzsche (tr. Carol Deithe), *On the Genealogy of Morality* (Cambridge: Cambridge University Press, 2006).

Friedrich Nietzsche (tr. R. J. Hollingdale), *Twilight of the Idols and The Anti-Christ* (London: Penguin, 2003).

David Nowell Smith, *On Voice in Poetry: The Work of Animation* (Basingstoke: Palgrave, 2015).

William Oddie, *Chesterton and the Romance of Orthodoxy: The Making of GKC, 1874–1908* (Oxford: Oxford University Press, 2008).

Walter J. Ong, *Orality and Literacy: The Technologizing of the Word* (London: Routledge, 1995).

Walter J. Ong, *The Presence of the Word: Some Prolegomena for Cultural and Religious History* (New Haven, CT: Yale University Press, 1967).

Walter J. Ong, *Ramus, Method, and the Decay of Dialogue* (Chicago: Chicago University Press, 2004).

George Orwell to Gleb Struve, 17 Feb. 1944, in *George Orwell, the Complete Works: I Have Tried to Tell the Truth, 1943–44,* ed. Peter Davison (London: Secker & Warburg, 1998), 99.

George Orwell to Naomi Mitchison, 17 June 1938, in *The Complete Works of George Orwell,* xi. *Facing Unpleasant Facts, 1937–1939,* ed. Peter Davison (London: Secker & Warburg, 2000), 163.

George Orwell to Stephen Spender, 15 April 1938, in *The Complete Works of George Orwell,* xi. *Facing Unpleasant Facts, 1937–1939,* ed. Peter Davison (London: Secker & Warburg, 2000), 132–3.

George Orwell, *Animal Farm: A Fairy Story* (London: Secker & Warburg, 1987).

George Orwell, *Animal Farm: A Fairy Story* (London: Penguin, 1989).

George Orwell, *A Clergyman's Daughter* (London: Secker & Warburg, 1998).

George Orwell, 'As I Please' 30 (*Tribune,* 23 June 1944), in George Orwell, *I Have Tried to Tell the Truth: 1943–44,* ed. Peter Davison (London: Secker & Warburg, 1998), 261–3.

George Orwell, 'Charles Dickens', in *Essays* (London: Penguin, 1994), 35–78.

George Orwell, 'Domestic Diary', in *The Complete Works of George Orwell,* xi. *Facing Unpleasant Facts, 1937–1939,* ed. Peter Davison (London: Secker & Warburg, 2000), passim.

George Orwell, 'Freedom and Happiness' (*Tribune,* 4 Jan. 1946), in *George Orwell, the Complete Works: Smothered under Journalism, 1946,* ed. Peter Davison (London: Secker & Warburg, 1998), 13–16.

George Orwell, *Homage to Catalonia* (London: Penguin, 1989).

George Orwell, 'Hop Picking' (*New Statesman and Nation,* 17 Oct. 1931), in *A Kind of Compulsion: 1903–1936,* ed. Peter Davison (London: Secker & Warburg, 1998), 233–5.

George Orwell, *Keep the Aspidistra Flying* (London: Secker & Warburg, 1998).

George Orwell, 'The Lion and the Unicorn: Socialism and the English Genius', in *A Patriot After All: 1940–41,* ed. Peter Davison (London: Secker & Warburg, 1998), 391–434.

Bibliography

George Orwell, 'Looking Back on the Spanish War', in *The Complete Works of George Orwell*, xiii. *All Propaganda is Lies: 1941–1942*, ed. Peter Davison (London: Secker & Warburg, 1998), 497–511.

George Orwell, *Nineteen Eighty-Four* (London: Secker & Warburg, 1997).

George Orwell, *Orwell's England*, ed. Peter Davison (London: Penguin, 2001).

George Orwell, 'Politics and the English Language', in *Essays* (London: Penguin, 1994), 348–59.

George Orwell, 'Review of Assignment in Utopia by Eugene Lyons', in *Facing Unpleasant Facts: 1937–1939*, ed. Peter Davison (London: Secker & Warburg, 1998), 158–60.

George Orwell, 'Review of Darkness at Noon', in *The Complete Works of George Orwell*, xii. *A Patriot After All: 1940–41*, ed. Peter Davison (London: Secker & Warburg, 1998), 357–60.

George Orwell, 'Review of Green Worlds by Maurice Hindus', in *The Complete Works of George Orwell*, xi. *Facing Unpleasant Facts, 1937–1939*, ed. Peter Davison (London: Secker & Warburg, 2000), 412–13.

George Orwell, 'Review of Power: A New Social Analysis by Bertrand Russell', in *The Complete Works of George Orwell*, xi. *Facing Unpleasant Facts, 1937–1939*, ed. Peter Davison (London: Secker & Warburg, 2000), 311–12.

George Orwell, 'Review of Russia under Soviet Rule by N. De Basily', in *The Complete Works of George Orwell*, xi. *Facing Unpleasant Facts, 1937–1939*, ed. Peter Davison (London: Secker & Warburg, 2000), 315–17.

George Orwell, *The Road to Wigan Pier* (London: Secker & Warburg, 1998).

George Orwell, 'Review of Teamsman by Crichton Porteous', in *The Complete Works of George Orwell*, xi. *Facing Unpleasant Facts, 1937–1939*, ed. Peter Davison (London: Secker & Warburg, 2000), 414–15.

George Orwell, 'Will Freedom Die with Capitalism', in *The Complete Works of George Orwell*, xii. *A Patriot After All: 1940–41*, ed. Peter Davison (London: Secker & Warburg, 1998), 458–64.

Peter Osborne, 'Global Modernity and the Contemporary: Two Categories of the Philosophy of Historical Time', in Chris Lorenz and Berber Bevernage (eds), *Breaking up Time: Negotiating the Borders between Present, Past and Future* (Göttingen: Vandenhoeck & Ruprecht, 2013), 69–84.

Our Correspondent, 'Soviet Lawyer Dismissed: More "Wrecking" Violent Attacks on Professor', *Manchester Guardian* (16 Apr. 1937), 15.

Our Moscow Correspondent, 'Professor Laski in Moscow, "Dogmatic Certitude of the Communist Mind", an Astonishingly Candid Discussion', *Manchester Guardian* (22 June 1934), 6.

Our Scientific Correspondent, 'Science Congress: A Neglected Branch of History—the Soviet Theory', *Manchester Guardian* (6 July 1931), 16.

Patrick Parrinder, *Science Fiction* (Abingdon; New York: Routledge, 2003).

Evgeny Bronislavovich Pashukanis (tr. Barbara Einhorn), *The General Theory of Law and Marxism* (New Brunswick, NJ; London: Transaction Publishers, 2002).

Ian Patterson, 'The Translation of Soviet Literature: John Rodker and PresLit', in Rebecca Beasley and Philip Bullock (eds), *Russia in Britain 1880–1940: From Melodrama to Modernism* (Oxford: Oxford University Press, 2013), 188–208.

Piotr Pavlenko, 'Nightpiece' (tr. Stephen Garry), in John Rodker (ed.), *Soviet Anthology* (London: Jonathan Cape, 1943), 101–9.

Bissera V. Pentcheva, 'The Performative Icon', *Art Bulletin*, 88/4 (Dec. 2006), 631–55.

Arthur Joseph Penty, *Means and Ends* (London: Faber & Faber, 1932).

Rachel Potter, *Modernist Literature* (Edinburgh: Edinburgh University Press, 2012).

Rachel Potter, *Obscene Modernism: Literary Censorship and Experiment 1900–1940* (Oxford: Oxford University Press, 2013).

Ezra Pound to Olivia Rosetti, 5 Apr. 1954, in *'I Cease Not to Yowl': Ezra Pound's Letters to Olivia Rosetti*, ed. Demetres P. Tryphonopolous and Leon Surette (Urbana, IL: University of Illinois Press, 1998), 145.

Ezra Pound, *The Cantos of Ezra Pound* (New York: New Directions Books, 1996).

Ezra Pound, *The Spirit of Romance: An Attempt to Define Somewhat the Charm of the Pre-Renaissance Literature of Latin Europe* (London: J. M. Dent, 1910).

J. B. Priestley, 'Answering You: J. B. Priestley, Leslie Howard, Geoffrey Crowther and George Strauss', *The Listener*, 27/690 (2 Apr. 1942), 439.

J. B. Priestley, *Russian Journey* (London: Writers Group of the Society for Cultural Relations with the USSR, 1946).

J. B. Priestley, *Summer Day's Dream in The Plays of J. B. Priestley*, iii (London: Heinemann, 1950), 403–76.

Preliminary Commission of Inquiry into the Charges Made Against Leon Trotsky in the Moscow Trials, *The Case of Leon Trotsky: Report of Hearings on the Charges Made Against him in the Moscow Trials* (New York: Harper & Bros., 1937).

D. N. Pritt to Otto Katz, 31 Jan. 1934, The National Archives, Kew (KV 2/1062).

D. N. Pritt, 'Foreword', in *The Reichstag Fire Trial: The Second Brown Book of the Hitler Terror, based on material collected by the World Committee for the Relief of the Victims of German Fascism* (London: John Lane the Bodley Head, 1934), pp. vii–ix.

D. N. Pritt, *From Right to Left* (London: Lawrence & Wishart, 1965).

D. N. Pritt, *Law, Class and Society*, ii. *The Apparatus of the Law* (London: Lawrence & Wishart, 1971), 83.

D. N. Pritt, *Light on Moscow: Soviet Policy Analysed, with a New Chapter on Finland* (Harmondsworth: Penguin, 1940).

D. N. Pritt, *The Moscow Trial was Fair, with Additional Material on the Personalities and Background of the Trial by Pat Sloane* (London: Russia Today, 1936).

D. N. Pritt, 'The Russian Legal System', in Margaret Cole (ed.), *Twelve Studies in Soviet Russia* (London: Victor Gollancz, 1933), 145–76.

D. N. Pritt, *The Zinoviev Trial* (London: Victor Gollancz, 1936).

Avril Pyman, *Pavel Florensky—A Quiet Genius: The Tragic and Extraordinary Life of Russia's Unknown da Vinci* (New York: Continuum, 2010).

John Quigley, *Soviet Legal Innovation and the Law of the Western World* (Cambridge: Cambridge University Press, 2007).

Anson Rabinbach, 'Staging Antifascism: The Brown Book of the Reichstag Fire and the Hitler Terror', *New German Critique,* 103/35/1 (Spring 2008), 97–126.

Dorothy M. Richardson, *Pilgrimage 3* (London: Virago, 1979).

Edgell Rickword, 'Notes on Culture and the War', *Poetry and the People,* 19 (July 1940), 7–8.

John Rodker to Ezra Pound, 29 June 1936, Rodker Papers, Harry Ransom Center, University of Texas at Austin, Box 39, Folder 9.

John Rodker, 'Five Plates of Soup', Rodker Papers, Harry Ransom Center, University of Texas at Austin. Box 37 Folder 2.

John Rodker, 'Harvest in the U.S.S.R.', Rodker Papers, Harry Ransom Center, University of Texas at Austin. Box 37 Folder 2.

John Rodker, 'Russian Impressions I', Rodker Papers Harry Ransom Center, University of Texas at Austin. Box 37 Folder 2.

Michael Rogers, *Nabokov and Nietzsche: Problems and Perspectives* (London: Bloomsbury, 2018).

H. S. Ruse, 'David the Intellectual', in C. H. Guest (ed.), *David Guest: A Scientist Fights for Freedom* (London: Lawrence & Wishart, 1939), 166–9.

Bertrand Russell, *The Analysis of Matter* (London: George Allen & Unwin, 1954).

Bertrand Russell, *The Practice and Theory of Bolshevism* (Rockville, MD: Arc Manor, 2008).

Bertrand Russell to Emma Goldman, 14 Feb. 1925, in Emma Goldmann Papers, Tamiment Library, New York University, Box 4 Folder 3.

Glyn Salton-Cox, *Queer Communism and the Ministry of Love: Sexual Revolution in British Writing of the 1930s* (Edinbugh: Edinburgh University Press, 2018).

Donald Sassoon, *One Hundred Years of Socialism: The West European Left in the Twentieth Century* (London: I. B. Tauris, 2010).

Michael Scammell, *Koestler: The Indispensable Intellectual* (London: Faber, 2009).

Robert Service, *A History of Modern Russia: From Nicholas II to Putin* (London: Penguin, 2003).

Gabriel Shapiro, 'Setting his Myriad Faces in his Text: Nabokov's Authorial Presence Revisited', in Julian W. Connolly (ed.), *Nabokov and his Fiction: New Perspectives* (Cambridge: Cambridge University Press, 1999), 15–35.

George Bernard Shaw, 'Basic & Spelling' (typescript), George Bernard Shaw Papers, Harry Ransom Center, University of Texas, Austin, Box 4 Folder 12.

George Bernard Shaw, 'Chesterton and Belloc', *The New Age* (15 Feb. 1908), 309–11.

George Bernard Shaw, 'Preface', to *On the Rocks: A Political Comedy,* in *Plays Political* (London: Penguin, 1986).

George Bernard Shaw, *The Rationalization of Russia* (Westport, CT: Greenwood Press, 1964).

George Bernard Shaw, 'Why Not Give the Intellectuals a Chance', *Nash's Pall Mall Magazine,* 92/486 (Nov. 1933), 95.

George Bernard Shaw et al., *The Stalin-Wells Talk: The Verbatim Record and a Discussion* (London: The New Statesman and Nation, 1934).

Morag Shiach, *Modernism, Labour, and Selfhood in British Literature and Culture, 1890–1930* (Cambridge: Cambridge University Press, 2004).

Adrian Smith, *The New Statesman: Portrait of a Political Weekly* (London: Frank Cass, 1996).

S. A. Smith, *The Russian Revolution: An Empire in Crisis* (Oxford: Oxford University Press, 2017).

S. A. Smith, *The Russian Revolution: A Very Short Introduction* (Oxford: Oxford University Press, 2002).

Olga Soboleva and Angus Wrenn, *From Orientalism to Cultural Capital: The Myth of Russia in British Literature of the 1920s* (Bern: Peter Lang, 2017).

Diana Souhami, *Mrs Keppel and her Daughter* (London: Flamingo, 1997), 123–334.

Stephen Spender, *Forward from Liberalism* (London: Gollancz, 1937).

Stephen Spender, *Trial of a Judge: A Tragic Statement in Five Acts* (London: Faber & Faber, 1938).

Stephen Spender, *World within World* (London: Faber & Faber, 1977).

Claire Sprague, 'Multipersonal and Dialogic Modes in Mrs Dalloway and The Golden Notebook', in Ruth Saxton and Jean Tobin (eds), *Woolf and Lessing: Breaking the Mold* (New York: St Martin's Press, 1994), 3–14.

H. St. L. B. Moss, 'The History of the Byzantine Empire: An Outline: (a) From A.D. 330 to the Fourth Crusade', in Norman H. Baynes and H. St. L. B. Moss, *Byzantium: An Introduction to East Roman Civilization* (Oxford: Oxford University Press, 1961), 1–32.

Gerald Stanton Smith, *D. S. Mirsky: A Russian-English Life, 1890–1939* (New York: Oxford University Press, 2000).

Frances Stonor Saunders, *Who Paid the Piper? The CIA and the Cultural Cold War* (London: Granta, 1999).

John Strachey, 'The Strangled Cry', *Encounter,* 15/6 (Dec. 1960), 23–37.

Harry Stevens to John Rodker, 31 Mar. 1942, Harry Ransom Center, Rodker Papers, Box 12 Folder 3.

Harry Stevens to Rodker, 28 July 1942, Harry Ransom Center, Rodker Papers, Box 12 Folder 3.

Matthew Taunton, 'Distributism and the City', in Matthew Beaumont and Matthew Ingleby (eds), *Chesterton, London and Modernity* (London: Bloomsbury, 2013), 203–27.

Matthew Taunton, *Fictions of the City: Class, Culture and Mass Housing in London and Paris* (Basingstoke: Palgrave Macmillan, 2009).

Matthew Taunton, 'Russia and the British Intellectuals: The Significance of the Stalin-Wells Talk', in Rebecca Beasley and Phillip Bullock (eds), *Russia in Britain, 1880–1940: Melodrama to Modernism* (Oxford: Oxford University Press, 2013), 209–24.

Elinor Taylor, *The Popular Front Novel in Britain, 1934–1940* (Leiden: Brill, 2018).

R. H. Tawney, *Religion and the Rise of Capitalism: A Historical Study* (London: John Murray, 1926).

Franklin Terrell, *A Companion to the Cantos of Ezra Pound* (Berkeley; Los Angeles; London: University of California Press, 1984).

E. P. Thompson, *The Making of the English Working Class* (New York: Random House, 1963).

George H. Thompson, *Notes on Pilgrimage: Dorothy Richardson Annotated* (Greensboro: ELT Press, 1999).

Michael E. Tigar and John Mage, 'The Reichstag Fire Trial, 1933–2008: The Production of Law and History', *Monthly Review*, 60/10 (Mar. 2009), <http://monthlyreview.org/2009/03/01/the-reichstag-fire-trial-1933-2008-the-production-of-law-and-history>[accessed Oct. 2016].

Fritz Tobias, *The Reichstag Fire* (London: Secker & Warburg, 1963).

Denys Trefusis, 'The Stones of Emptiness: A Picture of Soviet Russia' (typescript, 1926), Rare Book & Manuscript Library, Columbia University.

Frank Trentmann, *Free Trade Nation: Commerce, Consumption, and Civil Society in Modern Britain* (Oxford: Oxford University Press, 2008).

Ivan Turgenev (tr. Richard Freeborn), *Fathers and Sons* (Oxford: Oxford University Press, 1999).

Ivan Turgenev (tr. Constance Garnett), 'Prayer', in *Dream Tales and Prose Poems* (London: Faber & Faber, 2008).

Unsigned, 'British Lawyer's Moscow Trial Story—"Frame-Up Out Of Question"' *Daily Herald* (28 Jan. 1937), 1–2.

Unsigned, 'British Note to Moscow—Soviet Money for General Strike—a Strong Protest—Communist Plan', *The Times* (12 June 1926).

Unsigned, 'Critics of Moscow Trial Crushed by Lawyer Eye-Witness', *Daily Worker* (1 Oct. 1936), The National Archives, Kew (KV 2/1062).

Unsigned, 'From the Workers' Point of View: Some People are Never Pleased!', *Daily Herald* (17 Oct. 1924).

Unsigned, 'Harry Pollitt Trounces the Critics of the Moscow Trial', *Daily Worker* (30 Jan. 1937), 3.

Unsigned, 'Moscow Sentences' (leader), *Daily Herald* (30 Jan. 1937), 8.

Unsigned, 'Reconstruction in Russia.—IV.: Revolution by Tractor', *The Economist*, 110/4506 (4 Jan. 1930), 7–8.

Unsigned, 'Soviet Trial is Fair Says British Lawyer in Moscow', *Daily Worker* (27 Jan. 1937), 8.

Anna Vaninskaya, 'Janus-Faced Fictions: Socialism as Utopia and Dystopia in Willam Morris and George Orwell', *Utopian Studies*, 14/2 (2003), 83–98.

Claudia Verhoeven, 'Wormholes in Russian History: Events "Outside of Time" (Featuring Malevich, Morozov, and Mayakovsky)', in Berber Bevernage and Chris Lorenz (eds), *Breaking up Time: Negotiating the Borders between Present, Past and Future* (Göttingen: Vandenhoek & Ruprecht, 2013), 109–23.

Alexander Vucinich, 'Soviet Mathematics and Dialectics in the Stalin Era', *Historia Mathematica*, 27/1 (2000), 54–76.

Ian Watt, *The Rise of the Novel: Studies in Defoe, Richardson and Fielding* (London: Pimlico, 2000).

Sidney Webb, 'On the Emergence of a New World Religion', *International Journal of Ethics*, 43/2 (Jan. 1933), 167–82.

Sidney and Beatrice Webb, *Soviet Communism: A New Civilization*, 3rd edn, in 1 vol. (London: Longmans, Green & Co.: 1944).

Martin Weiner, *English Culture and the Decline of the Industrial Spirit 1850–1950* (Cambridge: Cambridge University Press, 1981).

Shane Weller, *Modernism and Nihilism* (Basingstoke: Palgrave Macmillan, 2011).

H. G. Wells, *The Discovery of the Future: A Discourse Delivered to the Royal Institution on January 24, 1902* (London: T. Fisher Unwin, 1902).

H. G. Wells, *Experiment in Autobiography: Discoveries and Conclusions of a Very Ordinary Brain (since 1866)*, 2 vols (London: Faber, 1984).

H. G. Wells, *The Shape of Things to Come: The Ultimate Revolution* (London: Hutchinson & Co., 1933).

Edith Holt Whetham, *The Agrarian History of England and Wales*, viii. *1914–39* (Cambridge: Cambridge University Press, 1978).

Alfred North Whitehead and Bertrand Russell, *Principia Mathematica* (Cambridge: Cambridge University Press, 1910).

Keith Williams, *British Writers and the Media, 1930–45* (Basingstoke: Palgrave Macmillan, 1996).

Raymond Williams, 'Base and Superstructure in Marxist Cultural Theory', *New Left Review*, 82 (1973), 3–16.

Raymond Williams, *The Country and the City* (New York: Oxford University Press, 1973).

Raymond Williams, *Culture and Society: Coleridge to Orwell* (London: Hogarth Press, 1993).

Raymond Williams, *Drama from Ibsen to Brecht* (New York: Oxford University Press, 1969).

Raymond Williams, *Keywords: A Vocabulary of Culture and Society* (London: Fontana, 1983).

Ludwig Wittgenstein (tr. Denis Paul and G. E. M. Anscombe), *On Certainty* (Oxford: Basil Blackwell, 1974).

Peter Womack, *Dialogue* (Abingdon: Routledge, 2011).

Virginia Woolf, 'Mr. Bennett and Mrs. Brown', in *Collected Essays,* i (London: Hogarth Press, 1966), 319–37.

Virginia Woolf, *To the Lighthouse* (London: Penguin, 1964).

Virginia Woolf, 'The Tunnel', *Times Literary Supplement*, 17 (13 Feb. 1919), 81.

Patrick Wright, *Iron Curtain: From Stage to Cold War* (Oxford: Oxford University Press, 2007).

Patrick Wright, 'Preface to the OUP edition', in *On Living in an Old Country: The National Past in Contemporary Britain*, OUP edn (Oxford: Oxford University Press, 2009), pp. xviii–ixx.

F. Yeats-Brown, 'Messiahs and Machines', *English Review*, 57/2 (Aug. 1933), 164–70.

Yevgeny Zamyatin (tr. Natasha Randall), *We* (London: Vintage, 2007).

Theodore Ziolkowski, *The Mirror of Justice: Literary Reflections on Legal Crises* (Princeton, NJ: Princeton University Press, 1997).

Slavoj Žižek, 'Introduction: Between the Two Revolutions', in V. I. Lenin, *Revolution at the Gates: A Selection of Writings from February to October 1917,* ed. Slavoj Žižek (London: Verso, 2002), 1–12.

Index

Index